HENRY JAMES
Selected Letters

HENRY JAMES

Selected Letters

EDITED BY

LEON EDEL

THE BELKNAP PRESS OF
HARVARD UNIVERSITY PRESS
CAMBRIDGE, MASSACHUSETTS
AND LONDON, ENGLAND

Library of Congress Cataloging-in-Publication Data

James, Henry, 1843–1916.
  Henry James, selected letters.

  Includes index.
    1. James, Henry, 1843–1916—Correspondence.
  2. Authors, American—20th century—Correspondence.
  I. Edel, Leon, 1907–   II. Title.   III. Title:
  Selected letters.
  PS2123.A4   1987   813'.4 [B]   87-8543
  ISBN 0-674-38793-7 (cloth)
  ISBN 0-674-38794-5 (paper)

The best letters seem to me the most delightful of all written things.

        —Henry James

I delight in a palpable imaginable *visitable* past . . . the poetry of the thing outlived and lost and gone.

        —Preface to "The Aspern Papers"

Acknowledgments

The selected letters published in this volume have been drawn from many sources in the United States and abroad, public institutions and private owners, as well as collections in universities and other libraries. The source of each letter is given at the top, beneath the name of the correspondent: Ms stands for the handwritten letter, Ts for typescript, Mf for microfilm. "Ms Unknown" means that a copy of the letter was seen by me but I no longer know its whereabouts—since letters change hands, are lost, or simply disappear, sometimes to be found at a later date. "Ms Private" means the holograph is in private hands. In some instances, with the consent of the private owners, I have given their names. "Dictated Ts" in the case of Henry James means a letter dictated by him directly to the typist seated at the typewriter, and usually signed by him. There are other typed letters that are copies, the originals of which may no longer exist.

Following are the institutions or collections whose documents I have used and to which I wish to express my thanks for access to Henry James documents during many years.

Barrett	C. Waller Barrett Collection, University of Virginia
Berg	Henry W. and Albert A. Berg Collection of English and American Literature, New York Public Library
Bodleian	Bodleian Library, Oxford
British Library	formerly the British Museum, London
Brown	John Hay Library, Brown University
Chester	Chester Public Records Office, U.K.
Colby	Colby College Library

Columbia	Butler Library, Columbia University
Congress	Library of Congress
Countway	Francis A. Countway Library of Medicine, Boston
Dartmouth	Baker Library, Dartmouth College
Duke	Duke University Library
Gardner	Isabella Stewart Gardner Museum, Boston
Glasgow	University of Glasgow Library
Harvard	The Houghton Library, Harvard University
Hillstead	Hillstead Museum, Farmington, Connecticut
Huntington	Henry E. Huntington Library, San Marino, California
Leeds	Brotherton Library, University of Leeds
Louvenjoul	Louvenjoul Collection, Chantilly, France
Lubbock	Typescripts in the Houghton Library assembled by Percy Lubbock for his two-volume edition of *The Letters of Henry James* (1920)
Mass. Historical	Massachusetts Historical Society, Boston
Morgan	Trustees of the Morgan Library, New York
N.Y. Historical	New York Historical Society
NYPL	Manuscript Division, New York Public Library, Astor, Lenox, and Tilden Foundations
Princeton	Princeton University Library
Royal Literary Fund	Royal Literary Fund, London
Scotland	National Library of Scotland, Edinburgh
Taylor	Robert H. Taylor Collection, Princeton University
Texas	Harry Ransom Humanities Research Center, University of Texas at Austin
Vaux	Robertson James Archive, Berkeley, California
Yale	Beinecke Rare Book and Manuscript Library, Yale University

I wish to thank in particular Lynn Jachney, for communicating the early letter found among her family papers (Letter 4); Adeline R. Tintner, for making available the original of the letter to Fanny Prothero about Stark Young (Letter 179); and the Royal Literary Fund of Britain (and in particular Janet Adam Smith) for the letter about Mrs. Dickens (Letter 120). I was much indebted to Robert H. Taylor during his lifetime for certain James letters and wish to thank Alexander D. Wainwright of the Princeton Library for help with the Taylor collection. The Harry Ransom Humanities Research Center at the University of Texas at Austin kindly provided its recently acquired letter to John Lane and one to Morton Fullerton. Lyall H. Powers, the editor of HJ's letters to Edith Wharton, generously helped me with the texts of those included here. My debts to many others are listed in the four-volume edition from which the present selection is mainly drawn. Not the least of my debts are to Alexander R. James, the novelist's grand-nephew, and to my editor at Harvard University Press, Camille Smith, who worked with me on earlier volumes and on this one.

Contents

Illustrations

Introduction
On Selecting Letters

When I completed my life of Henry James in 1971, I began work on an edition of his selected letters. I had read many thousands in writing the biography, copied a goodly number, and written a great many summaries, and I possessed copious notes as well as guides to the various repositories. Why did I settle on four volumes? The figure was based on a rough count of the letters I deemed most important, and on an appraisal of the James market at the time. There was no question of producing an edition of the total correspondence, which would have run to at least fifty volumes. James had expressed to his executor, Henry James III, his "utter and absolute abhorrence of any attempted biography or the giving to the world by 'the family,' or by any person for whom my disapproval has any sanctity, of any part or parts of my private correspondence." Such enterprises, he said, could be discredited and dishonored "even if one can't prevent them." His executor arranged for the publication of two volumes of letters by Percy Lubbock, an Eton-and-Cambridge man of letters, and hoped that these would satisfy public curiosity. The James family feared that an excess of James's social letters might give him too great an air of frivolity and superficiality. I think, too, that in the family's unspoken reservations there lay still another anxiety: that tell-tale letters might turn up revealing James's homoeroticism. We know that Henry III did veto publication by Hendrik Andersen of the novelist's letters to him—letters filled with avuncular affection. Viewed now, at more than half a century's distance, it might be said that perhaps the family was being over-protective. But at the time, when there survived nephews and a niece who had known and dearly loved their Uncle Henry, we can understand that "the real right thing" for them was a certain kind of caution and diffidence—the "hesitations and discretions" Lubbock found in them as he worked on the original volumes, which appeared very quickly, in 1920, four years after the novelist's death.

The four volumes I edited fifty years later, between 1974 and 1984, which appeared under Harvard's Belknap Press imprint, contain just over a thousand letters. Lubbock had published four hundred. From my collection I have now selected 166 letters. This may seem a very slight number, but James tended to run to length and it doesn't take many of his letters to fill a volume. I have added to my "selection from a selection" two dozen never printed before, which have a certain relevance and are now publishable in the new and freer climate of our time—our changed attitudes toward privacy. Some enlarge our knowledge of James's complicated involvements with Edith Wharton and her circle during the Edwardian years. Others offer bits of mosaic—information that biographers or critics, as well as the general reader, may find amusing or useful—for example James's feelings about the Baconians, who claimed he belonged to them; or his disavowal of his early review of Walt Whitman, which he said nothing would induce him to reveal, but which bibliographers long ago discovered without much difficulty.

In all, there are 191 letters in the present selection. It is mainly intended, I suppose, for the anonymous "general reader"—a reader who is not necessarily a scholarly specialist or a student researcher, or a Jamesian initiate, but who has read some of James's fiction and may want to know what sort of letter-writer he was. Others doubtless will study this book for their personal reasons: perhaps wondering—as I would myself of such selections—why certain letters were chosen rather than others. That becomes a paramount question from the moment letters are selected rather than published en masse. I am not sure that anyone making such choices can provide a satisfactory formula or guide to the decisions made, although I notice that some of my reviewers have spoken of my treating the four volumes as if they were an "annex" to the biography I published in several volumes between 1953 and 1972. In denying this soft impeachment I can only point out that a biographer most certainly uses important letters for the light they throw on a life and work and if they have this importance they obviously deserve inclusion in any subsequent collection of letters. There have also been certain critics who curiously developed a suspicion that I was trying to suppress sides of James's life, perhaps believing that I had acquired the "protectiveness" of his heirs. This is fantasy. My goal as a selector of James's letters has been not only to print as many significant letters as possible, but also to restore to certain letters in Lubbock passages trimmed by the family—largely to avoid hurting individuals then still alive and to conceal odd bits of family history, records of illnesses and constipations to which we would today pay very little attention.

The present selection, like my earlier volumes, has been guided by a search for letters that throw light on James's literary career, his life, his thoughts and fancies, his literary theories, and his most important friendships. These are the more obvious reasons for choosing certain letters and discarding others. Precious few actually discuss his day-to-day writings. The privacy of his desk was absolute in Bolton Street, where he wrote opposite the blank wall of a great house, and in De Vere Gardens, where he looked out on the western expanse of London. It is only later, when the elderly James shared his daily work with his typist, that we get a picture of "Henry James at work," and this not so much from the typed letters as from the memories and diaries of the typists. Most of James's letters (aside from the strictly business letters) are acts of friendship and personal relations. He was a supreme artist in the intimacies and connections that bind people together or tear them apart. When an epistolarium as grandiose as James's exists, every person reading the letters develops his or her own notion of their "importance," but I think it can be asserted that the individual who has read the largest number is likely to be in the best position to make comparisons and to offer judgment about what is most representative and significant. There are no absolutes, however, in the enterprise. Each person brings too many subjectivities to letter-reading to be wholly reliable, and this leads to frequent disagreement. Editors of "collected" or "complete" editions have no such problem. They, after all, are printing everything, and this makes possible the widest democratic judgment. The "completists" are also spared the doubts of "choice," and no aesthetic judgments are involved. Their problems are essentially of a practical order.

There are certain clear guides to selection: the stages of the writer's life, whatever crises were encountered (as in the case of James's failures in the theatre), periods of grief and mourning, journeys undertaken and carried out. Then there are the bits and pieces of information in letters—a casual sentence, a postscript, an allusion—one looks at all these hints and their verbalization. Letters sometimes have the same interest that has led generations of readers to cherish Defoe's *Robinson Crusoe*: they describe periods of stress as well as happiness, moments when the voyager is stranded and the ways in which some new mode or routine of life is established. James's early visits to the great houses of Britain, the formidable Victorian dinners he ate, the life he led in his clubs—clubs which so often are the refuge of the lonely—all reveal our subject. And then the liveliness and sparkle of his prose, the ways in which he adjusts his mask for each correspondent—all these aspects and elements play into selection of correspondence for publication. Such at any rate are the external reasons for making choices, and they are usually the ones that the more literal-minded scholars like to use.

There are less obvious reasons for choosing certain of Henry James's letters. Below the surface of his running handwriting—a handwriting often so rapid that the commas are turned around in a forward movement, as if they must not be allowed to act as a brake on his pace—we can discover a great deal of psychological content. This is not necessarily a matter for speculation: it is a matter of looking closely, of studying the formulations and the ways in which the young Henry James handles himself in his correspondence, particularly with his family. How does he assert himself? What are his strategies? Is he timid or outgoing? Is he urbane, dissimulating, aggressive? Or does he veil aggression in the smoothest of verbal cushioning? Answers can be found as we read, and these are neither guesses nor psychological "frames" and formulas. They involve simply studying a letter as we study the text of a poem. How does James deal with his seemingly penny-pinching mother—who in turn reveals a great deal about herself in her letters and the manner in which she attempts to manipulate her children? We must be careful when we use the word "manipulate"—but I use it in full awareness: for when there are a great many letters, it is possible to study stance and strategy behind the veiled politeness, and even lovingness, of a letter. In the case of James's mother we find her concerned with the funds he has drawn from his letters of credit. She shows her money worries. Sometimes she complains he is spending too much; at other times she wonders what he is living on. James's answers communicate a great deal, and not least in those passages where he explains to his mother how someone who wants to be a writer, like himself, is inclined not to be parsimonious; he must take advantage of his youthful sense of the picturesque and of observation, which is likely to become somewhat jaded as he grows older. Readers might offer different interpretations in such give and take, but the essence of this dialogue is clear enough. Henry James's own serene confidence, his clear feelings about what his destiny is to be, and his practical wisdom, are not only revealed but confirmed: and further letters show him paying back the money borrowed from his parents. His works are in demand. He achieves the fame he sought. Genius has its own measure and its own timetable.

This reading of letters in a psychological way can be of great help in making selections from a huge mass of documents. For the letters that tell us most are the ones of greatest use and interest to the reader—tell us most both of surface matters and those hidden behind the implicit dialogue that exists invariably in a correspondence.

The two large volumes Percy Lubbock edited offered certain problems. By the time I came to make my selection I had available not only the holographs but also some of the typescripts from which Lubbock had worked, and it was clear that he had used incomplete texts of certain of the family letters: these had been typed out for him in Cambridge by James's niece, and the texts approved by Mrs. William James; abundant ellipses in the volumes testify to the abridgments. In restoring the texts I accepted his selections although my desire was to print as many new letters as possible. Still, I felt it important to be a restorer as well as a selector. And then Lubbock had created a particular image of James, which I felt needed rounding out. Lubbock's edition printed only one hundred letters from James's twenty-sixth year to his fifty-fourth. The remaining three hundred covered his last two decades. The image of this collection is essentially that of the clean-shaven Master of Rye and Chelsea rather than the bearded, active, and more London-involved figure of Bolton Street and De Vere Gardens. Rebecca West described this Henry James long ago: "On London staircases," she wrote, "everyone turned to look at the American with the long, silky, black beard which I am told by one who met him then, gave him the appearance of 'an Elizabethan sea captain.'" Memoir writers have told us that his manner was grave and he was generally unsmiling, but by no means solemn; he was courteous and formal, and his wit was irresistible in its subtlety and syntactic adroitness.

This figure is absent from Lubbock for the most part; I restored it by drawing on large collections of early letters that surfaced after Lubbock. I also used James's business letters—to publishers, editors, and his agent—Lubbock's omission of which had given James an unworldly air. Indeed in Lubbock James's eminently practical side, his authorial professionalism, was entirely ignored. However, the friendly and affectionate side was abundantly present in admirable letters of an intimate and personal kind. James's hostesses were mostly disregarded, and of the younger generation only Hugh Walpole and Compton Mackenzie were on the scene. James's fanciful forms of address to Walpole, which worried the family, were deleted—the "dearest, dearest darlingest Hugh" or "belovedest Hugh." Walpole himself felt they might give a wrong impression.

I have used in this volume inevitably the same principles of selection which ruled for me in the four volumes. I have attempted to show the precocious Henry James of his adolescence and early maturity, the careful and meditative young man who was the friend of the Cambridge worthies, and then the traveler setting out in his twenty-sixth year for Europe. With his fortunate connections and his family's comfortable affluence, and under the experienced guidance of the Nortons, he moves around London with ease. Not many young men were as fortunate—to arrive in London and consort with Leslie Stephen and William Morris, to meet Rossetti and see the pre-Raphaelites in their studios. He hears Ruskin lecture. He has a meeting with Darwin. He visits George Eliot. A selection of letters throwing light on the young writer's impressions of London and the late Victorians gives us abundant insight. These are very good letters, for James's pen was vivid and descriptive and observant from the first. Some I have taken from Lubbock, restoring the deleted passages.

On he goes, the observant traveler, to Switzerland, carefully writing to different members of his family—if not to his parents, then to sister Alice, or brother William, knowing the letters are being shared and are all of a piece. He walks in Switzerland, descending into the Lombard plain for his first glimpses of Italy, sniffing from afar, he tells us, the country that will be for him the greatest repository of art and the finest background for American expatriates—sniffing the mustiness of the old museums and monasteries he will visit during his immersion into the Renaissance and history in those little walled towns, unpolluted by motor cars, that he came to love and know with a rare intimacy.

After the first ecstatic discoveries of his Italian journey, we glimpse some of his remarkable letters from the old cities and his now-classic effusion describing his first day in Rome. But something goes wrong. Perhaps it is the Italian food (James writes longingly of American vegetables) or too much pasta and olive oil: and with this unfamiliar diet, a certain amount of traveler's stress and tension and family complaints about his expenses—perhaps too a sense of loneliness as he walks the galleries in solitude. The letters begin to speak of his being unwell. And those to his brother, then a newly graduated Harvard M.D., tell us of Henry's constipation. Of course Henry had no television to tell him what pills to take; and the old Italian apothecaries offered we suspect simply old-fashioned purgatives. I remember when I read these letters that I had to tread lightly in the biography: the family was sensitive about the discussion of any kind of illness, and "constipation" seemed vulgar enough for me to dig up the word "costive" as substitute. But even that word bothered 95 Irving Street (the William James house, in which his second son lived). To modern eyes, Henry's discomfort may seem trivial and easily handled. But we are in 1869. Should he return to England and leave the delectable Italy to drink the waters at Malvern? In this volume I print for the first time three of his letters devoted to the commonplace subject. They are vivid enough and pathetic and one feels sorry for the sad interruption of James's travels. Readers will understand now his euphemisms like "hideous affliction" which Hemingway later, with his preoccupation with threats to his own manliness (as in *The Sun Also Rises*), translated into a fantasy of Henry's early impotence or castration by an imagined bicycle or riding accident. The sexual revolution of our time, the TV advertisements, our candor about the human body, have brought changed public attitudes. The modern reader will be inclined to less lurid fantasies than Hemingway's and see the dilemma of James's trying to deal in foreign cities, with foreign doctors—though he happily finds an Irish M.D. in Florence who proves helpful. Henry was clearly "up tight" during this journey in psychological as well as physical ways.

The various letters I have included in this volume not printed before should be of interest alike to general readers and researchers. I think with a certain amusement of the two I mentioned, the Shakespeare-Bacon controversy and the letter about the Walt Whitman review. These are to Manton Marble, an American journalist and later owner of the New York *World,* whom James had known during the months he was testing Manhattan as a place to live and write. Marble (a very Jamesian name) now lived in pleasant expatriation in a well-furnished and handsome house in Brighton: it was Edith Wharton's theory that Henry visited there often because Marble had a splendid modern American bathroom. I tell this anecdote to show the trials a searcher for letters sometimes undergoes. I read one day that the Library of Congress had Manton Marble's papers, and with a vision of a rare find, traveled to Washington expressly to search the archive. It was immense—great scrapbooks, a worldwide correspondence with bimetallists, for Manton Marble was an enthusiast about the monetary use of silver. For two or three days I leafed through these books, brought me by the library cartload, and found two thank-you notes from Henry James. Faced with spending a month or two at this job, and a running hotel bill, I decided life was too short, and Marble would probably be worth at best a sentence or two in the biography. Several years elapsed. Then, one morning, I received a letter from a London friend, the librarian of the London library, informing me that a lady had just walked into his office with over a hundred letters from Henry James "to one Manton Marble." The letters are now in the Houghton Library; I received at the time a typescript of them. I could congratulate myself, after the fact, on my biographical caution. For in due course I found that letters by James tended to be held out of archives: it seemed indeed that they were too precious to give away. (And I might add, the current auction prices for the novelist's holographs confirm this preciousness to the collectors of autographs.)

One never knows what scraps of information in a given letter will be of use to scholars or have appeal to general readers, and the individual who selects letters has to reconcile himself or herself to the idea that curious and searching readers will not always be satisfied. Each letter is a little bit of sovereign territory; and when a letter comes from the hand of genius it must be judged a valuable artifact. There are as we know all kinds of letters peculiar to personal careers and personal idiosyncrasies. There are letters I call "situational"—they illuminate a continuing situation among a group; and then there are letters of pure and undiluted gossip, some of it very old and no longer intelligible: this is true of the more than two hundred James wrote to Jessie Allen, the aristocratic lady whom he later named, because of her habit of bestowing such gifts on him as Venetian tapers or bearskin rugs, "Goody Twoshoes" after an old English verse. "Goody" Allen's letters, like the letters to Manton Marble, are amusing but would have little meaning to most readers. On the other hand, the "situational" letters involving the continuing friendship with Edith Wharton are of a high interest. For this reason I have added to this selection several new letters from James to Mrs. Wharton's one-time lover, William Morton Fullerton, a journalist I have always taken to be the original of Merton Densher in *The Wings of the Dove*. James and Fullerton had been acquainted for some fifteen years before James met Mrs. Wharton. The young American had turned up in London, suave and literary, and readily obtained a position on the London *Times*. But very soon that eminent journal moved him to its Paris bureau, for Fullerton, a Harvard graduate and the son of a clergyman, was well versed in French. Fullerton was a romantic, and the religiousness and idealism of his paternal home somehow became transformed into a very rich kind of sensuousness; he became one of the elegant seducers we find in the old novels, say Valmont in *Les Liaisons dangereuses*, a man of principle in some matters, but with a certain moral looseness—understandable since sex had been left out of his education in his father's church, and could be practiced with less guilt than the other sins. He was bisexual; his name is linked with such highly placed personages as the Ranee of Sarawak on the one hand and Lord Ronald Gower, the sculptor, on the other. As he got to know James better he seems to have offered the novelist well-edited accounts of his gallantries and escapades. By 1900 they were very good friends indeed, and James's letters reflect a constant regret at the rarity of Fullerton's visits to England. He wanted Fullerton's company and pleaded for it more and more in the loneliness of old age.

It was he who introduced Fullerton to Edith Wharton, gave a letter of introduction to the now middle-aged mustachioed Lothario. In due course James became a party to the developing liaison. Fullerton was a kind of liberator of Mrs. Wharton. She had lived two decades of her marriage to Teddy Wharton in a separate bedroom. Sex had proved a disaster between them. But the skilled libertine Fullerton restored her in her mid-forties to a sensual life and to a sexual appetite that seems to have been very great, and he endowed the experience with the romance and beauty of his refined nature. Readers of James might think of *The Ambassadors*—with Edith Wharton as Madame de Vionnet and Morton as a version of Chad Newsome, and James as the vicarious observer. To be sure, the novel had been written before the Wharton-Fullerton romance—but James had a way of predicting life and situations in his novels, of creating characters and then meeting them in actuality. The vicarious observer in *The Ambassadors* is Lambert Strether, and "it was nothing new to him . . . as we know, that a man might have—at all events a man such as he—an amount of experience out of any proportion to his adventures." James had his fantasies in his novels; and later he sometimes had the adventure of acting them out as if he had lived them.

My reason for dwelling on Fullerton is that I recently read some of the newly discovered correspondence of the lovers. Two brief sentences written by Edith caught my attention: "You write me like a lover, you treat me like a casual acquaintance! Which are you—what am I?" Good questions, given Morton's elusive nature. With the same directness she adds, "a certain consistency of affection is a fundamental part of friendship. One must know *à quoi s'en tenir*"—that is, where one stands. What emerges from these new letters in striking fashion is the double-edged nature of her affair: on the one hand it was liberating and profound, and on the other it was filled with the traditional *chagrin d'amour*.

Thus the triangle, Fullerton and Mrs. Wharton both friends of James; Mrs. Wharton loving and kept dangling; Fullerton receiving importuning letters from both asking him to make himself more available. That there had been a certain tenderness between Fullerton and James we know and we can read in one of the letters I print here for the first time. One remembers how in some of the letters to Hendrik Andersen James reveals his strong need for "touch"—he figures in many memoirs as a man who pats on the back, squeezes arms, embraces, and even kisses in the continental style on both cheeks. James wrote to Andersen: "I wish I could go to Rome and put my hands on you (oh, how lovingly I should lay them)." Other letters are filled with verbal embrace. His nephews often told how James used to say to them when they were young that they must not follow the bad Anglo-Saxon habit of not showing affection. Once, when they were boys, taking leave of one another, James told them he would turn his back so that they might without shyness give each other a fraternal hug or kiss. Knowing this, we can understand James's writing to Fullerton "hold me then *you* with any squeeze; grip me with any grip; press me with any pressure; trust me with any trust." The lonely bachelor issued, out of his Lamb House solitude, constant invitations to his younger friends, and it is interesting to find James writing in a 1900 letter here reproduced, "You are dazzling, my dear Fullerton; you are beautiful; you are more than tactful, you are tenderly, magically *tactile.*" This sentence is preceded by a confessional "I have told you before that the imposition of hands in a certain tender way 'finishes' me simply—and behold me accordingly more finished than the most *parachevé* of my own productions . . . You do with me what you will." Our literalists are likely to read these verbal extravagances with distinct reservations and suspicion of homosexuality: but I am inclined rather to see them as a part of the novelist's sheer joy in verbal playfulness, and he falls in, at the same time, with Fullerton's own tendency to gush flattery and flamboyance. In general, however, it is clear that Edith Wharton and Henry James shared certain affectionate feelings for Fullerton, and there is a distinct response to his sensuosity and romanticism. Beyond this, Mrs. Wharton loved him with a kind of compensatory emotion, as if to fill the blankness of her starved years.

Many indeed are the uses of old letters when they are filled with so much life and so much of the "visitable past." Readers of Henry James's tales know that his imagination created a masterpiece about a poet's love letters hidden in an old mattress in a shabby palace in Venice. That *tour de force* of storytelling, "The Aspern Papers," is one of the novelist's most popular works. There are minor stories on the same subject as well, like the one about a young man who buys an old desk and finds in a secret drawer a series of letters that might ruin a political reputation (perhaps an echo of the Parnell case). Like W. H. Auden in our time, Henry James enjoyed reviewing collections of letters, feeling all the while that he was invading privacy but relishing the revelations contained in the correspondence. There exists a little-known tale called "The Abasement of the Northmores," published at the turn of the century, which has a particular relevance to James's own letters. Lord Northmore has been an old windbag even if a personality in public life. He dies amid a flurry of solemn editorials, and his wife triumphantly publishes his collected letters. These prove "the text of his dullness and the proof of his fatuity." However, the letters of his old discreet and modest friend, Warren Hope, whose death provokes no editorials, are of a quite different sort—"natural, witty, vivid, playing with the idlest and lightest hand up and down the whole scale." His widow, reading them, reflects on "his easy power—his easy power; everything that brought him back brought back *that.*"

This is the very phrase for James's letters—their "easy power" resides in every sentence and even in the punctuation. James wrote with the lightest hand and played his themes and variations from letter to letter in a series of correspondences that are like Bach fugues—each having its own language and its own particular terms. In the Northmore story the widow of Warren Hope ends by printing a single volume of her husband's letters for her private reading, for the silent enjoyment of the easy power and the enchantment of their wit. In her will she orders the volume to be destroyed after her death, having herself burned the originals. This is the Jamesian doctrine about letters: the ultimate assertion of privacy. Was James thinking of his sister Alice's diary, printed in four or five copies for those closest to her? Deep in his own imagination and with his own distinct sense of his power he knew the fate of posthumous papers: that they can fall prey to all kinds of accidents no matter how cautious and specific the testament. There is a single sentence in the Northmore story that gives this feeling away—after describing all the precautions taken by the widow, the narrator remarks "if many were pages too intimate to publish, most of the others were too rare to suppress."

This must have been James's deepest and most private thought. "Too rare to suppress." The remark has guided me in all my selections of James's letters.

Chronology

1843	HJ born 15 April at 21 Washington Place, New York City, second son of Henry James of Albany and Mary Robertson Walsh of New York. Older brother, William, born 11 January 1842.
1843–44	Taken abroad by parents to Paris and London. Father, after breakdown, experiences conversion to Swedenborg.
1845–46	Garth Wilkinson James (Wilky) born 21 July 1845, New York City. Robertson James (Bob) born 29 August 1846.
1847–48	After sojourn in Albany, family settles in large house at 58 West 14th Street, New York City. Alice James, only daughter in the family, born 7 August 1848.
1848–55	HJ attends various day schools but receives no systematic education; much theatregoing and exposure to arts.
1855–58	Attends schools in Geneva, London, Paris, and Boulogne-sur-Mer and is privately tutored.
1858	School in Newport, Rhode Island, and friendship with T. S. Perry and John La Farge.
1859	Attends scientific school in Geneva and studies German in Bonn.
1860	Receives "obscure hurt" while serving as volunteer fireman, probably severe back strain. Studies painting briefly. Younger brothers are soldiers in Civil War.
1862–63	Spends term at Harvard Law School, and begins writing tales.
1864	Family settles in Boston and then at 20 Quincy Street, Cambridge. HJ publishes early anonymous story in *Continental Monthly* and begins writing reviews for *North American Review*. Spends autumn in Northampton, Massachusetts.
1865	Begins reviewing for *Nation*. First signed story, dealing with Civil War, published in *Atlantic Monthly*.
1869–70	Travels to England, France, and Italy. After brief period of ill health in Italy, goes to English spa. Death of beloved cousin, Minny Temple.

1870	Returns to Cambridge and writes first novel, *Watch and Ward*, serialized in *Atlantic*. Begins close friendship with William Dean Howells.
1872–74	Travels for summer in Europe with Alice and Aunt Kate; remains abroad writing travel sketches for *Nation*. Autumn in Paris, winter in Rome. Begins *Roderick Hudson*.
1874–75	Back home, completes *Roderick Hudson* and tests New York City as residence for his work. Writes much literary journalism for *Nation*.
1875	First three books published: *Transatlantic Sketches*, *Roderick Hudson*, and a collection of tales, *A Passionate Pilgrim*. Decides to live in Paris.
1875–76	Meets Turgenev, Flaubert, Daudet, Zola, Maupassant, and Edmond de Goncourt. Writes *The American*. Moves to London, settling in 3 Bolton Street. Revisits continent—Paris, Florence, Rome.
1878	"Daisy Miller," published in London, establishes fame. Brings out first volume of essays on French poets and novelists.
1879–82	Writes *The Europeans, Washington Square, Confidence, The Portrait of a Lady*. Elected to London clubs, accepted in British society, observes and studies British life and manners, forming many transatlantic friendships.
1882–83	Revisits Boston, pays first visit to Washington, seeing much of Henry Adamses. Death of mother. Returns to London and crosses Atlantic anew for death of father.
1884–86	Brother Garth Wilkinson (Wilky) dies in Milwaukee; sister Alice comes to be near HJ in London. Collected novels and tales published in 14 volumes. Writes *The Bostonians* and *The Princess Casamassima*.
1886	Moves to flat at 34 De Vere Gardens West, London.
1887	Long sojourn in Italy, mainly in Florence and Venice. Writes "The Aspern Papers" and *The Reverberator*. Friendship with Contance Fenimore Woolson and the Daniel Curtises.
1888	Publishes *Partial Portraits* and several collections of tales.
1889–90	*The Tragic Muse*.
1890–91	Dramatizes *The American*, which has short London run. Writes four comedies, which find no producers.
1892	Alice James dies in London. Friendship with W. Morton Fullerton.
1894	Miss Woolson dies in Venice, an apparent suicide.

1895	HJ is booed at first night of *Guy Domville*. Deeply depressed, he abandons the theatre and writes a series of ghost stories and tales of writers who are public failures and private successes.
1896–97	Writes *The Spoils of Poynton* and *What Maisie Knew*.
1898	Moves to Lamb House in Rye, Sussex. Writes "The Turn of the Screw."
1899–1900	Writes *The Awkward Age*, and *The Sacred Fount*. Friendship with Conrad, Ford Madox Hueffer (Ford), H. G. Wells, and Stephen Crane.
1902–04	Writes *The Ambassadors*, *The Wings of the Dove*, and *The Golden Bowl*. Friendships with sculptor Hendrik Andersen and Anglo-Irish socialite Jocelyn Persse. Meets and forms close friendship with Edith Wharton.
1905	Revisits the United States after 20-year absence. Travels to west coast and Florida, lecturing on Balzac and the American modes of speech.
1906–10	Writes *The American Scene* and final tales published in 1910 in *The Finer Grain*. Edits and revises 24-volume selected edition of novels and tales, the New York Edition. Friendship with Hugh Walpole.
1910	Long nervous illness. Returns to United States with brother William, who dies of heart ailment. Brother Robertson (Bob) dies in Concord, Massachusetts.
1911–12	In spite of infirmities, writes autobiographies: *A Small Boy and Others* and *Notes of a Son and Brother*. Moves into London flat at Carlyle Mansions.
1913	Sargent paints HJ's portrait as seventieth birthday gift from three hundred friends and admirers.
1914	Publishes *Notes on Novelists*. Begins visiting wounded in war hospitals.
1915	Becomes a British subject. In December, suffers a stroke.
1916	King George V bestows Order of Merit. HJ dies 28 February in Chelsea, aged 72. Funeral in Chelsea Old Church. Ashes buried in Cambridge, in James family plot.
1976	Commemorative tablet unveiled in Poets' Corner of Westminster Abbey, 17 June.

HENRY JAMES
Selected Letters

1 · Initiations
1855–1870

The early letters of Henry James are written largely to members of his family—his parents, his sister Alice, his older brother William—and to a few Newport and Cambridge friends. They deal with his early experiences in Europe, his period of schooling in Geneva, his life in Cambridge, and finally his first independent trip to England, France, and Italy, the traditional "grand tour" of young Americans of comparatively affluent families of the time. William James had had a year abroad during 1867–68 devoted to studies in Germany, and Henry was given his turn. He chose, instead of a program of study, "exposure" to the European past and particularly its artistic manifestations. Charles Eliot Norton and members of his family were abroad at the time, and James had the advantage of the American art-scholar's numerous connections, especially in England. James had been in France and England as a boy, but the trip to Italy was an entirely new experience. The letters reflect a certain loneliness and isolation once he gets to the Continent; and he suffered from a rather debilitating constipation, which took him back to England to a spa at Malvern. Once he returned to Cambridge the symptoms disappeared.[1]

1. HJ's allusions to his early physical problems and what he called his "obscure hurt," suffered while acting as a volunteer fireman at a Newport stable fire just before the Civil War, suggest a greater invalidism than actually existed. Doctors at the time found no injuries (this was why HJ used the word "obscure"). For details of James family illnesses, including the ways the young Jameses seemed to use their symptoms intuitively to manipulate their contradictory and demanding parents, see Jean Strouse, *Alice James* (1980), Howard M. Feinstein, *Becoming William James* (1984), Leon Edel, *Henry James, A Life* (1985), and Jane Maher's account of the younger brothers, Wilky and Bob, in *Biography of Broken Fortunes* (1986).

1 · To Edgar Van Winkle

Ms Harvard

Paris [1857?]

Dear Eddy,[1]

As I heard you were going to turn the club into a Theatre. And as I was asked w'ether I wanted to belong here is my answer. I would like very much to belong.

Yours truly
H. James

1. The earliest extant letter by HJ, written when he was thirteen, was addressed to a New York playmate, son of a lawyer. In A Small Boy and Others (1913), chapter 18, HJ describes the Van Winkle boy as walking "in a regular maze of culture."

2 · To Thomas Sergeant Perry

Mf Duke

Bonn, on the Rhine, Prussia
Wednesday, July 18th, 1860

Mein lieber, schönster Peri[1]—

If, on writing your letter of June 29th received by me this afternoon you had such an abundant stock of news to retail, that you did not know with which choice bit to commence, if *you* who have nothing but the gossip of a *little country village* to relate find yourself in such case, how much more perplexed must I be, *I* who can speak of the most hallowed spots of time-honoured historic Europe!!!!!! I think I must fire off my biggest gun first. One-two-three! Bung gerdee bang bang. . . . .!!! What a noise! Our passages are taken in the Adriatic, for the 11th of September!!!!!! We are going immediately to Newport, which is the place in America we all most care to live in. I'll tell you the reason of this as briefly as I can. Willie has decided to try and study painting seriously, and wished [to] return home and do so, if possible with Mr. Hunt.[2] That is the reason, at least in a great measure the reason (for his going home need not necessitate our all going) of this determination. Besides that, I think that if we are to live in America it is about time we boys should take up our abode there; the more I see of this estrangement of American youngsters from the land of their birth, the less I believe in it. It should also be the land of their breeding. I cannot devote my whole letter to this because I have so much more to say.

You ask me if I have made any of those courses³ on foot which seem so pleasant to you, and if so to tell you about them. I am glad to say I have. Before leaving Switzerland Willie and [I] had about a week's walking among the mountains. Although we did but little compared with what many people do and have done, we enjoyed more in a week than I thought possible to cram into so short a time. We went first from Geneva to Chamouni. Have you heard of it? It is the rendezvous of travellers of all nations who wish to "do" a few Swiss Mountains. It is down at the foot of Mont-Blanc (in Savoy or what now *miserabile dictu,* is France). We had but a day there, for the weather gave bad promise. We went over a mountain called the Moutonvert (two-hours) to the Mer de Glace. The M. de G. is a broad river of peaked, uneven ice that winds from the mountains down a deep ravine, and opens here and there into dark watery crevasses. We crossed—which with stout nails in your boots and a good spiked-pole is not a difficult business. We also crossed another glacier, the Gl. des Bassons which although smaller, is more beautiful than the M. de G. for the ice is much clearer and more sparkling. It is at the same time however, much more slippery and therefore I think more difficult of passage. We then crossed a mountain called the Tête-Noire to a place in the Canton du Valais called Martigny. It takes ten hours. We had a mule between us and I grieve to say that having hurt my foot the day before at Chamouni, I was obliged for a good part of the way to bestride the ugly beast. From Martigny we went up the great St. Bernard about whose good Father's and dogs we have both read, I am sure, in our primmers and geographys. The ascent takes about nine hours. I went almost all the way on foot for although we had a mule the guide profited most by him. At about three hours distance from the hospice the scenery becomes most wild dreary and barren. Everything indicates a great elevation. The growth of everything but the enormous rocks is stunted—not a blade of grass or straggling mountain pine. The tinkling of the last cattle bell dies away, you see the last hardy Alpine sheep climbing over desolate heights which would seem to afford no nourishment and then you enter upon the snow which lies all the year round. We had about an hour and a half's walk in it. It was very deep—far above our heads—but so hard on the surface that we didn't sink deeply in. It tires the legs to walk long in it, and it was bitter cold, so I was heartily glad when the high bleak hospice came in sight. We were received by one of the fathers who took us into a warm sitting-room, and gave us warm slippers and hot broth and roast mutton. He sat with us all the evening—a most kindly and courteous man. I asked him for pen and paper and sat me down to indite, by the light of a solitary tallow-candle a letter to you, dear friend. But sleep and chilliness with which I wrestled in vain soon overcame me and I retired to pass the night on a mattrass and pillow which were apparently stuffed with damp sand. In the morning we saw the dogs eight in number. They are noble majestic, tawny creatures and have (the old ones at least) the same stately courtesy in their bearing as the Fathers themselves. At a little distance from the Hospice is the house in which the corpses of those found in the snow are placed. As they cannot be buried they are stood around the walls in their shrouds and a grim and ghastly sight it is. They fall into all sorts of hideous positions, with such fiendish grins on their faces! faugh! I wish I could picture to you the appearance of that mournful region—I mean the colour. The sky is of a liquid twinkling sort of blue, and the gigantic gray and white rocks rise up against it so sharply-cut and so barren, and the stillness that reigns around and the apparent nearness of every object from the greater tenuity of the atmosphere! For all the courtesy and kindness which the priests expend nothing is asked. There is an alms-box in the chapel where one can drop what he pleases (nobody knows anything about it)—and that is all. The descent takes another day. On the following one we went by a carriage from Martigny to a place called Loèche-les-Bains, where there are warm medicinal baths which patients take in public tanks, sitting up to their chins in the nauseous places for hours together and reading and eating in them. Loèche stands at the foot of the ridge of the Gemmi over which one of the most wonderful passes in the Alps has been made; we crossed it the following day. From Loèche you see nothing but a vast towering surface of vertical rock naked and rugged. You cannot believe it possible that you can pass over it for no trace of a path can be discerned. And indeed the path is most curious. It is very narrow (five feet at the widest and generally about three) very steep and winds in such zigzags, that it turns so from right to left, that you never see whence you've come or whither you are going. In one place (so says the guide book, the spot escaped my notice) a plumb-line may be dropped over the precepice down a distance of 1600 ft. without any abuttement to interfere. On the plateau on the summit we had for a little over an hour of snow, and were down on the other side in seven hours from the time we started. That same evening we reached Interlaken where we found all the "folks" except Robby whom at that young gent's own earnest solicitation father left at school in Geneva, but who now is gone with his teacher and mates to travel on foot among the mountains, and to go into Italy as far as Venice. I wish I were in his place. The rest had been already some time at Interlaken which is a strangers' summer place full of hotels and English people and had thoroughly "done" the place and its neighborhood. We remained there for three days longer, saw what there was to be seen and then set out for Germany. We came almost directly here, stopping for a couple of days only at Wiesbaden and Frankfort. At the former place of which I suppose you have heard, we drank of course of the hot waters, and witnessed the gambling for which it is famous. Then we sailed up (or down) the Rhine. I am not the first person who has been disappointed in the Rhine and have a better reason than many for such sacreligiousness inasmuch as I had just come from among the mountains of Switzerland whose high privilege it is to make everything else look mean and small.

We are all three of us installed in German families for the learning of the German tongue. Wilky and I together, Willie alone.[4] The gentleman I am with is one Doctor Humpert Latin and Greek professor at the Gymnasium here. His family is composed of his wife and sister who are to aid him in the task of conversing ceaselessly with us (a task for which they might seem to be but ill-qualified as I don't believe that between them they can muster, Germanlike, more than half a dozen teeth). Also of his son Theodore aged seventeen, of whom I see little, as he is away at his lessons all day, and of five young Deutschers from six to fourteen years of age. With their company I am favoured only at meals. They are not his sons but are with him for intellectual cultivation, "all the comforts of a home" etc. This is an opportunity for me to see something of German life, in what would be called, I suppose the middle classes. I naturally compare it with the corresponding life at home, and think it truly inferior. The women stop at home all day, doing the housework, drudging, and leading the most homely and I should say joyless lives. I fancy they never look at a book, and all their conversation is about their pots and pans. The sister asked me the other day if we hadn't a king in the United States! The Doctor is a pleasant genial man with very little force of character and more book-learning, that is knowledge of Greek and Sanscrit than anything else. The other day, Sunday last, I think we went all of us, wife, sister and little Dutchers (a nice little party of eleven) to a place called Godesberg within ten minutes of this, by rail, to see a little mound, or mountain they call it, with a ruin on the top. Notwithstanding the stifling heat of the weather, and the dust, we went under a shed on the dusty road and partook of some steaming coffee and boggy loaf-cake, then strolled about and came back to drink some sweetened wine and water.

When I see you, which will be you see, much sooner than we either of us hoped I can tell you more in an hour than I can do in fifty letters. Your plan for the first of August savours of "Rollo,"[5] did you get the idea from him? Of course I will write you what I do, but I'm sure I shall feel all day as if I had the sword of Damocles suspended above my head. A fearful vengeance awaits Wilky's foolhardy imprudence in disclosing, as he did, my secret employment. You ask upon what style of work I am employed. I may reply that to no style am I a stranger, there is none which has not been adorned by the magic of my touch. I shall be most happy to send you fifty copies of each work, the payment of which can await my return.

I must now close as I have written all this at one breath, that is at one sitting, and am rather tired. I shall of course write before we sail. Good bye. Remembrances to all.

Yours sincerely
Henry James Jr.

P.S. I forgot to say that I received your letter of June 1st while at Interlaken.

The date of our sailing is the *eleventh* of Sept. not 15th, as I had first put it. Tant mieux!

1. Thomas Sergeant Perry (1845–1928), HJ's schoolmate at Newport, whose ancestors included the two commodores of history, the Perrys of Lake Erie and of Japan.

2. William Morris Hunt (1824–1879), the French-influenced American painter, had a studio in Newport.

3. An example of HJ's lapsing into French as if it were English—a consequence of his foreign schooling from 1855 to 1858 and his exposure to the language in Geneva.

4. Later recollections of this summer are recorded in *Notes of a Son and Brother* (1914), chapter 2.

5. An allusion to the juvenile "Rollo" series by Jacob Abbott (1803–1879), a Massachusetts educator and Congregationalist clergyman who published 28 volumes containing "instructive" stories for children.

3 · To Thomas Sergeant Perry

Mf Duke

New-York, Sunday
[1 November 1863]

Dear Sargy,

I am well aware that I might have answered your last letter sooner; you are well aware that I have not done so. What more need be said? Fancies will not alter facts and facts can do without them. A delay of this kind is always fatally prolonged by the dread existing in the mind of the delinquent of the excuses he will have to make when he *does* write. I make no excuses—I have none to make. I wrap myself in my immaculate Virtue. My foolish delay is, like the emancipation act,[1] a *fait accompli*. You know *that* cannot be receded from, need not be palliated etc etc; there it stands, stern, immutable, unchangeable.— Doubtless, if this strain is the result of my writing, you will prefer infinite silence.—Well, well, you know even Homer will sometimes nod.—Your letter is dated Oct. 24th—or rather 25th (Sunday). This also is Sunday—i.e. is a wet, nasty, black, horrid, damp-disgusting day. I have just finished breakfast and came up to my little roost to digest my rolls and coffee and pick my teeth, and gaze around at my four blank walls and at the white watery sky, and resolve the problem of extracting merriment—or at least, contentment, from these dismal surroundings. If my letter proves bald and blank and flat, revile it not—it will merely be from an excess of local colour. Here is a nice sentimental conundrum, such as free thinking young ladies would like: no, it is too nauseating; I will not give it.—I wish I had a novel to read. It cannot be denied that this desire is one of the elementary cravings of mankind. We take to it as to our mother's milk.—But I am

7

destitute and can procure nothing approaching a Romance unless I go out in the rain and buy the Sunday Herald. I shall certainly not go to church. I went twice last Sunday. In the morning to hear an old Scotch presbyterian divine under whom my mother sat in her youth. Darkly must her prospect of Heaven have been obscured! The old man is now eighty, but he still finds strength with great reinforcements of tobacco-juice, to fulminate against back-sliders and evil doers. I may emphatically say that he gave us hell. It is curious. People may allege the existence of such sermons and doctrines as those as a proof of the immobility of human developement; but the real measure of progress is in the way they are received. Seventy years ago, people were really moved and frightened, and convulsed, convinced and converted I suppose, by all such grim anathemas; but now, even when they are willing to pay a man for grinding them out, they are willing to let them pass for what they are worth. The brimstone fizzles up in the pulpit but fades away into musk and cologne-water in the pews. (Don't it strike you that I'm very epigrammatic?)—Well, in the evening, at the instance of Bob Temple,[2] I went to listen to the preaching of Mrs. Cora V. L. Hatch. She holds forth in a kind of underground lecture room in Astor Place. The assemblage, its subterraneous nature, the dim lights, the hard-working, thoughtful physiognomies of everyone present quite realised my idea of the meetings of the early Christians in the Catacombs, although the only proscription under which the Hatch disciples labour is the necessity of paying ten cents at the door. Three individuals from the audience formed themselves into a committee to select a subject for Cora to discuss—and they were marshalled out of the room by a kind of fat showman, who, as I wittily suggested, was probably Mr. Chorus V. L. Hatch.[3] They chose: "the Evidence of the continued existence of the Spirit after death." For some moments Cora remained motionless; probably, as Bob Temple said, "silently invoking her maker." Then she began to speak. Well, the long and short of it is, that the whole thing was a string of such arrant platitudes, that after about an hour of it, when there seemed to be no signs of a let-up we turned and fled. So much for Cora.

Your letter contains a little dissertation on prejudice, suggested by a book you had been reading (Locke on the Human Understanding), in which you do me the honour to ask me my opinion two or three times. It is a subject I have thought on not at all (like every other subject), and upon which I shrink from giving a judgement to you who have been reading Locke, even as a little child paddling among the chance waves that roll up about his feet on Newport beach, shrinks from following the strong man who ventures forth into the great ocean.—I agree with you perfectly that "prejudice is one of the worst evils which afflict humanity"; but I hardly think that it is one which each man can take in hand for himself and drive away. Every one knows the injustice of it, but few people are conscious that they possess it. Wilfully, intentionally prejudiced persons are very rare. Every one certainly is more or less prejudiced, but "unbeknown" to themselves. Is not a prejudice a judgement formed on a subject upon *data* furnished, not by the subject itself, but by the mind which regards it? (This is a very crude definition, but it will show you what I mean.) These *data* are the fruits of the subtlest influences,—birth, education, association. Unless carefully watched they insinuate themselves into every opinion we form. They grow to be the substance of our very being. So far are they from being subjects of consciousness that they almost become vehicles thereof. They exercise, then, a great weight in our judgements. They are so intimately connected with every mental process, that they insidiously pervert our opinions, discolour and distort the objects of our vision. The opinion is consciously formed, perhaps; but not appreciatively, critically. That is we are conscious of it when formed, but not during formation. Now, all opinions which we consciously hold for any time, receive in a measure the sanction of conscience. And then—who shall gainsay them? They have been stamped at the royal mint: let them pass current. However false they may be, however base the metal of which they are composed, they have undergone an ordeal which renders them supremely valid in our eyes. You will say we cannot impose them on others. Certainly not. But when others reject them they become doubly dear to ourselves. We treasure them up. We gloat over them in private. We become millionaires of self-complacency.—This of course is the very height of prejudice.—But there is no-one whose judgements are *all* pre-conceived. And even the most prejudiced people when convinced that they *are* so are willing to correct themselves. But the question is to find out where the prejudice lies, to distinguish the true from the false. This is immensely difficult—so much so, that I should fear a man setting to work on his own hook would find it impossible. We know when we lie, when we kill, when we steal;

when we deceive or violate others, but it is hard to know when we deceive or violate ourselves. You will say that a prejudice violates others—their rights, their claims, etc. Certainly it does when it is practically carried out; and *then* we can straightway take cognizance of it, measure it, reform it or cast it off. But as long as it is held as a mere opinion, I suppose it only violates some abstract standard of truth and justice. It cannot be denied, however, that we have mighty few opinions that we are not desirous to act upon.—Cannot you imagine the state of irresolution and scepticism and utter nothingness a man would be reduced to, who set to work to re-cast his old opinions, pick them clean of prejudice and build them up into a fairer structure? I'm afraid that he would find he had pulled out the chief corner stones, and that the edifice was prostrate, and he almost crushed in its ruins. In his desire to believe nothing but what his reason showed him to be true, I think he would end by believing nothing at all. It is a question whether he would not have attained the chief felicity of man; whether it is *not* better to believe nothing than to believe falsely; whether scepticism is not preferable to superstition. But it is a question which *I* can't answer. It seems to be like a choice between lunacy and idiocy,—death by fire—or by water. We were certainly born to believe. The truth was certainly made to be believed. Life is a prolonged reconciliation of these two facts. As long as we squint at the truth instead of looking straight at it—*i. e.* as long as we are prejudiced instead of fair, so long we are miserable sinners. But it seems to me that this fatal obliquity of vision inheres not wholly in any individual but is some indefinable property in the social atmosphere.—When by some concerted movement of humanity the air is purified then the film will fall from our eyes and (to conclude gracefully) we shall gaze undazzled at the sun!!!! How I *do* run on! You will certainly fear to broach any further question of morals THIS being the penalty. In reading the above over I am struck with its great dogmatism and crudity. It is probably all wrong or even all nothing. At all events, supply a query after every assertion and enclose the whole in a great parenthesis and interrogation point, or even scratch it all out.

9:30 P.M. I have just come in from another attempt at evening worship. *Monday morn.* My letter is delayed a day longer. I could not finish it last evening. I commenced to tell you about some religious performances I had just witnessed. As it had stopped raining and I was tired of having been in-doors so long I went with the ever faithful Bob Temple to a service held by the so-called "congregation of the new dispensation" just up Broadway. It was really wonderfully entertaining and worth telling about. I haven't time to describe it at length, tho' it was all extraordinary.—In fact my letter is so long already that I won't bother you with describing it at all. I enclose a little scribble of the platform. We had a grand oration (tremendous) from the female on the right and singing from her on the left. Love to Willie. *Is A. Porter in town?*

Yours very truly,
H.J.

1. President Lincoln's Emancipation Proclamation of 1 January 1863.
2. Robert Emmet Temple, Jr. (b. 1840), HJ's cousin. See *Notes of a Son and Brother*, chapter 5.
3. A foreshadowing of HJ's satirizing of secular preaching a quarter of a century later in *The Bostonians*.

4 · *To Mr. Haviland*

Ms Lynn Jachney

Boston, 13 Ashburton Place
May 17*th* [1865]

My dear Haviland[1]—

Many thanks for your letter and the enclosure from Mademoiselle Anna, whom I wish I knew otherwise than by letter. If her tongue is as ready as her pen she must be a very agreeable young lady "to have round." At Northampton, for instance, her presence would be a Great blessing—Northampton to me has become so completely a chapter in the past that it seems odd to read of my old friends still being there. I can readily believe that the place is looking beautiful in these Spring days. I am glad to hear that Mrs. Haviland improves—if only a little. Pray give her my best regards and good wishes when you next visit her. How often by-the-bye, does this event take place? Miss Wheeler too, you intimate, is still at N. I am very proud to learn that they regret my absence—or even notice it. They must both feel repaid for having staid out what must have been a pretty tedious winter, by the coming of these lovely days.—Elizabeth Rock must be looking charming just now.—I imagine myself in my little oblong apartment: I see once more the tattered old matting on the floor and the yellow paper on the walls. Outside, Fred is lugging—and hugging—a load of fire-wood. A tap at my door: yourself with hat and stick enter and propose a walk. *Je veux bien.* In the hall, Jenny proposing a bath to Miss Wheeler. At the front door, Ben proposing a journey into town, to the "Major." Down the road, the Doctor proposing damnation, generally, to a refractory Irishman.—You speak of having seen Howard, recently; where? in New York?—I have not heard from him for an age: but I suppose he has taken up his connexions, permanently, with Northampton. The warm weather must be bringing new patients. I saw Mr. Duncan Pell, recently, at Newport; and he told me that his brother was still there and not markedly better: which I was sorry to hear.—Is Miss Wheeler somewhat better. Please remember me to her in the kindest manner and tell her that my joy if she *is* better is only equalled by my sorrow if she is not. Has she the same little room over the kitchen?—And has Mrs. Haviland the same room too?—I don't mean as Miss Wheeler, but as she (Mrs. H.) always had.—So Miss Merritt has married and gone to house keeping: so I think your letter said. In default of being the husband, how I would like to be the *house,* which she keeps! Pardon me: on consulting your letter, I find that it *is* for her brother that Miss M. has assumed the office of housekeeper. My apprehensions are quieted. Remember me affectionately to Miss Merritt, please; and ask her if she would like to walk in to Kingsley's this afternoon and purchase some chocolate creams.—You speak of my photog. I have none on hand, unfortunately; but I have not forgotten my promise to Mrs. Haviland; and when (having made twenty other promises) the pressure of public opinion forces me to go thro' the torture of sitting once more, Mrs. Haviland shall have one [of] the results of the operation. You speak of my literary productions; thank you for your interest in them. There is nothing in the wind just now; but when there is I will let you know.

Ever truly yours
H. James Jr.

1. This letter, recently discovered, throws direct light on HJ's stay at Northampton, Massachusetts, from August to December 1864, when he was 21. The only other information we have is his own account in the preface to *Roderick Hudson,* the novel whose opening chapters are set in this watering town of his time.

5 · To Thomas Sergeant Perry

Ms Colby

Cambridge, Sept. 20th [1867]

Mon cher vieux Thomas:—

J'ai là sous les yeux depuis hier ta gentille lettre du 4 7bre. Je fus bien aisé de te savoir de retour a Paris, que tu n'as sans doute pas quitté. Je crois que tu ne regretteras jamais d'y avoir passé une grosse partie de ton temps; car enfin, quoiqu'on en dise, c'est une des merveilles de l'univers. On y apprend a connaître les hommes et les choses, et pour peu qu'on soit parvenu à y attraper le sentiment du *chez soi*, quelque genre de vie que l'on mène plus tard, on ne sera jamais un ignorant, un ermite—enfin un *provincial.*—Tu as depensé toute une page de ta lettre à me parler de l'Exposition.—Que le diable l'emporte, cette maudite baraque! Nous en avons bien assez, même ici à Cambridge. J'aurais bien mieux aimé que tu m'eusses parlé de toi, que tu m'eusses donné de tes nouvelles intimes. (En voilà, des imparfaits du subjonctif! Après cela dira qui voudras que je ne sais pas le Français!) Je me suis donné hier le plaisir d'aller chez tes camarades, Storey et Stratton,[1] recueillir de tes nouvelles. Ces messieurs ont été bien bien aimables, ils m'ont fait part des lettres qu' ils ont reçues de toi pendant l'été. J'en ai beaucoup ri, de ces lettres folles et charmantes. On ne peut avoir plus d'esprit, ni une gaillardise de meilleur ton. Ah mon cher, que je t'en porte envie, de tes courses et de tes aventures, et de ton humeur Rabelaisiaque!—Decidément, je plante là mon français: ou plutôt c'est lui qui me plante.—As I say, Storey and Stratton read me and lent me a large portion of your recent letters, beginning with a long one from Venice to the former. Many of your gibes of course I didn't understand, the context being absent. But I understood enough to enjoy the letters very much and to be able to congratulate you on your charming humour. (How detestable this *you* seems after using the Gallic *toi!*) Let me repeat in intelligible terms that I'm very glad to think of you as being as much as possible in Paris—city of my dreams! I feel as if it would count to my advantage in our future talks (and perhaps walks). When a man has seen Paris somewhat attentively, he has seen (I suppose) the biggest achievement of civilization in a certain direction and he will always carry with him a certain little *reflet* of its splendour.—I had just been reading, when your letter came, Taine's *Graindorge*,[2] of which you speak. It seems to me a truly remarkable book in the way of *writing* and description, but to lack very much the deeper sort of observation. As a writer—a man with a language, a vocabulary and a style, I enjoy Taine more almost than I do any one; but his philosophy of things strikes me as essentially superficial and as if subsisting in the most undignified subservience to his passion for description.—I have also read the last new Mondays of Ste. B., and always with increasing pleasure.³ Read in the 7th (I think) if you haven't already, an account of A. de Vigny. Truly, exquisite criticism can't further go.—Have you read M. *de Camours*, by Octave Feuillet?⁴—a sweet little story! Read by all means if you haven't, (I assume that you have the time), *Prosper Randoce*, by V. Cherbuliez.⁵ It's a work of extraordinary skill and power and I think takes the rag off all the French Romancers, save the illustrious G. Sand, *facile princeps*. I read recently, by the way, this lady's *Memoirs* a compact little work in ten volumes. It's all charming (if you are not too particular about the exact truth) but especially the two first volumes, containing a series of letters from her father, written during Napoleon's campaigns. I think they are the best letters I ever read. But you doubtless know the book.—In English I have read nothing new, except M. Arnold's *New Poems*, which of course you will see or have seen.—For real and exquisite pleasure read Morris's *Life & Death of Jason*. It's long but fascinating, and replete with genuine beauty.—There is nothing new of course in the universe of American letters—except the projected resuscitation of Putnam's Magazine.⁶ Great news, you see! We live over here in a thrilling atmosphere.—Well, I suppose there *are* thrills here; but they dont come from the booksellers—not even from Ticknor and Fields, publishers of *Every Saturday*. I applaud your high resolves with regard to work, when you get home. You will always have my sympathy and co-operation.—Have you in view a *particular office* here at Harvard, for which you are particularly fitting yourself, or meaning so to do?—Upon this point, on which I have long felt a natural curiosity I have as yet failed to obtain satisfaction. Tell me all about it and unfold your mind to your devoted H.J.—I should think that by the time you get home you will have become tolerably well saturated with the French language and spirit; and if you contrive to do as much by the German, you will be a pretty wise man. There will remain the classical and the English. On the first I say nothing. *That* you will take care of; and I suppose you will study Latin and Greek by the aid of German and *vice-versa*. But the English litera ture and spirit is a thing which we tacitly assume that we know much more of than we actually do. Don't you think so? Our vast literature and literary history is to most of us an unexplored field—especially when we compare it to what the French is to the French.—Deep in the timorous recesses of my being is a vague desire to do for our dear old English letters and writers *something* of what Ste. Beuve and the best French critics have done for theirs. For one of my calibre it is an arrogant hope. *Aussi* I don't talk about it.—To enter upon any such career I should hold it invaluable to spend two or three years on English soil—face to face with the English landscape, English monuments and English men and women.—At the thought of a study of this kind, on a serious scale, and of possibly having the health and time to pursue it, my eyes fill with heavenly tears and my heart throbs with a divine courage.—But men don't accomplish valuable results alone, dear Sarge, and there will be nothing so useful to me as the thought of having companions and a laborer with whom I may exchange feelings and ideas. It is by this constant exchange and comparison, by the wear and tear of living and talking and observing that works of art shape themselves into completeness; and as artists and workers, we owe most to those who bring to us most of human life.—When I say that I should like to do as Ste. Beuve has done, I don't mean that I should like to imitate him, or reproduce him in English: but only that I should like to acquire something of his intelligence and his patience and vigour. One feels—I feel at least, that he is a man of the past, of a dead generation; and that we young Americans are (without cant) men of the future. I feel that my only chance for success as a critic is to let all the breezes of the west blow through me at their will. We are Americans born—*il faut en prendre son parti.* I look upon it as a great blessing; and I think that to be an American is an excellent preparation for culture. We have exquisite qualities as a race, and it seems to me that we are ahead of the European races in the fact that more than either of them we can deal freely with forms of civilization not our own, can pick and choose and assimilate and in short (aesthetically etc.) claim our property wherever we find it. To have no national stamp has hitherto been a defect and a drawback, but I think it not unlikely that American writers may yet indicate that a vast intellectual fusion and synthesis of the various National tendencies of the world is the condition of more important achievements than any we have seen. We must of course have something of our own—something distinctive and homogeneous—and I take it that we shall find it in our moral consciousness, our unprecedented spiritual lightness and vigour. In this sense at least we shall have a national *cachet.*—I expect nothing great during your lifetime or mine perhaps: but my instincts quite agree with yours in looking to see something original and beautiful disengage itself from our ceaseless fermentation and turmoil. You see I am willing to leave it a matter of instinct. God speed the day.—But enough of "abstract speculation," marked as it is by a very concrete stupidity. I haven't a spark of your wit and humor, my boy, and I can't write amusing letters. Let me say, now while I think of it, that I was quite unaware until I heard it the other evening from Ben Peirce, of how serious your accident had been on Mt. Vesuvius. In writing to you after first hearing of it, I believe I didn't even speak of it. A thousand pardons for my neglect. My poor dear fellow: accept all my retrospective commiseration. It must have been the very devil of an exasperation. And you carry a classic wound—a Vesuvian scar!—Ah why was I not there (i.e. at the hotel) to sponge your gory face, and to change your poultices?—Well, thank the Lord it was no worse, I always said so when we used to walk on the hanging rock at Newport.—I have used up my letter with nonentities, and have no space nor strength for sweet familiar talk. No news. The summer (like a civil young man in the horse car) is giving its seat to the mellow Autumn—the glorious, the grave, the divine. We are having October weather in September: *pourvu que ca dure.* This is *American* weather— worth all the asphaltic breezes of Paris.—I have been all summer in Cambridge—*sans découcher une seule nuit.* Tiens! mon francais qui me retrouve!—It has been quite cool and comfortable, but "stiller than chiselled marble"—Vide Tennyson. I have a pleasant room with a big soft bed and good chairs, and with books and shirtsleeves I found the time pass rapidly enough.—I'm sorry to hear you say that your plans may not agree with Willie's for the winter.[7] I hope you may adjust them. You'll of course find it pleasant enough to be together; but I hope neither of you will sacrifice any thing to your serious interests. I should suppose of course that *you* will prefer Berlin. We are expecting daily to hear from W. He wrote eight weeks ago that he was feeling much better: news which gladded my heart.—I haven't seen John[10] all summer; but I heard from him yesterday.—Your sister is again a mother: a little girl, and doing well. But this you will have heard. I draw to a close. My letter is long but not brilliant. I can't make 'em brilliant until some one or something makes me brilliant. A hundred thanks for the photos. About has a capital, clever face;[8] and Sardou a highly refined and Parisian one.[9]—By all means send your own and others. Write punctually.—Farewell, *mon vieux. tout à toi*

H.J.

1. Perry's Harvard classmates Moorfield Storey (1845–1929), later an eminent lawyer and reformer, and Charles E. Stratton.

2. Hippolyte Taine, *Notes sur Paris: Vie et opinions de M. Frédéric-Thomas Graindorge* (1868), a series of ironical studies of Parisian life.

3. An allusion to the weekly literary column *Causeries du lundi* by the French critic and literary historian Charles-Augustin Sainte-Beuve (1804–1869). These columns, first published in the newspaper *Le Constitutionnel*, were collected in book form under the titles *Causeries du lundi* (15 vols., 1851–1862) and *Nouveaux lundis* (13 vols., 1863–1870). HJ kept these volumes in his library.

4. A novel reminiscent of *Les Liaisons dangereuses.*

5. Cherbuliez (1829–1899), a French novelist of Swiss origin, was a great favorite of the young HJ.

6. *Putnam's Monthly Magazine,* founded in 1853, suspended in 1857, was revived in 1868 as *Putnam's Magazine,* but lasted only two years.

7. WJ was studying in Germany, where he remained for 18 months during 1867 and 1868.

8. Edmond About (1828–1885), journalist and novelist. For an account of HJ's early impressions of About see *William Wetmore Story and His Friends* (1903), I, 359.

9. Victorien Sardou (1831–1908), the technique of whose "well-made" plays HJ greatly admired.

10. John La Farge; see Letter 10.

6 · To William James

Ms Harvard

Cambridge Nov. 22d [1867]

Dear Willy—

I haven't written to you for some time, because the others seemed to be doing so. We at last got some little news about your health. Praised be the Lord that you are comfortable and in the way of improvement!—I recd. about a fortnight ago—your letter with the review of Grimm's novel[1]—after a delay of nearly a month on the road, occasioned by I know not what. I am very sorry for the delay as it must have kept you in suspense, and even yet I am unable to give you a satisfactory reply. I liked your article very much and was delighted to find you attempting something of the kind. It struck me as neither dull nor flat, but very readable. I copied it forthwith and sent it to the *Nation*. I received no answer—which I take to be an affirmative. I expected it to appear in yesterday's paper; but I see it is absent, crowded out I suppose by other matter. I confess to a dismal apprehension that something may have happened to it on the road to New York and have just written to Godkin[2] to tell me whether he actually received it. But I have little doubt he has done so and that it is waiting, and will appear next week.—Were it not for the steamer I would keep your letter till I get his answer.—I hope you will try your hand again. I assure you it is quite worth your while. I see you scoffing from the top of your arid philosophical dust-heap and comission T. S. Perry to tell you (in his own inimitable way) that you are a d—d fool. I very much enjoy your Berlin letters. Don't try to make out that America and Germany are identical and that it is as good to be here as there. It can't be done. Only let me go to Berlin and I will say as much. Life here in Cambridge—or in this house, at least, is about as lively as the inner sepulchre. You have already heard of Wilky's illness—chills and fever. It finally became so bad that he had to come home. He arrived some ten days ago and is now much better; but he must have had a fearfully hard time of it. He eats, sleeps and receives his friends; but still looks very poorly and will not be able to return for some time. Bob went a few days ago out to his old railroad place at Burlington. He was very impatient to get something to do, but nothing else turned up, altho' he moved heaven and earth, *more suo.* I have no news for you. Aunt Kate is in N.Y., attending "Em" Walsh's wedding. The rest of us are as usual—whatever that may be called. I myself, I am sorry to say, am not so well as I was some time since. That is I am no worse but my health has ceased to improve so steadily, as it did during the summer. It is plain that I shall have a very long row to hoe before I am fit for anything—for either work or play. I mention this not to discourage you—for you have no right to be discouraged, when I am not myself—but because it occurs to me that I may have given you an exaggerated notion of the extent of my improvement during the past six months. An important element in my recovery, I believe, is to strike a happy medium between reading etc and "social relaxation." The latter is not to be obtained in Cambridge—or only a ghastly simulacrum of it. There are no "distractions" here. How in Boston, when the evening arrives, and I am tired of reading and know it would be better to do something else, can I go to the theatre? I have tried it *ad nauseam.* Likewise *"calling."* Upon whom?—Sedgwicks, Nortons, Dixwells, Feltons. I can't possibly call at such places oftener than two or three times in six months; and they are the best in Cambridge. Going into town on the winter nights puts a chill on larger enterprizes. I say this not in a querulous spirit, for in spite of these things I wouldn't for the present leave Cambridge, but in order that you may not let distance falsify your reminiscences of this excellent place. Tonight for example, I am going into town to see the French actors who are there for a week, give Mme. Aubray.[3] Dickens has arrived for his readings. It is impossible to get tickets. At 7 o'clock A.M. on the first day of the sale there were two or three hundred at the office, and at 9, when I strolled up, nearly a thousand. So I don't expect to hear him.[4] Tell Sargy I got his little note, enclosed by you, and am anxiously awaiting his letter. I *hope* (for his sake) he will be able to extend his absence. If not and he comes in March, I shall be first to welcome him. I haven't a creature to talk to. Farewell. I wanted to say more about yourself, personally, but I can't. I will write next week. *Je t'embrasse.*

H.J. Jr

1. Herman Grimm, *Unüberwundliche Machte,* which WJ reviewed in the *Nation,* 28 November 1867.

2. Edwin Lawrence Godkin (1831–1902), founder of the *Nation* in 1865 and later editor of the *New York Evening Post,* published the young HJ consistently and remained a devoted friend in later years.

3. *Les Idées de Mme Aubray* (1867), a play by Alexandre Dumas *fils.*

4. HJ had a momentary meeting with Dickens at the Nortons' during the British novelist's visit to Boston; see *Notes of a Son and Brother,* chapter 8.

7 · To Alice James

Ms Harvard

London 7 Half-Moon St. W.
March 10 [1869]

Ma soeur cherie[1]—

I have half an hour before dinner-time. Why shouldn't I begin a letter for Saturday's steamer. You will by this time have received my letter from Liverpool—or rather will just be receiving it. Mercy on us! What an age it seems to me since that letter was written and yet to think that it's only now finishing its dreary homeward voyage! On Friday last I despatched an immensely copious effusion to mother, which she will get in due time, and yet it seems to me that I now have matter for another chronicle on quite as large a scale. But I see you turn pale; *rassure toi;* I shall not yet repeat the infliction. I have now been in London some ten days and actually feel very much at home here—feel domesticated and naturalized in fact, to quite a disgusting extent. I feel that in proportion as I cease to be perpetually thrilled surprised and delighted, I am being cheated out of my fun. I really feel as if I had lived—I don't say a lifetime—but a year in this murky metropolis. I actually believe that this feeling is owing to the singular permanence of the impressions of childhood, to which my present experience joins itself on, without a broken link in the chain of sensation. Nevertheless, I may say that up to this time I have been crushed under a sense of the mere magnitude of London—its inconceivable immensity—in such a way as to paralyse my mind for any appreciation of details. This is gradually subsiding; but what does it leave behind it? An extraordinary intellectual depression, as I may say, and an indefineable flatness of mind. The place sits on you, broods on you, stamps on you with the feet of its myriad bipeds and quadrupeds. In fine, it is anything but a cheerful or a charming city. Yet it is a very splendid one. It gives you, here at the West End and in the city proper, a vast impression of opulence and prosperity. But you don't want a dissertation of commonplaces on London and you would like me to touch on my own individual experience. Well, my dear, since last week, it has [been] sufficient, altho' by no means immense. On Saturday I received a visit from Mr. Leslie Stephen[2] (blessed man) who came unsolicited and with the utmost civility in the world invited me to dine with him (early) the next day. This I did in company with Miss Jane Norton.[3] His wife made me very welcome and they both appear to much better effect on their own premises than they did in America. After dinner he conducted us by the underground railway to see the beasts in the Regent's Park, to which as member of the Zoological Society he has admittance "Sundays." This same underground railway, by the way, is a marvellous phenomenon—ploughing along in a vast circle thro' the bowels of London, and giving you egress to the upper earth in magnificent stations, at a number of convenient points. The trains are the same as above ground. As for cheapness, I went on Monday from the Nortons, in Kensington, to the Barings[4] in the heart of the city, first class, for sixpence. As for speed, owing to the frequent stoppages, I should have gone faster in a Hansom; but I should have paid several shillings. Of course at each end I had a little walk to the station.

12th A.M.

After we had seen the beasts I went back with Stephen to his house and had some tea and a little talk, after which I departed to my own residence. On Monday morning I breakfasted at the Nortons, "to meet" two gentlemen friends of theirs—Dr. Bridges a famous Comtist,[5] of the *Fortnightly Review* group and Mr. Simon[6] (pronounced *à la Francaise*) a very witty man, and occupying some high medical post in government. He politely asked me to dine at his house to meet Mr. and Mrs. Tom Taylor,[7] but I declined. (I forgot to say just now by the way, *apropos* of the Stephens, that Miss Thackeray[8] is absent on the Continent—gone to Rome to stay with the Storys[9]—else I should have seen her. Two other persons I have missed seeing are Mr. and Mrs. G. H. Lewes,[10] whom under the Nortons' auspices I should have met: they have seen much of the former and something of the latter.) On Tuesday I breakfasted with Rutson,[11] my neighbor above stairs, Charles Norton's friend, who initiated me here. He is private secretary to Mr. Bruce,[12] the Home Secretary, and he had invited a young member of Parliament to meet me. The banquet was not an immense success. The two gentlemen were oppressively political and high-toned; I had been invited only as a matter of grim duty by Rutson; I knew and cared nothing for my hosts and their interests; in short 'twas decidedly flat. Rutson must have loathed me for being thus rudely thrust into his existence. After breakfast I received another visit from Leslie Stephen, with renewed offers of service. He is evidently an excellent fellow and will make me adore him prostrate before he gets thro', if he goes on at this rate. Then remembering father's injunction to call on Mr. White,[13] I proceeded forth to Hampstead to perform the ceremony. He opened his door in person—received my name with blushes and "friendly greetings" and did his best to make me comfortable. His notion of hospitality however, seemed to be to get me out of the house as soon as possible, first under the pretext of calling on Father's old friend Mrs. Welford, who lives near him, and whom we didn't see, owing to her being laid up with "a bad face" (White says, by the way, that she has grown so fat she can't walk) and then for the purpose of walking me to death over the hills and dales of Hampstead. This I resisted, but he nevertheless showed me a good bit of it. It's a charming old town, nestling under oaks and ivied walls and sprawling over the deep misty verdure of its undulous heath. Mr. White is a little short-legged Scot with a vast bald head, a broad brogue and a red face—a shrewd little North British vulgarian. He asked many questions about Father. On my way home I called at the Wilkinsons[14] (to apologise for not having come on the Sunday, as I had partially agreed to do) and saw Mrs. W. alone, Mary to my sorrow having gone to Brighton to spend a month with Florence. Mrs. W. is very clever. I think however under the above circumstances that I shall not see much more of them, save, probably to dine there again. The Dr. is extremely busy. In the evening I dined with the invaluable Nortons and went with Charles and Madame, Miss S. and Miss Jane (via underground railway) to hear Ruskin lecture at University College on Greek Myths.[15] I enjoyed it much in spite of fatigue; but as I am to meet him someday thro' the N's, I will reserve comments. On Wednesday evening I dined at the N.'s (*toujours* Nortons you see) in company with Miss Dickens[16]—Dickens's only unmarried daughter—plain-faced, lady-like, (in black silk and black lace) and the image of her father. I exchanged but ten words with her. But yesterday, my dear old sister, was my crowning day—seeing as how I spent the greater part of it in the home of Mr. William Morris, Poet. Fitly to tell the tale, I should need a fresh pen, paper and spirits. A few hints must suffice. To begin with, I breakfasted, by way of a change, with the Nortons, along with Mr. Sam Ward,[17] who has just arrived and Mr. Aubrey De Vere, *tu sais*, the Catholic poet, a pleasant honest old man and very much less high-flown than his name. He tells good stories in a light natural way. After a space I came home and remained until 4.30 P.M. when I had given rendezvous to C.N. and ladies at Mr. Morris's door, they going by appointment to see his shop and C. having written to say he would bring me. Morris lives on the same premises as his shop, in Queen's Square, Bloomsbury, an antiquated ex-fashionable region, smelling strong of the last century, with a hoary effigy of Queen Anne in the middle. Morris's poetry you must know, is only his sub-trade. To begin with, he is a manufacturer of stained glass windows, tiles, ecclesiastical and mediaeval tapestry altar-cloths, and in fine everything quaint, archaic, pre-Raphaelite—and I may add exquisite. Of course his business is small and may be carried on in his house: the things he makes are so handsome, rich and expensive (besides being articles of the very last luxury) that his *fabrique* can't be on a very large scale. But everything he has and does is superb and beautiful. But more curious than anything is himself. He designs with his own head and hands all the figures and patterns used in his glass and tapestry and furthermore works the latter, stitch by stitch with his own fingers—aided by those of his wife and little girls. Ah, *ma chère,* such a wife!¹⁸ *Je n'en reviens pas*—she haunts me still. A figure cut out of a missal—out of one of Rossetti's or Hunt's pictures—to say this gives but a faint idea of her, because when such an image puts on flesh and blood, it is an apparition of fearful and wonderful intensity. It's hard to say [whether] she's a grand synthesis of all the pre-Raphaelite pictures ever made—or they a "keen analysis" of her—whether she's an original or a copy. In either case she is a wonder. Imagine a tall lean woman in a long dress of some dead purple stuff, guiltless of hoops (or of anything else, I should say,) with a mass of crisp black hair heaped into great wavy projections on each of her temples, a thin pale face, a pair of strange sad, deep, dark Swinburnish eyes, with great thick black oblique brows, joined in the middle and tucking themselves away under her hair, a mouth like the "Oriana" in our illustrated Tennyson, a long neck, without any collar, and in lieu thereof some dozen strings of outlandish beads—in fine Complete. On the wall was a large nearly full-length portrait of her by Rossetti, so strange and unreal that if you hadn't seen her, you'd pronounce it a distempered vision, but in fact an extremely good likeness. After dinner (we stayed to dinner, Miss Grace, Miss S.S.¹⁹ and I), Morris read us one of his unpublished poems, from the second series of his un-'Earthly Paradise,' and his wife having a bad toothache, lay on the sofa, with her handkerchief to her face. There was something very quaint and remote from our actual life, it seemed to me, in the whole scene: Morris reading in his flowing antique numbers a legend of prodigies and terrors (the story of Bellerophon, it was), around us all the picturesque bric-a-brac of the apartment (every article of furniture literally a 'specimen' of something or other,) and in the corner this dark silent medieval woman with her medieval toothache. Morris himself is extremely pleasant and quite different from his wife. He impressed me

most agreeably. He is short, burly and corpulent, very careless and unfinished in his dress, and looks a little like B. G. Hosmer, if you can
imagine B.G. infinitely magnified and fortified. He has a very loud
voice and a nervous restless manner and a perfectly unaffected and
business-like address. His talk indeed is wonderfully to the point and
remarkable for clear good sense. He said no one thing that I remember, but I was struck with the very good judgment shewn in everything
he uttered. He's an extraordinary example, in short, of a delicate sensitive genius and taste, served by a perfectly healthy body and temper.
All his designs are quite as good (or rather nearly so) as his poetry:
altogether it was a long rich sort of visit, with a strong peculiar flavour
of its own. You will have had enough, my dear, of this descriptive stuff
by this time and I stay my ruthless hand. When I stopped writing this
morning I went out and travelled over to the British Museum, with
regard to which I wish to stick in a pin. I found it a less formidable
process, going there, than I supposed. That is, there is only one region, the three or four Greek or Roman rooms, that I can pretend to
look at properly and these I shall hope to pay a couple more visits.
One may say indeed that the only thing to look at are the Elgin
Marbles; they vulgarize everything else so, that you are fain to rest
content with them. Of their wondrous beauty, my dear, I can say
nothing. Had I the pen of an immortal bard I would comment with a
Sonnet;[20] but failing this I must hold my tongue. I didn't say, I believe,
that I have been once to the great Kensington Museum—a vast store
house of art treasures. It's a marvel of richness and arrangement. I
hope to get a couple of hours there again. When I add that I have
done St. Paul's—I and Miss J. Norton together—and that to my infinite disgust the National Gallery is closed—I shall have finished the
tale of my pleasures and pains.—Ouf! What a repulsively long letter!
This sort of thing won't do. A few general reflections, a burst of
affection (say another sheet and I must close).—You can see for yourself that I see a great deal of the Nortons and I need hardly say that it is
everything to me, to have them here. But for their presence I should
have gone off (somewhere!) a week ago. In London you must have one
of two things (money being assumed)—friends or work. If I were able
to work (either at home or in the way of poking about and sightseeing
ad libitum) I might successfully contend with the loneliness and gloom
which is the necessary lot of a stranger here. As it is, the only basis on
which I can remain any time (save finish my month) is on the easy

social one furnished by the N's. I should have said instead of saying that they are as pleasant as ever, that they are much improved. They are decidedly more joyous, wild and free than before and are so kind and friendly to me that if I did as they would have me, I would in their house feel absolutely at home. So much for myself and my own affairs.—How I long to know something of thine, lovely child and of all the rest of your's—if that isn't grammar, it's love. Last Monday (I have waited till now to say it) I went over to Barings in quest of a letter and found mother's note of the 23rd. Woe, woe if I had found none. Of course the time seems so much shorter to you than to me and you don't feel as if you had anything to say; but for these first weeks, till I get used to the confounded thing, do try and send me some little scrap by each steamer and you will confer favour on a most deserving creature. On Monday next I shall scurry over to Barings on the wings of the wind—or rather the wheels of a Hansom—or most probably, economically on the top of a "bus." Perhaps, sweet maid, there will be a little note from you. Perhaps there will be one from Mother—from Father—from Bill. I hardly hope to hear from you all; I'm curious to see how you will arrange it. Meanwhile I thank Mother *de profundis* of my soul for her last: it was sweet. Even as the draught given by the Jewess of old to her little son in the Wilderness. What wilderness is equal to this tremendous London?—What Jewess to my Mother. I needn't say how I long to hear the sanitary record of the household—beginning with thine, dear child, *cette bonne petite santé à toi.* Has Willie felt my absence in any poignant—or rather any practical degree: if so—if he misses me "round the room" he mustn't scruple to send for me to return. I only want a pretext. My last letter was full of drivelling homesickness; do not think that I have not slain the enemy. A mild melancholy, at most, enshrouds my being. I know not why or what it is—whether I've come too late or grown too old, owlish and stupid, but I don't anticipate any rapturous emotions on this alien soil.—It must be confessed, however, that London is hardly the place for romances and raptures, and that when I leave it, they may attack me in earnest. The point I wish to make is simply that I am not homesick. I wouldn't go any further if I could.—On the chapter of bodily vigour, you see what has been the scale and programme of my performances, and that may imply a goodly share of it. The best thing I can say is that I'm *thoroughly* satisfied with my progress and condition. My venture is taking just the course I counted upon. There is no sudden change, no magic alleviation; but a gradual and orderly recurrence of certain phenomena which betray slow development of such soundness as may ultimately be my earthly lot. In short my life agrees and directly tends and administers to my recovery and will do so more and more as I get properly "attuned," as I may say to it. This is positive. I haven't felt better in I don't know when, than I felt last night when I reached home at the close of my busy day—breakfast at the Nortons and the long afternoon and evening at the Morris's. I have recovered my sleep, my appetite is enormous, especially for beer of which I drink largely. The climate creates and stimulates the taste. (I had torn off that leaf to make a ditch, as it were, for my run away pen to pull up at; but you see, it leaps the gulf.) I'm at my old trick of growing repulsively fat. If I only get as good news from Bill and you, I shall feel that I haven't lived in vain. You will receive in ten days (or at least see advertised, whereupon pray buy it) the *Galaxy* for April, with something of mine in it, which you will read.[21] It's sure to be badly printed. I came very near seeing a proof in New York but the man disappointed me at the last moment—confound him! Has anything more been heard from Youmans?—But I must pull in. I blush for the hideous magnitude of this letter. Don't read it, if it bores you. I want very much to know how Wilk and Bob took my departure. You will have heard and of course reported. Do give the dear fellows a brother's love and greetings. Tell T. S. Perry, with my love, that I await on this further shore the answer to that farewell note of mine. Give my love to Howells and tell him that I feel I owe him a letter in return for his last note. Is Aunt Kate at home? Farewell. Tell Arthur Sedgwick[22] that I have in mind that promised letter. Farewell, dear girl and dear incomparable all—

your

H.

1. Some of the feelings expressed in this letter were incorporated in HJ's later essay "London," reprinted in *Essays in London and Elsewhere* (1893).

2. Leslie Stephen (1832–1904) and his wife, Minnie, Thackeray's daughter, had met the Jameses during a journey to America. Stephen at this time was a literary critic in London.

3. Jane Norton (1824–1877), sister of Charles Eliot Norton (1827–1908), professor of art history at Harvard from 1873 to 1898.

4. HJ's bankers.

5. Dr. John Henry Bridges (1832–1906) translated Comte into English.

6. Sir John Simon (1816–1894), sanitary reformer, pathologist, and friend of Ruskin's.

7. Tom Taylor (1817–1880), prolific writer of thrillers and plays. See Edel, *Henry James: A Life* (1985), 464–467, for Taylor's profound influence on HJ's work, notably "The Turn of the Screw."

8. Anne Isabella Thackeray (1837–1919), later Lady Ritchie, eldest daughter of the novelist and herself a writer of fiction.

9. William Wetmore Story (1819–1895), an American sculptor who lived in Rome for many years and whose biography HJ wrote in 1903.

10. Mary Ann Evans (George Eliot) (1819–1880), who had lived for years out of wedlock with George Henry Lewes (1817–1878).

11. Albert Rutson figures in HJ's posthumously published autobiographical fragment *The Middle Years* (1918).

12. Henry Austin Bruce, First Baron Aberdare (1815–1895), Home Secretary in Gladstone's first government of 1868.

13. William White, English Swedenborgian, wrote a two-volume life of Swedenborg published in 1868.

14. J. J. Garth Wilkinson (1812–1890), an eminent Swedenborgian. The James and Wilkinson families had formed a close friendship during the Jameses' stay abroad in 1843.

15. Ruskin's lectures on 8 and 15 March 1869, dealing with Greek myths of storm, were later published as *The Queen of the Air*.

16. Kate MacCready Dickens (b. 1839), later Mrs. Perugini.

17. Sam Ward (1814–1884), U.S. banker.

18. Jane Burden Morris (1839–1914) sat for many of the paintings of the pre-Raphaelites.

19. Grace Norton (1834–1926), Charles Eliot Norton's sister, to whom HJ wrote some of his finest letters, and C. E. Norton's sister-in-law Sara Sedgwick (1839–1902), who later married Charles Darwin's son, William.

20. An allusion to Keat's sonnet "On Seeing the Elgin Marbles."

21. The April *Galaxy* (VII, 538–549) published one of HJ's early experiments in the dramatic form, a sketch called "Pyramus and Thisbe," reprinted in *Collected Plays*, ed. Edel (1949).

22. Arthur Sedgwick (1844–1915), Charles Eliot Norton's brother-in-law, a lawyer and journalist, later associated with HJ on the *Nation*.

8 · To William James

Ms Harvard

Oxford April 26*th* [1869]
Randolph Hotel

Dearest Bill—

I found here today on my arrival your letter of April 9th which I was mighty glad to get. It seemed strange, foul and unnatural to have heard from you only once in all these weeks. What you say of yourself and your prospects and humor interested me deeply and half pleased, half distressed me. I thoroughly agree with you that to exonerate your mind in the manner you speak of will of itself conduce to your recovery, and I fancy that the result of such a decision will be to smooth the way to convalescence in such a manner that much sooner than you seem inclined to believe you will be able to redeem your pledges and find that you have been even too much reconciled. For heavens sake don't doubt of your recovery. It would seem that on this point I ought to need to say nothing. My example is proof enough of what a man can get over. Whenever you feel downish, think of me and my present adventures and spurn the azure demon from your side. At all events I am heartily glad that your reflections have cleared up your spirits and determined you to take things easy. *À la bonne heure!*—Altho' it lacks some days of mail-time I can't resist putting pen to paper for a few minutes this evening and getting the start of any possible pressure of engagements or fatigue later in the week. I feel as if I should like to make a note of certain recent impressions before they quite fade out of my mind. You know, by the way, that I must economise and concentrate my scribblements and write my diary and letters all in one. You must take the evil with the good. These same impressions date from no earlier than this evening and from an hour and a half stroll which I took before dinner thro' the streets of this incomparable town. I came hither from Leamington early this morning, after a decidedly dull three days in the latter place. I know not why—probably in a measure from a sort of reaction against the constant delight—the tension of perception—during my three days run from Malvern—but the Leamington lions were decidedly tame. I visited them all faithfully. Warwick Castle is simply a showy modern house with nothing to interest save a lot of admirable portraits, which I couldn't look at, owing to my being dragged about by a hard alcoholic old housekeeper, in the train of a dozen poking, prying, dowdy female visitants. Kenilworth, for situation and grandeur, reminded me forcibly of the old stone-mill, and at Stratford, too, my enthusiasm hung fire in the most humiliating manner. Yesterday afternoon I drove over to Coventry. I enjoyed the drive but the place disappointed me. It would seem decidedly odder if it didn't seem quite so new. But I investigated a beautiful old church, alone worth the price of the drive. These English Abbeys have quite gone to my head. They are quite the greatest works of art I've ever seen. I little knew what meaning and suggestion could reside in the curve of an arch or the spring of a column—in proportions, and relative sizes. The Warwickshire scenery is incredibly rich and pastoral. The land is one teeming garden. It is in fact too monotonously sweet and smooth—too comfortable, too ovine, too bovine,[1] too English, in a word. But in its way it's the last word of human toil. It seems like a vast show region kept up at the expense of the poor.—You know, as you pass along, you feel, that it's not poor man's property but rich man's. *Àpropos* of Leamington, tell Alice that I found at the hotel her friend the late Julia Bryant and family. I called and had a pleasant visit. I don't find in myself as yet any tendency to flee the society of Americans. I never had enough of it in America to have been satiated and indeed, from appearance, the only society I shall get here will be theirs.—

27*th* A.M. I turned in last evening without arriving at the famous "impressions". Mrs. Norton gave me a letter to A. Vernon Harcourt Esq.[2] fellow of Christ Church and at about 5 P.M. I strolled forth to deliver it. Having left it at his college with my card I walked along, thro' the lovely Christ Church meadow, by the river side and back through the town. It was a perfect evening and in the interminable British twilight the beauty of the whole place came forth with magical power. There are no words for these colleges. As I stood last evening within the precincts of mighty Magdalen, gazed at its great serene tower and uncapped my throbbing brow in the wild dimness of its courts, I thought that the heart of me would crack with the fulness of satisfied desire. It is, as I say, satisfied desire that you feel here; it is your tribute to the place. You ask nothing more; you have imagined only a quarter as much. The whole place gives me a deeper sense of English life than anything yet. As I walked along the river I saw hundreds of the mighty lads of England, clad in white flannel and blue, immense, fair-haired, magnificent in their youth, lounging down the stream in their punts or pulling in straining crews and rejoicing in their godlike strength. When along with this you think of their haunts in the grey-green quadrangles, you esteem them as elect among men.[3] I received last evening when I came in a note from Harcourt, telling me he would call this morning and asking me to dine at his college commons in the evening. I have also from Jane Norton a note to Mrs. Pattison, rectoress of Lincoln College which may shew me something good. As this letter promises to become long, I will here interpolate a word about my physics, *en attendant* Harcourt, whose hour is up. I gave you at Leamington, a list of my *haut faits* in Monmouthshire. What I then said about my unblighted vigor is more true than ever. I felt my improvement in the midst of my fatigue; I feel it doubly now. There is no humbug nor illusion about it and no word for it but good honest *better*. If my doings at Oxford have the same result I shall feel as if I have quite established a precedent.

29*th*. Harcourt turns out to be simply angel no. 2. He is tutor of chemistry in Christ Church and a very modest pleasant and thoroughly obliging fellow. He came for me the other morning and we started together on our rounds. It is certainly no small favor for a man to trudge about bodily for three hours in the noon-day sun with a creature thus rudely hurled into his existence from over the sea, whom he neither knows nor cares for. His reward will be in heaven. He took me first to Convocation—a lot of grizzled and toga'd old dons, debating of University matters in an ancient hall and concluding with much Latin from one of them. Thence to lunch with the rector of Lincoln's—Harcourt having kindly arranged with Mrs. Pattison beforehand to bring me there. The Rector is a dessicated old scholar, torpid even to incivility with too much learning; but his wife is of quite another fashion—very young (about 28) very pretty, very clever, very charming and very conscious of it all.[4] She is I believe highly emancipated and I defy an English-woman to be emancipated except coldly and wantonly. As a spectacle the thing had its points: the dark rich, scholastic old dining room in the college court—the languid old rector and his pretty little wife in a riding-habit, talking slang. Otherwise it was slow. I then went about with Harcourt to various colleges, halls, and gardens—he doing his duty most bravely—and I mine for that matter. At four I parted from him and at six rejoined him and dined with him in Hall at Christ Church. This was a great adventure. The Hall is magnificent: an immense area, a great timbered and vaulted roof and a hundred former worthies looking down from the walls between the high stained windows. I sat at the tutors' table on a platform, at the upper end of the Hall, in the place of honor, at the right of the Carver. The students poured in; I sat amid learned chat and quaffed strong ale from a silver tankard. The dinner and the service, by the way, were quite elaborate and elegant. On rising *we tutors* adjourned to the

Common-room across the court, to dessert and precious wines. In the evening I went to a debating club, and to a soirée at Dr. Acland's[5] (I've quite forgotten who and what he is) where I saw your physiological friend Mr. Charles Robin. 'Twas mortal flat. All this was well enough for one day. Yesterday I kindly left Harcourt alone and drove in the morning out to Blenheim, which was highly satisfactory. The palace is vast cold and pretentious but the park is truly ducal. As far as you can see, it encircles and fills the horizon—"immense, ombreux, seigneurial." (T. Gautier) *Enfin,* I could talk a week about the park. But the great matter is the pictures. It was with the imperfect view at War-wick, the other day, my first glimpse (save Ruskin's Titian and the poorish things at Dulwich) of the great masters: thank the Lord it is not to be the last. There is a single magnificent Raphael and two great Rembrandts, but the strength of the collection is in the Rubenses and Vandykes. Seeing a mass of Rubenses together commands you to believe that he was the first of painters—of *painters,* in fact, I believe he was.[6] A lot of his pictures together is a most healthy spectacle—fit to cure one of any woes. And then the noble, admirable modern Van-dyke! His great portrait of Charles I on horse-back is a thing of infinite beauty—I strolled slowly away thro' the park, watching the great groves and avenues, murmuring and trembling in the sunny breeze and feeling very serious with it all. On my return I went out alone and spent the afternoon in various college gardens. These same gardens are the fairest things in Oxford. Locked in their own ancient verdure, behind their own ancient walls, filled with shade and music and per-fumes and privacy—with lounging students and charming children—with the rich old college windows keeping guard from above—they are places to lie down on the grass in forever, in the happy belief that the world is all an English garden and time a fine old English after-noon. At 6 o'clock, I dined in hall at Oriel with Mr. Pearson (the author of the early English History who was in America while you were away.)[7] It was Christ Church over again on a reduced scale. I stole away betimes to get a little walk in Magdalen Gardens—where by way of doing things handsomely they have, in the heart of the city—an immense old park or Chase filled with deer—with deer, *pas davantage. Ce detail,* it seems to me, gives, as well as anything, a no-tion of the scale of things here. Today I am to lunch with Harcourt but shall take things quietly. Tomorrow I shall depart. I received yesterday a note from Frank Washburn[8] saying he had just arrived in England *en route* for home, May 11th. We shall probably meet. If I feel as well tomorrow as today I shall satisfy my desire for seeing a little more in the Cathedral line by going to London (roundabout) *via* Salisbury and Winchester. My present notion is to stay a fortnight in London in lodgings and then make for Geneva. There is much in and about London that I want still to see. My letter has been long and I fear, boresome.—Do in writing give more details gossip etc. I am glad you've been seeing Howells: give him my love and tell him to expect a letter. Tell T. S. Perry *I* expect one. Do tell me something about Wendell Holmes.[9] One would think he was dead. Give him my compliments and tell him I'm sadly afraid that one of these days I shall have to write to him.—I suppose all is well within doors, from your silence. What demon prompts Father to direct the letters he doesn't write? It is really cruel. If he only would write a few lines I'd as lief Isabella should direct them. You must have received my message about the *Nation:* I miss it sadly. I repeat I heartily applaud your resolution to lie at your length and abolish study. As one who has sounded the *replis* of the human back, I apprise that with such a course you cannot fail to amend. Love to Mother and Alice, to Wilk and Bob. Aunt Kate will have sailed. Regards to Ellen and Isabella. Is Eliza's successor a success?—Another piece of mine will have appeared in the *Galaxy*[10]—probably very ill printed. You will of course have sent it. Howells will send Father a proof to correct. I am haunted with the impression that it contains an imperfect quotation of a Scripture text to the effect that out of the lips of babes and sucklings cometh knowledge.[11] If there is such a text or anything like it ask him to establish it; if not suppress it. But farewell—

yours

H.J. Jr

1. HJ used this description in his essay "Lichfield and Warwick," which appeared in the *Nation*, 25 July 1872, and was republished in *Transatlantic Sketches* (1875) and much later in *English Hours* (1905).

2. A. Vernon Harcourt (1840–1919), a distinguished chemist.

3. HJ used a portion of this passage in his story "A Passionate Pilgrim" (1875).

4. Mark Pattison (1813–1884), rector of Lincoln from 1861, believed by some critics to have been George Eliot's model for Casaubon in *Middlemarch*. His widow, Emilia Frances Strong (1840–1904), later married Sir Charles Dilke.

5. Henry Wentworth Acland (baronet 1890), Regius Professor of Medicine at Oxford from 1858 to 1894.

6. Later HJ changed his mind and described Rubens as reigning with magnificent supremacy among the "coarse" painters.

7. Charles Henry Pearson (1830–1894), British historian, had lately visited the United States to study Southern blacks. He wrote considerably on the history of England in the Middle Ages.

8. Frank Washburn, a Cambridge friend of the Jameses described by HJ as having "a most charming and generous mind."

9. Oliver Wendell Holmes, Jr. (1841–1935), later an Associate Justice of the U.S. Supreme Court (1902–1932).

10. "Pyramus and Thisbe," a short play.

11. An allusion to HJ's "Gabrielle de Bergerac," forthcoming in the *Atlantic*. The biblical line appears in the tale paraphrased as "The truth comes out of the mouths of children."

9 · *To Henry James, Sr.*

Ms Harvard

23 Sackville Street
Monday May 10*th* [1869]

Dear father—

It is a rare satisfaction at last to hear from you—which I did this morning per date of April 29, as well as from Mother and Willy. I am much obliged to you all for your good advice—altho' I confess that I have been acting somewhat against the spirit of it. You will by this time have received my letters written *en voyage* and have perceived that I was executing a little tour. To have you think that I am extravagant with these truly sacred funds sickens me to the heart, and I hasten in so far as I may to reassure you. When I left Malvern, I found myself so exacerbated by immobility and confinement that I felt it to be absolutely due to myself to test the impression which had been maturing in my mind, that a certain amount of regular lively travel would do me more good than any further treatment or further repose. As I came abroad to try and get better, it seemed inexcusable to neglect a course which I believed for various reasons to have so much in its favor. After lying awake therefore as usual on the subject, I grimly started and proceeded. You know what I did and where I went. I am sufficiently justified I think by success. I have now an impression amounting almost to a conviction that if I were to travel steadily for

a year I would be a good part of a well man. With such a conviction ahead of me, you will cease to wonder that I should have been
tempted to put forth a feeler. As to the expense of my journey, in telling that tale about the £60. I acted on gross misinformation. I was
circulated for nearly three weeks and spent less than £25.00, seeing a
very great deal on it. I am obliged of course, on account of the seats, to
travel first class. My constant aim is to economise and make my funds
minister, not to my enjoyment,—which may take care of itself—it
wasn't assuredly for that I came hither—but to my plain physical improvement, for which alone I live and move. I think I have moved for
it to some purpose. I have got quite my £25's worth of flexibility in the
back, of experience and insight into my condition. I may declare, in
fact, that when I started on my journey it seemed to me an absolute
necessity to do so. I indulge in this somewhat diffuse elucidation, dear
Father, because I attach not only so much value to the money you
have given but so much respect and gratitude to the temper in which
you gave it and I can't bear to have you fancy I may make light of your
generosity. I incline I think to take my responsibilities to my little fortune too hard rather than too easy and there have been moments
when I have feared that my satisfaction here was going to be very seriously diminished by a habit of constant self-torturing as to expense.
You will perhaps think that the fear is superfluous when I tell you that
during my eleven weeks in England I shall have spent about 120£. The
sum sounds large but on investigation, it will scarcely turn out to be
excessive, distributed as it is among five weeks in London, three at an
expensive water-cure and three in travelling. It covers the purchase of
considerable clothing and other articles of permanent use—or such as
will last me during much of my stay here. It covers on the other hand
very little trivial, careless or random expenditure—altho' it indicates
perhaps some inexperience, which I am rapidly getting over. It involves for one thing a large amount of cab-hire. I have treated you to
this financial budget as a satisfaction to myself rather than because I
suppose you expect it. I leave London on Friday 14th inst. the day my
week is up in these lodgings. I proceed to Geneva *via* Paris, arriving
there if possible Saturday evening. What Geneva will bring forth for
my amelioration remains to be seen. You shall hear. I should have
gone on immediately but that I thought it best to rest here a few days
on my return from Lincolnshire, before undertaking so long a journey,

and as you can't take a lodging for less than a week, I'm in for that period. The one marvel as yet, of my stay, is having finally seen Mrs. Lewes,[1] tho' under sadly infelicitous circumstances. I called on her yesterday (Sunday) afternoon, with Grace Norton and Sara Sedgwick—the only way in which it seemed possible to do it, as she is much hedged about with sanctity and a stranger can go only [under] cover of a received friend. I was immensely impressed, interested and pleased. To begin with she is magnificently ugly—deliciously hideous. She has a low forehead, a dull grey eye, a vast pendulous nose, a huge mouth, full of uneven teeth and a chin and jaw-bone *qui n'en finessent pas*. By far the best description of her is to say that she is an ugly image of Mrs. Sam Ward.[2] The likeness is most strange. The whole air, the dress, the pose of the head, the smile, the motion, recall Mrs. W. Now in this vast ugliness resides a most powerful beauty which, in a very few minutes steals forth and charms the mind, so that you end as I ended, in falling in love with her. Yes behold me literally in love with this great horse-faced blue-stocking. I don't know in what the charm lies, but it is thoroughly potent. An admirable physiognomy—a delightful expression, a voice soft and rich as that of a counselling angel—a mingled sagacity and sweetness—a broad hint of a great underlying world of reserve, knowledge, pride and power—a great feminine dignity and character in these massively plain features—a hundred conflicting shades of consciousness and simpleness—shyness and frankness—graciousness and remote indifference—these are some of the more definite elements of her personality. Her manner is extremely good tho' rather too intense and her speech, in the way of accent and syntax peculiarly agreeable. Altogether, she has a larger circumference than any woman I have ever seen. The sadness of our visit was in the fact that Mrs. Lewes's second son, an extremely pleasant looking young fellow of about twenty four, lay on the drawing-room floor, writhing in agony from an attack of pain in the spine to which he is subject. We of course beat a hasty retreat, in time to have seen G. H. Lewes come in himself in all *his* ugliness, with a dose of morphine from the chemists.

Wednesday, 12th. I have had no adventures since Monday and am chiefly engrossed in thinking of those that are in store for me in Switzerland. I leave as I think I have said, Friday A.M. I have seen the Nortons again several times. They have finally concluded to go to the Lake of Geneva for the summer which may make us neighbors again, for a time—a circumstance which I regard philosophically. In very sooth I have had enough of them—and all of my own seeking, too,—to last me for ever and ever. In fact I shouldn't mind seeing the ladies again repeatedly—but Charles inspires me with a terrible lack of sympathy and unfortunately, there's a popular delusion between us that he is my guide, philosopher and bosom friend. I must be an arrant hypocrite. But I must do Charles the justice to say that he has come out strong since he has been in England and is very much of a man. I was to have gone to Queen's Gate Terrace this evening to meet Mr. Arthur Helps,[3] who has been dining there; but on coming in late from dinner, after spending three hours steady in the National Gallery, and then taking a walk in St. James's park, then working hard at my eating house as interpreter to a terribly obscure Frenchman who turned up in my neighborhood—after all this, coming up to my room in a certain languor of spirit with a fresh copy of the Pall-Mall in my pocket—the idea of thrusting myself into my finery and travelling faraway to Kensington in a costly cab in order to grin away half an hour in the Nortons' drawingroom quite frowned me out of countenance. So here I am in dressing gown and slippers conversing with my Papa. Part of the fun of seeing Mr. Helps was to have been, by the way, in conversing about this same Papa; inasmuch as Charles Norton tells me that he is (by his own account) a great reader of Swedenborg and carries a richly annotated copy of it about his person—or very near it. If I had seen him, therefore, I might have had something to tell you; but you will probably value my not having gone, against my bodily inclination more than his compliments. I dined yesterday at the Wilkinsons' rather stupidly. The Doctor seems pre-occupied and lacking in light conversation. Mary spoke with very real pleasure, evidently, of having got a letter from Mother. Her young man was present and after dinner they sang duets together. He seems a very nice fellow and a truly fine singer. He has a noble and delicious voice.—I was very glad to hear from Mother of Bob's being at home and in such good spirits and health. Do give him a brother's love and benison. I wish he would drop me a line. To Wilky too when he comes up, commend me most affectionately. I wish I could once more improve his elastic abdomen. It does my soul good to hear that he is in any way up to time with his crops. I'm mighty glad Alice is dropping her elegant invalidity; I think she will find a proper state of health so becoming that she will decide

to stick to it. I send a kiss or so, to encourage her in the path of propriety. To Willy I enclose a short note: to Mother I enclose everything
that my letter contains. The great subject here is the American quarrel. It is evident that the English have pronounced their *ultimatum*.
Sumner's speech has produced a great irritation: I observed it greatly
in Dr. W. If we want war we shall be served to our taste. But heaven
forbid that we should want it. If Sumner's speech seems half as unrea-
sonable at home as it does here, there is little danger.[4]—At next writing let something be said about your summer plans.—I am watching
for Aunt Kate's arrival but I don't expect to see her in some time. Farewell. Now that you've begun to write, dear Father, do continue. What
of your *Swedenborg?*[5] Of course I shall hear of it.

With much love
your ancient child
H. James Jr

1. HJ describes this visit to George Eliot in *The Middle Years.*
2. The former Medora Grymes, daughter of John Randolph Grymes of New Orleans
and Suzette Bosque of a French-Spanish family, widow of the first governor of Louisiana.
See Maude Howe Elliott, *Uncle Sam Ward and his Circle* (1938), where Medora is described
as having "powers of fascination . . . a peerless charmer."
3. Sir Arthur Helps (1813–1875), a historian, wrote a series of popular works on ethical and aesthetic questions. HJ reviewed his *Social Pressure* in the *Nation,* 18 March 1875.
4. Senator Charles Sumner (1811–1874) attacked Britain's concessions to the Confed-
erate States and demanded satisfaction for U.S. "national claims."
5. The elder HJ had just completed his book *The Secret of Swedenborg,* which was to be
published later in the year.

10 · *To John La Farge*

Ms New York Historical

Hotel du Righi-Vaudois
Glion, Lake of Geneva
June 20*th* [1869]

My very dear John[1]—

Your letter of June 3d was handed me last night, just at a moment
when I was recording a silent oath that today and not a day later, I
should execute my long designed and oft-deferred letter to you. Truly,
I have most earnestly been meaning to write to you. I felt the need of

so doing: our parting in New York was so hurried and unsatisfactory that I wished to affix some sort of supplement or correction. Happily now, what I write may be a greeting rather than a farewell.

I am deeply delighted to hear that there is a prospect of your getting abroad this summer. Don't let it slip out of your hands. That your health has continued bad, I greatly regret; but I can't consider it an unmitigated curse, if it brings you to these parts. You must have pretty well satisfied yourself that home-life is not a remedy for your troubles, and the presumption is strong that a certain amount of Europe may be.—As you see I am already in Switzerland: in fact I have been here for the past five weeks. I came directly to Geneva (giving but a day to Paris, and that to the Salon) and spent a month there; and then came up to this place which is at the other extreme of the lake, beyond Vevey, perched aloft on the mountain side, just above the Castle of Chillon. It is what they call a *hotel-pension:* a number of people, capital air, admirable scenery. Unhappily the weather is bad and seems determined to continue so. Heaven defend us from a rainy summer—no uncommon occurrence here. My actual plans are vague; they are simply to continue in Switzerland as long as I can, but as I am not a regular tourist, I shall distribute my time between two or three places.—I enjoyed most acutely my stay in England. If you can only touch there, I think you will find it pay. Of people I saw very few, of course: and of places no vast number, but such of the latter as I did get a glimpse of, were awfully charming. I did see Rossetti, Charles Norton having conducted me to his studio—in the most delicious melancholy old house at Chelsea on the river. When I think what Englishmen *ought* to be, with such homes and haunts! Rossetti however, does not shame his advantages. Personally, he struck me as unattractive, poor man. I suppose he was horribly bored!—but his pictures, as I saw them in his room, I think decidedly strong. They were all large, fanciful portraits of women, of the type *que vous savez,* narrow, special, monotonous, but with lots of beauty and power. His chief inspiration and constant model is Mrs. William Morris (wife of the poet) whom I had seen, a woman of extraordinary beauty of a certain sort—a face, in fact quite made to his hand. He has painted a dozen portraits of her—one, in particular, in a blue gown, with her hair down, pressing a lot of lilies against her breast—an almost great work. I told him I was your intimate friend and he spoke very admiringly of three of your drawings he

had seen.—I saw also some things of another man (tho' not himself),
one Burne Jones,[2] a water-colorist and friend of Charles Norton. They
are very literary &c; but they have great merit. He does Circe preparing for the arrival of Ulysses—squeezing poison into a cauldron, with
strange black beasts *dans les jambes:* thro' the openings of a sort of
cloister you see the green salt ocean, with the Greek galleys blowing
up to land. This last part is admirably painted. I enjoyed vastly in London the National Gallery, which is a much finer collection than I supposed. They have just acquired a new Michael Angelo—Entombment
of Christ—unfinished, but most interesting, as you may imagine.
Then they have their great Titian—the Bacchus and Ariadne—a
thing to go barefoot to see; as likewise his portrait of Ariosto. Ah,
John! What a painter. For him, methinks, I'd give you all the rest. I
saw in the country (i.e. at Blenheim near Oxford and at Wilton House
near Salisbury) some magnificent Vandykes. The great Wilton Van-
dyke (the Earl of Pembroke and family—an immense canvas) is I
think worth a journey to contemplate. A *propos* of such things, I
oughtn't to omit to say that I dined at Ruskin's, with the Nortons. R.
was very amiable and shewed his Turners. The latter is assuredly great:
but if you wish to hold your own against exaggeration, go to see him at
the National Gallery, where some thirty of his things stand adjoining
the old Masters. I think I prefer Claude. He had better taste, at any
rate.—In England I saw a lot of Cathedrals—which are good things
to see; tho' to enjoy them properly, you mustn't take them quite as
wholesale as I was obliged to do.—You ask my intentions for next
winter. They are as yet indefinite, and are not firmly fixed upon Paris.
That is, I am thinking a little of Italy. If I give up Italy, however, of
course I shall take up Paris. But I do most earnestly hope we shall be
able to talk it over face-to-face. Of course, if you decide to come, you
will lose no time. I wish greatly that your wife were to come with you;
short of that, I must hope that your visit if it takes place, will really
pave the way for her. Give her my love and tell her, persuasively, that
if Europe does not wholly solve the problem of existence, it at least
helps the flight of time—or beguiles its duration. You give me no local
or personal news, beyond that of your illness. I hope other matters are
of a more cheerful complexion. I can hear nothing better than that
you have sailed. If you determine to do so, write to me (Lombard,
Odier & Cie, Genève) and give your own address. Meanwhile, till fur-

ther news, farewell. *Portez vous mieux*, at least. Regards to J. Bancroft,[3] if you see him. Most affectionate messages to your wife and youngsters and a *bon voyage*, if any, to yourself.

Yours, always
H. James jr.

1. John La Farge (1835–1910), American painter and early friend of HJ's in Newport.
2. Edward Burne-Jones (1833–1898), then at the beginning of his long career as a painter. His principal subjects were medieval and mythical.
3. John Chandler Bancroft, son of the historian George Bancroft.

11 · To Mrs. Henry James, Sr.

Ms Harvard

Glion sur Montreux
Hotel du Righi. Vaudois
June 28th [1869]

My dearest Mother—

Glion last week and Glion, as you see, still. Glion has produced however, in the interval, your most amiable letter of June 7th or 8th (I conjecture: it has no date.) Besides this, it has brought forth nothing so wonderful as to be particularly described or related. Nevertheless, I can't help writing, at the risk (I persist in suspecting) of boring you by my importunity. It is a warm Sunday afternoon: I have come up to my room from dinner, and after lying down snoozingly on the sofa for half an hour find a thousand thoughts and memories of home invade my languid mind with such pertinacity that there is nothing for it but to seize the pen and work off my emotions. Since I last wrote, the situation has changed very much for the better. The weather has cleared up and we have had nearly a week of fine warm days. I have found it possible to profit by them to my very great satisfaction. Every afternoon I have taken a long lonely lovely ramble of some three or four hours. The walks hereabouts are extremely numerous and singularly beautiful. It is true that they are all more or less on the perpendicular; nevertheless I have learned them almost all. Judge of my improvement since leaving Malvern, where I found the little hills a burden and a nuisance. Now I think nothing, so to speak, of a mountain, and climb one, at least, on an average every afternoon. I should extremely like to be able to depict the nature of this enchanting country; but to do so requires the pen of a Ruskin or a G. Sand. Back from the lake, at Montreux, stretches the wide deep gorge or ravine, on one side of which, on a little plateau, this hotel is planted. Into this gorge, above, below, horizontally, you can plunge to your heart's content. Along its bottom rolls the furious course of a little mountain river, hurrying down to the lake. Leaving the hotel and striking into the fields, a winding footpath, wandering up and down thro' meadows and copses and orchards, leads down to a heavenly spot where a little wooden bridge spans this tremendous little torrent. It is smothered in the wilderness; above your head tangled verdure shuts out the hillsides; beneath, the racketing stream roars and plunges far down in its channel of rocks. From here you can cross up and ascend the opposite side of the gorge, pursue it along its edge, to its innermost extremity, where the great mountain walls close sheer about it and make it lonely, awful and Alpine. There you can again cross the river and return thro' the woods to Glion. This is one walk in a dozen. I enjoy them all: I relish keenly the freedom of movement, the propulsion of curiosity, the largeness and abundance of the scenery—and for that matter its richness and gentleness too. Crossing the bridge aforesaid and turning out toward the lake and along the hillsides above you can walk to Vevey thro' a region of shady meadows and slanting orchards as tranquil and pastoral as an English park.—Nevertheless this is not yet real Switzerland and I am preparing to take myself thither. I want to get into genuine alpine air and scenery. I went over to Vevey by train a few days since and paid a second visit to the Nortons. I have made up my mind on leaving this place to go and spend a week in the farmhouse adjoining their premises. They are so utterly buried and lonely that I think they would be somewhat grateful for my society and I can thereby do something to pay off their hospitalities to me in London and cancel a possibly onerous obligation.

They enjoy extremely their seclusion and rusticity and find it a very pleasant relief after England. It is well they do, for it is absolute and without appeal. In this house I shall probably remain a week longer. It is a little more expensive than what I expect to find elsewhere, but it affords a number of comforts which I am glad to have at this stage of my initiation into mountain habits. A fortnight hence I shall be better able to rough it. With this view I shall proceed to the Lake of Lucerne, seek out an abode and remain there probably to the 1st of September. I have about given up the idea of going to St. Moritz. I am deterred by the stories I hear about the extreme cold and the severity of the climate. I want the air of some great altitude, but enough is as good as a feast; I want the summer too. But of all this, you will hear when it takes place. I duly noted your injunction to spend the summer quietly and economically. I hope to do both—or that is, to circulate in so far as I do, by the inexpensive vehicle of my own legs. You will by this time have received a letter written nearly a month ago in Geneva on this matter of travelling and expenditure containing propositions somewhat at variance with the spirit—or rather with the letter of the above advice. I don't know in what manner you have replied to it; exactly as you felt you ought, of course. When you speak of your own increased expenses etc. I feel very guilty and selfish in entertaining any projects which look in the least like extravagance. My beloved mother, if you but knew the purity of my motives! Reflection assures me, as it will assure you, that the only economy for me is to get thoroughly well and into such a state as that I can work. For this consummation, I will accept everything—even the appearance of mere pleasure-seeking. A winter in Italy (if I feel two months hence as I do now) enabling me to spend my time in a certain way, will help me on further than anything else I know of—more than a winter in Paris and of course, so long as the very semblance of application is denied me—than one in Germany. But it will by so much hasten (so I reason) the moment when I can spend a winter or some months at any rate, in Germany without damage and with positive profit. If before I left home I had been as certain as I have now become, that to *pay,* my visit here must at present be a real change—a real active taking hold of the matter—we could have talked over the subject far better than we can do in this way. In effect when I consider how *completely,* during the three or four months before I sailed I was obliged to give up all reading and writing (Willy can tell you) I see that it was a very absurd extension of my hopes to fancy that mere change of place would enable me to take them up again—or that I could lead the old life with impunity in Paris more than in Cambridge. Having lost all the time I have, you see I naturally wish to economise what is left. When I think that a winter in Italy is not as you call it a winter of "recreation" but an occasion not only of physical regeneration, but of serious culture too (culture of the kind which alone I have now at twenty-six any time left for) I find the courage to maintain my proposition even in the face of your allusions to the need of economy at home. It takes a very honest conviction thus to plead the cause of apparently gross idleness against such grave and touching facts. I have trifled so long with my trouble that I feel as if I could afford now to be a little brutal. My lovely mother, if ever I am restored to you sound and serviceable you will find that you have not cast the pearls of your charity before a senseless beast, but before a creature with a soul to be grateful and a will to act.—There are two things which I hardly need add. 1st, that of course you will be guided in your rejoinder simply by the necessities of the case, and will quite put aside any wish to please or any fear to displease me; and 2d that whether I go to Italy or to Paris I shall be as economical as possible. After all, there are two months yet; so much discussion of protestation will strike you as premature. I may find that by the 1st of September I am quite strong enough to face the *dulness* of Paris.

Wednesday 30*th* I left my letter standing and shall add but a few words before closing it. I have had an adventure worth mentioning. On Monday evening (night before last) I agreed with three gentlemen here (two Englishmen and a German) to make with them the ascent of a certain mountain hard-bye, by name the Roche de Neige. (For the various localities hereabouts, by the way, tell Willy to shew you M. Arnold's two poems on *Obermann*). We started accordingly at midnight, in order to be on the summit to see the sunrise. We reached the top after four hours steady walking—the last part by moonlight. The sunrise was rather a failure owing to an excess of clouds: still, the red ball shot up with the usual splendid suddenness. The summit was extremely cold—tho' we had brought a guide with overcoats etc. We descended in about half the time and reached the hotel by 7 A.M. in time for a bath and breakfast. I was of course tired but not to excess and today finds me alright again. The expedition was a stupid one, however, and I shall undertake no more night feats. They don't pay. But the rocks of Naye are about as high as Mt. Washington. What would you have thought last summer of my starting off at midnight to scale the latter? As far as impunity is concerned I feel perfectly disposed to start off tomorrow, with a pleasant companion, by daylight, on the same errand.—I have just received with gratitude, the July At-

lantic. My story strikes me as the product of a former state of being.[1] The second part, I fancy, is better. I heard recently from John La Farge to the effect that he would probably come out to Switzerland this summer. I hope much he may, but I doubt it. Minny Temple writes me that she *may* appear in Rome next winter. This too I hope somewhat faintly. I hear often from Aunt Kate who evidently is enjoying things hugely. You must be on the point of starting for Pomfret. Write me all about it. Address me until I give you a more permanent address to the Nortons, *la Pacotte, Vevey.* Farewell, my dearest Mother. Tell Willy I shall speedily answer his last. My blessings upon Father and Alice. Make Wilky write.

Your devoted son
H. James jr

1. "Gabrielle de Bergerac" appeared in three installments in the *Atlantic,* July–September 1869, 55–71, 231–241, 352–361.

12 · To William James

Ms Harvard

Florence, Hotel de l'Europe
October 16*th* Sunday [1869]

My dear Wm.

I wrote you a week ago a letter such as ought to be followed up, I feel, by some further communication. I don't want to incur the charge of harrowing you up—without at least raking you over. I hoped by this time to have got a letter from you; but I receive nothing but cold head-shakes from the *portier.* Since, then, I've undertaken this "startling exposé" of my condition, I will proceed to draw the curtain altogether. I felt very blue at having to write to you as I did; but I was glad I had done so; inasmuch as after I had sent my letter, matters came to a crisis which made me feel that they were truly serious and that if you were to give me any hints, the sooner I got them the better. I have just written to mother, without speaking of being unwell. But you had better let father know that I am not quite all that I should be, since if I should be obliged (as I still hope not to be, however) to do anything or go anywhere for this special reason, so much of this tiresome story may be known.—I was feeling very badly when I wrote you: *je ne tardai pas* to feel worse. For a week, owing to the state of my bowels, my head and stomach had been all out of order.[1] What I have called the "crisis" was brought on by taking two so-called "antibilious" pills, recommended me at the English druggist's. They failed to relieve me and completely disagreed with me—bringing on a species of abortive diarrhoea. That is I felt the most re-iterated and most violent inclination to stool, without being able to effect anything save the passage of a little blood. Meanwhile my head got much worse and this was accompanied by a gradual violent chill. Whereupon I took to my bed, and here the chill began to merge into a fever, with cramps in my feet and legs—my bowels horribly stuffed and my head *infernal.* Of course I sent for the English (or rather, as he turned out the Irish) physician. (I believe there are several here.) He concentrated his energies upon getting me a stool as speedily as possible. That is he made me take an injection, of some unknown elements, which completely failed to move me. I re-peated it largely—wholly in vain. He left me late in the morning ap-parently quite in despair; and between my abdomen and my head, I passed a very hard night and one such as I should be sorry to endure the repetition of. Towards morning some pills which he had given me began to procure me comparative relief, tho' my head was slow to clear up. Eventually however with reiterated pills I began to mend and that afternoon went out into the air. Several days have now passed. I have seen the doctor repeatedly as he seems inclined (to what extent as a friend and to what as a doctor I ignore) to keep me in hand. He has prescribed me a peculiar species of alactic pill, to be taken an hour before dinner, which he hopes if kept up long enough will evac[uate] me into an habitual action. *Je ne demande pas mieux,* so long as that in the interval, I can keep tolerably comfortable—which is the difficult point. He says, what is doubtless true—that my bowels have been more injured by large injections in the past, than by the abuse of medi-cine. He examined them (as far as he could) by the insertion of his finger (horrid tale!) and says there is no palpable obstruction. He seemed surprised however that I haven't piles; you see we have always something to be grateful for. On the whole nevertheless I find it hard to make him (as I should anyone who hadn't observed it) at all under-stand the stubbornness and extent—the length and breadth and depth, of my trouble. He indulges in plenty of vague remarks about diet, exer-

cise and not reading—which you will admit that I have earned the
right to dispense with.—Of course all this business has left me uncomfortable in the present and apprehensive of the future. At this present
moment of my writing, I know neither how I'm to do without a stool,
nor how (in spite of the doctor's pills, as yet) I am to get one. The
whole matter occupies perforce (how gracefully!) the foreground of my
thoughts and oppresses equally my mind and my body. It seems hardly
worth while to be in this great Italy on such a footing: but *enfin* circumstances are what they are; and mine might be very much worse.
My trouble is a bad one, but the circumstances are very well: especially this of my sitting scribbling to you. Of course I feel even more
than when I last wrote that some change is imperative and that this
state of things must discontinue *au plus tôt*. But as you see however I
am not much nearer to finding an issue, and meanwhile my daily life
becomes rather less than more comfortable. Let me not however use
too dark colors. I find the best restaurant here—the Café de Paris—
very sufficient to my dietetic needs. I can get things done quite *à l'anglaise*. I have entered into renewed engagements with myself with regard
to eating and drinking, and by means of these, the doctor's pills and
the form [of] active life that I [have] been leading so long (tho' with
only *this very* result against which I now appeal to it!) I hope to hold
out till the dawning of some change.—But this matter of an active life
suggests precisely the most serious point in these late developments.
They have brought with them a rapidly growing sense of the relation
between the state of my bowels and my *back*. My actual situation is
complicated by the fact that this recent terrible constipation has made
itself *directly* felt in my back (the lower part, across the base, loins and
hips) to such a degree that it becomes an added effort to take that
amount of exercise needful to combat this same constipation. I feel
this heaviness of the bowels across my loins more palpably and unmistakeably than I can express to you. I have always felt in a general
way that if my bowels were regular, my back would be better; but it is
only within the past few weeks that I have realized keenly the connection between the two and been able to measure the load of which my
back would be lightened if I could keep my abdomen free. Formerly I
had two distinct troubles—my constipation and my pain in my back. I
now see that what I still retain of the latter is in a sharp degree but
another phase of the former. I draw from this fact a stupendous hope—
it shines to me as a light out of the darkness: and I depend upon it for

running to your mind, by its clearing influence, the barbarity of this appeal to your sympathies. To put it in a word, I feel justified in believing that if, say at the end of a month, (no matter how—by some miracle!) I had established a healthy action of my bowels, my back would by a corresponding movement have made a leap not of a *month* but of a year—of two, three—what you please. I should feel in other words IMMEDIATELY an improvement which I have been used to consider a thing of very distant days. I don't mean to say that the relation between these two localities has always been the same: but there came a moment in the march of improvement when the one overtook and outstripped the other, and has ever since been clogged and held back by it. Disengaged from this fatal grasp it would at once advance to the end of its own chain—a longer one than I have yet ventured to fancy. —These reflections fill me with a perfectly *passionate* desire for a reformation in my bowels. I see in it not only the operation of a special localized affection, but a large general change in my condition and a blissful renovation of my life—the reappearance above the horizon of pleasures which had well-nigh sunk forever behind that great murky pile of undiminishing contingencies to which my gage had so long been accustomed. It would mean in the course of a comparatively short time, a return to repose—reading—hopes and ideas—an escape from this weary world of idleness. But I needn't descant further: a word to the wise is enough. —You may imagine that there's nothing I am not ready to do to compass my desire. At present the prescription seems to be that hardest of all things—to wait. Well—I'll even wait. I shall remain in Florence until one way or the other I get some news of a change. I shall do so almost *mechanically,* for I confess that in my present physical condition—with this perpetual oppression of the inner and outer man—to enjoy things keenly is difficult. If I get no better, I shall not push on to Rome. Such at least is my present disposition. It would *spoil* Rome to see it under this perpetual drawback. To go there simply as travelling and as therefore beneficial would moreover not be worthwhile, as here for some time to come I can get a sufficiency of movement. If I leave Florence *not* for Rome, I don't see what is left for me but to go to *Malvern*—a matter on which I touched in my last. I am not wrong I think, in attributing to Malvern my condition during the last part of my stay in England; and I feel now that once possessed of a similar *start,* I should not let it slip from me as before. I should, however, deeply regret being forced to take this step

47

and to turn my back upon Italy. The thought is horrible. Not only should I lose what may possibly be the most delightful and valuable part of this Italian experience; but I should find my subsequent plans grievously disarranged. It is my dearest desire to get three months of England, in the fine season, before my return—to sail if possible thence. To take them now in midwinter would of course be a poor substitute.— On the other side, if I should make a solid gain by a couple of months at Malvern, it would reconcile me to everything. Such a start, I say, I would undertake to keep; and with my bowels thus regenerated I would laugh Italy to scorn. I should then feel comparatively small need of leading a life of sight-seeing and should not hesitate to claim from the days a fair allowance of reading. With this consolation—I should ask but for a moderate daily sitting—I should either remain in England (i.e. London) or revert to Paris and abide there till such a moment as I should feel prepared to venture on Germany. Then after a sojourn the duration of which I don't now pretend to fix—I should return to Cambridge and I devoutly trust to work.—"The thought grows frightful, 'tis so wildly dear." All this hangs as you see—on a feeble thread—but it *does* hang.—Meanwhile I eat brans and peas and grapes and pears and walk—walk—walk—in the hope of an *occasional* stool.—This is the end of my long story. I feel the better for having written it: I hope you will feel none the worse for reading it. It's because I know you not to be a maudlin and hysterical youth that I have let myself out. But don't think me a great fail[ure] if you should suddenly get a letter from me from England. I can imagine being *forced* to fly, in desperation. For instance I don't think I could withstand the effects of another attack like that last—for tho' the "crisis" was accelerated by improper medicine I'm sure I felt all ripe for it. But I have good hopes of evading such miseries and remaining here—at any rate. Having opened up the subject at such a rate, I shall of course keep you informed.—To shew you haven't taken this too ill, for heaven's sake make me a letter about your own health—poor modest flower!—Commend me most lovingly to my parents and sister. Write to me to as good purpose as (without worrying) you may and believe me your brother

H.J. jr.

P.S. It's no more than just that the family should in some form repay themselves for your medical education. And what is a doctor meant for but to listen to old women's *doléances?* Don't lose sight of that good news about my back.

Give my love, when you see him to Frank Washburn and tell him I long for news of him—and that if he should ever feel like sending me a line the gracious act would rank among benefits remembered. Let him remember Pisa and that Florence is but a larger part of Pisa.

I get no news at all of O. W. H[olmes] jr.—Tell him—I hate him most damnably; I never knew till the past few months how much; but that I yet think I shall write to him.

19*th.* I have kept my letter till today, hoping I might have one from home to acknowledge.—But I close it, sick unto death of vain wait-ing.—I see in it nothing to alter—and nothing to add save the adjura-tion to TAKE IT EASY! The Malvern plan is very thin: I don't see how I *can* leave Italy.—While there is life there is hope.—Address me as I wrote you: MM. Em. Fenzi et Cie. Banquiers, Florence, Italy. If I go to Rome they will forward and if I am likely to be there more than a month I will give you a new address. Pray stop the *Atlantic* coming from the office. It keeps coming like the *Nation* whereof I wrote you, thro' Lombard Didier & Cie, and after them thro' a string of Bankers who each charge a commission, I suppose. If you could have it sent you from the office and mail it yourselves as you do my letters I should prefer it. I made this same request about the *Nation.* If this is inconve-nient, it would be better to suppress them.

1. This letter is published here for the first time. It was kept by HJ for ten days and dispatched on 26 October, when he also wrote Letter 13. HJ's bout of constipation seems to have had a variety of causes: the Continental food and water; his loneliness and home-sickness; his being "uptight" because of his parents' insistence that he be economical; the stress of feeling himself an idler in pursuit of aesthetic experience compared with his brother William, who had followed a course of systematic reading and study during his own recent period abroad. HJ recovered by the time of his return to Cambridge, and in later years he had no troubles of this nature.

13 · *To Henry James, Sr.*

Ms Harvard

[Florence, 26 October 1869]

My dearest Daddy—[1]

I feel as if I should write a very dismal letter; nevertheless, write I must, tho' it be but three lines. There are moments when I feel more keenly than ever the cheerlessness of solitude and the bitterness of exile. Such a one is the present. The weather has turned fearfully bleak and cold, and gloomy skies and piercing winds are the order of the day. The dusk has fallen upon my small and frigid apartment and I have lit my candle to warm my fingers—as I begin this letter to warm my thoughts. Happy Florence is going to dine *en famille* and to enjoy the delights of mutual conversation.—Well; so be it: Well it's something to have a *famille* to write to if not to dine and converse with.—I have recently come in from a long walk in the *Cascine*—the great Bois de Boulogne of Florence—a lovely verdurous park, skirting the Arno, with no end of charming outlooks into the violet-bosomed hills. The Florentine *beau-monde* and *bourgeoisie* were there in force—a remarkably good looking set of people they are: the latter—the pedestrians—especially. I've been vastly struck throughout with the beauty of the Italian race, especially in the men. After the hideous population of German Switzerland, they are most delightful to behold; and when hand in hand with their charming smiles come flowing the liquid waves of their glorious speech, you feel positively ashamed of your Anglo-Saxon blood. Never in my life as since I've been in Florence have I seen so many young men of princely aspect. The charm of it all too is that it's the beauty of intelligence and animation quite as much as of form and feature.—Their beauty, however, consoles me little in my sorrow—my sorrow at the cold silence of my home—owing to which I have had no letter—no sign or sound of life or love—for nearly three weeks. I got a letter from Mother on my arrival here; but I've waited in vain for further news.—I seek not to complain; but I feel lonely and weak minded and if I mention the fact cannot pretend to be indifferent. I devoutly trust soon the stillness will soon be broken.—I set you all a good example by writing even tho' I've very little to tell. My life in Florence is very quiet and monotonous and unless I go in for a *catalogue raisonné* of the two great galleries, my letter must perforce be brief. Such a catalogue indeed would be as good an account of my time as anything I could give; inasmuch as I have spent it chiefly in looking at pictures. I feel able to say now with a certain amount of truth that I *know* the Uffizi—and the Pitti. How much the wiser I am for my knowledge I hope one of these days to learn—if not to teach. These two Galleries are unutterably rich and I hope before I leave Florence to transmit to William a few glittering generalities on their contents.

Monday evening. 25th. I was obliged to give up writing yesterday because my room was too cold to abide. A fierce *tramonta[na]* has been blowing for several days and Florence is like Boston in January. I adjourned for warmth and cheer to a very good English reading-room near at hand; and there, having spent an hour, I made my way across the river to call upon Mrs. Huntington and daughters, whom I have already mentioned. I found them seated with Mrs. Horatio Greenough and daughter,[2] round a jolly fire which it was a joy to behold. In the centre of this rich group of my fair country-women, I spent a very pleasant evening. Today too I have tasted of society. Charles Norton arrived here this morning from Pisa, where he had left his family, in quest of an apartment. I went about the city with him and parted with him in the afternoon, he returning to Pisa. We saw two good places— a large handsome apartment in town in the same house as the Huntingtons and a most delightful old Villa, a good bit out of the city gates. Charles inclines to the latter—and indeed with friends and books it would be hard to contrive a brighter lovelier home: the house capacious, elderly, Italian—and the garden and all the outside prospect Italianissimi—Florence lying at your feet and the violet snow-tipped Apennines ornamenting the distance. In one way or another I suppose they will settle themselves within a week. I am very glad to have looked at that Villa, at all events. It gave me a most penetrating sense of the peculiar charm of Florence—of the general charm indeed of Italy—a charm inexpressible, indefineable, which must be observed in its native air, but which, once deeply felt, leaves forever its mark upon the sensitive mind and fastens it to Italian soil thro' all its future wanderings by a delicate chain of longings and regrets. I wish I could get you and Mother and Alice implanted for a while in some such habitation—feeding on its picturesqueness and drinking the autumn sunshine—which like everything about Florence seems to be colored with a mild violet, like diluted wine. But it's a very silly wish. You would die of loneliness and you'd curse your antique privacy.—I have placed myself half under a promise to go down to Pisa within a day or two, to see the Nortons 'ere they come to Florence. I hesitate somewhat to do it because if I turn my back upon Florence now, I'm afraid I shall turn it upon Italy altogether. I'm very sorry to say that I am anything but well. Not that I have any new and startling affliction, but an old trouble which I had most confidently hoped by this time to have got the mastery of, has settled down upon me during the last six weeks with a most inexorable weight. Willy will tell you what it is: I wrote him on the subject soon after I came to Florence. I fought a hard battle all summer with it in Switzerland; but I left the country with a painful sense that I hadn't gained an inch of ground. Ever since I have been in Italy I have been rapidly losing ground and now I have scarcely a square inch to stand on. During my stay in Venice my journey hither and the three weeks of my being here I have been in a very bad way. Shortly after getting here I was so knocked up that I had to take to my bed and have the doctor and I have since then been in his hands. He plies me with drugs, but to no purpose: I only seem to get worse. But I'll not treat you to a string of details: I recommend you to Willy for information. I don't know whether to think that Italian air has anything to do with the matter: I'm utterly unable to explain so violent an aggravation of my state, in the very face of a mode of life magnificently calculated (as one would say) to ensure a steady improvement. But the fact remains and I must come to some sort of terms with it. I feel as if I couldn't live on a week longer in my present pernicious condition. I'm not impatient: I have given the thing a fair chance and my present condition, which is all that has come of my patience, is quite unendurable. I would give a vast deal to be able to believe that all I have to do is to hang on in Italy and change will come. Experience assures me that I have no reason whatever to look for a change on these terms and without a change I absolutely can't remain. It makes a sad trouble of what ought to be a great pleasure. My malady has done a great deal towards spoiling Florence for me: I should be sorry to have it meddle with other places. The question is of course what to do, inasmuch as I've pretty nearly exhausted expedience. I have almost made up my mind to depart straight from Italy and take refuge at Malvern again. The sole period of relief that I have enjoyed since I've been abroad came to me during the last part of my stay there and the subsequent month of my travels in England. On leaving England I immediately relapsed. I therefore feel justified in hoping that if I buckle down to a good two months at M[alvern] (or whatever shorter time may seem sufficient) I may gain a solid benefit. I have come to this decision with much cogitation and infinite regret. In leaving Italy now I shall be doing I think, the hardest thing I ever did. But I don't see that any other way is open to me. To be at the very gates of Rome and to turn away requires certainly a strong muscular effort. A very faint ray of light ahead would make me advance with a rush. But I cannot undertake to see Rome as I have seen Florence: the sooner I do it the better. This will be a great disappointment to your dear sympathetic souls at home, just as it is to my own: place on the other side the chance of my recovery by going to M. There will be no Rome and no Italy like the Rome and Naples of my getting really relieved of this dismal burden. They will be utterly vulgar in comparison. You may measure the *need* of my bolting thus out of Italy, by the simple fact of things having reached that point that it's easier to go than to stay.

Tuesday morning. I was driven to bed last night by the cold and before going out this morning I take up my shaky pen to finish my letter. It's such a dismal effusion that the sooner I bring it to a close the better. Don't revile me and above all don't pity me. Simply be as comfortable and jolly as you can yourselves and I shall get along very well. Don't wholly give up writing to me, however; such an extravagance of jollity I should wholly deprecate.—Dear Father, if once I can get rid of this ancient sorrow I shall be many parts of a well man. Remember this and give me your good wishes. This trouble now is the only rock in my path: if I remove it I shall march straight ahead, I think, to health and work.—I spent a good portion of last night wondering whether I *can* manage not to go to Rome. *Nous verrons:* I shall go to Pisa for a couple of days and may there with a change of circumstances and a little society receive an impulse for the better, on which I shall perhaps try Rome for a couple of weeks. I shall drop you a line from there saying whether I am to move North or South, so that you may know where to write. Meanwhile farewell. *Je vous embrasse*—I *squeeze* you all.—I have invented for my comfort a theory that this degenerescence of mine is the result of Alice and Willy getting better and locating some of their diseases on me—so as to propitiate the fates by not turning the poor homeless infirmities out of the family. Isn't it so? I forgive them and bless them.

Your ever affectionate young one
H. James jr

1. Like the preceding letter, this is published here for the first time.

2. The American Greenoughs and Huntingtons had resided in Florence from the earlier part of the century. Horatio Greenough (1805–1852), a Boston-born sculptor, was among the first American artists to work in Italy. His nephew Gordon, also a sculptor, became the subject of HJ's short story "The Tree of Knowledge" (1900); see HJ, *The Complete Notebooks* (1986), 182, 184.

14 · *To William James*

Ms Harvard

Rome Hotel d'Angleterre
Oct. 30*th* [1869]

My dearest William—

Some four days since I despatched to you and Father respectively, from Florence, two very doleful epistles, which you will in course of time receive. No sooner had I posted them, however than my spirits were revived by the arrival of a most blessed brotherly letter from you of October 8th, which had been detained either by my banker or the porter of the hotel and a little scrap from Father of a later date, enclosing your review of Mill and a paper of Howells—as well as a couple of *Nations.* Verily, it is worthwhile pining for letters for three weeks to know the exquisite joy of final relief. I took yours with me to the theatre whither I went to see a comedy of Goldoni most delightfully played and read and re-read it between the acts.—But of this anon.— I went as I proposed down to Pisa and spent two very pleasant days with the Nortons. It is a very fine dull old town—and the great Square with its four big treasures is quite the biggest thing I have seen in Italy—or rather was, until my arrival at this well-known locality.—I went about a whole morning with Charles Norton and profited vastly by his excellent knowledge of Italian history and art. I wish I had a small fraction of it. But my visit wouldn't have been complete unless I had got a ramble *solus,* which I did in perfection. On my return to Florence I determined to start immediately for Rome. The afternoon after I had posted those two letters I took a walk out of Florence to an enchanting old Chartreuse—an ancient monastery, perched up on top of a hill and turreted with little cells like a feudal castle.[1] I attacked it and carried it by storm—i.e. obtained admission and went over it. On coming out I swore to myself that while I had life in my body I wouldn't leave a country where adventures of that complexion are the common incidents of your daily constitutional: but that I would hurl myself upon Rome and fight it out on this line at the peril of my existence. Here I am then in the Eternal City. It was easy to leave Florence; the cold had become intolerable and the rain perpetual. I started last night, and at 10½ o'clock and after a bleak and fatiguing journey of twelve hours found myself here with the morning light. There are several places on the *route* I should have been glad to see; but the weather and my own condition made a direct journey imperative. I rushed to this hotel (a very slow and obstructed rush it was, I confess, thanks to the longueurs and lenteurs of the Papal dispensation) and after a wash and a breakfast let myself loose on the city. From midday to dusk I have been roaming the streets. *Que vous en dirai-je?* At last— for the first time—I live! It beats everything: it leaves the Rome of your fancy—your education—nowhere. It makes Venice—Florence— Oxford—London—seem like little cities of pasteboard. I went reel- ing and moaning thro' the streets, in a fever of enjoyment. In the course of four or five hours I traversed almost the whole of Rome and got a glimpse of everything—the Forum, the Coliseum (stupendis- simo!), the Pantheon, the Capitol, St. Peter's, the Column of Trajan, the Castle of St. Angelo—all the Piazzas and ruins and monuments. The effect is something indescribable. For the first time I know what the picturesque is.—In St. Peter's I stayed some time. It's even beyond its reputation. It was filled with foreign ecclesiastics—great armies en- camped in prayer on the marble plains of its pavement—an inexhaust- ible physiognomical study. To crown my day, on my way home, I met his Holiness in person[2]—driving in prodigious purple state—sitting dim within the shadows of his coach with two uplifted benedictory fin- gers—like some dusky Hindoo idol in the depths of its shrine. Even if I should leave Rome tonight I should feel that I have caught the key- note of its operation on the senses. I have looked along the grassy vista of the Appian Way and seen the topmost stone-work of the Coliseum sitting shrouded in the light of heaven, like the edge of an Alpine chain. I've trod the Forum and I have scaled the Capitol. I've seen the Tiber hurrying along, as swift and dirty as history! From the high tri- bune of a great chapel of St. Peter's I have heard in the papal choir a strange old man sing in a shrill unpleasant soprano. I've seen troops of little tonsured neophytes clad in scarlet, marching and countermarch- ing and ducking and flopping, like poor little raw recruits for the heav- enly host. In fine I've seen Rome, and I shall go to bed a wiser man than I last rose—yesterday morning.—It was a great relief to me to have you at last give me some news of your health. I thank the Lord it's no worse. With all my heart I rejoice that you're going to try loaf- ing and visiting. I discern the "inexorable logic" of the affair; courage, and you'll work out your redemption. I'm delighted with your good report of John La Farge's pictures. I've seen them all save the sleeping woman. I have given up expecting him here. If he does come, *tant mieux*. Your notice of Mill and Bushnell seemed to me (save the opening lines which savored faintly of Eugene Benson)³ very well and fluently written. Thank Father for his ten lines: may they increase and multiply!—Of course I don't know how long I shall be here. I would give my head to be able to remain three months: it would be a liberal education. As it is, I shall stay, if possible, simply from week to week. My "condition" remains the same. I am living on some medicine (aloes and sulphuric acid) given me by my Florentine doctor. I shall write again very shortly. Kisses to Alice and Mother. Blessings on yourself. Address me *Spada, Flamine* and Cie. Banquiers, Rome. Heaven grant I may be here when your letters come. Love to Father.

À toi

H.J. jr

1. HJ describes the visit to the Carthusian monastery outside the Porta Romana in *Italian Hours* (1909), 299–302.

2. Pope Pius IX.

3. Eugene Benson (1839–1908), an American artist and devotee of the Venetian school, the author of numerous articles published in book form as *Art and Nature in Italy*. He may have been the original for Singleton in *Roderick Hudson*.

15 · To William James

Ms Harvard

Rome

27 [Dec. 1869]

Beloved Bill,—

I have just found at my bankers a long letter from you (Dec. 5th) which has gratified me so inexpressibly that altho' I despatched home a document only a couple of days since, I feel powerfully moved to write to you directly,—the more especially as my letter contained a promise that I would. Your letter fills me with a divine desire to occupy for an hour that old cane-bottomed chair before your bedroom fire. One of these days it will hold me for many hours. I am extremely glad you like my letters—and terrifically agitated by the thought that Emerson likes them.¹ I never manage to write but a very small fraction of what has originally occurred to me. What you call the "animal heat" of contemplation is sure to evaporate within half an hour. I went this morning to bid farewell to M. Angelo's *Moses* at San Pietro in Vincoli, and was so tremendously impressed with its sublimity that on the spot my intellect gushed forth a torrent of wisdom and eloquence; but where is that torrent now? I *have* managed tolerably well however, which is the great thing, to *soak* myself in the various scenes and phenomena. Conclusions occasionally leap full-armed from my Jovine brain, bringing with them an immensely restful sense of their finality. This morning I think I definitively settled the matter with regard to Michael Angelo. I believe, by the way, I never explicitly assured you of the greatness of the "Moses."—or of the vileness of that calumnious photograph. It is a work of magnificent beauty,—beauty very nearly equal to that of the statue of Lorenzo d'Medici. I now feel as if I could judge of Michael Angelo's merits in tolerably complete *connaissance de cause*. I have seen the Great Greek things; I have seen Raphael and I have seen all his own works. He has something—he retains something, after all experience—which belongs only to himself. This transcendent "something" invested the *Moses* this morning with a more melting, exalting power than I have ever perceived in a work of art. It was a great sensation—the greatest a work can give. I sat enthralled and fascinated by that serene *Aristides* at Naples; but I stood agitated this morning by all the forces of my soul. The beauty of such a thing as the Aristides is in the effect achieved; that of the *Moses*, the *Lorenzo*, the figures on the Sistine roof in the absence of a limited effect. The first take no account of the imagination; the others the largest. They have a soul. Alack! 'tis poor work talking of them; *je tenais seulement* to work off something of the tremor in which they have left me, and to gratify myself by writing down in black and white and, if need be, taking my stand on it against the world, the assertion that Michel Angelo is the greatest of artists. The question remained solely as between him and the Greeks; but this morning settled it. The *Moses* alone perhaps wouldn't have done it; but it did it in combination with the vision of Lorenzo's tomb—which I had it with the deepest distinctness. It's the triumph of feeling: the Greeks deny it—poor stupid old Michel proclaims its sovereign air a regenerated world:—and affords a magnificent pretext for making a stand against it *en suite*. It's the victorious cause: the other will never be so well pleaded. It behoves therefore the generous mind to take up the latter. It was worth the trouble going, afterwards, as we did this morning, to San Agostino and Sta. Maria della Pace to look upon Raphael's two wretchedly decayed frescoes of Isaiah and the Sybils, in which *il a voulu faire du Michel Ange.* There was in him none but the very smallest Michel Angelesque elements. —I fancy that I have found after much fumbling and worrying—much of the deepest enjoyment and of equal dissatisfaction—the secret of his incontestable thinness and weakness. He was incapable of energy of statement. This may seem to be but another name for the fault and not an explication of it. But *enfin* this energy—positiveness—courage,—call it what you will—is a simple, fundamental, primordial quality in the supremely superior genius. Alone it makes the real man of action in art and disjoins him effectually from the critic. I felt this morning irresistibly how that Michel Angelo's greatness lay above all in the fact that he *was* this man of action—the greatest, almost, considering the temptation he had to be otherwise, considering how his imagination embarrassed and charmed and bewildered him—the greatest perhaps, I say, that the race has produced. So far from perfection, so finite, so full of errors, so broadly a target for criticism as it sits there, the *Moses* nevertheless by the vigor with which it utters its idea, the eloquence with which it tells the tale of the author's passionate abjuration of the inaction of fancy and contemplation—his willingness to let it stand, in the interest of life and health and movement as his *best* and his only possible,—by this high transcendent spirit, it redeems itself from subjection to its details, and appeals most forcibly to the generosity and sympathy of the mind. Raphael is undecided, slack and unconvinced—I have seen little else since my return from Naples. I have been staying on from day to day—partly from the general difficulty there is in leaving Rome, partly from the Christmas doings, and partly because it's a certain comfort to Aunt Kate[2] and Helen Ripley. My departure however is fixed for tomorrow. You will have heard from Aunt K. of the steady hideousness of the weather. It tells sadly upon her party and reduces to a very small amount the utmost that can be done in a day. I have seen very little of the Christmas ceremonies. I got my fill so completely at the Council[3] of a crowd and a struggle that I made no attempt to go out on Christmas Eve. On Christmas Day I roamed about St. Peter's. I saw nothing of the Mass or the Pope—but the crowd there is immensely picturesque and well worth seeing. Aunt K. and Helen R. (cousin Henry having been laid up for a week with a violent cold) went with their Courier, got beautiful places and saw to perfection. I'm sick unto death of priests and churches. Their "picturesqueness" ends by making you want to go strongly into political economy or the New England school system. I conceived at Naples a tenfold deeper loathing than ever of the hideous heritage of the past—and felt for a moment as if I should like to devote my life to laying rail-roads and erecting blocks of stores on the most classic and romantic sites. The age has a long row to hoe.—Your letter was full of delightful things. I can't too heartily congratulate you on your plan of visiting. *Vous allez bien voir.* You will live to do great things yet.

Assisi. Tuesday, Dec. 28th.—Since writing the above I have been taking a deep delicious bath of mediaevalism. I left Rome this morning by the 6.40 A.M. train and under a villainous cloudy sky, and came along in a mortally slow train (all the better to see from) thro' the great romantic country which leads up to Florence. Anything *more* romantic—more deeply and darkly dyed with the picturesque and all the happy chiaroscuro of song and story, it would be impossible to conceive. Perpetual alternations of the landscape of Claude and that of Salvator Rosa—an unending repetition of old steel engravings—raised to the hundredth power. Oh! *Narni*—oh! *Spoleto!* who shall describe your unutterable picturesqueness?—What words can shadow forth your happy positions aloft on sinking mountain spurs,—girt with your time-fretted crumbling bastions—incrusted with the rich deposit of history? I've seen such passages of color and composition—such bits—such effects—as can only be reproduced by a moan of joy. It's *dramatic* landscape. The towns are all built alike, perched on a mountain summit and huddled together within the dark-belted circuit of their walls. At 2.30, after a long morning of delight (despite occasional grievous showers) I arrived at this famous little spot—famous as the birthplace of St. Francis and the seat of that vast wondrous double church of which you, perhaps, remember the description in Taine. The town lies away up on the mountain and the church is built sheer upon its side. I got the one little *carriole* at the station to convey me thither, and found to my delight that I had time to see it tolerably well and get a hasty ramble through the terrific little city before dark. I have made a magnificent afternoon of it, and I am now scribbling this in the strangers' room of the *Leone d'Oro,* having just risen from an indigestibilissimo little repast.—The church is a vast and curious edifice of a great deal of beauty and even more picturesqueness—a dark cavernous solemn sanctuary below—and above it another, high, aspiring and filled with light—and with various sadly decayed frescoes of Giotto. The position is glorious. A great aerial portico winds about it and commands a tremendous view. The whole thing is intensely mediaeval, and the vocabulary of Michelet alone could furnish a proper characterization of it.[4] And if such is the church—what are the strange, tortuous, hill-scaling little streets of the city? Never have I seen the local color laid on so thick. They reek with antiquity. The whole place is like a little miniature museum of the *genre*—a condensation of the elements of mediaevalism—or the effect it produces at least, a condensation of one's impressions of them.

I am to go on this evening by the 8.30 train to Perugia. The man who brought me up has promised me to return with his vehicle and convey me down the mountain and across the plain to the station. Meanwhile however, the wind howls wofully, the storm seems to be rousing itself, and our transit may perhaps be uncomfortable. But I am bent on reaching Florence tomorrow night, and I wish to see Perugia in the morning. I am haunted with the apprehension that the host has bribed the little driver *not* to return, so that I may be kept over night.— I have vilely calumniated the establishment: the *padrona,* with the loveliest and most beaming Italian face I have ever seen, has just come in, to herald the approach of the *vetturino. Buona sera!* I shall add a word at Florence.

Florence. Jan. 1st 1870. A happy new-year! I have been here nearly three days but have been unable until now to get at my letter. I made with success the transit from Assisi to Perugia and now feel as if I had [laid] up a store of thrilling little memories which will last for many a year and witness many a recurrence of this would-be festive day. I spent at Perugia (which I found decorated with a snow-storm which would have done no discredit to the clime of obstructed horse-cars) a morning of unalloyed enjoyment. I put myself for the first time in Italy in the hands of a valet-de-place and found him a capital investment. So if there is one spot in Europe I know it's Perugia—Perugia the an-

tique, the high-created—the Etruscan-walled, the nobly-palaced—
the deeply darkly densely curious. It's the centre of that fine old Um-
brian school of art, of which Perugius and he of Urbino were the
brightest efflorescence and I saw there a number of noble specimens of
the former painter which almost reconciled me to his eternal monotony and insipid sweetness. What a summer could be spent in a long
slow journey of long lingering days between Florence and Rome—
every town stopped at—every landscape stared at—and lofty grim old
Roman Cortona not whizzed by in the pitiless train near the Lake of
Thrasymene barely glanced at through a gust of cinders. With these
reflections and under these annoyances I arrived in Florence. But the
sweetness of Florence restores me to perfect equanimity. I feel once
more its delicate charm—I find it the same rounded pearl of cities—
cheerful, compact, complete—full of a delicious mixture of beauty
and convenience. There is for the moment at least a return of fine
weather, but the cold is simply devilish. The streets, the hotels, the
churches and galleries all strive to out-freeze each other. I begin to
appreciate now the mildness of Rome and Naples. Yesterday, however,
the sun was glorious and I got a good warming up in a sweet lone walk
all beside the rapid Arno to the uttermost end of the charming Cascine, where, sheltered from the north by a magnificent wall of perpetual verdure and basking full in the long-sealed smile of the South,
all happy graceful Florence was watching the old year decline into its
death-shroud of yellow and pink. I have spent a long day with the
Nortons who are established in a cold capacious Villa not too far from
one of the city gates, to their apparent perfect contentment. They
made me as welcome as ever and we talked about Rome and Naples.
Charles seems sufficiently well and is working in a way it does one
good to see so many-burdened a man work, on Italian history and art.
The rest are excellent and pleasant, *comme toujours*. I took a turn yesterday thro' the Uffizi and the Pitti. All my old friends there stood
forth and greeted me with a splendid good-grace. The lustrissimo
Tiziano in especial gave me a glorious Venetian welcome. I spent half
an hour too in Michel Angelo's chapel at the San Lorenzo. Great
Lorenzo sits there none the less, above that weary giantess who re-
clines at his feet, gazing at the future with affrighted eyes and revolving the destinies of humanity. He has not yet guessed his riddle or

broken his awful stillness. Such lines were never conceived in other vision as Michel Angelo has there wrung out of his marble. For the notion of real grandeur we must knock at that door.—

But I am scribbling on without remembering that before I close I must thank you for your further counsel upon what you term so happily my moving intestinal drama. I wrote you before I went to Naples that I had consulted Dr. Gould, the "popular" American physician at Rome. He recommended me a mineral water, which I tried without the least success. Meanwhile, however Dr. Duffy's pills began to resume their action and at Naples (owing I think to the concurrent influence of many oranges) became decidedly efficacious. They are slacking up once more, but I continue to take them, wear a sort [of] bandage and get along very decently. Dr. Gould recommended fluid extract of senna, of which I procured a supply but have as yet held off from going into it. I am extremely glad to hear that you tested on yourself the virtues of the sulfuric acid. It has evidently an especial application to this matter. I don't know where Dr. D. got hold of it. I mean to see him again and will ask him.—Meanwhile I am gravitating northward. You bid me not hope to escape wholly the bore of Malvern. I don't in the least. I am determined to get rid of this thing before my return home, if not without Malvern, then with it. I wish to put off my visit there till such a moment as that when I leave, the season will be advanced enough for me to remain in England without disadvantage. I shall try and hold off therefore till the 1st of March. But you will be hearing from me again before I leave Florence. I don't know that there is anything more to say upon this solemn theme.—In reading over what I have written it occurs to me that you will reproach me with brevity and paucity of *data* regarding Aunt Kate. But there is nothing very startling to communicate. The three ladies apparently found my presence a useful distraction from the unbroken scrutiny of each other's characters. I think they are a little bit tired of each other and owing partly to the presence of an insane[5] and partly to the absence of a sane, gentleman among them, have not introduced a "foreign element" into their circumstances to the degree they would have liked. Aunt Kate's energy, buoyancy, and activity are magnificent. With a male companion and without a courier (a very stupefying as well as a very convenient appendage) she would have had a better chance to exercise them. Helen Rogers is very observant and very American (both for better and worse). She regrets somewhat, I fancy, the "good time" which she might have had under different circumstances. Cousin Henry seems mild and gentle and patient of her adventures rather than actively interested in them. I did what I could for them all but was very sorry I couldn't do more.—But I must bring this interminable scrawl to a close.—I am perpetually and deliciously preoccupied with home—as little as I can help to the detriment of European emotions—but to a degree which condemns me decidedly of being less in the intellect than the affections. But my intellect has a hand in it too. When you tell me of the noble working life that certain of our friends are leading in that clear American air, I hanker wofully to wind up these straggling threads of loafing and lounging and drifting and to toss my ball with the rest. But having waited so long I can wait a little longer.—I rejoice in the felicity of Minny Temple's visit—and deplore her disappointment with regard to California. But I mean to write her. The *Nation* has ceased to come to me; but I felt a most refreshing blast of paternity, the other day in reading Father's reply to a "Swedenborgian," in a number I saw at the bankers. But was there ever so cruel a father? He writes to the newspapers but not to his exiled child. I have not yet got his letter to England. I saw Ripley and Mrs. R. on my return to Rome. The former sent his love to Father: the latter looked very pretty and related an "audience" she had had of the Queen of Wurtemburg, who was living at the same hotel.—But a truce to my gossip. *Addio.* A torrent of love and longing to my parents and sister.

Your brother
H.

P.S. Since T. S. Perry is so hard at work on philology, ask him the Persian for a faceless and perjured friend!—

1. HJ's father had been circulating his son's travel letters among his friends.

2. HJ's aunt Catharine Walsh (Aunt Kate), his mother's sister, who had lived for years with the Jameses, was in Rome with friends, Helen Ripley and Helen Rogers.

3. An allusion to the meeting of the Ecumenical Council that took place while HJ was in Rome, which drew the boundaries of Vatican City and proclaimed anew the doctrine of Papal Infallibility.

4. Jules Michelet (1798–1874), the French historian, celebrated for his eloquent style.

5. HJ wrote the name Henry, crossed it out, and substituted the words "an insane." The reference is to his cousin Henry, who was in the ladies' party.

16 · *To Henry James, Sr.*

Ms Harvard

Genoa Hotel Feder
Jan. 14*th* 1870

Dearest father—

I drew from my bankers in Florence the day before I left your excellent and most welcome letter of Dec. 22d. You speak of having written me along with Mother and Willy, on the receipt of my bad news from Florence.[1] Your letter is probably destined soon to come to hand. I imagine it to be the document I am now in treaty for with the P.O. at Naples—it having gone there after I had left the place thro' the carelessness of my Roman bankers, and various complexities since having clustered about its fate. When I next write I hope to be able to announce its arrival. Meanwhile, for the present, your last is good enough to content me—tho' it pleases you to call it a sermon. For heaven's sake don't fear to write exactly as the spirit moves you. I should be as sorry to have you delay any injunction on your natural humor as to have you not write at all. Be very sure that as I live more I care none the less for these wise human reflections of yours. I turn with great satisfaction to any profession of interest in the fate of collective humanity—turn with immense relief from this wearisome European world of idlers and starers and self-absorbed pleasure seekers. I am not prepared perhaps to measure the value of your notions with regard to the amelioration of society, but I certainly have not travelled a year in this quarter of the globe without coming to a very deep sense of the absurdly clumsy and transitory organization of the actual social body. The only respectable state of mind, indeed, is to constantly express one's perfect dissatisfaction with it—and your letter was one of the most respectable things I have seen in a long time. So don't be afraid of treating me to a little philosophy. I treat myself to lots. With your letter came two *Nations*, with your Swedenborgian letters, which I had already seen and I think mentioned. I read at the same time in an *Atlantic* borrowed from the Nortons, your article on the woman business[2]—so you see I have had quite a heavy blow of your genius. Your *Atlantic* article I decidedly liked—I mean for matter. I am very glad to see someone not Dr. Bushnell and all that genus insist upon the distinction of sexes. As a mere piece of writing moreover I enjoyed it immensely:—I had been hoping before I left Florence to write a good long "descriptive" letter to Willy; but between my various cares it never came to the light. But it's only adjourned. Florence is the one thing I mean to talk about when I reach home. Talk alone can deal with it—talk as light and delicate and many shaded as its own inestimable genius. At present I feel as if I could hardly speak of it: all my instincts are sunk in the one dull dismal sensation of having left it—of its holding me no more. I sit here and wonder how my departure effected itself. The better man within me—the man of sympathies and ideas—soul and spirit and intellect, had certainly not the least little finger in the business. The whole affair was brutally and doggedly carried through by a certain base creature called Prudence, acting in the interest of a certain base organ which shall be nameless. The angel within me sate by with trembling fluttering wings watching these two brutes at their work. And oh! how that angel longs to spread these wings into the celestial blue of freedom and waft himself back to the city of his heart. All day yesterday, in the train as it dragged me along I could hardly believe that I was doing the hideous thing I was. Last night I spent—so to speak, in tears. Today I have been *more meo* trudging over Genoa, trying hard to make it do service, as an humble step-sister—a poor fifth cousin, of my Florence. But it's wretched work. The divine little city has no mortal relationships. She has neither father nor mother, nor brother nor child. She sits alone in the great earth with nothing but a lover—and that lover *moi!*—I was there about a fortnight—making six weeks in all. Day by day my fondness ripened into this unhappy passion. I have left my heart there and I shall be but half a man until I go back to claim it.—I should be now however in some degree a consoled and comforted man, dear father if I could give you some sufficient statement—some faithful account, of this delightful object of my choice. But in truth no mere account of Florence—no catalogue of her treasures or colloquy of her charms—can bring you to a knowledge of her benignant influence. It isn't this that or the other thing; her pictures, her streets or her hills— it's the lovely genius of the place—its ineffable spirit—its incalculable felicity. It's the most feminine of cities. It speaks to you with that same soft low voice which is such an excellent thing in women. Other cities beside it, are great swearing shuffling rowdies. Other cities are mere things of men and women and bricks and mortar. But Florence has an immortal soul. You look into her deep grey eyes—the Florentines have great cheap brown eyes, but the spiritual city has orbs of liquid grey—and read the history of her early sympathies and her questing youth—so studious, so sensitive, so human. Verily, of the history of Florence I as yet know the very smallest amount. I should be sorry to establish my passion on deeper foundations than really belong to it. No—Florence is friendly to all men and her beauty is equal to her wisdom. I spent a couple of days before I came away in going about to take a farewell look at the places I had more or less haunted. It was then that my heart was wrung with its deepest pain. To know all this and yet to forswear it—is there any sense in life, on such a basis? In point of fact, after all, there are very few individual objects in Florence of transcendent excellence. Michel Angelo's tombs stand first—then the Raphael's and Titian's portraits in the Uffizi and Pitti and then the Fra Angelicos at the Marco and half a dozen specimens of the early Florentine masters (Ghirlandaio, Lippo Lippi, Botticelli etc.) in various places. There is no great church; no great palace (a dozen capital *fine* ones) and save Leonardo, there was no great Florentine painter—(counting M.A. as a Roman).—Which he wasn't!

Mentone. H. de Gde. Bretagne. Jan. 17th P.M. I stayed my hand three nights ago at Genoa—since when I haven't had time to add a word. Tonight finds me on French soil—too tired with four days of constant exertion to hope to finish my letter; which I must keep till I get to Nice and rest my bones and my mind. But I don't want to fail to make a note of my impressions at the close of this memorable journey—the famous drive along the upper Riviera—the so-called Cornice Road. I had the good luck—the most blessed good fortune indeed I must call it—to find at Genoa a return carriage to Nice—the proprietor whereof was glad to take me at about a fourth of the rate of the regular journey—but little more than I should have had to pay for my *coupe* in the diligence. I left Genoa yesterday morning at five A.M. by train for *Savona* (two hours) where I met my carriage, which turned out thoroughly comfortable. How can I tell you what followed? how can words express it or minds conceive it? The naked facts are that I started from Savona at eight o'clock, halted and lunched at the little sea-side village of *Loano* and slept at *Onegha*: that I started this morning again at the same hour, lunched at *San Remo* and reached Mentone this evening at five: that tomorrow finally I am to take the short remnant of the drive (four hours) to Nice. Amid all that I have seen and done and felt in Europe, this journey stands forth triumphant. I have been *too*, too happy—and at the same time too utterly miserable—the latter to think that some parent or brother or sister was not at my side to help to dispose of such overwhelming impressions. The weather has been simply perfect—which in this particular region means a good deal.

Nice, Grand Hotel. Jan. 18th. P.M. I have carried out my programme. I spent this morning at Mentone and established myself in my carriage at about one. We reached this place at five. The drive is said to be the most beautiful part of the Riviera. Beautiful indeed it is. It leaves the shore and climbs and winds aloft among the mountains, giving you on one side a succession of the grandest masses of hill-scenery, all clad in purple and spotted and streaked with broken lights—and on the other, seen thro' the open portals of shady seaward gorges, the vast blue glitter of the Mediterranean. But it lacks the lovely swarming detail—the lingering clinging *Italianism* of the earlier portions of the road. Mentone is delicious and I am *tout desolé* to find myself in this ugly pretentious sprawling Nice. I speak on the evidence of half an hour's stroll I got before dinner. Here Italy quite gives it up and Imperial France reigns supreme—France which I used to love—but somehow love no more. That passion is dead and buried.—But what *shall* I tell you of this transcendent journey? Great heavens! That while he has breath in his body and a brain in his head a man should leave that land of the immortal gods! Never never never have I got such a sense of the essential enchantment—the incomparable "distinction" of Italy. Happy, thrice happy, the man who enters the country along that road! Proportionately deep and serious the melancholy of one who leaves it. No, one has not *lived* unless one has left Italy by the Cornice, in the full mid-glow of enjoyment, in the divinest weather that ever illumined the planet!—I have been journeying, as I suppose you know, thro' a belt of eternal spring. It has been a revelation of the possible kindness of nature. And that such a power should be the power of storm and darkness and cold! The country is a land of universal olive—a foliage as gentle and tender as the feathers on the breast of a dove—of olives and lusty cacti and fierce fantastic date-palms, perfect debauches of light and heat. Two moments stand out beyond the rest in my memory of the last three days—the night I spent at Oneghi—and the two sweet morning hours I passed at San Remo, yesterday. The first had a peculiar sanctity from the fact that it was my last night on Italian soil. I still had a good long hour of day-light after arriving and well I used it to roam thro' the little sea-side town. But it was the moon-light which set its stamp on the event—the biggest brightest highest moon I ever beheld—a few pale stars looking on and the Mediterranean beneath, a sheet of murmurous silver. At San Remo, as the Italian coast draws to a close it gathers up on its lovely bosom the scattered elements of its beauty and heart-broken at ceasing to be that land of lands, it exhales towards the blind insensate heavens a rapturous smile, more poignant than any reproach. There is something hideous in having at such a place to get back into one's carriage. The color of the Mediterranean there is something unutterable—as blue as one has dreamed the skies of heaven—as one's seen the Rhone at Geneva. There, too, the last sweet remnant of the beautiful Italian race looks at you with kindly dark eyed wonder as you take your way to the stupid unlovely North. I made a hundred notes of things I wanted to describe to you but I give it all up. The details overwhelm me. I can only bid you come and see it for yourself—come and see what you feel as you drive thro' a wide low plantation of olives, with their little tender sparkling leaves all interwoven overhead into a filter of grey-green light and their little slender twisted stems and trunks forming on the grassy hill-side an upper and lower horizon, and a foot-path trodden in the grass making a vista to shew in the distance two young Italians strolling arm in arm.—I made one note, tho', which I shan't forebear to dwell upon—a note relating to the deep gratitude I feel to the beloved parents to whom I owe all the rich acquisitions of these inestimable days. My second thought is always of them.

19th. I was so tired last night that I knocked off just after the above little spurt of filial affection. Tho' I had nominally driven from Mentone, yet so much of the way was up the mountains that I walked for miles together, to ease the horses: I was consequently a bit jaded by ten o'clock. Meanwhile however, the days are treading on each other's heels and you will have been an age without hearing from me. I don't forgive myself for not having managed to write in Florence: it was a rare occasion lost. I did however write three long letters, the two first of which you had better get hold of: one to Mr. Boott[3] (thro' Father) one to A. G. Sedgwick and one to M. Temple.—Tonight again I am rather tired and in view of this and of your probable impatience will make short work of what I have left to say. I oughtn't to abuse Nice, she has given me a charming day—charming, that is, by getting away from her. I plucked up my energies after breakfast and walked over to the beautiful little adjoining bay and town of Villefranche—where my heart beat proudly at seeing a noble American Man of War riding alone and glorious in the still blue basin of the harbor. Once at Villefranche I walked about promiscuously for hours (as I may say) among the loveliest conceivable olive-shaded paths, beside the sweet blue coves that look across the outer sea toward the bosky cliffs of Italy. I took a little carriage home, just in time for dinner. I have never seen anything so unmitigatedly innocent and sweet as all this coast region. It but—Italy's England [*sic*]. I mean to hang on as many days as I think I can afford to get some more walks.—Woe betide me! All this time I see I have told you nothing about Genoa. I was there but two days but I saw it tolerably well, and be-walked it, I fancy, as few mortals have ever done before. It's an extremely curious and interesting place—a sort of prosaic Naples; full moreover of a magnificent second-rate architectural picturesqueness. Lots of tremendous ornate palaces whose rusty cornices take the afternoon light, as the sun descends to the ocean, with a grand glaring melancholy. Of especial sights the one chiefly worth mentioning is the beautiful collection of paintings at the Brignole-Sale Palace: four tremendous Vandykes. I can't write of them. Before their immortal elegance I lay aside my plebeian pen. I enclose a poorish photo. of the greatest (one of the early marquises of B.S.) for Alice. It's not Rafael—it's not Titian; it's not an Italian. But it *is* Vandyke—transcendent Dutchman!—I have already hinted of my probable course on leaving this place. I shall *filer sur Paris*, stopping en route at three or four places—chiefly Avignon Arles and Nîmes and be settled in Paris by Feb. 1st.—settled for three or four weeks. To this has fizzled down my youthful dream of spending *years* in the brilliant capital! No: If I had any extra years on hand I should have given them to Florence. By the first week in March I hope to have reached Malvern. But enough of projects.—These are dreary days in respect of letters. You will have been directing I suppose to Bowles frères, as I asked you. I hope to find at least a dozen, teeming with news and health and happiness. Farewell. I read in the last *Atlantic* Lowell's poem and Howells's Article.[4] I admire them both largely—

especially the latter. Tell H. I haven't been waiting for him to write, to write again myself, but simply for the convenient moment. It will soon come. *Addio.* Unsachliche Liebe.—

Your H.

1. His recent constipation.
2. "Is Marriage Holy?" *Atlantic* XXV (1870), 360–368.
3. Francis Boott (1813–1904), an old friend of the James family who spent many years in Florence, where he reared his daughter Elizabeth (1846–1888).
4. William Dean Howells (1837–1920) was sub-editor of the *Atlantic Monthly* from 1866 and editor from 1871. He had been receptive to HJ's writings from the first and they had formed a warm friendship. Howells's article, "A Pedestrian Tour," appeared in the *Atlantic* XXIV (November 1869), 591–603.

17 · To William James

Ms Harvard

Great Malvern
March 8th '70

Beloved Bill—

You ask me in your last letter so "cordially" to write home every week, if it's only a line, that altho' I have very little to say on this windy Sunday March afternoon, I can't resist the homeward tendency of my thoughts. I wrote to Alice some eight days ago—raving largely about the beauty of Malvern, in the absence of a better theme: so I haven't even that topic to make talk of. But as I say, my thoughts are facing squarely homeward and that is enough. The fact that I have been here a month today, I am sorry to say, doesn't even furnish me with a bundle of important tidings. My stay as yet is attended with very slight results—powerful testimony to the obstinacy of my case. Nevertheless I have most unmistakeably made a beginning—or at least the beginning of one and in this matter it is chiefly a *premier pas qui coût.* On the whole I am not disappointed, when I think of from what a distance I have to return. It is unfortunate here that the monotony and gross plainness of the diet (mutton, potatoes and bread being its chief elements) are rather calculated in this particular trouble to combat the effect of the baths. Ye powers immortal! How I do find myself longing for a great succulent swash of American vegetables—

for tomatoes and apples and Indian meal! The narrowness of English
diet is something absolutely ludicrous. Breakfast cold mutton (or chop)
toast and tea: dinner leg or shoulder, potatoes and rice pudding; tea
cold mutton again (or chop) toast and tea. I sometimes think that I
shall never get well until I get a chance for a year at a pure vegetable
diet—at unlimited tomatoes and beans and peas and squash and tur-
nips and carrots and corn—I enjoy merely writing the words. I have a
deep delicious dream of someday uniting such a regimen with a daily
ride on horseback—walking having proved inefficient. So you see I
have something ahead of me to live for. But I have something better too
than these vain impalpable dreams—the firm resolve to recover on my
present basis—to fight it out on this line if it takes all summer—etc! It
would be too absurd not to! A fortnight hence I count upon being able
to give you some definite good news—to which period let us relegate
the further discussion of the topic. It constantly becomes more patent
to me that the better I get of this—the more I shall be able to read—
up to a certain point. During the past month I have been tasting
lightly of the pleasure—reading among other things Browning's Ring
and Book,[1] in honor of Italy, the President de Brosses's delightful
letters,[2] Crabb Robinson's memoirs[3] and the new vol. of Ste Beuve.
Browning decidedly gains in interest tho' he loses in a certain mystery
and (so to speak) infinitude, after a visit to Italy. C. Robinson is disap-
pointing I think—from the thinness of his individuality, the superficial character of his perception and his lack of descriptive power.
One of your letters contains something to make me think you have
been reading him. I have quite given up the idea of making a few retrospective sketches of Italy. To begin with I shall not be well enough (I
foresee) while here; and in the second place I had far rather let Italy
slumber in my mind untouched as a perpetual capital, whereof for my
literary needs I shall draw simply the income—let it lie warm and nu-
tritive at the base of my mind, manuring and enriching its roots. I remember by the way that you recently expressed the confident belief
that I had made a series of notes for my own use. I am sorry to say that
I did nothing of the sort. Mere bald indications (in this I was very
wrong) seem to me useless, and for copious memoranda I was always
too tired. I expect however to find that I have appropriated a good
deal from mere "soaking": i.e. often when I *might* have been scribbling
in my room I was still sauntering and re-sauntering and looking and

"assimilating."—But now that I am in England you'd rather have me talk of the present than of pluperfect Italy. But life furnishes so few incidents here that I cudgel my brain in vain. Plenty of gentle emotions from the scenery etc: but only man is vile. Among my fellow-patients here I find no intellectual companionship. Never from a single English man of them all have I heard the first word of appreciation or enjoyment of the things here that I find delightful. To a certain extent this is natural: but not to the extent to which they carry it. As for the women I give 'em up: in advance. I am tired of their plainness and stiffness and tastelessness—their dowdy beads, their dirty collars and their linsey woolsey trains. Nay, this is peevish and brutal. Personally (with all their faults) they are well enough. I revolt from their dreary deathly want of—what shall I call it?—Clover Hooper[4] has it—intellectual grace—Minny Temple[5] has it—moral spontaneity. They live wholly in the realm of the cut and dried. "Have you ever been to Florence?" "Oh yes." "Isn't it a most peculiarly interesting city?" "Oh yes, I think it's so very nice." "Have you read *Romola?*" "Oh yes." "I suppose you admire it." "Oh yes I think it's so very clever." The English have such a mortal mistrust of anything like criticism or "keen analysis" (which they seem to regard as a kind of maudlin foreign flummery) that I rarely remember to have heard on English lips any other intellectual verdict (no matter under what provocation) than this broad synthesis—"So immensely clever." What exasperates you is not that they can't say more, but that they wouldn't if they could. Ah, but they are a great people, for all that. Nevertheless I should vastly enjoy half an hour's talk with an "intelligent American." I find myself reflecting with peculiar complacency on American women. When I think of their frequent beauty and grace and elegance and alertness, their cleverness and self assistance (if it be simply in the matter of toilet) and compare them with English girls, living up to their necks among comforts and influences and advantages which have no place with us, my bosom swells with affection and pride. Look at my lovely friend Mrs. Winslow. To find in England such beauty, such delicacy, such exquisite taste, such graceful ease and laxity and freedom, you would have to look among the duchesses—*et encore!*, judging from their photos. in the shop windows. Not that Mrs. Winslow hasn't her little vulgarities, but taking one thing with another they are so far more innocent than those of common English women. But it's a graceless task, abusing women of any clime or country. I can't help it tho', if American women have something which gives them a lift!—Since my return here there is one thing that I have often wished for strongly—i.e. that poor John La Farge were with me sharing my enjoyment of this English scenery—enjoying it that is, on his own hook, with an intensity beside which I suppose, mine would be feeble indeed. I never catch one of the perpetual magical little "effects" of my walks without adverting to him. I feel sorry at moments that a couple of months ago I didn't write to him proposing a rendezvous at Malvern, March 1st, where he could stay and be doctored too, and whence we might subsequently roam deliciously forth in search of the picturesque. If I were at all sure of my condition a couple of months hence and of the manner I shall spend the spring and summer I would write to him and ask him if it is at all in his power to take a three or four months holiday. We might spend it together and return together in the Autumn. I feel sure that as a painter he would enjoy England most intensely. You may be a little surprised at my thus embracing for a whole summer the prospect of his undivided society. But for one thing I feel as if I could endure his peculiarities much better now than formerly; and then I feel too as if in any further travelling I may do here—I should find it a great gain to have a really good companion: and for observation what better companion than he? The lack of such a companion was in Italy a serious loss. I shall not write to him (if at all) with any such idea until I see myself fairly on the way to be better; but meanwhile, you, if you see him, might make some tentative enquiry and transmit me the result. I have no doubt that he would vastly like the scheme; but little hope of his finding it practicable.—Of Wendell Holmes I get very much less news than I should like to have. I heard recently from Arthur Sedgwick who mentioned his being appointed at Harvard College instructor in Constitutional Law. This has a very big sound; but I never doubted of his having big destinies.—Do speak of him in your next. Nor of Gray[6] do I hear anything. Do you often see him and how does he wear? I am very nervous about a letter from Howells which Mother some months ago mentioned his being on the point of sending. It hasn't yet turned up and I am utterly sickened at the idea of its being lost. Do ascertain from him whether it was ever sent. His letters are really things of value and I should find it a great feast to get one. Heaven speed it and guard it!—I received a few days since thro' Father a letter from Bob: very pleasant but with a strangely quaint and formal tone about it. But I was very glad to hear from him. It fills me with wonder and sadness that he should be off in that Western desolation while I am revelling in England and Italy. I should like extremely to get a line out of Wilky: but fate seems adverse. I very much wish by the way, that someone would let me know *who and what* is William Robeson, his partner. I simply know that he is not Andrew R. A propos of the family property, you've bought the house—an event I don't quarrel with. Since I began my letter the afternoon has waned into dusk and by my firelight and candles Cambridge looks like the sweetest place on earth. And it's a good old house too and I'm not ashamed of it. This reminds me of what you said in your last about getting photos, and books. I sometime since sent home a statement of my complete non-purchase of the former, save four very handsome statues I got for Alice in Rome which Aunt Kate will bring her, viz. the great Augustus, the boy Augustus, the Demosthenes and the so called "Genius of the Vatican" (Praxitiles). As soon as I arrived in Italy I saw that I must either buy more than I believed I had means for or leave them quite alone. The mere going into shops to buy an occasional one would have been fatal: besides you can't carry a few; if you get many, you provide a particular receptacle. Oh then! The delicious things I left unbought. If I return to the Continent I will do what I can to repair discreetly my abstinence. I very much regret now that I didn't immediately demand of Father and Mother a commission of purchase. But I seem condemned to do things in a small way. I am sure that as notes for future reference photos. are unapproached and indispensable.—As for books you rather amuse me by your assumption that in Italy I went in for a certain number of *vellum bindings*. Not for one. To get books seemed to me at that stage of my adventures to needlessly multiply my cares: and I felt like waiting till I had read a few of the vast accumulation on my hands before swelling the number. I shall probably pick up a few before going home; I fancy not many. If you want any particular ones you'll of course let me know. A very good way to get books in England—modern ones—is to buy them off Mudies' Surplus Catalogue—frequently great bargains.—But I must put an end to my stupid letter. I have been shut up all day and the greater part of yesterday with a bad sore throat and feel rather muddled and stultified. In a couple of days or so I hope again to be hearing from home. I look very soon for a letter from you correcting that last account of your relapse. I re-echo with all my heart your impatience for the moment of our meeting again. I should despair of ever making you know how your conversation *m'a manqué* or how when rejoined, I shall enjoy it. All I ask for is that I may spend the interval to the best advantage—and you too. The more we shall have to say to each other the better. Your last letter spoke of Father and Mother having "shocking colds." I hope they have melted away. Among the things I have recently read is Father's *Marriage* paper in the *Atlantic*—with great enjoyment of its manner and approval of its matter. I see he is becoming one of our prominent magazinists. He will send me the thing from *Old and New*. A young Scotchman here gets the *Nation*, sent him by his brother from New York. Whose are the three female papers on Woman? They are "so very clever." À *propos*—I retract all those brutalities about the Englanderinnen. They are the mellow mothers and daughters of a mighty race.—I expect daily a letter from Aunt Kate announcing her arrival in Paris. She has been having the inappreciable sorrow of a rainy fortnight in Florence. I hope very much to hear tho' that she has had a journey along the Riviera divinely fair enough to make up for it. But I must pull in. I have still lots of unsatisfied curiosity and unexpressed affection, but they must stand over. I never hear anything about the Tweedies.[7] Give them my love when you see them. T. S. Perry I suppose grows in wisdom and virtue. Tell him I would give a great deal for a humorous line from him. Farewell. Salute my parents and sister and believe me your brother of brothers

H. James jr.

1. *The Ring and the Book* had been published in the preceding year.

2. Charles de Brosses (1709–1777), a magistrate of the *parlement* of Burgundy, whose *Lettres familières écrites d'Italie en 1739 et 1740* remained permanently in HJ's library.

3. Henry Crabb Robinson (1775–1867), journalist, barrister, friend of many literary personalities, whose diaries had just been published.

4. Marion (Clover) Hooper (1843–1883), later Mrs. Henry Adams.

5. Mary (Minny) Temple (1845–1870), HJ's cousin, died on the day this letter was written.

6. John Chipman Gray (1839–1915), friend of Minny Temple, later a professor of law at Harvard.

7. Mary (Temple) Tweedy was a daughter of Col. Robert Emmet Temple (1808–1854) in his first marriage. His second wife was Catherine Margaret James (1820–1854), a sister

of HJ Sr. On the death of the colonel and his wife in 1854, Mary Tweedy undertook to rear four of their daughters, one of whom was Mary (Minny) Temple.

18 · *To William James*
Ms Harvard

Great Malvern
March 29, 1870

Dear Willy—

My mind is so full of poor Minny's death[1] that altho' I immediately wrote in answer to mother's letter, I find it easier to take up my pen again than to leave it alone. A few short hours have amply sufficed to more than reconcile me to the event and to make it seem the most natural—the happiest, fact, almost in her whole career. So it seems, at least, on reflection: to the eye of feeling there is something immensely moving in the sudden and complete extinction of a vitality so exquisite and so apparently infinite as Minny's. But what most occupies me, as it will have done all of you at home, is the thought of how her whole life seemed to tend and hasten, visibly, audibly, sensibly, to this consummation. Her character may be almost literally said to have been without practical application to life. She seems a sort of experiment of nature—an attempt, a specimen or example—a mere subject without an object. She was at any rate the helpless victim and toy of her own intelligence—so that there is positive relief in thinking of her being removed from her own heroic treatment and placed in kinder hands. What a vast amount of truth appears now in all the common-places that she used to provoke—that she was restless—that she was helpless—that she was unpractical. How far she may have been considered up to the time of her illness to have achieved a tolerable happiness, I don't know: hardly at all, I should say, for her happiness like her unhappiness remained wholly incomplete: but what strikes me above all is how great and rare a benefit her life has been to those with whom she was associated. I feel as if a very fair portion of my sense of the reach and quality and capacity of human nature rested upon my experience of her character: certainly a large portion of my admiration of it. She was a case of pure generosity—she had more even than she ever had use for—inasmuch as she could hardly have suffered at the hands of others nearly as keenly as she did at her own. Upon her limitations, now, it seems idle to dwell; the list of her virtues is so much longer than her life. My own personal relations with her were always of the happiest. Every one was supposed I believe to be more or less in love with her: others may answer for themselves: I never was, and yet I had the great satisfaction that I enjoyed *pleasing* her almost as much as if I had been. I cared more to please her perhaps than she ever cared to be pleased. Looking back upon the past half-dozen years, it seems as if she *represented,* in a manner, in my life several of the elements or phases of life at large—her own sex, to begin with, but even more *Youth,* with which owing to my invalidism,[2] I always felt in rather indirect relation.

Poor Minny—what a cold thankless part it seems for her to have played—an actor and setter-forth of things in which she had so little permanent interest! Among the sad reflections that her death provokes for me, there is none sadder than this view of the gradual change and reversal of our relations: I slowly crawling from weakness and inaction and suffering into strength and health and hope: she sinking out of brightness and youth into decline and death. It's almost as if she had passed away—as far as I am concerned—from having served her purpose, that of standing well within the world, inviting and inviting me onward by all the bright intensity of her example. She never knew how sick and disordered a creature I was and I always felt that she knew me at my worst. I always looked forward with a certain eagerness to the day when I should have regained my natural lead, and one friendship on my part at least might become more active and masculine. This I have especially felt during the powerful experience of the past year. In a measure I had worked away from the old ground of my relations with her, without having quite taken possession of the new: but I had it constantly in my eyes. But here I am, plucking all the sweetest fruits of this Europe which was a dream among her many dreams—while she has "gone abroad" in another sense! Every thought of her is a singular mixture of pleasure and pain. The thought of what either she has lost or won, comes to one as if only to enforce the idea of *her* gain in eternal freedom and rest and ours in the sense of it. Freedom and rest! one must have known poor Minny to feel their value—to know what they may contain—if one can measure, that is, the balm by the ache. I have been hearing all my life of the sense of loss

77

which death leaves behind it—now for the first time I have a chance to learn what it amounts to. The whole past—all times and places—seems full of her. Newport especially—to my mind—she seems the very genius of the place. I could shed tears of joy far more copious than any tears of sorrow when I think of her feverish earthly lot exchanged for this serene promotion into pure fellowship with our memories, thoughts and fancies. I had imagined many a happy talk with her in years to come—many a cunning device for cheering and consoling her illness—many a feast on the ripened fruits of our friendship: but this on the whole surpasses anything I had conceived. You will all have felt by this time the novel delight of thinking of Minny without the lurking impulse of fond regret and uneasy conjecture so familiar to the minds of her friends. She has gone where there is neither marrying nor giving in marriage! no illusions and no disillusions—no sleepless nights and no ebbing strength. The more I think of her the more perfectly satisfied I am to have her translated from this changing realm of fact to the steady realm of thought. There she may bloom into a beauty more radiant than our dull eyes will avail to contemplate.

My first feeling was an immense regret that I had been separated from her last days by so great a distance of time and space; but this has been of brief duration. I'm really not sorry not to have seen her materially changed and thoroughly thankful to have been spared the sight of her suffering. Of this you must all have had a keen realization. There is nevertheless something so appealing in the pathos of her final weakness and decline that my heart keeps returning again and again to the scene, regardless of its pain. When I went to bid Minny farewell at Pelham before I sailed, I asked her about her sleep. "Sleep," she said, "Oh, I don't sleep. *I've given it up.*" And I well remember the laugh with which she made this sad attempt at humor. And so she went on, sleeping less and less, waking wider and wider, until she awaked absolutely!

I asked mother to tell me what she could about her last weeks and to repeat me any of her talk or any chance incidents, no matter how trivial. This is a request easier to make than to comply with, and really to talk about Minny we must wait till we meet. But I *should* like one of her last photos, if you can get one. You will have felt for yourself I suppose how little is the utmost one can *do*, in a positive sense, as regards her memory. Her presence was so much, so intent—so strenuous—so full of human exaction: her absence is so modest, content with so little. A little decent passionless grief—a little rummage in our little store of wisdom—a sigh of relief—and we begin to live for ourselves again. If we can imagine the departed spirit cognizant of our action in the matter, we may suppose it much better pleased by our perfect acceptance of the void it has left than by our quarreling with it and wishing it filled up again. What once was life is always life, in one form or another, and speaking simply of this world I feel as if in effect and influence Minny had lost very little by her change of state. She lives as a steady unfaltering luminary in the mind rather than as a flickering wasting earth-stifled lamp. Among all my thoughts and conceptions I am sure I shall never have one of greater sereneness and purity: her image will preside in my intellect, in fact, as a sort of measure and standard of brightness and repose.

But I have scribbled enough. While I sit spinning my sentences she is *dead*: and I suppose it is partly to defend myself from too direct a sense of her death that I indulge in this fruitless attempt to transmute it from a hard fact into a soft idea. Time, of course, will bring almost even-handedly the inevitable pain and the inexorable cure. I am willing to leave life to answer for life; but meanwhile, thinking how small at greatest is our change as compared with her change and how vast an apathy goes to our little measure of sympathy, I take a certain satisfaction in having simply written twelve pages.—

I have been reading over the three or four letters I have got from her since I have been abroad: they are full of herself—or at least of a fraction of herself: they would say little to strangers.[3] Poor living Minny! No letters would hold you. It's the *living* ones that die; the writing ones that survive.

One thought there is that moves me much—that I should be here delving into this alien England in which it was one of her fancies that she had a kind of property. It was not, I think, one of the happiest. Every time that I have been out during the last three days, the aspect of things has perpetually seemed to enforce her image by simple contrast and difference. The landscape assents stolidly enough to her death: it would have ministered but scantily to her life. She was a breathing protest against English grossness, English compromises and conventions—a plant of pure American growth. None the less tho' I had a dream of telling her of England and of her immensely enjoying my stories. But it's only a half change: instead of my discoursing to her, I shall have her forever talking to me. Amen, Amen to all she may say! Farewell to all that she was! How much this was, and how sweet it was! How it comes back to one, the charm and essential grace of her early years. We shall all have known something! How it teaches, absolutely, tenderness and wonder to the mind. But it's all locked away, incorruptibly, within the crystal walls of the past. And there is my youth—and anything of yours you please and welcome! turning to gold in her bright keeping. In exchange, for you, dearest Minny, we'll all keep your future. Don't fancy that your task is done. Twenty years hence we shall be loving with your love and longing with your eagerness and suffering with your patience.

30th P.M. So much I wrote last evening: but it has left me little to add, incomplete as it is. In fact it is too soon to talk of Minny's death or to pretend to feel it. This I shall not do till I get home. Every now and then the thought of it stops me short, but it's from the life of home that I shall really miss her. With this European world of associations and art and studies, she has nothing to do: she belongs to the deep domestic moral affectional realm. I can't put away the thought that just as I am beginning life, she has ended it. But her rare death is an answer to all the regrets it provokes. You remember how largely she dealt in the future—how she considered and planned and arranged. Now it's to haunt and trouble her no longer. She has her present and future in one.

To you, I suppose, her death must have been an unmitigated relief—you must have suffered keenly from the knowledge of her sufferings. Thank heaven they lasted no longer. When I first heard of her death I could think only of them: now I can't think of them even when I try.

I have not heard from you for a long time: I am impatiently expecting a letter from you. With this long effusion you will all have been getting of late an ample share *de mes nouvelles*. From Alice too I daily expect to hear. Yesterday came to me a very welcome and pleasantly turned note from Mr. Boott.—I hope I haven't hitherto expressed myself in a way to leave room for excursive disappointment when I say that after now nearly eight weeks of this place, I have made materially less progress than I hoped. I shall be here about ten days longer. In town I shall immediately go to see a couple of as good and *special* physicians as I can hear of. Unhappily my sources of knowledge are few.[4]

1. Minny Temple had died of tuberculosis on 8 March.

2. There is abundant evidence that in his youth HJ regarded himself as more "invalidical" than he ever was. His most serious illness was typhus, at Boulogne in 1857. He strained his back when acting as volunteer fireman at Newport, and his recent constipation may have exacerbated this condition. See Edel, *Henry James: A Life* (1985), 95–96, 101–104, 720–722, for a detailed inquiry into the novelist's various illnesses.

3. These letters survived HJ's burning of his personal papers late in life.

4. The remainder of this letter is missing.

19 · To Grace Norton

Ms Harvard

Malvern
April 1st 1870

Dear Grace—

If I possessed in anything like such perfection as yourself the noble art of *printing*, I would assure you forthwith, in the very largest and fairest capitals, that I received no longer than an hour ago, with "unfeigned delight," your good gracious graphic letter of—a certain "Monday evening." I say a truce to all incriminations and explanations. What matters a wave more or less in the ocean?—A letter more or less in the fathomless floods of affection and sympathy which discharge their equal tides on English and Italian shores? In the letter, as in the spirit, let me believe that we are "square." Let me nonetheless thank you for this last note with as much *effusion* as if it were a fruit of pure generosity (which indeed, I strongly suspect.) And no remote response to any appealing utterance of mine.—Inexpressibly sweet it is to hear from you and Florence—from Florence in you. How shall I tell you what a strange look of contradictory nearness and distance overlies all that you remind me of? so near is it all in time—so incalculably remote in character from the medium in which I here live and move. I could treat you to five pages of the flattest platitudes about Italy as she dwells in my mind *entre cour et jardin*—between memory and hope. But with the infinite reality before you what need have you for the poor literary counterfeit? "Oh how the March-sun feels like May!"—

exquisite truth! And what does the April sun feel like? and what do the April hills look like? And what does the lengthening April twilight put into one's heart—down in the city piazzas, in front of the churches? For all your mention of your various household facts I am duly grateful—tho' hardly for the facts themselves. I sincerely hope that by this time the colds have melted away before the breath of the older and kindlier spring—the real Florentine season. Of Charles's and Susan's[1] projected visit to Rome I am delighted to hear. If Rome will only do a little in the way of health-giving to Charles I will freely forgive it all its sins and follies. For Susan—she can dispense with even the most pious adjurations—and going to Rome for the first time can easily snap a scornful finger and thumb at poor me who have in the vague future but the prospect of a poor second.—But in what utterly ungracious and unlikely attitudes am I thus fantastically treating Susan? Since I have done her a wrong, let me profit by it to do her the right (the fullest I know) of begging of her a favour—that once in a while—at St. Peter's—at the Vatican, in the Coliseum, in the Campagna—out of a dozen long glances that she takes for herself and you in Florence, she will take one short one for me in England; and that into a hundred deep thoughts which she bestows upon the ancient Romans, she will insinuate one little heart-beat of regret that a luckless modern American was able to see only half as much *de tout cela* as he wanted.—Of immediately personal news I have none to give you; save that in repeating to you the tidings which I had a week ago from home, I shall tell you of what has been for me a great personal sorrow. You will possibly have learned them by your own Cambridge letter. My cousin Minny Temple died most suddenly some three weeks ago. I am not sure that you ever knew her well enough to understand how great a sense of loss this fact brings with it to those who really knew her—as *I* did. I knew her well and her friendship had always been for me one of the happiest certainties of the future. So much for *certainties!* But already, after the lapse of a week, I am strangely—most serenely—familiar with the idea of her death. The more I think of it, the more what there is to accept—almost with thanks—gains upon and effaces what there is to deplore and quarrel with. She is one about whom there would be much to say—much which I know, as the lapse of time tends to clarify and simplify, as it were, her memory, will seem to me so much more and more that one of these days I shall surely say to you a large part of it. She was a divinely restless spirit—essentially one of the "irreconcilables"; and if she had lived to great age, I think it would have been as the victim and plaything of her constant generous dreams and dissatisfactions. During the last year moreover it had become obvious that her life would be one of immense suffering—suffering far harder to think of than (to me at least) even the death which has cut short the sweetness of her youth. A fortnight before she died she had her lungs examined by some great New York authority, who told her point blank that she had less than two years to live. From this moment she sank. Other physicians offered her far more cheerful hopes and her family (on the testimony of Dr. Metcalf) had made up their minds that she would even recover. But she had never been afraid of the truth: and it seemed as if she had no care to accept the respite which had been granted her in charity. She died apparently from simple exhaustion. Her memory will be full of interest and delight to all her friends. I feel not only much the wiser for having known her, but—I find—really the happier for knowing her at absolute peace and rest. Her life was a strenuous, almost passionate *question*, which *my* mind, at least, lacked the energy to offer the elements of an answer for. It would be really a great spirit that should contain a power to affirm and illumine and satisfy, equal to her exquisite energy of wonder, conjecture and unrest.—Her peculiar personal charm and grace you will doubtless remember. This had never been greater, I am told, during the year before her death. She was to have come abroad this next summer—but one little dream the more in a life which was so eminently a life of the spirit—one satisfied curiosity the less in a career so essentially incomplete on its positive side—these seem to make her image only more eloquent and vivid and purely youthful and appealing. She had a great fancy for knowing England.—Meanwhile here I sit stupidly scanning it with these dull human eyes!—But in speaking of her one must return to what one begins with—her rare simple superficial charm of physiognomy and presence. Amen! Her absence, too, has its sweetness.—But I am scribbling all this my dear Grace, in a wretchedly cold room—made tolerable only by the thought that I am writing to a very warm heart.—For the moment farewell. I can talk of *moments:* I feel as if I were going to write so soon again. I am full of wonder and sympathy and interest in all your coming days of spring and summer. It's a great boon to my imagination to have you there on duty for me in Italy. To Baron Mackay, if he comes, you might venture, tentatively, to present my warm regards. To your mother—abruptly, recklessly—my love. The same to Susan, Charles and Jane—as opportunity—of time and humour, seems to favor. To Jane I will write *not*—when inclined—which she is not to confound with "when *not* inclined." Happy Spain-faring Sara! *Addio.* Get well of everything—save a lingering kindness for

Yours most faithfully
H. James jr.

Address me next please to *Barings.* I shall be in London ten days hence. "The rest is *silence.*"

1. Charles Eliot Norton and his wife, the former Susan Sedgwick.

2 · Saturations
1870–1880

The second phase of Henry James's advance to literary power and fame can be described as his period of saturations. He himself suggested this when he said "the great thing is to be *saturated* with something—that is, in one way or another, with life." To which he added, "I chose the form of my saturation."

The letters of the decade following his return from his first adult journey to Europe reveal the particular forms of James's exploration and assimilation of the life of his time. His worldly view, guided by his intellectual strength, was aesthetic and sensual. In this he rose above the genteel class in which he had been reared. He studied the higher reaches of society and the uses of wealth. But he did not close his eyes to poverty and social disorder in his own land and the lands he visited. His early work dealt with the dilemmas of artists attempting to accommodate themselves to hostile and materialistic societies. His portraits of the artists as young men and young women went beyond personal struggle and affront: for he insisted that the form he chose to practice, the novel of art, was essentially a history of the ways in which men and women arranged their lives—a record, as Flaubert had said, of *moeurs* or, as we would say, of *mores*. It was by a society's manners and customs and taboos that an artist could read its inherent human values and the strengths and weaknesses of the social order.

James's letters show him consistently "taking possession" of Europe's cities—the cities he would use for his novels when he went outside America—London, Paris, Rome, Venice. We see him constantly exploring and stocking his memory with notes on social creation and artifacts, the signatures of the "visitable past." At the same time he catches, in those early Darwinian days, the effect on and control of individuals by their environment and the pressures of society and social contracts, the tyrannies of civilization without which there would exist chronic anarchy.

Occasionally in his letters he speaks, especially to his brother William, of his accumulation of "impressions." He is troubled a little by a feeling that a career of active observation, such as he practiced, might be deemed indolence—for he consistently refused to seek a job or to "settle down" like other young upper-middle-class Americans. "I have gathered more impressions, I am sure, than I suppose," he writes to William, "impressions I shall find value in when I come to use them." And indeed when he came to use them he revealed the extraordinary extent of his saturation, the power of his memory for visual detail and his grasp of human behavior. Nor could it be said that he was as indolent as he feared—the consequence, we might say, of a certain guilt induced by his rather demanding family. For within two or three years he began to earn his way in a number of magazines and repay all his debts to his father.

He went abroad for a second time in 1872, and then stayed on in Europe assimilating life in Paris, Rome, and Venice, turning himself into an accomplished cosmopolitan. In 1875 he emerged from his ten-year apprenticeship by publishing three books in a single year, each illustrative of a side of his varied genius: *A Passionate Pilgrim*, his early tales of American wanderers abroad; *Transatlantic Sketches*, the literary productions of his own wanderings; and his remarkable portrait of the American artist as a young man, *Roderick Hudson*. Having obtained a modest but secure reputation, he settled in Paris, where he met Ivan Turgenev, the Russian writer whose cosmopolitanism and sensibility, compassion and sympathy resembled his own. Turgenev introduced him to the Flaubertian *cénacle*, where he met the French master himself and such writers as Zola, Daudet, Edmond de Goncourt, Maupassant, and others. After a year in Paris, which yielded the romantic novel *The American*, he moved to London and began his absorption of British society. "A position in society," he said, "is a legitimate object of ambition." Like one of Balzac's or Thackeray's heroes, he rose in society with firm footsteps. He was soon in considerable demand at Victorian dinners and known to the British literary establishment. His wit, his urbanity, his discretion, and his writings found favor with the English, and he enjoyed, as he said, "a certain show of fame."

The circle of James's correspondence widened as he led this life of worldly relations even while he spent his private hours in Bolton Street spinning his early good-humored inventions. He had regularly corresponded with his family and his Cambridge and Newport friends. Now his letters reach high British figures in the nobility and in the ranks of his own artistic contemporaries. He handles his personal publishing affairs with singular business acumen. Letter-writing to him is not a drudgery as it is to some authors. It is a part of the work of his busy pen: and his letters are as literary, and contain the same charm and style, as his stories. He passes with ease from the exigencies of his art to the pleasures of intimate personal relations. Absent only from his epistolary calendar are love letters. About his personal life, he is a cautious and secretive Victorian. His emotional warmth goes into graceful verbal forms, into the finesse of addressing the society he has cultivated. His best letters reflect his ease with the world and his large human sympathies; and those to his closest friends contain his acute appraisal of his "London life."

20 · To Grace Norton

Ms Harvard

Cambridge
May 20th 1870

My dear Grace.

Nothing more was needed to make me feel utterly at home—utterly *revenu* and awake from my dream again—than to get your letter of May 2d. Hearty thanks for it! Here I am—here I have been for the last ten days—the last ten years. It's very hot! the window is open before me: opposite thro' the thin trees I see the scarlet walls of the president's *palazzo*.[1] Beyond, the noble grey mass—the lovely outlines, of the library: and above this the soaring *campanile* of the wooden church on the *piazza*. In the distance I hear the carpenters hammering at the great edifice in process of erection in the college yard—and in sweet accordance the tinkle of the horse-cars. Oh how the May-wind feels like August. But never mind: I am to go into town this P.M. and I shall get a charming breeze in the cars crossing the bridge.—Nay, *do* excuse me: I should be sorry wilfully to make you homesick. I could find in my

87

heart to dwell considerately only on the drawbacks of Cambridge life: but really I know of none: or at least I have only to look at that light elegant *campanile*—that simple devout Gothic of the library—or indeed at that dear quaint old fence of wood, of stone (which is it most?) before the houses opposite—to melt away in ecstasy and rapture.— My voyage I am happy to say, was as prosperous as if I had received your good wishes at its beginning instead of its close. We made it in nine days and a half, without storms or serious discomforts. I will agree with you in any abuse of the cabins and state-rooms of the Scotia: but the deck is excellent and there I chiefly spent my time. I find all things here prosperous, apparently, and all people decently happy. My own family may be well reported of. My sister is in strength and activity quite an altered person and my brother inspires me with confident hopes. My parents are particularly well. I lately spent an evening in Kirkland Street where of course I found many questions to answer; and boasted hugely of all your favors. Miss Theodora[2] is a most delightful young lady: I say it because I don't believe you adequately know it. Arthur I have seen several times: we enjoy very much reminding each other of you. The Gurneys too I have seen and the Howells—all very well. Howells is lecturing very pleasantly on Italian literature. I go to the lecture room in Boylston hall; and sit with my eyes closed, listening to the sweet Italian names and allusions and trying to fancy that the window behind me opens out into Florence. But Florence is within and not without. When I'm hopeful of seeing Florence again not ten years hence—that *is* Florence!—all that you tell me is delightful. I can fancy what a game Florence and May are playing between them. Poor May just here has rather an irresponsible playmate. But when May is a month older she will amuse herself alone.—I congratulate you on Charles and Susan having returned from Rome. When I think that in this latter season they have made that journey thro' the very vitals of Italy, I feel almost as if it were a merry world. Indeed when I hear that you really think of summering (not simmering) in Venice, I pronounce it altogether a mad world—using the term in no invidious sense. Thrice happy thought! I could say horrible things—invent the fiercest calumnies, about Siena, to drive you to Venice. If you write to me not from Venice—I shall—I shall almost delay to answer your letter. Siena would be all very well if you had never thought of Venice—but having done this I don't see how you

can escape going there. There are things the immortal gods don't forgive. Beware them.—I wish I were able to tell you where I am going to
outlast the genial season—or what, now that I have got America
again, I am going to do with it. Like it enormously *sans doute:* they say
there is nothing like beginning with a little aversion. My only fear is
that mine is too old to end in a grand passion. But America is American: that is incontestable, and consistency is a jewel. I wish I could
tell you how characteristic every thing strikes me as being—everything from the vast white distant sky—to the stiff sparse individual
blades of grass.

22*d.* A.M. I went yesterday to lunch at Shady Hill.[3] Don't think me
very cruel when I tell you how lovely it was—in the very sweetest
mood of the year—the fullness of the foliage just all but complete and
the freshness of the verdure all undimmed. The grass was all golden
with buttercups—the trees all silver with apple blossoms, the sky a
glorious storm of light, the air a perfect hurricane of zephyrs. We sat
(Miss C. Hooper, Miss Boott[4] &c) on a verandah a long time immensely enjoying the fun. But oh my dear Grace it was ghostly. For me
the breeze was heavy with whispering spirits. Down in that glade to
the right three women were wading thro' the long grass and a child
picking the buttercups. One of them was you, the others Jane and
Susan—the child Eliot. Mesdemoiselles Hooper and Boott talked of
Boston, I thought of Florence. I wanted to go down to you in the glade
and we should play it was the Villa Landor. Susan would enact Miss
Landor. But the genius of my beloved country—in the person of Miss
Hooper—detained me. I don't know indeed whether I most wanted
you to be there or to be myself in Florence. Or rather I do very well
know and I am quite ashamed of my fancy of robbing that delightful
scene of its simple American beauty. I wished you all there for an hour,
enjoying your own.—But my intended note is turning into a very poor
letter. One of these days I shall intend a letter.—I ought to tell you by
the way, that my having taken a turn for the worse in England, was
partly concerned in my return home. I was wise in doing as I did apparently: for I am already vastly better. At all events, economy had
begun to make my return necessary. I don't feel very much further
from you here than I was in England. I may safely assume—mayn't
I?—that you are to be abroad two or three years yet. Largely within
that time we shall meet again. When I next go to Italy it will be not

for months but years. These are harmless visions, but I utter them only to you.—Wherever you go this summer, remember that—*I* care most about hearing the whole story. This is not modest, but I maintain it. Live, look, enjoy, write a little for me. Tell all your companions how fondly I esteem them. I implore your mother to exert her maternal authority in favor of Venice. I perceived no bad smells there: and as for mosquitoes, I imagine that a private house properly furnished with curtains needn't in the least fear them. Howells tells me *they* never suffered. Wherever you go, however, I shall be happy in your contentment and shall believe you blessed with peace and prosperity. Farewell. Love to one and all. Believe me dear Grace your's most faithfully

Henry James jr.

I don't ask about Sara because I have just written to her and have hopes of an answer if she has time before her return.

1. The Quincy Street residence of President Eliot of Harvard was located opposite the home of the Jameses.

2. Maria Theodora Sedgwick (1851–1916).

3. Shady Hill, the Phillips-Ware-Norton house, northeast of Harvard Yard, had been the home of Andrews Norton, father of Charles Eliot Norton, who now lived in it.

4. Elizabeth, daughter of Francis Boott, was then visiting Cambridge from her home in Florence.

21 · To Charles Eliot Norton

Ms Harvard

Cambridge

Feb. 4th '72

My dear Charles—

I hear of you from time to time but I have an unsatisfied desire to hear from you—or at any rate, to talk *at* you directly, myself. Alice received a couple of days since a charming note from Susan, which was an approach to immediate news of you and has done much to put my pen into my hand. Let me use it first to thank Susan most tenderly for her altogether amiable mention of myself—both as man and author!—I am in constant expectation of a letter from Jane or from Grace and I come down to breakfast every morning and stride to my plate with a spiritual hunger for this possible letter hugely in excess of that which coffee and rolls can satisfy. But as yet I have to content myself grimly with the coffee and rolls. Jane and Grace may be affected by the knowledge that this state of things is not conducive to that breakfast-table cheerfulness and smilingness which I presume figures in their programme for a Christian life.—It is not that I have anything very new and strange to relate. In fact, when one sits down to sum up Cambridge life *plume en main,* the strange thing seems its aridity. A big hustling drifting snowstorm is the latest episode—and we try to believe that, owing to the remarkable "open weather" that has preceded it, it has a certain charm. I have been spending a quiet stay-at-home winter, reading a good deal and writing a little. Of people or things in which, or whom, you are interested especially I have seen little. But who and what are the particular objects of your interest? You must write and tell me—for I hardly know what tastes and sympathies you may be forming in these many months of silence and absence. To the formation of what tastes does a winter in Dresden conduce? A few *distastes,* possibly come into shape. Tell me of these too, for I want to be assured that in the interest of "general culture" a winter in Germany is not *de rigueur.*—I have vague impressions of your being disappointed in the gallery. But happy man, to have a gallery even to be disappointed in!—But it will be made up to you in New York, when you come back, by the rare collection of old masters who are to form the germ of what it seems so odd to have the *Revue des Deux Mondes* calling the *Musée* de New York.[1] You will of course adjourn thither from shipboard!—But I'll not talk of your coming back yet awhile, but try rather to forward you some native odds and ends.—The public mind seems to be rather vacant just now, save as to a vague contemplation of the close of the English Treaty. I fancy there is something irrational and premature in the present English irritation on the subject. I doubt whether our directing demands, in so far as the country supports them, are not such as can be fairly satisfied. The English seem exasperated by the very copious setting forth of our injuries. I suppose we have stated our case strongly, to gain moderately. At all events the matter is not, thank heaven, in the hands of the two big foolish nations, but, I trust, in that of men of the last discretion, who feel that the vexing ghost *must* be laid.[2]—Among those who ask about you when we meet is Gurney[3]—though we meet but rarely. I don't know whether it's fancy, but he has to me the air of a man almost oppressed and silenced and saddened by perfect comfort and happiness.—Lowell, to my regret, I never see. With Longfellow I lately spent a pleasant evening and found him bland and mildly anecdotical. Have you seen his new book—the *Divine Tragedy?* I believe it's noted but a partial success. He is not quite a Tintoretto of verse. Howells is making a very careful and business-like editor of the *Atlantic.* As a proof of his energy—he has induced me to write a monthly report of the Fine Arts in Boston!!⁴ It's pitiful work and I shall of course soon collapse for want of material.—You, like all the world here I suppose, have been reading Forster's *Dickens.*⁵ It interested, but disappointed me—through having too many opinions and "remarks" and not enough facts and documents. You have always I think, rated Dickens higher than I; so far as the book *is* documentary, it does not, to my sense, add to his intellectual stature. But this we shall discourse in coming days over the succeeding volumes.—Have I come to the end of our common acquaintance? You know, I suppose, the Charles Perkinses—with whom I lately spent an evening. Mrs. P. is spicy and Mr. P.—sugary, shall I say?—No, full of sweetness and light—especially sweetness. He is repeating before the Lowell Institute a course of lectures on Ancient Art, which he gave last winter to the University. Careful and sound, but without the divine afflatus.—There is more or less good lecturing going on. John Fiske is giving a long course in town on Positivism—quite a large performance, in bulk and mass, at any rate;⁶ and Wendell Holmes is about to discourse out here on Jurisprudence. The latter, some day, I think, will *percer,* as the French say, and become eminent—in a speciality but to a high degree.⁷ He, my brother, and various other long-headed youths have combined to form a metaphysical club, where they wrangle grimly and stick to the question. It gives me a headache merely to know of it—I belong to no club myself and have not great choice of company either to wrangle or to agree with. If it didn't sound weak-mindedly plaintive and fastidious, I would say I lacked society. I know no "nice men"—that is, passing few, to converse withal. The only one we often see is Arthur Sedgwick—who by the way, has gone to New York to comfort and assist Godkin in his present illness.—I suppose of course you always see the *Nation.* I don't know whether it strikes you as it does us; but I fancy its tone has been a good deal vitiated—and in a miserable, fatal sort of way. Godkin seems to me to come less rather than more into sympathy with our "institutions." Journalism has brutalized him a good deal, and he has too little tact, pliancy and "perception."—I confess that my best company now-a-days is that of various vague moonshiny dreams of getting to your side of the world with what speed I may. —I carry the desire (this confession is mainly for Jane) to a morbid pitch, and I exaggerate the merits of Europe. It's the same world there after all and Italy isn't the absolute any more than Massachusetts. It's a complex fate, being an American, and one of the responsibilities it entails is fighting against a superstitious valuation of Europe. —It will be rather a sell, getting over there and finding the problems of the universe rather multiplied than diminished. Still, I incline to risk the discomfiture!

Feb. 5th A.M. I was obliged to interrupt myself yesterday and must now bring my letter to a close—if not to a point! the twenty-four hours have brought forth nothing momentous—save a little party last night at Mrs. Dorr's (*arida nutrix leonum!* as someone called her) where I communed with a certain Miss Bessy Minturn of N.Y., whom Mrs. D. tenders you as "*probably* the most learned woman now living!" Imagine the grimace with which you accept her! But if she's blue—it's a heavenly blue. She's a lovely girl. —I was going on to say above that no small part of this scandalous spiritual absenteeism of mine consists of fantastic encounters with you and yours in various choice spots of the shining Orient—so that I shall listen with infinite zeal to any hint of your future movements and tendencies. —It seems to me I have now been about as egotistical as the most friendly heart can desire. Be thus assured of the value I set on the practise! Tell me how you are and where you are,—morally and intellectually. I suppose you can bring yourself once in a while to read something not German. If so, I recommend: Taine's *Notes sur l'Angleterre* and Renan's *Reforme Morale:*[8] the latter curiously fallacious in many ways, but a most interesting picture of a deeply conservative soul. And in the way of a novel, Cherbuliez's last. I don't see how *talent* can go further. I have heard of Grace, Theodora and Eliot's journey to Berlin. If I might have the story from Grace! Your mother, I trust, continues well. Give her my filial regards—and commend me fraternally to Susan, Jane and the rest. Your children, I suppose, are turning into so many busy little heroes and heroines for Otto Pletsch. Farewell, dear Charles. Respond only at your perfect convenience and believe me ever yours

H. James Jr.

1. The Metropolitan Museum of Art had been incorporated in New York in 1870 and would move into its present building in Central Park in 1880.

2. The British had recently agreed to arbitrate the claims of their destruction of American shipping during the Civil War.

3. Ephraim W. Gurney, historian and Dean of the Faculty at Harvard.

4. HJ wrote a few papers on art shows. See John L. Sweeney, ed., *The Painter's Eye* (1956), a selective anthology of HJ's art criticism.

5. John Forster's life of his friend appeared during the years 1872–1874.

6. John Fiske (1842–1901), the chief popularizer of Victorian philosophy and science in the United States.

7. HJ accurately predicts Holmes's future, which would lead him to the U.S. Supreme Court.

8. HJ reviewed Taine's English notes in the *Nation*, 25 January 1872, 58–60. He would be a close reader of the philologist and historian Ernest Renan (1823–1892). The full title of Renan's book was *La Reforme intellectuelle et morale* (1871).

22 · To His Parents

Ms Harvard

Heidelberg
Sept. 15th P.M. [1872]

Dear father and mother.

I think I should manifest an energy more becoming a child of yours if I were to sustain my nodding head at least enough longer to scrawl the initial words of my usual letter:—and as I have now been tolerably well waked up by chasing a mosquito I think I may manage it. We are travellers in the midst of travel.[1] You heard from me last at Innsbrück—or rather, I think, at Botzen, just before Innsbrück. That was a week since. We gave one day and night to Innsbrück—a place beautiful by nature but most ugly by man and came by an admirable five hours' run through the remnant of the Tyrol to Munich, where we spent two rather busy days. It's a singular place and one difficult to write of with a serious countenance. It has a fine lot of old pictures, but otherwise it is a nightmare of pretentious vacuity: a city of chalky stucco—a Florence and Athens in canvas and planks. To have come thence from Venice is a sensation! We found reality at last at Nüremburg, by which place, combined with this, it seemed a vast pity not to proceed rather than by stupid Stuttgart, where there is nothing but poor little Hugh Walsh to see. Nüremberg is excellent—and comparisons are odious; but I would give a thousand Nürembergs for one day of Verona! We spent there yesterday a capital afternoon and examined things exhaustively—or almost, and this A.M. came on hither by a goodly morning and noon of railway, which has not in the least prevented a goodly afternoon and evening at the Castle here. The castle (which I think you have all seen in your own travels) is an incomparable ruin and holds its own against any Italian memories. The light, the weather, the time, were all, this evening most propitious to our visit.—This rapid week in Germany has filled us with reflections and observations, tossed from the railway windows on our course, and irrecoverable at this late hour. To me, this hasty and most partial glimpse of Germany has been most satisfactory; it has cleared from my mind the last mists of uncertainty and assured me that I can never hope to become an unworthiest adoptive grandchild of the fatherland.[2] It is well to listen to the voice of the spirit—to cease hair splitting and treat oneself to a good square antipathy—when it is so very sympathetic! I may "culti‑vate" mine away, but it has given me a week's wholesome nourishment.

Sept. 15th. Strasbourg—I broke off last night, but I must add these closing words and despatch my letter without further delay. We came straight hither this A.M.—passed Baden‑Baden which we had momen‑tary thoughts of giving a day to, so great is our impatience to reach Paris, letters and rest. On the train we met Frank Loring and his sister, just from Baden who shewed me a recent *Nation* with Willy's *Taine*. It did my heart good to see it and I shall find it, I trust, in Paris. We have seen Strasbourg—a palpably conquered city—and the Cathedral, which beats everything we have ever seen. Internally, it amazed me, which somehow I hadn't expected it to do. Strasbourg is gloomy, battered and painful; but already, apparently, much Germanised. The shops are full of French prints representing its down‑trodden condition. We take to‑morrow the formidable journey to Paris, and shall reach the Hôtel de l'Amirauté (Rue Neuve St. Augustin) at 9 P.M. Alice is wonderfully well and indefatigable. We have been travelling *hard*, one may call it now, for a month, with languid Italy, included, and yet she has never yet seemed to me better than these last few days. My first steps in Paris will be to Munroe's and I shall then despatch a supplementary letter acknowledging what I find there. I must send this off now. Good‑night.

Your's in hope and love
H. James Jr.

1. HJ was escorting his Aunt Kate and his sister, Alice, on a summer's tour of Europe.

2. The novelist would maintain this opinion of Germany, in contrast to WJ, who had lived and studied there.

23 · *To Henry James, Sr.*

Ms Harvard

Paris
[Nov. 1872]

Dear father:

I received promptly your letter of Oct. 14th: and I had a couple of days before received the last *Atlantic*. For both many thanks. The photograph from John La Farge's drawing, and Bob Temple's letter were both welcome, too, in their respective and very different manners. The drawing seems to be a weaker thing than John ought to be doing, now-a-days, (though certainly very pretty); and Bob's letter is touching in its amiable demoralizations. It's an event worthy of Thackeray that his *spelling* should have degenerated!—I have not yet heard from Aunt Kate and Alice; I must allow them a few days more. By this time, I suppose, you feel as if they had never been away. The dresses are unpacked, and the photographs, and the stories told, and Alice is all ready to take ship again. You must remind her that she is to write me the most *intime* details of her impressions of home. My love to Aunt Kate, who will have written me, I trust, whatever she is able to do. May she, on reaching home, have found this more than it seemed to be here!—I am fast becoming a regular Parisian *badaud;* though, indeed, I led a far madder and merrier life in Cambridge than I seem likely to do here. The waiters at the *restaurants* are as yet my chief society. The weather, since my return, has been wet but soft, and I have had a blissful respite from suffering with the cold. This little room of mine, in the Hotel Rastadt, is a most delightful spot: hardly larger than a state room on the *Algeria,* but with everything needful and all the warmer for its smallness. Today is bright and the sun is pouring in over the opposite house tops in a way that I wish Aunt Kate could see. A gentleman has just come in to try me on a shirt. Imagine Mr. Chaffin calling in Quincy Street for this purpose or entertaining the idea that a shirt could be tried on! Mine is an elegant fit and *très echanchré* in the neck.—I did wrong just now to speak slightingly of my society; for I have struck up a furious intimacy with James Lowell,[1] whom I lived side by side with for so many years in Cambridge without sight or sound of. I called on him the other day, with a message from Charles Norton; he returned my call, the next day and we went out to walk and tramped over half Paris and into some queer places which he had discovered on his own walks. There is a good deal of old Paris left still. Lowell is very pleasant and friendly, and apparently very happy: driving great bargains in old books, some wonderfully handsome and cheap. The cheapness of books here must make Paris a paradise of bibliophilists. A few days later I went over and dined at Lowell's *table d'hôte* in the Rue de Beaune, just off the Quai Voltaire. He lives in a little old genuine French hotel, in a snug little apartment, with fabulous cheapness. The dinner at 3 frs. 50 was the cheapest entertainment I ever enjoyed, not only on account of the food which was very *savoureux*, but of the company, which was more succulent still. The scene was indescribable; I only wish Willy could have seen it. It consisted of a political fight between four conservatives (one the Marquis de Grammont, a deputy and legitimist), and a solitary republican, a Wallachian by birth. All the classic qualities of the French nature were successively unfolded before us, and the *manner* of it beat the best comedy. One of the conservatives, a doctor of the complacent sapient epigrammatic sort, was a perfect specimen of a certain type of Frenchman, and the way he rolled his eyes and chucked his epigrams into the air with his chin (as if he were balancing a pole on the end of it) was something not to miss. He clamored for a despotism stronger than any France has ever had, absolute suppression of the press and that all radicals should be *fusillés*. The Marquis de Grammont thought *suppression* of the press a little severe, but went in for *lois très répressives* and declared that his party hoped to carry such in the next session of the chamber. He then worked himself into a rage, against the Wallachian, more purple, more frantic, more grotesque, than anything you can imagine. The wildest parody couldn't approach it, and it was wondrous to see the rest of them quietly eating their dinner instead of running for a straight-jacket. I shall know in future what to *s'échauffer* means. The state of mind exhibited by the whole thing was incredibly dark and stupid—stupidity expressed in epigrams. If the discussion was really as typical as it seemed to be, the sooner France shuts up shop the better. I mean to return often to the Hotel de Lorraine, and if the other table d'hôtes in that region are as good, I shall take them all in turn. Mr. John Holmes,[2] by the way, is with the Lowells, with his aroma of Cambridge quite undiluted.—Rowse and C. Wright have gone and the latter, I suppose, will have turned up in Cambridge before this reaches you. I know of no one else in Paris whom I am likely to see, except the Masons and Bob James, whom I mean to reserve till every other resource has failed.—For your liberal advice about drawing money, beloved father, many thanks. I shall do very well without ruining you. I mean to act in accordance with what you say about having my cheques sent to you; it is the best plan.[3] Tell Alice and Willy to read the *full correspondence* of Henri Regnault, just published. I have just sent a review of it to the *Nation*.[4] You say nothing about the boys, so that I suppose there is nothing new with them. Tell Willy I mean soon to write to him. Love to my incomparable mammy. Address Hotel Rastadt etc. Farewell.

Ever your loving son
H. James jr.

1. James Russell Lowell (1819–1891), poet, abolitionist, linguist, was fifty-six at this time and HJ twenty-nine.

2. Brother of Oliver Wendell Holmes.

3. HJ arranged to have magazines send payment for his work directly to his father as reimbursement for money advanced for his travels.

4. Unsigned review of *Correspondance de Henri Regnault* in the *Nation*, 2 January 1873, 13–15.

24 · *To Henry James, Sr.*

Ms Harvard

Rome
March 4*th* [1873][1]

Dearest father—

I haven't written for a longer time than usual, because I have been waiting for a letter from home—which doesn't come. The last, now more than a fortnight since, was from you. Since then I have written to mother, and I hope my letter will not be lost, as possibly one of yours has in this interval. But I hope not. I had rather you had not written at all. I am well and happy and still rejoicing in Rome. The spring has begun in earnest and the sun is getting decidedly fierce. I foresee that my generous south-window will become a nuisance before long and that I shall incline to change my room. I am sick of hotel-life to which I have now been restricted for nearly ten months and long for perfect privacy.—*Vedrèmo!*—Since I last wrote the Carnival has died and been buried—greatly to the relief of everyone lodged on the Corso, which for ten days was transformed into a squeaky pandemonium. But I am on the point of enclosing some remarks on it to Howells, to which I refer you for details. Lent has now begun and I am hoping that the unprofitable little invitations to which I have been sacrificing myself for the last two months in the hope of some latent profit, will die a natural death. What do you think—what does Alice think—of my having to go tonight to the Greenoughs—having declined them before? There I shall bury my dress coat. Last night I was bidden again to the Archbishop of Dublin's (who seems fairly *hungry* for my society) and to Miss Sarah Clarke's[2] to meet the Emersons, back from Egypt. I let them both alone; but in the morning I had called on the E's and had had the pleasure of serving them by giving them my passes to the Vatican. They are very serene and appreciative and Emerson was as lovely as ever. Of course you will see them and learn everything about their travels.—The Tweedies and Bootts rub along and I rub against them as usual. Tweedy is quite himself again—but poor Aunt Mary is passably erratic and uncomfortable. She is in a state of chronic dissatisfaction with everything. Mrs. William Temple has just come to them for a month. The Bootts I see pretty often, especially now that I have begun to ride pretty regularly with Lizzie. I have taken a very nice little horse for a month, as that was the only way to get him—he being engaged twice a week to follow the hounds and to be had neither on those days nor the morrow's. I didn't judge myself *de force* to go round trying horses promiscuously: so now for a month I am master of a great privilege. He has a charming little character and yet is sufficiently lively to assist me somewhat; to learn to ride. For some ten days past, I have been incapacitated by—to speak plainly—a *boil*; but before that I had one day a famous ride with Mrs. Sumner and Miss Bartlett:[3] both admirable horsewomen, especially Miss B., and both very handsome in the saddle. We went far away in to the rolling meadows, where the shaggy-vested shepherds feed their flocks and had a series of magnificent gallops, of which I acquitted myself *à mon honneur*. But for me and my infirmities, they ride at rather a tiring rate, and as Lizzie depends upon me, I shall be chiefly her companion.—The rival houses of Story and Terry[4] have each been having theatricals—each indifferently good—in spite of the two clever heads presiding at each—Story himself and Miss Annie

Crawford. The latter (Miss C.) is quite the most remarkable person I have seen in Rome. She has every gift (including a face so mobile and expressive that it amounts almost to beauty) but she is as hard as flint and I am pretty sure will never have an adorer. He will have to be a real Lion-tamer.[5] She is supposed to lead her step-father (poor Mr. Terry) a terrible life. She told me a few evenings since right under his nose, that she *hated* people who had no "modelling" in their faces; and I have no doubt that poor Terry who has as roughly-finished a plebian a countenance as you often see, keenly realizes the fact.—A much sweeter girl, as well as a very clever one, on whom I occasionaly call in the dusky half hour before dinner, is Miss Lowe[6] (of Venice) of whom Alice will have heard Lizzie Boott speak. She is very handsome, very lovely, very reserved and very mysterious, and ought to have many adorers. But I am not yet regularly enlisted as one of them. I have seen no one else in society here (the very small society I have been in) who has caused a pulse of curiosity in the least to beat. Mrs. Wister has beautiful hair; but on the whole I don't at all regret that I'm not Dr. Wister.—Your little admirer, Eugene Benson, has called on me twice; in consequence of which I went lately to his studio and saw several careful and conscientious but very uninspired little pictures. I don't know whether I have mentioned going also to the Storys'. *His* inspiration is very unequal: though his cleverness is always great. His things, on the whole though, are fatally un-simple.—Everyone seems to be in Rome and I constantly pass in the street carriage-loads of people I know. But I fix a stony stare on some merciful column or statue: for life is too short to go to see them all.—The Andrews have left this hotel and gone to a smaller, where I dutifully called on them and found them happy. But I *almost* notified them it must serve for evermore.—These shoals of American fellow-residents with their endless requisitions and unremunerative contact, are the dark side of life in Rome. They really abridge very much the sense of all that one comes for, and make one ask very often whether under such circumstances Rome pays. If I come here again next winter, I shall break with them altogether. The trouble here is that there is apparently no interesting or "cultivated" native society, as in Paris and London. On the side of "culture" Rome seems pitifully barren and provincial.—Here is enough gossip, in conscience: it may beguile the family fireside—the fireside near which, I suppose, you are still unhappily huddling.—Not a word about my moral life or my intellectual!—I have enough of each left to think Cherbuliez's last novel in the *Revue des Deux Mondes* very inferior to anything he has done.[7] It seems to me *almost* poor. I suppose you have been reading it.—My moral life all goes to wondering how you are and what you are doing, and why I don't hear from you. I hope much that William will soon be able to send me a line or so. I am very well *indeed,* and ought to be able to work along prosperously enough. I shall do so better, when all this stale party-going subsides. I gave myself up to it thinking it wouldn't be stale, and that new and various forms of life would be revealed to me: but it is in Rome as in Cambridge. Peace be with it!—How is society with you?—with Alice especially? I should like much to hear from her, what she is doing and whom seeing. Has she been going into Boston at all?—I swore just above at the Greenoughs. But I advise Alice on their return (this summer, I believe) to make their acquaintances: for they are both very nice girls, and I should think she might take very kindly to the elder one (Fanny).—Mr. Emerson sent you (father) very friendly messages, and asked me what you are now writing. But I couldn't tell him—and the fault is yours. I hope you are better of your late discomforts and able to do your work. Enlighten me about it and don't abate your recent frequency in writing to me. I am always homesick, but in the midst of this lavish loveliness of the Roman spring—the thought—even of certain March-moods of our Yankee heavens, causes me to groan with filial tenderness.—Farewell, dearest father. It is not the moods of the skies only, but those of the paternal and maternal souls conjoined, that make me hanker for home.—I suppose Aunt Kate is still in New York and I hope well and prosperous.—Mention always the last news from the boys. I would give my hand for a talk with William. But farewell, again. Furious kisses to mother and sister.—

Your everlasting H.

1. HJ had been in Rome since December 1872.

2. Sarah Freeman Clarke, a transcendentalist friend of HJ's father and an amateur painter.

3. Mrs. Sumner, the former Alice Mason, later resumed her own name after her divorce from Sumner; Alice Bartlett, a southerner, shared Mrs. Sumner's apartment in the Via della Croce, where HJ visited frequently.

4. The sculptor William Wetmore Story lived in a vast apartment in the Palazzo Barberini: painter Luther Terry (1813–1900) in a more modest apartment in the Odescalchi Palace.

5. HJ was prophetic: Annie Crawford married a Prussian and became the Countess von Rabe.

6. Elena Lowe of Boston, who was probably the original of HJ's Christina Light in *Roderick Hudson* and *The Princess Casamassima*.

7. Cherbuliez's latest novel, then being serialized, was *Meta Holdenis*.

25 · To Grace Norton

Ms Harvard

Rome
March 5th 73

Dear Grace—

Your letter was a letter to have been answered the day it came. It was not answered, because there were several sterner duties to perform on that day (and the following ones)—and by keeping it constantly before me, as one does an unanswered letter, I have learned its great merits, as one does, with time, those of all supremely best things. I've carried about with me, meanwhile a heart full of sympathy for poor Charles. What a miserable season! Your letter gives me a painful sense of far-away unhelpfulness to your troubles. But they are melting away I trust, and Charles's cold being thawed out of him and his patience rewarded by even such lukewarm whiffs of spring as a London March affords. How all your trouble, in so far as it's a physical matter, would dissolve in the influence of this vernal sun of Rome! But a little endurance more and you will have an English April—a thing I know well, for I drank deep of it for two successive years.—Already here, in the sunny places, there is a certain scorchingness: but such a loveliness everywhere—such a solid blue in the sky and such a carpeting of anemones and violets in the untrodden places in the Villas.—It would all have been worth waiting for, even if the winter had been half as goodly as it has.—Your picture of your London fog-world was really Turnersque, and Charles lying in the midst of it ill—and with Smollett (has it one *l* or two?) for his healer a truly pathetic image. Has Smollett done his share of the work? If so, I will treat him tenderly when I come to write my great projected work—*A History of Prose Fiction since Cervantes.*[1] Seriously dear Grace, give Charles my tenderest love and my heartiest congratulations, if he is as much better as I hope he is. Your mother, I would fain believe, is out of her room and her serenely vigorous self again—and the children enlivening the high respectability of Cleveland Square by the vocal music of their sports.—Thank you for envying me all these Roman opportunities so much: your good opinion of them reminds me how precious they are. Of regular sightseeing, *Murray* in hand, I have done little this winter—owing partly to want of time, partly to the cold damp atmosphere of most places of resort and partly to a strange feeling of familiarity with most of the lions, begotten I suppose, by intensely zealous scrutiny of them on my former visits. But I have had lovely random walks and rambles and droppings into places, and have perhaps been taking the best course really to know Rome—I have surrendered myself freely to the current of "society" here—but it has landed me on rather sandy shores, enriched chiefly by the stern experience of its unprofitableness. One's inevitable (or almost so) entanglements with the American colony here are a dark side to a brilliant picture, and make one think twice about deciding on a second winter here. It contains nothing novel, individual or picturesque enough to repay one for any great expenditure of time. I doubt that any society here does. There must be some very good scattered individuals: but I haven't met them. On the other hand, (not to be misanthropic) I have met lots of amiable people.—Your own hints about your London world excited my curiosity more than they satisfied it. Some day, perhaps, I shall have a glimpse of it, and shall walk safely by the light of your impressions. In the way of scattered individuals, Mr. Emerson is here with his daughter, back from the Nile, serene and urbane and rejuvenated by his adventures. He is on his way to London, and will relate them of course to you, as quaintly as he did—a little—to me.— Of people you know, I doubt that I see anyone but the Storys, who give pleasant enough parties, at which their handsome daughter sings with a delightful voice, with the strangest most tremulous sort of vibration in it. (Privately) I imagine the touching effect is a matter of voice rather than of *âme.* —I went lately to Story's studio and found him in the midst of an army of marble heroines, which were not altogether unsuggestive of Mrs. Jarley's waxworks.[2] They are extremely (though unequally) clever, but I think almost fatally unsimple.—However criticism in the case is really ungrateful: for they offer a perfect feast of ingenuity, inventiveness and fancy.—Àpropos of criticism, the Nation *Middlemarch* is not at all mine—*mais pas du tout!* It is by Mr. Albert Dicey (I am told) whom I think you know. I had sent them a notice, but at the eleventh hour they displaced it for this one, which is doubtless better as going more into details. But if mine is printed elsewhere you shall see it.[3] What you write me about Lewes's anecdotes was most interesting and welcome. I wondered whether you were hearing anything about George Eliot. Her book, with all its faults, is, it seems to me, a truly immense performance. My brother William lately wrote me that he was "aghast at its intellectual power." This is strong—and what one says of Shakespeare. But certainly a marvellous *mind* throbs in every page of *Middlemarch*. It raises the standard of what is to be expected of women—(by your leave!) We know all about the female heart; but apparently there is a female brain, too. In fact, dear Grace, there are two of them!—I have read very little else this winter and written little, though something. Thank you for liking the Bethnal Green notice. *Criticism* of pictures is less and less to my taste and less and less useful—to my perception.[4] An easy-going profession of amusement in them is more philosophic, I think. In fact criticism of all kinds seems to me overdone, and I seriously believe that if nothing could be "reviewed" for fifty years, civilization would take a great stride. To produce some little exemplary works of art is my narrow and lowly dream. They are to have less "brain" than *Middlemarch*; but (I boldly proclaim it) they are to have more *form*.—I don't know whether I mentioned in my last that I had lately taken to the saddle and been exploring the wondrous Campagna. I see indescribable things, many of which you can doubtless close your eyes and see glowing in faint violet through the mists of years. Yes, it's all solemnly beautiful, and strange and still as you remember it. I ride often with Lizzie Boott, who is a very nice girl, and who, when you go back to Cambridge, will rejoice to know you.—Do you know Mrs. Charles Sumner? I went the other day with her and like her much. With her great beauty (which on horseback is enormous) she has great honesty, frankness and naturalness—I gave your message to the Tweedies who received it gratefully. They are enlivened (though perhaps that is hardly the word just now) by having Mrs. Captain Temple (Mrs. T's sister in law) with them. Not that she is not a particularly nice woman, I only meant she is a little drooping. Mr. T. is altogether salubrious and happy. The Storys profess to believe that *Lowell* is still to turn up: but I doubt it, from what he told me in Paris.—Farewell, dear Grace. I wrote lately to Jane; my letter must have crossed yours. My universal love. I should like extremely a single line, saying that Charles is better—and your

mother. I shall soon write to Charles. I think of Jane and you, as always, as of two things in heaven.

> Your perpetual worshipper
>
> H.J. jr.

1. HJ is apparently being facetious. He seems never to have planned a work of historico-
criticism of this nature. It was the sort of book that might have been written by his friend
Perry.
2. In Dickens's *The Old Curiosity Shop*.
3. The review was published unsigned in the New York magazine *Galaxy*, March 1873.
4. "The Bethnal Green Museum" appeared in the *Atlantic*, January 1873. HJ disliked
criticism of painting, although he wrote a considerable body of it during his early years (see
Letter 21, note 3).

26 · To Charles Eliot Norton

Ms Harvard

> Rome
>
> March 13*th* 73

Dear Charles—

Some days since I heard from Grace the sad story of your last illness
and this morning comes a letter from Jane with further mention of it,
of a kind that makes me feel how trying it must have been. Ten days
ago—a week ago—you were still in your room, with the single compensation, apparently, that though that was dismal, the outside world
was more dismal still, and you had not the torment—as you would
have had here—of seeing squares of deep blue sky in your window and
long streams of sunshine over your walls and carpet.—But whatever
your skies and winds, I hope by this time you have made their acquaintance again and have even had another walk or so with Carlyle.
You have had all my sympathy in your illness and you would have a
good deal of my envy (perhaps not quite *all*) in those walks. I have
been seeing a great *mess* of people this winter and they have none of
them diminished my sense of the value of the company of a man of
genius. For instance: I a few nights since heard W. W. Story read (at
Mrs. Wister's, to an audience composed simply of herself, her husband, Mrs. Kemble and myself, whose presence was accidental)—a
five-act tragedy on the history of *Nero!*[1] He got through three acts in

three hours, and the last two were resumed on another evening when I was unavoidably absent. The performance was the result much less of an inward necessity, I surmise, than of a most restless ambition, not untinged with—what an impertinent little word stands for, beginning with v and ending with y^2—as I say, I should have enjoyed particularly just afterwards, half an hour of Carlyle's English and Carlyle's imagination.—I gather from Jane and Grace as I did from your letter received several weeks since and which I now tardily acknowledge, that you have been having a rather interesting winter but not an especially cheerful one. You must have had a dreary dose of climate—and I think of all that with a shudder; but I inevitably think of the moral climate of London as a murky, dusky, oppressive medium too;—only to be comfortably outweathered if you have laid up a private store of intellectual sunshine. Yet I also confess that I am fond of English *chiaroscuro,* in the material landscape and relish it somewhat in the social as well. And you have some opportunities that are foreign enough to us—such as the show of old masters at the Royal Academy which Jane speaks of in her today's letter. You remember how quickly one can number the first-rate pictures in Rome.—Fortunately Rome is itself a picture—now in these mild March days more than ever. Of the charm that is stealing over the place with every deepening breath of spring, I can hardly soberly speak; and you have your memory and Jane's and Grace's to consult.—I know how your memory has been charged of late with another burden. Your illness has at any rate done you the service of helping you to be alone with your thoughts.—Jane tells me that you are to sail on May 15*th*—sooner even than I supposed—not too soon, I hope for a peaceful voyage and a—what shall I call it?—philosophical arrival. I suppose you'll hardly see much of Cambridge before the summer is over, but I shall nevertheless feel tempted to beg you to interpret my absence to our fellow-citizens as eloquently as you may feel moved to.—I ought myself to justify it by doing much more than I have done this winter. But how can I write good tragedies when I am liable to find myself in for a three hours' audition—a poor one?—Your children I hope are better of their colds and are able to watch the hawthorne springing as I suppose it does or soon will, in Cleveland Square. Your mother, I trust, has had no cold nor any other small misfortune, to get rid of and will be able to await serenely the day of your departure. My affectionate remembrances to her—please thank Jane profusely for her letter, and mention (the Roman postoffice is rather lax) to Grace that I despatched her one, in answer to her own, about a week since. Farewell dear Charles, with vigorous wishes for a return of strength and of all good influences.

Yours most truly
H. James jr.

1. For an account of this evening, remembered many years later, see *William Wetmore Story and His Friends*, II, 254.
2. The word, fairly obviously, is "vanity."

27 · *To Mrs. Henry James, Sr.*

Ms Harvard

Rome
March 24*th* '73

Dearest Mammy.

Since writing last, almost a fortnight since, I have been blessed with three letters: one from Willy, one from you, and one, yesterday, from father. All were supremely welcome and all excellent in their diverse manners. I am well and undisturbed, in spite of my long silence, and have not written chiefly because of much other occupation. I have rejoiced in your home news when it was good—and deplored it when it was not, as for example when you touch upon your furious snows and frosts—you, dearest mammy, upon your grievous domestic fatigues and woes, and Willy upon Alice's spoiled dinner parties.—But I hope by this time the tender grass is peeping up along the border of the Brattle street fences, where I used to watch it so lovingly last year,—that Maria and Lizzie[1] have recovered their health, and Alice has ornamented all the feasts to which she has been bidden.—Here, midspring is already upon us and I walk abroad in my summerest clothes and am warm therewith. Yesterday I spent the whole afternoon rambling in the Borghese Villa, drinking in the vernal influences with a satisfaction tempered only by the regret that you, sweet mother, might not be trampling the anemones, in the shadow of the grim old walls of Rome and plucking the violets from the roots of the high-stemmed pines. The days follow each other in gentle variety, each one leaving me a little more *Roman* than before. Lent is well on and party giving, though I continue to get pitifully entangled in stupid little engagements which deprive me of the pleasure of spending my evenings in meditative solitude. But every day now brings a little more liberty. The Bootts leave in a week, the Wisters the same (also for America) and various other people are more or less shutting up shop. The Tweedies thrive, somewhat ponderously, and Mrs. Temple who is staying with them, stands forth in scintillating relief. I continue to dine there quite often, in spite of the sufferings engendered by Tweedy's passion for converting his rooms into an oven. I have had no fire in five weeks but he still revels in a temperature which is positively fabulous, and Aunt Mary, Mrs. Temple and I fan violently by the hour. The Butler was recently threatened with expulsion, but has been kept and the pantry still flourishes. I see a good deal of the Bootts and can't help thinking that Lizzie will miss her Roman resources in Cambridge more than she apprehends, and that their stay there will be short. Going up early the other morning to make a riding appointment with her, I found her in her studio with a certain little Peppina—the most enchanting little nut-brown child model you can imagine: in structure, color, costume, everything, the handsomest little miniature woman. There sat Lizzie happily painting this delicious object. Where will she get a Peppina in Cambridge? The Park doesn't grow them alas. Lizzie, by the way, has painted much this winter and has enormously, or at least, strikingly improved. I was present the other evening at an exhibition she gave of all her things (including a lot of sepia and watercolor sketches) to a couple of young artists, Boit and Crowninshield,[2] and they, like myself, were much surprised at her fertility, inventiveness and general skill. She ought now to paint, or more especially, to draw well enough, to sell her things and make herself if she wishes, a career.—I have been riding with her a good deal, and also with Mrs. Wister. I have now had for some three weeks the luxurious, the *princely*, sensation—of keeping a saddle-horse. I am a little disappointed in the immediate profitableness of riding, which I thought would be a very good muscular exercise. It is a fair one, but I find it doesn't take the place of walking. In a general way, however, and morally and intellectually, it is magnificent. The only drawback is that at present and for sometime back, the mild weather gives too little *tone* to the air for really exhilarating movement. If to the boundless Campagna, Rome added a climate with a little snap and lift to it, riding here would be Paradise. I went out the other day with Mrs. Wister and her husband. They led me rather a dance, but I took four ditches with great serenity and was complimented for my close seat. But the merit was less mine than that of my delightful little horse, who is a brave jumper, and would just suit Alice if she would come out and try him. To cease this heartless jesting. I am now in the position of a creature with *five* women *offering* to ride with him: Mrs. Sumner, Mrs. Wister, Mrs. Boit, Miss Bartlett and Lizzie Boott. I shall fight shy of Mrs. Boit who, I believe, is an equestrian terror. Pray don't repeat these fatuous speeches.—Everyone, more or less, is here—several in whom Alice will be interested. I called the other night on the Dixwells, and found them fresh and hearty and wholesome. Tell Alice our *Whitwells* of Berne are here, Miss W. handsomer than ever, and with a wondrous pretty but less satisfying sister, who fell into my arms and asked about her (Alice). *À propos* of our last summer's friends, she will be interested in hearing that I met Mr. *Duggin* of the Algeria etc. Imagine my horror on learning from him that our lovely friend Miss Bailey had *died* in Paris, in October last, of congestion of the brain brought on by the excitement and fatigue of shopping for her *trousseau.* She was to be married on her return. Alice will tell you all about her: she was an enchanting creature. (Send this on to Aunt Kate)—Your three letters contained a good deal of home talk, which was all devoutly relished. Thank Willy, to whom I will soon write a specific answer. I owe father one too, which he shall soon have. Thank him meanwhile greatly for his story of *Mr. Webster.* It is admirable material, and excellently presented: I have transcribed it in my notebook with religious care, and think that some day something will come of it.[3] It would require much thinking out. But it is a first class theme. Thank him also for his trouble in discussing with Osgood[4] the matter of my bringing out a volume. He mentioned it sometime since and it has been on my mind to respond. Briefly, I don't care to do it, just now. I value none of my early tales enough to bring them forth again, and if I did, should absolutely need to give them an amount of verbal retouching which it would be very difficult out here to effect. What I desire is this: to make a volume, a short time hence, of tales on the theme of American adventurers in Europe, leading off with the *Passionate Pilgrim.*[5] I have three or four more to write: one I have lately sent to Howells and have half finished another. They will all have been the work of the last three years and be much better and maturer than their predecessors. Of these there is only one—*A Light Man*[6] (published in the *Galaxy*) I should not rather object to reissue. That

showed most distinct ability. The money I should get would not (probably) be enough to make a sacrifice for—so long as (as I properly) I can
keep making enough to get on with comfortably.—I should loathe,
too, to have you spending money on my plates—though it's noble to
offer it.—If I should think better of this a few days hence I will let you
know. But there is the impossibility of the thing's being printed as they
stand, uncorrected. They are full of thin spots in the writing which I
should deplore to have stereotyped, besides absolute errors, to which
I was always very subject.—A blessing on all that concerns you. The
letter enclosed by mother from Bob, was lovely. Happy boy! Mention
to Wilky I lately wrote him.—My especial love to Sara Sedgwick, and
my friendliest sympathy in her disturbed health. Happy Arthur with
his *work* and his 2500$!!—Is Aunt Kate back? My love to her always,
and send her my letters.—Where is Mrs. Lombard and does anyone
hear from her? I thought she might write me. Farewell, farewell,
dearest Mother. A smoother kitchen and many happy months ahead.
Love to sister and to her poor head, and to Father and William

Your fondest H

1. Apparently domestics in Quincy Street.

2. Edward D. Boit (1840–1915) and Frederic Crowninshield (1845–1918) were
among the painters HJ came to know in Rome and used in his novel of American artists,
Roderick Hudson.

3. HJ used this subject, an anecdote about a man's self-sacrifice to a demanding wife,
several years later in "Crawford's Consistency," *Scribner's Monthly* XII (August 1876),
569–584.

4. James R. Osgood (1836–1892), Boston publisher.

5. *A Passionate Pilgrim and Other Tales*, HJ's first volume of fiction, was published by
Osgood in 1875.

6. "A Light Man," *Galaxy* VIII (July 1869), 49–68, revised and reprinted in *Stories by
American Authors*, V (Scribner, 1884).

28 · To William James

Ms Harvard

Rome 101 Corso

April 9th 73

Dear William:—

I have had in hand from you for some time a letter of Feb. 13th
which gave me great pleasure on its arrival and of which I have just

been refreshing my memory. Three days since too came a letter from father of March 18, which I shall answer at my next writing. Many thanks to him meanwhile. As always, when I write, I feel that in some mood a week or two before, I would have had a good deal more to say and that the full stream of utterance is not turned on at this particular hour. But we must say what we can—and *read* it. From all my letters as they come, you get, I suppose, a certain impression of my life, if not of my soul. In fact, my soul has not been quite as active as a well regulated soul should be. (By soul, here, I mean especially brain.) The winter is at last fairly over, and I can look at it as a whole and decide that though under the circumstances I am fairly satisfied with it, I shouldn't care to spend another just like it. All of it that has been of pure Rome (with the exception of one point) has been delightful: but there is little left here now of which that can be said and the mark of the fiend—the American fiend—is on everything. I surrendered myself with malice prepense when I came, to whatever social entanglements should come up. They multiplied actively and took up my evenings pretty well for three months; but on retrospect they don't seem to have been very remunerative. I have seen few new people and no new types, and met not a single man, old or young, of any interest. There have been several interesting women "round"—Mrs. Wister being the one I saw most of—but none of the men have *fait époque* in my existence. Mrs. Wister has gone, to bury her regrets in Germantown, Penn., and I have of late been seeing a good deal of Mrs. Sumner and Miss Bartlett, who live together, are now my neighbors, and since I have given up my horse have amiably invited me several times to ride one of theirs—having three. They are both superior and very natural women, and Mrs. Sumner a very charming one (to Miss B. I feel very much as if she were a boy—an excellent fellow)—but they are limited by a kind of characteristic American want of culture. (Mrs. Wister has much more of this—a good deal in fact, and a very literary mind, if not a powerful one.) For the rest society (for Americans) is very thin and such at home as we would dream of coming somewhere else to get something superior to. Storys and Terrys soon pall, and such is our fatal capacity for getting *blasé* that it soon ceased to be for me, what it was at first, a kind of pretty spectacle to go to their houses. At the Storys' however, the other night I met and conversed for a few minutes with Matthew Arnold, whom, if I had more ingenuity, I suppose I might have managed to see more of. He is handsome but not as handsome as his fame or his poetry and (to me) he said nothing momentous. But I think I mentioned all this in my last. This in parenthesis. I suppose there are interesting individuals to know in Rome, but I doubt that there is any very edifying society. And I doubt that one meets interesting—generally interesting—individuals anywhere by going round and hungering for them. If you have some active prosperous speciality, it introduces you to fellow-workers, and the interest of such is the one, I suppose that wears best.—My own speciality has suffered a good deal, for the immediate hour, by my still unformed and childish habits of application having been much at the mercy of the distractions and preoccupations of my daily goings and comings, innocent as they have been. I have written less than I have supposed I should and read not at all. But in the long run I have gained for it has all after all been "quite an experience" and I have gathered more impressions I am sure than I suppose—impressions I shall find a value in when I come to use them. And for the actual writing now that life is growing quieter, I shall sufficiently overtake myself. The point at which, above, I took exception to Rome in itself is one I have only gradually made up my mind about—namely, the influence of the climate. (This has had much to do with my intellectual idleness.) When I first came and the winter gave it a certain freshness, I felt nothing but its lovely mildness; but for the past eight or ten weeks I have been in a state of ineffable languefaction. The want of "tone" in the air is altogether indescribable: it makes it mortally flat and dead and relaxing. The great point is that it is all excessively pleasant and you succumb to languor with a perfectly demoralized conscience. But it is languor (for me at least) languor perpetual and irresistible. My struggles with sleep have been heroic, but utterly vain, and to sit down with a book after eight P.M. (and after a rousing cup of *caffè néro*) and not snore the evening ignobly away has been a dream never realized. It seems to me that I have slept in these three months more than in my whole life beside. The soft divine, enchanting days of spring have of course made matters worse and I feel as if, for six weeks past, I have been looking at the world from under half-meeting eyelids. But I am going to fight it out to the end, for I don't know when I shall ever be here again. Nothing of all this means that I find the air unwholesome: on the contrary. It makes me thick-headed and a little head-achy; but the languor and the "fever" are two very different matters, and I have

been steadily living and still live, in the most salubrious conditions.—
Of Rome itself, otherwise, I have grown very fond, in spite of the inevitable fits of distaste that one has here. You feel altogether out of the
current of modern civilization and in so far, very provincial, but (as I
believe I have more than once said) I often hanker for the high culture
and high finish of Paris—the theatres and newspapers and booksellers
and restaurants and boulevards. But the atmosphere is nevertheless
weighted—to infinitude—with a something that forever stirs and
feeds and fills the mind and makes the sentient being feel that on the
whole he can lead as complete a life here as elsewhere.—Then there is
the something—the myriad somethings—that one grows irresistibly
and tenderly fond of—the unanalysable *loveableness* of Italy. This fills
my spirit mightily on occasions and seems a sort of intimation of my
learning how to be and do something, here. These last—or first—
weeks of spring have been strangely delicious, and it has seemed a sort
of crime to be keeping them to myself. The weather has been perfect;
as it has been constantly since my arrival, and perfect Roman weather
seems somehow, beyond all others, the weather for the *mind.* My riding has put me in the way of supremely enjoying it and of course has
doubled the horizon of Rome. Physically, I doubt that it will ever do
wonders for me; but morally and intellectually it is wondrous good.
Life here (after one has known it) would be very tame without it and
to try it is to make it an essential. Like everything that is worth doing,
riding well is difficult; but I have learned to sit a well-disposed horse
decently enough—the Campagna, with its great stretches of turf, its
slopes and holes and ditches, being a capital place to acquire vigilance
and firmness. I wish *fratello mio,* that you might come and take a turn
at it.—But you'll soon be thinking that my only mission in life is to
preach amusement.—Of Italian, *per se,* I have learned much less than
I had dreamed of doing—not having (with so many other things to
do) hired the intelligent young Roman of my vision to come daily and
converse with me. But I read it fairly well and to speak it after the
fashion of a rank foreigner is not hard. I lately formed a contract with
Miss Bartlett to come twice a week and read *Tasso* with her (delicious
stuff!) and this I hope will progress as finely as my inevitably falling
into a three hours' dead sleep over my dictionary will allow. I have
been now for a fortnight in these rooms on the Corso (extremely good
ones) where I have more observation of *moeurs Italiennes* than at my

hotel. The *padrone* keeps a little shop of Catholic images in the basement and lives with all his family (wife, three children, sister-in-law, maid servant and various female hangers-on) behind a curtain, in an alcove off the vestibule to my two rooms, which being on the front, with a balcony, are the main source of his subsistence. It's a pathetic old-world situation and I feel as if (if I were not a brute) I would invite them in to air themselves in my apartment.—Your letter was full of points of great interest. Your criticism on *Middlemarch* was excellent and I have duly transcribed it into that *note-book*[1] which it will be a relief to your mind to know I have at last set up. Better still was your expression of interest in your lectures and of their good effect on you.—Without flattery, I don't see how you could fail to please and stimulate your students, and hope the thing will develop and bring you larger opportunities. That your health too, should keep pace with them is my cordial wish. Your praise of my articles was of great value. I feel myself that I constantly improve, and I have only now to strive and to let myself go to prosper and improve indefinitely. So I think! I mean to spend a not idle summer. Our friends here are in eclipse. The Tweedies, with Mrs. Temple, have gone to Albano, for a change of air, poor Mr. Tweedy having lately been suffering acutely from rheumatism. Rome doesn't agree with him and I should think he would be glad to get away. His brother (John T.) has had his daughter ill at Albano for many weeks with typhus fever (brought from Naples); so that the whole family has been roughly used. Aunt Mary is on the whole rather tragical (not to call it comical) and I pity their want of a central influence or guiding principle. (Such as their children would have been.) They don't know where to go, what to do, or why to do it. They have been full of hospitality to me.—The Bootts after a few days at Albano, are gone to Naples, prior to a month at Bellosguardo again. I have seen a good deal of them all winter; and miss them now. Lizzie wears better than her father, whose dryness and coldness and tendency to spring back to calling you Mr. again like a bent twig, is ineffable. But still, if you get him laughing (as you so easily can) you forgive him everything. Lizzie still makes one pity her—though I don't know why. Her painting has developed into a resource that most girls would feel very thankful to possess, and she has had a very entertaining winter. Her work will always lack the last delicacy, but if she would only paint a little less *helplessly,* she would still go far—as women go.

But with her want of *initiation,* it is remarkable that she does as well. I should think she might make very successful little drawings for books. She has made a lot of excellent sketches.—In the way of old friends we have been having Henry Adams and his wife, back from Egypt and (last) from Naples, each with what the doctor pronounced the germs of typhus fever. But he dosed them and they mended and asked me to dinner, with Miss Lowe, (beautiful and sad) and came to Mrs. Sumner's, where I dined with them again, and shewed me specimens of their (of course) crop of bric-à-brac and Adams's Egyptian photos (by himself—very pretty)—and were very pleasant, friendly and (as to A.) improved. Mrs. Clover has had her wit clipped a little I think—but I suppose has expanded in the "affections."—I have been meeting lately at dinner for ten days young *Ireland* (Miss I's brother) who used to dine with us on Sundays. He is travelling hereabouts and spending a month in Rome and seems rather helpless and listless and lonely and thankful for chance company. He has a more amiable air than in former days.—There have been hordes of other people here, before-seen, most of whom I have contrived to elude. The Andrews have gone to Florence, having much enjoyed Rome. I surrendered lately an evening to the Dixwells—who were very wholesome and lively, especially Mrs. D., whom Europe animates and beautifies. I have first or last seen in a cab in the Corso every one I ever saw anywhere before—including (tell Alice) Ella Eustis and mamma—the latter, apparently, with the same ink stain on her nose she had at Oxford! Also the Dr. Kings and in fine, every one!—But my letter is eternal. Continue to say all you can about the boys. Bob evidently will thrive, and our blessings and hopes must go with Wilky. I'm glad Alice was to have been in New York, and hope it will have tuned her up to writing me a line. My blessings on her. Did Aunt Kate come back with her? If so, a line from her again when she can, will be welcome.— Love to every one else. There were some things in father's letter I wanted to answer but I must wait. Kisses in profusion to my inestimable mammy. I am wearing all my old under garments, though in rags, because they have her needle work.—Farewell, dear Bill. I haven't said twenty things I meant but it must serve.

Ever yours
H.J. jr.

1. This notebook did not survive among those published in *The Complete Notebooks*, but HJ used portions of it in "From a Roman Notebook," *Galaxy* XVI (November 1873), 679–686.

29 · *To William Dean Howells*

Ms Harvard

Florence

March 10th [1874]

Dear Howells[1]—

This is grim business, and yet I must be brief. Your dear friend Dr. Holland[2] has just proposed to me to write a novel for *Scribner*, beginning in November next. To write a novel I incline and have been long inclining: but I feel as if there were a definite understanding between us that if I do so, the *Atlantic* should have the offer of it. I have therefore sent through my father a refusal to Dr. H. to be retained or forwarded according to your response. Will the *Atlantic* have my novel, when written? Dr. H's offer is a comfortable one—the novel accepted at rate (that is if terms agree,) and to begin, as I say, in November and last till the November following. He asks me to name terms, and I should name $1200. If the *Atlantic* desires a story for the year and will give as much, I of course embrace in preference the *Atlantic*. Sentimentally I should prefer the A.; but as things stand with me, I have no right to let it be anything but a pure money question. Will you, when you have weighed the matter, send me a line through my father or better, perhaps, communicate with him *viva voce*—This is not a love-letter and I won't gossip. I expect to be in Europe and, I hope, in Italy, till mid-summer. I sent you lately, at three or four weeks' interval, the two parts of a tale.[3] You have them, I hope? Farewell, with all tender wishes to your person and household.

Yours ever

H. James jr.

1. William Dean Howells was now editor-in-chief of the *Atlantic Monthly*.

2. Josiah Gilbert Holland (1819–1881), Massachusetts author and the first editor of *Scribner's Monthly*.

3. The two-part tale "Eugene Pickering."

30 · To the James Family

Ms Harvard

Story's Hotel, Dover St.
Piccadilly Sunday Nov. 1st [1875]

Dear People all—

I take possession of the old world—I inhale it—I appropriate it![1]
I have been in it now these twenty-four hours, having arrived at Liverpool yesterday at noon. It is now two o'clock, and I am sitting, in the
livid light of a London November Sunday, before a copious fire, in my
own particular sitting-room, at the establishment mentioned above.
I took the afternoon train from Liverpool yesterday, and having tele-
graphed in advance, sat down at 10 P.M. to cold roast beef, bread and
cheese and ale in this cosy corner of Britain. I have been walking up
Piccadilly this morning, and into Hyde Park, to get my land-legs on; I
am duly swathed and smoked and chilled, and feel as if I had been here
for ten years.—Of course you got my letter from Sandy Hook, and
learned that my voyage began comfortably. I am sorry to say it didn't
continue so, and I spent my nights and my days declaring that the sea
shouldn't catch me again for at least twenty years. But of course I have
already forgotten all that and the watery gulf has closed over my miseries. Our voyage was decently rapid (just ten days) owing to favoring
winds; but the winds were boisterous gales, and after the second day
we tumbled and tossed all the way across. I was as usual, but I kept
pretty steadily on deck, and with my rugs and my chair, managed to
worry thro'. The steamer is a superb one, but she was uncomfortably
crowded, and she presumably bounced about more than was needful. I
was not conversational and communed but little with my multitudinous passengers. My chief interlocutor was Mrs. Lester Wallack,[2] whose
principal merit is that she is the sister of Millais the painter. She offers
to take me to his studio if he returns to town before I have—which he
won't. We had also Anthony Trollope,[3] who wrote novels in his state
room all the morning (he does it literally every morning of his life, no
matter where he may be), and played cards with Mrs. Bronson[4] all the
evening. He has a gross and repulsive face and manner, but appears
bon enfant when you talk with him. But he is the dullest Briton of
them all. Nothing happened, but I loathed and despised the sea more
than ever. I managed to eat a good deal in one way and another, and
found it, when once I got it well under way, the best help to tran-

quillity. It isn't the eating that hurts one, but the stopping.—I shall remain in this place at most a week. It is the same old big black London, and seems, as always, half delicious, half dismal. I am profoundly comfortable, thanks to Mr. Story, the usual highly respectable retired butler, who gives me a sitting room, a bedroom, attendance, lights and fire, for three guineas a week. Everything is of the best, and it is a very honorable residence. Why didn't Aunt Kate and Alice bring me here in '72? I shall probably start for Paris a week from tomorrow, and hope to find there a line from home. If anything very interesting befalls me here I will write again, but in my unfriended condition this is not probable. I hope the Western journey has been safely and smoothly executed and count upon hearing full particulars. If Aunt Kate has gone to New York let her see this. Each of you hold Dido an hour against your heart for me.[5] The sight of all the pretty genteel dogs in Hyde Park a while since brought tears to my eyes. I think that if I could have had Dido in my berth I would have been quite well. But perhaps *she* would have been sea-sick. I have been haunted since I left home by the recollection of three small unpaid bills, which I pray mother to settle for me.

1. At Dollard's, the cobbler's. About 2 dollars.

2. Schönhof and Moellers. About $3.00

3d. At Smith's, the tailor's, 7$ for that summer coat: not 7.50, as his bill said, which I left on my bedroom table. Excuse these sordid details. This sitting still to write makes me swim and roll about most damnably.

> Your all-affectionate
> H. James jr.

1. The statement was prophetic: this was indeed the beginning of HJ's expatriation. After contracting with the *Atlantic* for his novel *Roderick Hudson,* of which he wrote a large part in Florence, he had traveled in the Low Countries and then returned to Cambridge in late 1874. He had spent the winter in New York but found he had to do too much hackwriting to support himself there. By early summer 1875, he had decided to try Paris and promised to write a series of Paris letters for the New York *Tribune.* This letter was written on his arrival in England en route to the French capital.

2. Wife of the English actor Lester Wallack (1820–1888).

3. HJ would later recall this voyage in his essay on Trollope in *Partial Portraits* (1888).

4. Katherine De Kay Bronson, wife of Arthur Bronson and future hostess of HJ and Browning in Venice.

5. The James family pet.

31 · To Mrs. Henry James, Sr.

Ms Harvard

Rue de Luxembourg 29
Jan. 24*th* [1876]

Dearest mother:

I have just received a letter from you, of January 11th; and a week ago I got one from William of Jan. 1st. I answer yours first as most becoming, and most urgent. Thank William meanwhile for his, which was a great blessing, and every way agreeable and comfortable.

I passed a wretched hour this morning over that part of your letter which mentioned that my drafts of money had been excessive and inconvenient. I am very sorry to learn that father's income has been disturbed, and I shall be very careful to do nothing more to disturb it. Of course I know I had drawn more largely and at shorter intervals than could be at all agreeable to you; but it seemed, for the moment, a necessity of my situation. Not that, as you seem to suppose, I was "living extravagantly." On the contrary; I have hardly had my expenses off my mind an hour since I have been abroad, and I had arranged my life here, in Paris, well within my means. It was my stay in England, my tailor's bill etc, there and my journey hither and first *frais d'installation,* that made necessary—or helped to make necessary—what seemed so large a sum of money. I am living comfortably, but nothing more. Paris is of course not cheap—far from it; but it is not so dear as New York; and once under way, as I am now, I am in for nothing that I cannot face. I knew you would be somewhat bothered by my drafts, and I have already written to you about it—a letter which you seemed not yet to have received: but I had no idea that father's resources were curtailed, or I should have been doubly and triply careful. This I was not; but it is only in that sense that I have been extravagant. I *am* to receive my moneys for my writing myself as you suppose; which accounts for father's receiving nothing. I am sorry to say that the mistake which I supposed to exist in Osgood's account and which would have made him owe me (on the sum paid to father) somewhat more was a mistake of mine. The sum was correct. I cannot say how soon any returns from *Roderick Hudson* will come in; but of course as they do they are all father's, to whom they will be sent. I strongly hope, and have reason to expect, that the three drafts you mention are all I shall, for the present, have had need to make. I have made none since, and have no prospect of making any for some time. If I make none for three months to come, I shall probably be so far ahead of my expenses that I shall not need to make any more at all—unless in case of sickness; which is not probable, happily. Of this at any rate, I am sure; that by the end of the year I shall have a balance in my favor and I shall be able to refund and compensate inconveniences. I tend, all the while, to work more smoothly and abundantly. I heartily subscribe to what you say about poor Bob's dues in the way of assistance, and I should feel like a profligate monster, if I in any way obstructed them. I hope your Syracuse trouble will be short-lived, and shall do nothing in the world to increase your embarrassment. But let me add that I beg you to banish from your mind your visions of my extravagance. I am living simply as well as physical well-being, and decent mental cheerfulness (so far as it depends on circumstances) seem, in a lonely life, to demand. Unquestionably, the mere daily process of life in Paris is a conspiracy against one's purse, but I repeat that all things considered, it is cheaper than home. The money in question does not simply cover two months, but has covered me up for the future.

But enough of this, which doubtless you do not wish too much descanted on. It is nine o'clock in the evening; and I am going in three quarters of an hour—where do you think?—to a reception of the Duc d'Aumale's,[1] for which Mme Laugel has very kindly sent me an invitation—as well as to another, which follows in a fortnight hence. She has also invited me tomorrow to dine, to meet M. and Mme Ernest Renan: so you see that she does at the least her duty. I must go and dress, in five minutes, for the Duke, but I shall finish my letter when I come in, as we are invited but from 9 to 11.—I wrote you a short time since, giving you an impression, I am afraid, that I was not seeing much of the world. This was true enough at the time: but since then I have seen more. I have taken a desperate plunge into the American world, and have lately been to two balls and a dinner party: one of the former given by Mrs. Harrison Ritchie of Boston (a very nice woman) and the other by Mrs. Kernachan, who I believe is chiefly celebrated for having, as Miss Winthrop, been engaged to George Curtis. The dinner was given by some very good people named Reubell, whom I know thro' Mrs. Crafts, and who have always lived in Paris. I sat next a very nice Mme Autrey, formerly Miss Helen Russell of Newport.

12 P.M. I have just come back from the Duc d'Aumale's, where I spent an entertaining hour, in the bosom of the Orléans family, assisted by a few Ambassadors and their wives. All the Orléans family was there, except the Comte de Paris; and I was presented to the Duke and to a Princess of Saxe Coburg—the latter old, corpulent and deaf, and ignorant of my literary fame, and yet in spite of these drawbacks so gracious and "chatty" as to give me a realising sense of what princesses are trained to. The Orléans people are a great collection of ugly women—and indeed there was not a beauty in the assembly. Laugel introduced me also to John Lemoinne, and Louis de Loménée.[2] The former is a dwarfish man with a glittering eye: the other began to talk to me immediately about American anti-slavery orators!—and their "*style biblique.*" I also renewed acquaintance with Mme Autrey, whom I mentioned above, and with the Nortons' friend Edward Lee Childe,[3] who called upon me the other day, struck me as a good fellow, and invited me to dine on Saturday.—I saw Tourgénieff the other day—he being laid up with gout, from which he is a great sufferer. He was on his sofa, and I sat with him an hour. I returned a few days later, but he was too unwell to see me, and sent word that as soon as he went out he would come to my house. I continue to like him as much as ever: all his talk is full of sense and feeling and *justesse.* I also spent a Sunday afternoon again at Flaubert's with his *cénacle:* E. de Goncourt, Alphonse Daudet etc. They are a queer lot, and intellectually very remote from my own sympathies. They are extremely narrow and it makes me rather scorn them that not a mother's son of them can read English. But this hardly matters, for they couldn't really understand it if they did. If I'd gone the Sunday before I should have found Taine, who is a frequenter, and a great friend of Turguéneff and Flaubert. I was surprised to learn from T. that he has a very bad convergent squint. I have further made the acquaintance of an amiable family named Turguéneff, remote relations of Ivan, at whose house I have been twice, and who seem amicably inclined.[4] This is all the amusing gossip I can think of; I will give you more when I gather it. A lady some time since sent me a particular message to father—her *warmest love.* She is by name Mrs. Albert Gallatin,[5] who said she knew him at Fort Hamilton twenty years ago, and that he used to sit with her on the piazza and delight and edify her with his conversation. She is an elderly widow, very pretty, and rather silly, and has lived in Paris ever since. But father must acknowledge her message, for she affirmed that it is her belief that he is *the best man in the world!* He must send her something very handsome.—I am glad, dear mother, that your own parties succeed, that the little dog flourishes, and that your winter is comfortable. I wish I could contribute to your social pleasure, but I can't—save by scribbling you thus what I see and hear. I would gladly give Alice and William my chance at the theatre here, of which I am extremely tired. I have given up everything but the Théâtre Français. I am sorry poor Wilky suffers still: I hope Aunt Kate continues well. Tell William I will answer his letter, but this is for all of you. I enclose a pair of gloves for Alice, which were meant to go with the other pair. Love to father who I hope will soon write.

Ever, dearest M. your
H.—

1. The Duc d'Aumale (1822–1891) wrote articles on politics and military subjects.

2. John Lemoinne (1815–1892), journalist and critic. HJ dealt with his election to the French Academy in a letter to the *Tribune*, 1 April 1876. Louis de Loménie (1815–1878) was the author of many biographical works. Auguste Laugel (1830–1914), a French authority on British and American history, wrote on French politics for the *Nation*.

3. Edward Lee Childe (1836–1911), a nephew of General Robert E. Lee, spent the greater part of his life in France.

4. Ivan Turgenev (1818–1883), the Russian novelist, much admired by HJ, who had written an article about him. He introduced HJ to the family of Nicholas Turgenev, political exiles, at whose home HJ was often received.

5. The former Louisa Bedford Ewing (1842–1922).

32 · To William Dean Howells

Ms Harvard

Paris, Rue de Luxembourg 29
Feb. 3rd [1876]

Dear Howells—

Ambiguous tho' it sounds, I was sorry to get your letter of the 16th ult. Shortly after coming to Paris, finding it a matter of prime necessity to get a novel on the stocks immediately, I wrote to F. P. Church, offering him one for the *Galaxy*, to begin in March, and I was just sending off my first instalment of MS. when your letter arrived. (The thing has been delayed to April.) It did not even occur to me to write to you about it, as I took for granted that the *Atlantic* would begin nothing till June or *July*, and it was the money question solely that had to determine me. If I had received your letter some weeks before I think my extreme preference to have the thing appear in the *Atlantic* might have induced me to wait till the time you mention. But even of this I am not sure, as by beginning in April my story, making nine long numbers, may terminate and appear in a volume by next Christmas. This, with the prompter monthly income (I have demanded $150 a number), is a momentous consideration. The story is *The American*— the one I spoke to you about (but which, by the way, runs a little differently from your memory of it). It was the only subject mature enough in my mind to use immediately. It has in fact perhaps been used somewhat prematurely; and I hope you find enough faults in it to console you for not having it in the *Atlantic*. There are two things to add. One is that the insufferable *nonchalance*, neglect and ill-manners of the Churches have left me very much in the dark as to whether my conditions are acceptable to them: and I have written to them that if they are not satisfied they are immediately to forward my parcel to you. The other is that I would, at any rate, rather give a novel to the *Atlantic* next year, (beginning, that is, in January) than this.[1] So far as one party can make a bargain, I hereby covenant to do so. I expect to have the last half of the summer and the autumn to work on such a tale; for I shall have obviously to settle down and produce my yearly romance. I am sorry, on many accounts, that the thing for the present, stands as it does, but I couldn't wait. I hope you will find something that will serve your turn.

Why didn't you tell me the name of the author of the very charming notice of *Roderick Hudson* in the last *Atlantic*, which I saw today at Galignani's? I don't recognize you, and I don't suspect Mrs. Wister. Was it Lathrop? If so please assure him of my gratitude. I am doing as I would be done by and not reading your story in pieces.[2] Will you mail me the volume when it appears? I should like to notice it.

Yes, I see a good deal of Tourguéneff and am excellent friends with him. He has been very kind to me and has inspired me with an extreme regard. He is everything that one could desire—robust, sympathetic, modest, simple, profound, intelligent, naif—in fine angelic. He has also made me acquainted with G. Flaubert, to whom I have likewise taken a great fancy, and at whose house I have seen the little *coterie* of the young realists in fiction. They are all charming talkers—though as editor of the austere *Atlantic* it would startle you to hear some of their projected subjects. The other day Edmond de Goncourt (the best of them) said he had been lately working very well on his novel—he had got upon an episode that greatly interested him, and into which he was going very far. *Flaubert:* "What is it?" E. *de* G. "A whore-house *de province.*"

I oughtn't to give you any news—you yourself were so brief. Indeed I have no news to give: I lead a quiet life, and find Paris more like Cambridge than you probably enviously suppose. I like it—(Paris)—much, and find it an excellent place to work.—I am glad my *Tribune* letters amuse you.[3]—They are most impudently light-weighted, but that was part of the bargain. I find as I grow older, that the only serious work I can do is in story-spinning.—Farewell. With a friendly memory of your wife and children

Yours very truly
H. James Jr.

1. *The American* was published in the *Atlantic,* June–December 1876 and January–May 1877.

2. HJ seems to allude here to *Private Theatricals* by Howells, published in the *Atlantic,* November 1875–May 1876.

3. HJ wrote in all twenty letters to the *Tribune;* they were later published as *Parisian Sketches* (1957), ed. Leon Edel and Ilse Dusoir Lind.

33 · To William James

Ms Harvard

29 Rue de Luxembourg
Feb. 8*th* [1876]

Dear William.

I am in your debt for many letters—for all of which I have been devoutly grateful. The last, arrived yesterday, was of Feb. [January] 22d. I wrote home, last, I think, about a fortnight ago. Today I could believe I am at home. The snow is falling from a leaden sky, and the opposite house tops are piled thick with it. But the winter is drifting rapidly away and the European spring is not very far off. The days bring me nothing much to relate, and I am ashamed of myself that, living in Paris, I have not more rich and rare things to tell you. I do my best to collect such material, and it is not my fault if I haven't more of it.—I keep seeing a little of the few people I know. I dined a while since at the Laugels' with Renan and his wife, and am invited there tomorrow evening to encounter the Duc d'Aumale, who is their great social card. Renan is hideous and charming—more hideous even than his photos, and more charming even than his writing. His talk at table was really exquisite for urbanity, fineness and wit—all quite without show-off. I talked with him for three quarters of an hour, in the corner, after dinner, told him that I couldn't measure his writings on the side of erudition, but that they had always been for me (and all my family!!) "*la plus haute perfection de l'expression,*" and he treated me as if I were a distinguished savant.—I saw Tourguénieff the other day, again—he having written me a charming note (I enclose it, if I can find it, for Alice) telling me he was still ill, and asking me to come and see him. So I went and passed almost the whole of a rainy afternoon with him. He is an *amour d'homme*. He talked more about his own writings etc. than before, and said he had never *invented* anything or any one. Everything in his stories comes from some figure he has seen—tho' often the figure from whom the story has started may turn out to be a secondary figure.[1] He said moreover that he never consciously *puts anything into* his people and things. To his sense all the interest, the beauty, the poetry, the strangeness, etc., are there, *in* the people and things (the definite ones, whom he has seen) in much larger measure than he can get out and that (what strikes him himself as a limitation of his genius) touches that are too *raffiné*, words and phrases that are too striking, or too complete, inspire him with an instinctive *méfiance*; it seems to him that they *can't* be true—for to be true to a given individual type is the utmost he is able to strive for. In short, he gave me a sort of definition of his own mental process, which was admirably intelligent and limpidly honest. This last is the whole man; and it is written in his face. He also talked much about Flaubert, with regard to whom he thinks that the great trouble is that he has never known a decent woman—or even a woman who was a little interesting. He has passed his life exclusively "*avec des courtisanes et des rien-du-tout.*"[2] In poor old Flaubert there is something almost tragic: his big intellectual temperament, machinery, etc., and vainly colossal attempts to press out the least little drop of *passion*. So much talent,

and so much naïveté and honesty, and yet so much dryness and coldness.—I have seen a little of the Lee Childes, the Nortons' friends,
who seem agreeable and kindly people, tho' a trifle superfine and
poseurs. I dined there the other day with a large and gorgeous party—
all American; and I call in the afternoon and find Mme Lee Childe in
black velvet by her fire (she is a very graceful, elegant and clever
Frenchwoman), with old decorated counts and generals leaning against
the mantlepiece. Mme Viardot[3] has invited me to a *bal costume* on the
19th, to which I shall probably go, if I find a domino doesn't cost too
much. There are some amiable Boston people here, the Harrison
Ritchies by name, with whom I dined a couple of days since, and took
in Mme Bonaparte—an American with beautiful eyes. She was a Mrs.
Edgar, I believe, and is now wife of the American-born grandson of
old Gérôme. He is now recognised by the Empress and Prince Imperial
as against Prince Napoléon; and the ci-devant Mrs. Edgar (she is a
grand-daughter of Daniel Webster, whom she strikingly resembles) is
moving heaven and earth in the Bonapartist cause, as if it ever comes
up again she will be a princess, or a great swell. She is very charming,
very clever, and quite capable of playing a part. Bonaparte is a *bel
homme,* but stupid.—

Que vous dirai-je encore? I keep on scribbling—sending stuff to the
Nation and the *Tribune* (whose headings and editorial remarks over my
letters sicken me to the soul) and working at the novel I have begun
for the *Galaxy*. The *Galaxy*'s printing is as usual. I write (in that last
thing) "a quiet and peaceful *nun*"—and it stands "a quiet and peaceful
man!" Little Henry Mason ("Sonny") came the other day to see me—
a very nice, gentle, sweet-faced youth of twenty-two—living in the
Latin Quarter and working at painting in Gérôme's studio. I believe
he has been summoned home by his father.—It was true, in Laugel's
letter, that the Right and Left combined to exclude the Right Centre
(the Orléanists). But this was only after the O's had refused with much
arrogance to admit a single Left or Extreme Right name to their Sena-
torial list. "It must be all ours or nothing!" they said. "It shall be
nothing, then!" said the others, and clubbed together to make it so. It
was a regular chopping off of their own head by the O's. But they have
lost nothing, because they have nothing to lose; they have no hold on
the country—partly because they are too good for it. "*Ils n'ont pas de
prestige*" I heard a Frenchman say the other day—and they haven't—a

grain. And yet they are the only party in France who hasn't pro-
scribed, murdered, burnt etc. That is "prestige."—But I think there is
a very fair chance now for the conservative republicans. In the elec-
tions, just over, the Bonapartists have been heavily beaten.—Love to
all, and blessings on yourself.

Yours ever
H. James Jr.

1. Many years later HJ embodied his memories of this conversation in his New York
Edition preface to *The Portrait of a Lady*.

2. Flaubert's affair with Louise Colet was not known to Turgenev at the time.

3. Pauline Viardot-Garcia (1821–1910), the celebrated singer, with whom Turgenev
had formed an attachment that would be lifelong.

34 · To William Dean Howells

Ms Harvard

29 Rue de Luxembourg, Paris
May 28th [1876]

Dear Howells—

I have just received (an hour ago) your letter of May 14th. I shall be
very glad to do my best to divide my story so that it will make twelve
numbers, and I think I shall probably succeed. Of course 26 pp. is an
impossible instalment for the magazine. I had no idea the second number would make so much, though I half expected your remonstrance.
I shall endeavour to give you about 14 pp., and to keep doing it for
seven or eight months more. I sent you the other day a fourth part, a
portion of which, I suppose, you will allot to the fifth.

My heart was touched by your regret that I hadn't given you "a great
deal of my news"—though my reason suggested that I couldn't have
given you what there was not to give. *"La plus belle fille du monde ne
peut donner que ce qu'elle a."* I turn out news in very small quantities—
it is impossible to imagine an existence less pervaded with any sort of
chiaroscuro. I am turning into an old, and very contented, Parisian: I
feel as if I had struck roots into the Parisian soil, and were likely to let
them grow tangled and tenacious there. It is a very comfortable and
profitable place, on the whole—I mean, especially, on its general and
cosmopolitan side. Of pure Parisianism I see absolutely nothing. The

great merit of the place is that one can arrange one's life here exactly as one pleases—that there are facilities for every kind of habit and taste, and that everything is accepted and understood. Paris itself meanwhile is a sort of painted background which keeps shifting and changing, and which is always there, to be looked at when you please, and to be most easily and comfortably ignored when you don't. All this, if you were only here, you would feel much better than I can tell you—and you would write some happy piece of your prose about it which would make me feel it better, afresh. *Ergo,* come—when you can! I shall probably be here still. Of course every good thing is still better in spring, and in spite of much mean weather I have been liking Paris these last weeks more than ever. In fact I have accepted destiny here, under the vernal influence. If you sometimes read my poor letters in the *Tribune,* you get a notion of some of the things I see and do. I suppose also you get some gossip about me from Quincy Street. Besides this there is not a great deal to tell. I have seen a certain number of people all winter who have helped to pass the time, but I have formed but one or two relations of permanent value, and which I de-sire to perpetuate. I have seen almost nothing of the literary fraternity, and there are fifty reasons why I should not become intimate with them. I don't like their wares, and they don't like any others; and be-sides, they are not *accueillants.* Tourguéneff is worth the whole heap of them, and yet he himself swallows them down in a manner that ex-cites my extreme wonder. But he is the most loveable of men and takes all things easily. He is so pure and strong a genius that he doesn't need to be on the defensive as regards his opinions and enjoyments. The mistakes he may make don't hurt him. His modesty and naïveté are simply infantine. I gave him some time since the message you sent him, and he bade me to thank you very kindly and to say that he had the most agreeable memory of your two books. He has just gone to Russia to bury himself for two or three months on his estate, and try and finish a long novel he has for three or four years been working upon. I hope to heaven he may. I suspect he works little here.

I interrupted this a couple of hours since to go out and pay a visit to Gustave Flaubert, it being his time of receiving, and his last Sunday in Paris, and I owing him a farewell. *He* is a very fine old fellow, and the most interesting man and strongest artist of his circle. I had him for an hour alone, and then came in his "following," talking much of Émile Zola's catastrophe—Zola having just had a serial novel for which he was being handsomely paid interrupted on account of protests from provincial subscribers against its indecency.[1] The opinion apparently was that it was a bore, but that it could only do the book good on its appearance in a volume. Among your tribulations as editor, I take it that this particular one at least is not in store for you. On my [way] down from Flaubert's I met poor Zola climbing the staircase, looking very pale and sombre, and I saluted him with the flourish natural to a contributor who has just been invited to make his novel last longer yet.

Warner[2] has come back to Paris, after an apparently rapturous fortnight in London, and the other morning breakfasted with me—but I have not seen him since, and I imagine he has reverted to London. He is conspicuously amiable. I have seen no other Americans all winter—men at least. There are no men here to see but horribly effeminate and empty-pated little *crevés*. But there are some very nice women.—I went yesterday to see a lady whom and whose *intérieur* it is a vast pity you shouldn't behold for professional purposes: a certain Baroness Blaze de Bury—a (supposed) illegitimate daughter of Lord Brougham. She lives in a queer old mouldy, musty *rez de chaussée* in the depths of the Faubourg St. Germain, is the grossest and most audacious lion-huntress in all creation and has the two most extraordinary little French, emancipated daughters. One of these, wearing a Spanish mantilla, and got up apparently to dance the cachacha, presently asked me what I thought of *incest* as a subject for a novel—adding that it had against it that it was getting, in families, so terribly common. *Basta!* But both figures and setting are a curious picture.—I rejoice in the dawning of your dramatic day, and wish I might be at the *première* of your piece at Daly's. I give it my tenderest good wishes—but I wish you had told me more about it, and about your comedy. Why (since the dramatic door stands so wide open to you) do you print the latter before having it acted? This, from a Parisian point of view, seems quite monstrous.—

Your inquiry "Why I don't go to Spain?" is sublime—is what Philip Van Artevelde says of the Lake of Como, "softly sublime, profusely fair!" I shall spend my summer in the most tranquil and frugal hole I can unearth in France, and I have no prospect of travelling for some time to come. The Waverley Oaks seem strangely far away—yet I remember them well, and the day we went there. I am sorry I am not to see your novel sooner, but I applaud your energy in proposing to change it. The printed thing always seems to me dead and done with.

I suppose you will write something about Philadelphia—I hope so, as otherwise I am afraid I shall know nothing about it. I salute your wife and children a thousand times and wish you an easy and happy summer and abundant inspiration.

Yours very faithfully,
H. James Jr.

1. Zola's novel was *L'Assommoir* (1877).
2. Charles Dudley Warner (1829–1900), novelist and essayist, born in Massachusetts and reared in western New York.

35 · To William James

Ms Harvard

Etretat
July 29th [1876]

Dear William,

Your long and charming letter of July 5th came to me just before I left Paris—some ten days since. Since then, directly after my arrival here, I wrote a few words to Alice by which you will know where I am "located." Your letter, with its superior criticism of so many things, the Philadelphia Exhibition especially, interested me extremely and quickened my frequent desire to converse with you. What you said of the good effect of the American pictures there gave me great pleasure; and I have no doubt you are right about our artistic spontaneity and sensibility. My chief impression of the Salon was that four-fifths of it were purely mechanical (and *de plus*, vile). I bolted from Paris on the 20th, feeling a real need of a change of air. I found it with a vengeance here, where as I write I have just had to shut my window, for the cold. I made a mistake in not getting a room with sun, strange, and even loathesome, as it may appear to you! The quality of the air is delicious—the only trouble is indeed that it has too shipboard and mid-ocean a savor. The little place is picturesque, with noble cliffs, a little Casino, and your French bathing going on all day long on the little pebbly beach. But as I am to do it in the *Tribune*, I won't steal my own thunder.[1] The company is rather low, and I have no one save Edward Boit and his wife (of Boston and Rome)[2] who have taken a most charming old country house for the summer. Before I left Paris, I spent an afternoon with the Bootts, who are in Paradise—though with Ernest Longfellow and lady as fellow-seraphs. They have a delightful old villa, with immense garden and all sorts of picturesque qualities, and their place is (as I found by taking a walk with Boott) much prettier than I supposed—in fact very charming, and with the air of being 500 miles from Paris. Lizzie and Longfellow are working with *acharnement*, and both, I ween, much improving. I have little to tell you of myself. I shall be here till August 15–20, and shall then go and spend the rest of the month with the Childes, near Orléans (an ugly country I believe), and after that try to devise some frugal scheme for keeping out of Paris till as late as possible in the Autumn. The winter there always begins soon enough. I am much obliged to you for your literary encouragement and advice—glad especially you like my novel. I can't judge it. Your remarks on my French tricks in my letters are doubtless most just, and shall be heeded. But it's an odd thing that such tricks should grow at a time when my last layers of resistance to a long-encroaching weariness and satiety with the French mind and its utterance has fallen from me like a garment. I have done with 'em, forever and am turning English all over. I desire only to feed on English life and the contact of English minds—I wish greatly I knew some. Easy and smooth-flowing as life is in Paris, I would throw it over tomorrow for an even very small chance to plant myself for a while in England. If I had but a single good friend in London I would go thither. I have got nothing important out of Paris nor am likely to. My life there makes a much more succulent figure in your letters, as my mention of its thin ingredients, comes back to me, than in my own consciousness. A good deal of Boulevard and third rate Americanism: few retributive relations otherwise. I know the Théâtre Français by heart!—Daniel Deronda (Dan'l himself) is indeed a dead, though amiable failure. But the book is a large affair; I shall write an article of some sort about it.[3] All desire is dead within me to produce something on George Sand; though perhaps I shall, all the same, mercenarily and mechanically—though only if I am forced. *Please make a point of mentioning,* by the way, whether a letter of mine, upon her, exclusively, *did* appear lately in the *Tribune*.[4] I don't see the *Tribune* regularly and have missed it. They misprint sadly. I never said e.g. in announcing her death, that she was "*fearfully* shy": I used no such vile adverb, but another—I forget which.—I am hoping, from day to day, for another letter from home, as the period has come round. I hope father is getting on smoothly and growing able to enjoy life a little more. I am afraid the extreme heat does not help him and I fear also that your common sufferings from it have been great—though you, in your letter, didn't speak of it. I hope Alice will have invented some plan of going out of town. Is there any one left in Cambridge whom the family sees? I am glad you went to Mattapoissett, which I remember kindly, tho' its meagre nature seems in memory doubly meagre beside the rich picturesqueness of this fine old Normandy. What you say of nature putting Wendell Holmes and his wife under a lens there is very true. I see no one here; a common and lowish lot; and the American institution of "ringing in" is as regards the French impossible. I hope your own plans for the summer will prosper, and health and happiness etc. be your portion. Give much love to father and to the ladies.—

Yours always—

H. James Jr.

1. "A French Watering Place" appeared on 26 August 1876 and was reprinted in *Portraits of Places* (1883).

2. HJ had met the painter Edward Boit and his wife in Rome three years before (see Letter 27).

3. An unsigned note on *Daniel Deronda* had already appeared in the *Nation* in the issue of 24 February 1876; in December 1876 HJ published in the *Atlantic* "Daniel Deronda: A Conversation," later reprinted in *Partial Portraits* (1888).

4. HJ's letter about George Sand had appeared on 22 July 1876.

36 · To Mrs. Henry James, Sr.

Ms Harvard

Varennes
Amilly par Montargis
Loiret
Aug. 24*th* [1876]

Dearest Mother:

I received this A.M. your letter of August 7th speaking of Janet Gourlay's death, and enclosing the duplicate of William's cheque, and etc. I was much distressed by your further mention of your resentment at my failure to acknowledge the draft from Houghton some weeks since. It was certainly a most culpable omission and I cannot think how it came about. The draft reached me so as a matter of course that

I treated acknowledging it too much as a matter of course. I didn't
appreciate, either, that *you*, sweet mother, had had all the trouble of
procuring it. I am covered with shame, I thank you most tenderly and
I assure you that I will never sin in the same way again! I had not
heard of poor Jeanette's death and am very sorry for Libby. Still, one
can't desire that Jeanette should have lived in suffering to give Libby
occupation or companionship. If Libby should by chance come to stay
with you give her my love.—I am especially delighted to hear that
your terrible temperature had cooled—it was high time—your sufferings must have been extreme. For your good account of father I am
also grateful: I wrote to him just leaving Etretat. I hope his days are
brightening more and more.—I have been at this place for four days,
having come hither directly from Etretat, *via* Paris where I spent the
night. I shall never forget the whole journey; the heat was colossal,
sickening (even Etretat had become a prey to it)—and travelling in
such a temperature was a torture. But on my arrival here the weather
changed, with the help of a little terribly needed rain, and I have had
nothing but quiet enjoyment. (I am staying, as I suppose you divine,
with the Childes—who are perfect hosts and hospitality and *préve-
nance* incarnate.) It is a very entertaining little glimpse of French *vie
de château.* The little chateau itself I wish you could see, with its rare
and striking picturesqueness—(unfortunately it isn't photographed).
It stands on a little island in a charming little river which makes a
wide clear moat all around it, directly washes its base, and with its
tower, its turret, its walls three feet thick (it's of the 15th century!) and
its originality of construction, it is as pretty as a *décor d'opéra.* The
estate[1] is a very large one and contains two other chateaux, one occupied by the old Baronne de Triqueti, Mrs. Childe's aunt (Mrs.
Childe inherits the property from her uncle[2] and the aunt has a life-
interest in it) and the other by the Comte de Bréssieux, nephew of the
hideous and amusing old baronne. Both of these places are also delightfully picturesque and characteristic, and the estate, with meadows
and streams and woods, is of the prettiest (tho' the country in general,
the ancient Gâtinais, I believe, is rather dull and tame). Here, I am in
clover of the deepest sort, the house being as luxurious and elegant
within as it is quaint without. I dwell all alone in a detached pavillion,
in a charming Blue Room, with a *cabinet de toilette* in a turret, and a
valet detailed to do my peculiar bidding. I find everything agreeable
and even interesting, and am very glad that I mustered energy to

come;—for I had a real wrench in leaving Etretat, of which I had become most fond, and which seemed up to the last, delightfully safe, serene and salubrious. The *châtelaine* is decidedly the most agreeable and accomplished of women, and Childe shines as a country gentleman. They propose every day some pleasant little excursion. Yesterday I went with Madame to make a *tournée* among the peasants in two or three villages, where she plays Lady Bountiful. It was as good as a chapter in *La Petite Fadette* or the *Maîtres Sonneurs*.[3] We made a dozen visits, in a dozen queer little smoke-blackened big-bedded, big-clocked kitchens, and every where I was charmed with the nature of the people—their good manners, quaintness and *bonhomie* and the way they did the honors of their little huts. This morning Mrs. Childe drove me first over to Changy (one of the other chateaux) to call on Mme de Bressieux, a nice little woman, in such a perfect French *entourage*, and then further on to see the curé of the neighboring village, who is a particular friend of hers and whom she wished to ask to breakfast. This little visit was delicious—the old curé, charming, candid and polite, in his queer little rustic *presbytère*, was like a figure out of Balzac. Another time I went to the Perthuis to see old Mme de Triqueti, who is an old lady quite *à la Balzac* also; tomorrow Mrs. Childe is to drive me to Montargis (five miles off) and the next day she is to give a large dinner-party to certain Montargeois and others, which will probably be, to an observant mind, something of a collection of types. So you see I am entertained. Among the attractions of the house is a lovely infant of about six years—a little orphan nephew of Mrs. Childe whom she has adopted. He is by name Paul Harvey, has eyelashes six inches long and is a source of much delectation to me, at the rare moments when the superior discipline of the house permits him to appear.[4] I shall probably remain here to September 1st, when I shall return to Paris for a day or two. But I have no desire to face (for the winter) either its pleasures or its pains (i.e. its expenses) so early in the season; though where I shall descend I don't yet know. (My address is always 29 Rue de Luxembourg.—I have taken the rooms for next winter again.)—I am very glad you answered my question as to how father's affairs are affected by the financial troubles at home, but I am sorry you had to answer it so unfavorably. I hope you are not too sensibly incommoded. The sight of the troubles of the more unfortunate classes must indeed be distressing. I am glad I don't see them—that I see only this strange, thrifty, grasping, saving, prospering France, where alone the commercial disasters of the day are not felt. (Some of the "peasants" we saw yesterday are worth sixty and eighty thousand dollars—made franc by franc.) You say nothing of William's or Alice's movements; so I suppose they were at home. But I hope they have moved about a little and are well. Tell Alice that this letter was to have been for her, but the receipt of yours this morning makes me address you. 'Tis all one. Did Alice ever receive two photos (large) of Dubois' statues that I sent her some time before leaving Paris? You shall have no more trouble about the *Century*, dear, dear mother; I wish to hold on to the club, for national sentiment's sake, but I will deal with the undertaking directly.[5] I am sorry about the poor boys' troubles—I trust they are waning. Great love to father, sister, aunt and brother. I embrace you, dearest mammy and remain yours ever

H.J. Jr.

1. The estate was known as Le Perthuis, and the Baron Eugène de Triqueti had acquired in 1833 the small Château de Varennes nearby. It had been restored a few years before James stayed there. HJ gives a charming account of this visit in his essay "From Normandy to the Pyrénées" in *Portraits of Places* (1883).

2. Mrs. Edward Lee Childe, the former Blanche de Triqueti, had inherited Le Perthuis in 1866. The Childes usually spent their summers at the Château de Varennes and their winters in Paris. James would use certain aspects of this Franco-American family in his short novel *The Reverberator* (1888).

3. Novels by George Sand, published respectively in 1848 and 1852.

4. Harvey was the son of Mrs. Childe's brother, Edward. He was to become a British diplomat, a knight, and erudite compiler of the Oxford Companions to English and French literature.

5. HJ had been elected to the Century Association, New York's famous club of the arts, just before his departure for Europe. He resigned in 1878 when he recognized that his expatriation was more or less permanent.

37 · To Whitelaw Reid

Ms Brown

Château De Varennes (near Montargis)
August 30, 1876

Dear Mr. Reid:[1]

I have just received your letter of August 10th. I quite appreciate what you say about the character of my letters, and about their not being the right sort of thing for a newspaper. I have been half expecting to hear from you to that effect. I myself had wondered whether you could make room for them during the present and coming time at home, and I can easily imagine that the general reader should feel in-disposed to give the time requisite for reading them. They would, as you say, be more in place in a magazine. But I am afraid I can't assent to your proposal that I should try and write otherwise. I know the sort of letter you mean—it is doubtless the proper sort of thing for the *Tribune* to have. But I can't produce it—I don't know how and I couldn't learn how. It would cost me really more trouble than to write as I have been doing (which comes tolerably easy to me) and it would be poor economy for me to try and become "newsy" and gossipy. I am too finical a writer and I should be constantly becoming more "literary" than is desirable. To resist this tendency would be rowing upstream and would take much time and pains. If my letters have been "too good" I am honestly afraid that they are the poorest I can do, espe-cially for the money! I had better, therefore, suspend them altogether. I have enjoyed writing them, however, and if the *Tribune* has not been the better for them I hope it has not been too much the worse.[2] I shall doubtless have sooner or later a discreet successor. Believe me, with the best wishes,

Yours very truly
Henry James Jr.

1. Whitelaw Reid (1837–1912) was editor of the New York *Tribune*, for which HJ had been writing his series of letters from Paris.

2. See *Complete Notebooks*, 109–110, 123–124, for HJ's memory of this experience with the *Tribune*, which he used in his story "The Next Time," published in the *Yellow Book* (July 1895).

38 · To William Dean Howells

Ms Harvard

29 Rue de Luxembourg
Oct. 24*th* [1876]

Dear Howells—

Many thanks for your letter and the promise of *Hayes*, which I shall expect.[1] Thanks also for your good opinion of the notice of *Daniel Deronda*, which charmed and reassured me.[2] I was rather afraid that you would think its form beneath the majesty of the theme. Many thanks, furthermore, for your continuing to like the *American,* of which I shall send you by the next mail another installment. (I sent you one by the last, and I shall very soon send you the closing pages.) Your appeal on the subject of the *dénouement* fairly set me trembling, and I have to take my courage in both hands to answer you. In a word Mme de Cintré doesn't marry Newman, and I couldn't possibly, possibly, have made her do it. The whole point of the *dénouement* was, in the conception of the tale, in his losing her: I am pretty sure this will make itself clear to you when you read the last quarter of the book. My subject was: an American letting the insolent foreigner go, out of his good nature, after the insolent foreigner had wronged him and *he* had held him in his power. To show the good nature I must show the wrong and the wrong of course is that the American is cheated out of Mme de Cintré. That he should only have been scared, and made to fear, for a while, he was going to lose her, would have been insufficient—*non è vero?* The subject is sad certainly but it all holds together. But in my next novel I promise you there shall be much marrying. *Apropos* of this I have it on my conscience to mention that I am in correspondence with Scribner about a serial to begin in this magazine in June next. Nothing is yet settled, but I suppose something will be.[3] The vision of a serial in Scribner does not, I may frankly say, aesthetically delight me; but it is the best thing I can do, so long as having a perpetual serial running has defined itself as a financial necessity for me. When my novels (if they ever do) bring me enough money to carry me over the intervals I shall be very glad to stick to the *Atlantic.* Or I would undertake to do this if I could simply have money down for my MS., leaving the Magazine to publish at its leisure. My novel is to be an *Americana*—the adventures in Europe of a female Newman, who of course equally triumphs over the insolent foreigner.[4]—Yes, I couldn't help translating those [illegible]—verses of Turgénieff,[5] tho' I don't share the Russian eagerness for War. T. himself is full of it, and I suspect it is coming. The air is full of it and all the world here expects it.—I think I shall thrive more effectually than here in London, to which city I propose before long to emigrate—if I don't go to Italy. But I shan't, at any rate, winter here. You managed to tell me very little about yourself. What are you writing?

Yours very truly, with love at your fire-side,

H. James Jr.

1. Howells had just written a campaign biography of Rutherford B. Hayes, his wife's cousin, who was elected to the American presidency that autumn.

2. See Letter 35, note 3.

3. Nothing came of this plan.

4. Here HJ foreshadows *The Portrait of a Lady*.

5. HJ's prose rendering of Turgenev's verses appeared in the *Nation*, XXIII (5 October 1876), 213.

39 · To Alice James

Ms Harvard

Address regularly:—3 Bolton St. Piccadilly W.

Dec. 13*th* [1876]

Dearest Sister—

Quincy Street will have been without a letter from me for some time, but you will doubtless have sagely reflected that the mighty cares of a *déménagement* from the rue de Luxembourg to Bolton Street have been the cause of my silence. This tremendous move made, I am once more at liberty to speak. I am sorry that the first thing I have to say is a sad one. I am afraid I have lost—temporarily—a letter from you, sent after the 15th of last month—to Brown and Shipley. They turn out to have stupidly sent such a letter (received on the 27th) to a person of my name in Baltimore, who had just left London and ordered his letters to follow him. They, however, at my behest, immediately wrote in pursuit of it, and I shall before long recover it. I have an idea that the document in question was from your too-rarely-exercised hand and on this assumption put a *high* price upon it. If it was not, so much the better, and I shall still hear from you. If it was, I must possess my soul in patience for two or three weeks longer. The letter will of course return.

—Meanwhile I am in London, having crossed over on the 10th ult., very agreeably, on a Channel as smooth as this paper: a wondrous sensation.[1] I lost no time *à me caser*, which I did yesterday morning in the most satisfactory manner. I have an excellent lodging in this ex-cellent quarter—a lodging whose dusky charm—including a house-maid with a fuliginous complexion, but a divine expression and the voice of a duchess—are too numerous to repeat. I have just risen from my first breakfast of occasional tea, eggs, bacon, and the exquisite English loaf, and you may imagine the voluptuous glow in which such a repast has left me. *Chez moi* I am really very well off—and it is a rare pleasure to feel warm, in my room, as I sit scribbling—a pleasure I never knew in Paris. But after that charming city London seems—superficially—almost horrible; with its darkness, dirt, poverty and general unaesthetic *cachet.* I am extremely glad however to have come here and feel completely that everything will improve on acquaintance. I am moreover much pleased with the economical character of my move. I shall evidently live here much more cheaply than in Paris, where I had fallen into expensive ruts. My rooms, which are highly genteel, are very much cheaper than my habitation in the rue de Luxembourg. I have seen no one here as yet, of course,—save James Crafts[2] and his wife who have been here for some time doctoring, greatly to the advantage of the former, in consequence of the advice of a physician who has made him walk willy-nilly and drink coffee ditto. He is so much better that his wife is going to leave him in England, alone, to visit at country-houses while she joins her poor more and more suffering sister at Cannes. And only a month ago in Paris, Crafts was living almost entirely in bed! It remains to be seen, of course, whether his improvement continues.—Paris was Paris up to the last; the weather was beautiful and it was hard to come away. Before doing so I spent a last morning with Tourguéneff—beside his gouty couch—and parted with him in the most affectionate manner. He expressed a flattering desire to correspond with me even frequently, and gave me an "*adieu, cher ami*" which went to my heart. My last impression of him is as good as my first, which is saying much.—I likewise became strangely intimate with Mrs. Tappan,[3] who apparently desired to have me to dinner every day, and on my praising a very clever picture in Goupil's window, went off and bought it on the spot for 7000 frs. (It is a Russian snow-scene, with superb horses, by Chelmanski.) I am afraid she and Mary (who has greatly "improved") will have a dullish winter in Paris. They scan the horizon vainly for people to dine with them; and when one thinks of all the clever people there are there who would be glad to eat their excellent dinners it seems a pity they shouldn't be put *en rapport.*—All this while I have been a long time without letters, and don't know how you are feeling and thinking about the dreadfully mixed matter of Tilden and Hayes.[4] I won't hazard the expression of conjectures derived solely from the London

Times, but await private information. Is the "agitation" so great as is here supposed?—are you alarmed, depressed, impoverished? Write me all about it. Here the conference at Constantinople[5] occupies all men's thoughts, and the wind seems turning a little to peace: very little though.—I have written a longer letter than I deemed I had time for, and can only add my blessings on all of you. I hope father grows more and more lusty and that in general your winter *s'annonce bien.* I have of course seen the news of the Brooklyn theatre: but it is too horrible to allude to. Farewell dear child. I send you herein *one* pair of gloves, and will follow it by others, sent individually. I brought them from Paris, purposely, to post here, as I have heard of French letters with soft contents being confiscated by the New York Custom House. These gloves are *not* Bon Marché, but a very superior article. Farewell—farewell from your affectionate brother

H. James Jr.

1. HJ described his move between the two capitals in "An English Easter," *Lippincott's Magazine,* XX (July 1877), 50–60, reprinted in *Portraits of Places* (1883).

2. James Mason Crafts (1839–1917), an eminent chemist, later president of MIT, who lived much abroad.

3. Mrs. William A. Tappan, the former Caroline Sturgis, was an old friend of the Jameses, having met them abroad in the 1850s. HJ described her as having "an admirable intelligence, of the incurably ironic or mocking order." See *Notes of a Son and Brother,* chapter 7.

4. In the presidential election of 1876, Samuel J. Tilden received 184 electoral votes and Rutherford B. Hayes 165; another 20 were in dispute. A bipartisan committee of 15 members, 8 Republicans and 7 Democrats, ultimately voted along straight party lines, giving all 20 votes to Hayes. The election was described as the "most deeply corrupt" of that time.

5. Attempting to avert a Russo-Turkish war and pacify the Balkans, the European powers called a conference of the nations involved, in Constantinople, in November 1876. The parley failed, and Tsar Alexander II attacked Turkey in April 1877.

40 · To Mrs. Henry James, Sr.

Ms Harvard

3 Bolton St., Piccadilly. W.

Christmas eve [1876]

Dearest mammy—

I lately received your two letters: the one involving William's, and the note enclosing Bob's verses. William will forgive me for addressing my answer to you, rather than to him; but it is meant for both of you. Many thanks for all. I have already written to you since my arrival here, and you know that I am fairly established. It is only a fortnight today, but it seems a long time—which I don't mean in an invidious sense. This is rather a combination of two drearinesses—a London Sunday afternoon and a London detached Christmas eve. The weather is, and has been, beyond expression vile—a drizzle of sleet upon a background of absolutely *glutinous* fog, and the deadly darkness of a London holiday brooding over all. To relieve the monotony of the situation I could do nothing better than commune a bit with the mammy of my love. You are not to suppose from this that I am in low spirits. Oh no; my spirits never were higher. I take very kindly indeed to London, and am immensely contented at having come here. I must be a born Londoner, for the place to withstand the very severe test to which I am putting it: leaving Paris and its brilliancies and familiarities, the easy resources and the abundant society I had there, to plunge into darkness, solitude and sleet, in mid-winter—to say nothing of the sooty, woolsy desolation of a London lodging—to do this, and to like this murky Babylon really all the better, is to feel that one is likely to get on here. I like the place, I like feeling in the midst of the English world, however lost in it I may be; I find it interesting, inspiring, even exhilarating. As yet, no great things have happened to me; but I have not objected to being quiet: on the contrary. I have been glad to do some quiet work. I have besides, seen two or three people. I breakfasted only this morning, at the Arts Club, with a very pleasant young Englishman whom I met last summer at Etretat, and have renewed my acquaintance with here. He is a journalist and you may read him in the "Occasional Notes" of the Pall Mall Gazette, many of which he does. He is likewise a Jew and has a nose, but is handsome and looks very much like Daniel Deronda.[1] Gurney gave me a letter to a young Benson who was in America while I was away and who a couple of days since invited me to dine with him very kindly, at the Oxford and Cambridge Club, where were two other men, one of them Andrew Lang,[2] who writes in the *Academy* and who, though a Scotchman, seemed a quite delightful fellow. Benson is not exciting, but most gentle and *bon comme du pain*. That is the only introduction I have brought with me to England: but I have written home to two or three persons for two or three more, which I suppose in the course of time will arrive and fructify. As Henry Adams had sent me a message through William

I wrote to him; and also to Mrs. Wister, who had made me offers of that sort of old. I have also called upon G. W. Smalley,[3] who had called upon me in Paris; and who has a very pretty house and wife, and is very civil.—That is as much, for the present, as I have seen of the *vie intime* of London; as other vistas open out before me I will let you know. I feel, keenly, that it is an excellent thing for me to have come here. I expected it would prove so, but it *feels* so, even more than I expected. I am very glad I wasted no more time in Paris. I shall work here much more and much better, and make an easier subsistence. Besides it is a comfort feeling nearer, geographically, my field of operation at home. I feel very near New York. I have been revelling in a subscription to Mudies:—All this about myself, a subject which you will desire that I should not scant. I was deeply grieved to hear from William that he had been weak and disabled, thro' his dysentery, so much longer than I supposed. I fondly believed he was well again, and I trust he is now. Tell him I thank him much for his strictures on some of Newman's speeches in *The American* of which I quite admit the justice. It is all along of my not seeing proof—I should have let none of those things pass. The story, as it stands, is full of things I should have altered; but I think none of them are so inalterable but that I shall be easily able in preparing the volume, to remove effectually, by a few verbal corrections, that Newmanesque taint on which William dwells.[4] I wish any of you would point out anything more you think subject to modification.—I have received since being here a letter from Aunt Kate (written before she had gone to Cambridge to see Bob's baby) in which she speaks of father's having been a trifle less well. But I hope this was but a fleeting shadow. Give him all my love and blessing and ask him if I can do anything for him in London.—The advent of Bob and his Babe must have been a very interesting and agreeable episode. I wish I could have shared in it; and that, failing that, Alice would write me about the Babe. Bob's verses are surprising, and very touching: fearfully so, in fact. They have, as you say, a touch of inspiration; and are a strange proof of the reality of the need for poetic utterance— for expressing that which transcends our habitual pitch. It is an affecting groping for form—and finding it. I am sorry for his domestic troubles, which seem strange over here, where there are so many hungry servants looking for work. I wish I could do something for Mary. Is there any modest thing I can *send* her—not a trinket or a ribbon, which would be a mockery. Think of s'thing, and let me know. I have (as I said) just heard from Aunt Kate to whom, as I may not be able to answer her letter directly, (I mean instantly), pray make a point of forwarding this. It will tell her about me *en attendant*. Tell my sister, with a kiss, that I am now daily awaiting the return of that missing letter of her's. Farewell sweet mother.

Your fondest

H. J. Jr.

P.S. I have it at heart to add that just before leaving Paris I was obliged to draw for the first time in a year, on my letter of credit. The expense of breaking up there and coming here compelled it. But don't imagine from this that I am going to begin and bleed you again. I regard the thing as a temporary loan—and I have amply sufficient money coming in to me in these next weeks to repay it in two or three remittances. I shall not draw again for another year—and had not done so, up to this time, from the first few weeks of my coming abroad. You needn't commiserate me for my *Tribune* cessation, as it was only two days since that I received payment for my last letters, written six months ago. If it had come sooner, I shouldn't have had to use my credit. I don't miss the *Tribune* at all; I can use my material to better advantage.—I am forgetting to wish you a Merry Christmas. I shall eat a solitary Christmas dinner tomorrow—if indeed one can be procured at an eating-house, which Sabbath-wise, here, I doubt. If not I shall fast! But I hope your own feast will be succulent and sociable and that you will spare a thought to the lone literary exile.

1. The young man was Theodore E. Child of Merton College, Oxford, later Paris correspondent to London newspapers and editor of an Anglo-French journal, the *Parisian*. The warm friendship between Child and HJ, rooted in their common love of France and French letters, endured until Child's death in 1892, "prematurely and lamentedly, during a gallant professional tour of exploration in Persia," as HJ put it, in the preface to volume 14 of the New York Edition.

2. Andrew Lang (1844–1912) wrote much literary journalism, poetry, folklore, fiction, and anthropology and translated from the Greek.

3. George Washburn Smalley (1833–1916), an American journalist, famous for his Civil War reporting in the New York *Tribune*, was now a correspondent in London.

4. *The American* is one of the most extensively revised novels in HJ's New York Edition.

41 · To Henry James, Sr.

Ms Harvard

Athenaeum Club
Pall Mall
Feb. 13*th* [1877]

My dearest Dad—

I received this A.M. your letter about sending you the weekly *Times* etc.—besides having received a long and excellent letter from William of Jan. 28th. Many thanks for both, especially for yours, as a proof of recovered vigor. I have been meaning any day for a week to do what you ask about the *Times,* and have delayed it only because a journey over into the City is a serious enterprise, taking time. But I shall do it immediately. I shall likewise be very happy to send the *Graphic* to Bob—but where shall I send it? This morning came to me a note from Carry (to thank me for some gloves I had sent her on Christmas), telling me that she "supposed I know all about Bob's Mary's having come back to Milwaukee") and speaking as if they intended to remain. You don't mention this, and I am anxious to know whether poor Bob has found himself forced to suspend farming. I hope not and should be glad to hear. Meanwhile, subscribing to a journal for a long time I don't know where to have it sent. But I will try Whitewater.—I am writing this in the beautiful great library of the Athenaeum Club.[1] On the other side of the room sits Herbert Spencer, asleep in a chair (he always is, whenever I come here) and a little way off is the portly Archbishop of York with his nose in a little book. It is 9:30 P.M. and I have been dining here. An old gentleman put himself at the table next me and soon began to talk about the "autumn tints" in America—knowing, heaven knows how, that I came thence. Presently he informed me that he was the son of Sir Richard Westmacott, the sculptor; and that the old gentleman on the other side of him was a nephew of Lord Nelson etc. etc. I give you this for local color (it is a great blessing, by the way to be able to dine here, where the dinner is good and cheap. I was seeing arrive the day when London restaurants, whose badness is literally fabulous, would become impossible, and the feeding question a problem so grave as to drive me from the land. I am not sure that some day it won't). I have been spending of late rather quiet days and have not seen anyone in particular. But I go to break-

fast tomorrow with Lord Houghton, who invited me of his own movement. H. Adams and Mrs. Wister had each sent me a letter for him;
but I have not presented them, first, because I heard his house had
lately been burnt down; second, because I had an idea he was much
battered, bored and beset. But if the mountain comes to Mahomet, it
is all right. He wrote to me (as "Dear Mr. James," which, indeed, is
what all the English do, before they have ever seen you) and asked me
to breakfast, having heard of my existence I don't know how. On
Thursday I breakfast with Andrew Lang, at his club, to meet J. A.
Symonds, and tomorrow I dine with the spasmodic but excellent little
Dicey (who was in America) and whom, with his ugly but equally
excellent wife, I met the other day at James Bryce's. I lunched a
few days since at Lady Pollock's. with a lot of people, whom Lady P.
left to scramble after her to the dining-room as they could, she,
an aged woman, having marched out with a little infantile Lord
Ronald Gower—not so handsome as his name. Lunched also with the
Cunliffes, very kindly, but mildly-interesting people, and sat next
Samuel Laurence, the artist who did your bad portrait in the dining-
room—a very kind, soft little man: who when I told him he had done
my father's portrait, said that was what every American told him.
I went today to see Thomas Woolner, the sculptor, to whom H. Adams
had given me a letter—a good plain, conceited fellow and respectable
artist, living, with an intensely pre-Raphaelite wife, in a charming old
house, full of valuable art-treasures: a delightful place. Adams' other
letter was to F. T. Palgrave, on whom I left it a week ago, but who has
taken no notice of it. But perhaps he will, yet. *Don't breathe a word of
this.* Tell William I prized his letter highly, and make Alice get from
the Athenaeum, Mackenzie Wallace's *Russia,* a new book which every
[one] here is talking about.[2] It is most interesting. Farewell, dearest
dad. Write me again when you can and believe me your loving son—

H. James Jr.

1. John Lothrop Morley (1814–1877), the American historian, obtained for HJ guest
privileges at the Athenaeum. Among the names of celebrities sprinkled through this letter
are Herbert Spencer (1820–1903), founder of evolutionary philosophy; John Addington
Symonds (1840–1893), who, behind his Hellenism and major writings on the Italian Renaissance, was a campaigner for homosexuality; Albert Venn Dicey (1835–1922), professor of English law at Oxford, opponent of Irish Home Rule; James Bryce (1838–1922),
author of *The Holy Roman Empire* and later *The American Commonwealth;* Lord Houghton

(Richard Monckton Milnes) (1809–1885), first biographer of Keats and an eminent Victorian.

2. HJ wrote an unsigned review of this book for the *Nation*, XXIV (15 March 1877), 165–167.

42 · To Alice James

Ms Harvard

> Athenaeum Club
> Pall Mall S.W.
> (3 Bolton St. Picc.)
> March 2 [1877]

Dearest sister:

I enclose you a letter from Ivan Tourguéneff which I received this a.m. in the belief that it will entertain you and the domestic circle.[1] Tho' slight it is pleasant. *Please show it to no one outside of the family,* and return it, in the envelope, by the first person who writes.—This is not meant to be a letter, *chère sœur.* It is very late at night and I am in the delightful great drawingroom of the Athenaeum Club where I have been reading the magazines all the evening, since dinner, in a great deep armchair with such a comfortable place to repose my book and such a charming machine to sustain my legs! I don't want to excite your animosity—but I might, were I to depict the scene that one may usually view here—in this same drawing room, at 5 o'clock in the afternoon:—all the great chairs and lounges and sofas filled with men having afternoon tea—lolling back with their laps filled with magazines, journals, and fresh Mudie books, while amiable flunkies in knee-breeches present them the divinest salvers of tea and buttered toast! I don't write, because I sent William a long letter three days since. But write me, then!

> Ever your
> H.J. Jr.

1. The letter from Turgenev, dated from Paris 28 February 1877 and written in French, speaks of the failure of his new novel, *Virgin Soil;* expresses regret at HJ's absence from the French capital; and alludes to Zola's *L'Assommoir* as "not an immoral book—but devilishly dirty." Turgenev adds: "If I were a cartoonist for *Punch* I'd amuse myself by representing Queen Victoria reading *L'Assommoir.*"

43 · *To William James*

Ms Harvard

Athenaeum Club, Pall Mall
March 29*th* [1877]

Dear William—

—I will write you a few lines before I leave this place this evening. I thanked you for your last letter thro' mother a few days since—a letter of which I forget the exact date; (you described your brain-lecture etc.) I have been dining here, and then sitting awhile to read the last number of the *Nineteenth Century* (I won't send it you as I send it to Mrs. Lockwood, who can't afford to buy it and would never see it otherwise.) Vidi in the same Prof. Clifford's thing[1] at the end.— London life jogs along with me, pausing every now and then at some more or less succulent patch of herbage. I was almost ashamed to tell you thro' mother that I, unworthy, was seeing a bit of Huxley. I went to his house again last Sunday evening—a pleasant easy, no-dresscoat sort of house (in our old Marlboro' Place, by the way.)[2] Huxley is a very genial, comfortable being—yet with none of the noisy and windy geniality of some folks here, whom you find with their backs turned when you are responding to the remarks that they have very offensively made you. But of course my talk with him is mere amiable generalities. These, however, he likes to cultivate, for recreation's sake, of a Sunday evening. (The slumbering Spencer I have not lately seen here: I am told he is terribly "nervous.") Some mornings since, I breakfasted with Lord Houghton again—he invites me most dotingly. Present: John Morley, Goldwin Smith (pleasanter than my prejudice against him), Henry Cowper, Frederick Wedmore and a monstrous cleverly, agreeably-talking M.P., Mr. Otway. John Morley has a most agreeable face, but he hardly opened his mouth. (He is, like so many of the men who have done much here, very young-looking.) Yesterday I dined with Lord Houghton—with Gladstone, Tennyson, Dr. Schliemann (the excavator of old Mycenae, etc.)[3] and half a dozen other men of "high culture." I sat next but one to the Bard, and heard most of his talk which was all about port-wine and tobacco: he seems to know much about them, and can drink a whole bottle of port at a sitting with no incommodity. He is very swarthy and scraggy, and strikes one at first as much less handsome than his photos: but gradually you see that it's a face of genius. He had I know not what simplicity, speaks with a strange rustic accent and seemed altogether like a creature of some primordial English stock, a thousand miles away from American manufacture.—Behold me after dinner conversing affably with Mr. Gladstone—not by my own seeking, but by the almost importunate affection of Lord H. But I was glad of a chance to feel the "personality" of a great political leader—or as G. is now thought here even, I think, by his partisans, ex-leader. That of Gladstone is very fascinating—his urbanity extreme—his eye that of a man of genius— and his apparent self-surrender to what he is talking of, without a flaw. He made a great impression on me—greater than any one I have seen here: though 'tis perhaps owing to my naïveté, and unfamiliarity with statesmen. Dr. Schliemann told me two or three curious things. 1. he is an American citizen having lived some years in America in business. 2.—though he is now a great Hellenist he knew no word of Greek until he was 34 years old, when he learned it in *six* weeks (!!) at St. Petersburg. *Ce que c'est d'être Allemand!* The other men at Houghton's dinner were all special notabilities. Next me sat a very amiable Lord Loucke—noted as the unhappy young peer who a short time since married a young wife who three or four months after her marriage eloped *bel et bien* with a guardsman.—Did I tell you that I some time since spent an evening with F. T. Palgrave? Strictly between ourselves—i.e. as regards H. Adams, and everyone else,—I don't particularly like him: but he is evidently very respectable. He is a tremendous case of culture, and a "beggar for talk" such as you never faintly dreamed of. But *all* his talk is kicks and thrusts at every one going, and I suspect that, in the last analysis, "invidious mediocrity" would be the scientific appellation of his temper. His absence of the *simpatico* is only surpassed by that of his wife. (This sounds pretty scornful; and I hasten to add that I imagine he very much improves on acquaintance. I shall take a chance to see.)

Did I tell you that I had been to the Oxford and Cambridge boat-race? But I have paragraphed it in the *Nation*,[4] to which I refer you. It was for about two minutes a supremely beautiful sight; but for those two minutes I had to wait a horribly bleak hour and a half, shivering, in mid-Thames, under the sour March-wind. I can't think of any other adventures: save that I dined two or three days since at Mrs. Godfrey Lushington's (they are very nice *blushing* people) with a parcel of quiet folk: but next to a divine little Miss Lushington (so pretty English girls can be!) who told me that she lived in the depths of the City, at Guy's Hospital, whereof her father is administrator. Guy's Hospital, of which I have read in all old English novels. So does one move all the while here on identified ground. This is the eve of Good Friday, a most lugubrious day here—and all the world (save 4,000,000 or so) are out of London for the ten days' Easter holiday. I think of making two or three excursions of a few hours apiece, to places near London whence I can come back to sleep; Canterbury, Chichester etc. (but as I shall commemorate them for lucre I won't talk of them thus).

Farewell, dear brother, I won't prattle further. Thank father for the two cuts from the *Galaxy*—tho' I wish he had sent a line with them. I enclose $2.00 I accidently possess. Add them to that $12.00 to expend them for any cost I may put you to. Have you received your *Maudsley?* Don't you think very well of Hayes, and are not things in a brightening way? Encourage Alice to write to me. My blessings on yourself from your fraternal

H.J. jr.

1. William Kingdon Clifford (1845–1879), Victorian mathematician and philosopher. HJ had a close friendship for many years with his widow.

2. Thomas Henry Huxley (1825–1895), professor of natural history at the Royal School of Mines and an influential supporter of Darwin's theories. The Jameses had lived in a house in Marlborough Place during their stay in London in the mid-1850s.

3. This was HJ's first meeting with Alfred Lord Tennyson (1809–1892), the Bard, who had been poet laureate since 1850. Heinrich Schliemann (1822–1890), discoverer of Troy, was then being feted in London.

4. Described by HJ in an unsigned *Nation* note, XXIV (12 April 1877), 221–222.

44 · *To William Dean Howells*

Ms Harvard

3 Bolton St. W.
March 30th [1877]

Dear Howells—

I am supposed to be busily scribbling for lucre this morning; but I must write you three lines of acknowledgment of your welcome long letter. Its most interesting portion was naturally your stricture on the close of my tale, which I accept with saintly meekness. These are

matters which one feels about as one may, or as one can. I quite understand that as an editor you should go in for "cheerful endings"; but
I am sorry that as a private reader you are not struck with the inevitability of the American dénouement. I fancied that most folks
would feel that Mme de Cintré *couldn't*, when the finish came, marry
Mr. Newman; and what the few persons who have spoken to me of the
tale have expressed to me (e.g. Mrs. Kemble t'other day) was the fear
that I should really put the marriage through. *Voyons*; it could have
been impossible: they would have been an impossible couple, with an
impossible problem before them. For instance—to speak very materially—where would they have lived? It was all very well for Newman to
talk of giving her the whole world to choose from: but Asia and Africa
being counted out, what would Europe and America have offered?
Mme de Cintré couldn't have lived in New York; depend upon it; and
Newman, after his marriage (or rather *she,* after it) couldn't have
dwelt in France. There would have been nothing left but a farm out
West. No, the interest of the subject was, for me, (without my being
at all a pessimist) its exemplification of one of those insuperable difficulties which present themselves in people's lives and from which the
only issue is by forfeiture—by losing something. It was cruelly hard for
poor N. to lose, certainly: but *que diable allait-il faire dans cette galère?*
We are each the product of circumstances and there are tall stone walls
which fatally divide us. I have written my story from Newman's side of
the wall, and I understand so well how Mme de Cintré couldn't really
scramble over from *her* side! If I had represented her as doing so I
should have made a prettier ending, certainly; but I should have felt as
if I were throwing a rather vulgar sop to readers who don't really know
the world and who don't measure the merit of a novel by its correspondence to the same. Such readers assuredly have a right to their entertainment, but I don't believe it is in me to give them, in a satisfactory
way, what they require.—I don't think that "tragedies" have the presumption against them as much as you appear to; and I see no logical
reason why they shouldn't be as *long* as comedies. In the drama they
are usually allowed to be longer—*non è vero?*—But whether the *Atlantic* ought to print unlimited tragedy is another question—which
you are doubtless quite right in regarding as you do. Of course you
couldn't have, for the present, another evaporated marriage from me!
I suspect it is the tragedies in life that arrest my attention more than

the other things and say more to my imagination; but, on the other hand, if I fix my eyes on a sun-spot I think I am able to see the prismatic colors in it. You shall have the brightest possible sun-spot for the four-number tale of 1878.[1] It shall fairly put your readers' eyes out. The idea of doing what you propose much pleases me; and I agree to squeeze my buxom muse, as you happily call her, into a hundred of your pages. I will lace her so tight that she shall have the neatest little figure in the world. It shall be a very joyous little romance. I am afraid I can't tell you at this moment what it will be; for my dusky fancy contains nothing joyous enough: but I will invoke the jocund muse and come up to time. I shall probably develop an idea that I have, about a genial, charming youth of a Bohemianish pattern, who comes back from foreign parts into the midst of a mouldering and ascetic old Puritan family of his kindred (some imaginary locality in New England 1830), and by his gayety and sweet audacity smooths out their rugosities, heals their dyspepsia and dissipates their troubles. *All* the women fall in love with him (and he with them—his amatory powers are boundless;) but even for a happy ending he can't marry them all. But he marries the prettiest, and from a romantic quality of Christian charity, produces a picturesque imbroglio (for the sake of the picturesque I shall play havoc with the New England background of 1830!) under cover of which the other maidens pair off with the swains who have hitherto been starved out: after which the beneficent cousin departs for Bohemia (*with his bride, oh yes!*) in a vaporous rosy cloud, to scatter new benefactions over man—and especially, woman-kind!— (Pray don't mention this stuff to any one. It would be meant, roughly speaking, as the picture of the conversion of a dusky, dreary domestic circle to epicureanism. But I may be able to make nothing of it. The merit would be in the amount of *color* I should be able to infuse into it.) But I shall give you it, or its equivalent, by November next:—It was quite by accident I didn't mention the name of your admiress. Nay there are two of them! The one I spoke of, I think, is Lady Clark[2]—a handsome charming woman, of a certain age, the wife of a retired and invalid diplomatist who lives chiefly on her estate in Scotland. She takes in the *Atlantic* and seems to affect you much. The other is Mrs. Coltman, a modest, blushing and pleasing woman, who also has the *Atlantic,* and who can best be identified by saying that she is the sister of the widow of A. H. Clough, the poet—Lowell's friend. She is to take me some day soon down to Eton to show me an inside-view of the school, where her rosy little British boys are. Both of these ladies descanted to me on the *Atlantic,* and your productions and said nary a word to me of my own masterpieces: whereby I consider my present action magnanimous! Àpropos: the young girl in your comedy is extremely charming; quite adorable, in fact; and extremely real. You make them wonderfully well.—What more shall I say?—Yes, I find London much to my taste—entertaining, interesting, inspiring, even. But I am not, as you seem to imply, in the least in the thick of it. If I were to tell you whom I see; it would make a tolerably various list: but the people only pass before me panoramically, and I have no relations with them. I dined yesterday in company with Browning, at Smalley's—where were also Huxley and his wife and the editor and editress of the *Daily News:* among the cleverest people I have met here.[3] Smalley has a charming house and wife, and is a very creditable American representative; more so than the minister who, I am told, has never returned a dinner since he has been here. Browning is a great chatterer but no *Sordello* at all.—We are lost in admiration of Mr. Hayes; may his shadow never grow less. Blessings on your home.

Yours always truly
H. James Jr.

1. HJ outlines his plan for *The Europeans,* published in the *Atlantic,* July–October 1878.

2. Lady Clark was the wife of Sir John Clark, with whom HJ became good friends. See Letter 54.

3. Mr. and Mrs. F. H. Hill.

45 · To Henry James, Sr., and Alice James
Ms Harvard

Embley,
Romsey. Hants.
May 20*th* [1877]

Dearest father and sister.

I address you both together for economy's sake, and I pray you to divide my letter impartially between you. I have favors from both of you to acknowledge: from sister the charming gift of an American blotter brought me by Sara Sedgwick:[1] from father the letter of May 2d received three or four days (or more) ago. I was very grateful for the letter, as it was a long time since I had seen the paternal hand. The blotter gave me an exquisite joy, and sister could not have chosen a more sympathetic gift. It adorns my table and transfigures my room. *Apropos* of Sara Sedgwick I will give you news of her without more delay. I went down to Tilgate to see her on Tuesday last, and by Mrs. Nix's invitation dined and spent the night. Sara looked to me old and shrunken, but she seemed very cheerful and happy: though I should think the very dull life she must be booked for at Tilgate would be a rather severe test of her cheerfulness. Her cousin, Mrs. Nix, is an extremely pretty, charming and attractive woman—a most lovely being, in fact, to whom I quite lost my heart, and whom I am greatly indebted to Miss Ashburner (*tell her this*) for having introduced me to. She is married however, to a man grossly and painfully her inferior— a snob of the snobbish, I should say. The place is very beautiful (at least I thought so until I had seen *this* abode of bliss); but the life is I should think of a quietness beside which Kirkland Street is Parisian and Quincy Street a boulevard.—I must take up the thread of my London life where I left it last, I suppose: only I forget exactly where I left it, and I find I tend more and more to forget where I have been and whom I have seen. *Apropos* of this Sara S. tells me that you labor under the impression that I "go out immensely" in London, have a career etc. Disabuse yourself of this: I lead a very quiet life. One must dine somewhere and I sometimes dine in company; that is all. I have been to several dinners the last fortnight, two or three of which I can't for my life recall, though I have been trying for the last ten minutes in order to enumerate them all. I can mention however that I dined one day at Lady Rose's, a big sumptuous banquet where I sat on one side, next to Lady Cunliffe. (Lady Rose[2] is one of the easiest, agreeablest women I have seen in London.) Then I dined at the banquet of the Literary fund, invited nominally by Lord Derby, the chairman, in reality by good Frederick Locker.[3] I sat next to young Julian Sturgis, and opposite his papa (Russell S.)[4] but the thing was dull and the speechmaking bad to an incredible degree—dreary, didactic and witless. As many Americans would certainly have done better. Then I feasted at Mme Van de Weyer—a feast and nothing more, some unrememorable fine folk. Then a pleasant dinner at Hamilton Aïdé's,[5] whom Alice will remember as the author of novels which she used to read in the days of the "Fanny Perry intimacy." He is an aesthetic bachelor of a certain age and a certain fortune, moving apparently in the best society and living in sumptuous apartments. The dinner was in particular to George Du Maurier of *Punch* a delightful little fellow, with a tall handsome wife like his picture-women. I sat on one side next Mrs. Procter,[6] widow of Barry Cornwall, (mother of Adelaide P.) a most shrewd, witty and juvenile old lady—a regular London diner-out. *H.J.* "Tennyson's conversation seems very prosaic." *Mrs. P.* "Oh dear yes. You expect him never to go beyond the best way of roasting a buttock of beef." She has known everyone. On t'other side was a very handsome and agreeable Mrs. Tennant,[7] an old friend and flame of Gustave Flaubert. She was brought up in France. I dined a week ago at Lady Goldsmid's— a very nice, kindly elderly childless Jewess, cultivated, friend of George Eliot etc. who is of colossal fortune and gives banquets to match in a sort of country house in the Regents' Park. *H.J. to a lady after dinner.* "It's a very fine house." *The lady.* "Ow—it's like a goodish country house." I sat at Lady G's next to Mlle de Peyronnet, a very nice English-French youthful spinster, whose mother with whom I afterwards talked (Mme de P.) is, though an English-woman, the Horace de Lagardie who used to write *causeries* in the *Journal des Débats*, and of whom there is a tattered volume somewhere in Quincy Street. I met the mother and daughter (there is another daughter, Lady Arthur Russell, whose husband I have been introduced to and talked with at the *Cosmopolitan*) again at an evening crush at Lord Houghton's, of which the Princess Louise (a charming face) was the heroine; and where also, much *entourée*, was the Miss Balch whom Alice will remember at Newport, red-faced and driving in a little pony-trap, and who now figures in England as a beauty, a fortune and a fast person. She *is*, strange to say, divinely fair, not at all red-faced, smothered in pearls and intimate with the Marchioness of Salisbury (with whom, that is, I saw her hob-nobbing and who looks as if she had just cooked the dinner). Such is life—or rather Balch; who is living with another American spinster of the *décolleté* order, a Miss Van Rensselaer to whom Anthony Trollope (at Lord Houghton's) introduced me on the strength of having overheard her say that she heard I was present, and that I was the person she desired most to see!! *Notez bien* that the rooms swarmed with famous grandees. Miss V.R. by her American "chattiness" exhilarated me more than any *anglaise* I have talked with these six months, and though she was vulgar, made me think worse of these latter, who certainly are dull, and in conversation quite uninspired. (Anecdote of Mrs. Kemble's. *Frenchman sitting next to young Anglaise at dinner, who has said nothing for three quarters of an hour. "Eh, Mademoiselle, risquez donc quelque-chose!"*) *Apropos* of Lord Houghton: I breakfasted with him again lately—a very numerous breakfast—of the *Philobiblions*: mostly ancient gentlemen, and pretty dull. I went some time or other to another dinner at Mrs. Rogerson's, promiscuous and easy like most of her dinners, and with men preponderating: Mackenzie Wallace (*Russia*) Augustus Hare (*Walks in Rome* etc.) old Alfred Wigan, the actor, Lady Gordon, etc. I have dined furthermore at the Morton Lothrops' (of Boston) who has been staying in London, and in rather solemn and dullish fashion, at Mrs. Coltman's who is a sister of Mrs. A. H. Clough, with whom (strange as it may appear) I am staying since yesterday P.M., and until tomorrow A.M. at this beautiful place. Tho' you don't suspect it, this is Whitsunday, and all the world leaves London. Mrs. Clough sent me a very kind note (through her other sister, Mrs. Godfrey Lushington) asking me to come down here and stay with her aged parents, Mr. and Mrs. Smith. I had determined for the present to "stay" nowhere in England; but the temptation to get out of London for thirty six hours was great—to say nothing of seeing this lovely Hampshire country. The rest of the household have gone properly to church, and I sit in the library in a great deep window, looking out, while I scribble all this base gossip, into green gardens, and the oaks and beeches and cedars of a beautiful park. The place is a very vast and very fine one, tho' as Mr. Smith (a charming rosy old gentleman of eighty-two) tells me, not at all a "crack" one. In America however it would be "goodish," having a drive of rhododendrons four miles long! These kind and friendly people have come into it only two or three years since, I believe, through the death of Mrs. Smith's brother, Mr. Nightingale, uncle of Florence N. Mrs. Smith is also a rosy octogenarian and the old couple are even now creeping about together on the lawn, like Philemon and Baucis. Mrs. Clough is a stout and genial widow, of, I should suppose, mildly—very mildly—"liberal" tendencies, but not of commanding intellect or irresistible brilliancy. The whole household however *respire d'honnêteté* and kindness; Mrs. Coltman's rosy children, with their German governess, are sporting down one of the avenues, before me. There are of course several other people staying in the house, and I have a plan, after the lunch, to take a long walk, over to the New Forest, with a very nice young fellow who is one of the number. The place and the country are of course absurdly, fantastically fair. But I must break off, as I must go out on the lawn and say a word to Mr. and Mrs. Smith, who don't come to breakfast and whom I haven't saluted for the day. I will finish this evening.

3 *Bolton St. May 22d.* I had no time to resume my letter at Embly, and I hastily close it here, having returned last night. I have just received Alice's note enclosing Grace Norton's, and the thought of poor Jane's approaching end saddens me too much to write more. It is a great shock to me, as Sara Sedgwick had spoken as if she were quite on the way to recovery. What a strange fate for that genial, generous woman, so willing to live and with so many reasons to live! If all this were less true she might be living longer! I have just written to Grace.— I stopped over, another day at Embly, and drove yesterday through the New Forest: an enchanting country. On my way home I stopped at Winchester and saw the Cathedral. I have just received (*tell her, mother, when you write*) a long and delightful letter from Aunt Kate. Farewell. I fancy you all feel a personal grief as to poor Jane Norton—I send a few poor photos.

Ever your loving
H. James Jr.

1. Sara Sedgwick, the sister of Charles Eliot Norton's first wife, married Charles Darwin's son, William.

2. Lady Rose, before her marriage to Sir John Rose, was Charlotte Temple, an aunt of HJ's Temple cousins and sister of Mrs. Edmund Tweedy.

3. Frederick Locker (1821–1895), who took the name of Locker-Lampson in 1885, was a British civil servant and bibliophile who wrote light verse.

4. Russell Sturgis was a senior partner in the banking house of Baring Brothers and probably the original of Mr. Touchett in *The Portrait of a Lady.*

5. Charles Hamilton Aïdé (1826–1906), a Londoner of versatile artistic accomplishments and familiar figure in British society.

6. The witty Ann Benson Procter had known all the poets of the century from Shelley to Browning and was "an extraordinary compendium of wisdom and experience" (HJ to Grace Norton, 4 January 1879).

7. Mrs. Charles Tennant, the former Gertrude Collier, daughter of a naval attaché at the British embassy in France, had met Flaubert at Trouville. See Steegmuller, ed., *Letters of Gustave Flaubert, 1857–1880* (1982), p. 263.

Henry James and his father, 1854

Henry James's mother,
Mary Walsh James

Henry James in Boston,
age 16 or 17

Portrait of Henry James, age 17, by John La Farge

William James at 21

Alice James at 19 or 20

Henry James in Geneva, 1860

Portrait of Henry James by Abbott H. Thayer, 1881

Henry James in the 1890s; photo inscribed to an unknown friend

Constance Fenimore Woolson

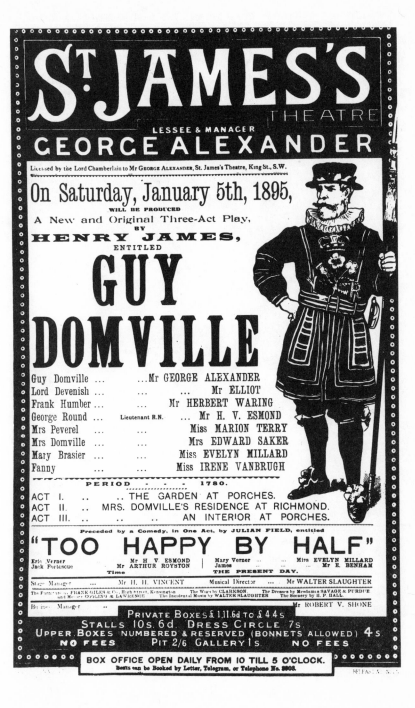

Poster for Henry James's play *Guy Domville*

Edith Wharton in 1905

Morton Fullerton in Paris, around 1907

Henry James in 1905

Portrait of Henry James by Jacques-Emile Blanche, 1908

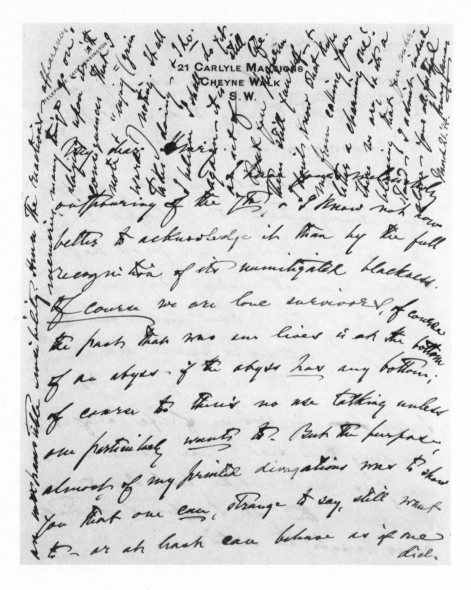

First page of letter to Henry Adams, March 21, 1914 (Letter 182)

46 · *To Gustave Flaubert*

Ms Louvenjoul

Londres

ce 15 avril [1878]

Cher monsieur Flaubert.[1]

J'ose penser que vous n'aurez pas oublié le bon accueil que vous me faisez il y a deux ans, lorsque je venais chez vous le dimanche avec notre ami Tourguéneff. Le souvenir de ces causeries auxquelles j'assistais un peu en étranger mais bien en admirateur, me permet de croire que vous aurez la même bienveillance pour la personne très-distinguée qui vous remettra cette lettre—Lord Houghton—homme d'état et écrivain anglais, est amateur de tout ce qui se produit en France de neuf et de frappant. Il serait très-flatté que vous lui accordiez votre connaissance et s'estimerait heureux s'il recontrait chez vous ce petit cercle de vos habitués du dimanche que j'avais souvent le plaisir d'y trouver: MM. Daudet, Zola, de Goncourt, etc. Lord Houghton s'intéresse vivement aux écrits d'Émile Zola et serait volontiers auprès de lui l'interprète du public très-nombreux et très-attentif qu'il possède en Angleterre. Je suis fort heureux, pour moi-même, de trouver une occasion aussi propice de me rappeler à votre bon souvenir et de vous remercier de nouveau de ces procédés amicaux par lesquels vous m'avez donné le droit de vous adresser un ami. Un homme de la valeur de Lord Houghton se trouve tout présenté rien qu'en le nommant, et j'ai voulu surtout le charger de vous exprimer mes amitiés et voeux très-sincères pour votre prospérité personnelle et votre travail. Voici le second hiver que je passe à Londres, mais je me promets d'année en année le plaisir de me retrouver à Paris au moment où vous y serez et de frapper bien discrètement à votre porte. Tout à vous, cher Monsieur Flaubert, d'admiration et de reconnaissance.

Henry James Jr.

1. Dear Monsieur Flaubert.

    I am permitting myself to believe that you have not forgotten the warm welcome you gave me two years ago when I visited you on Sundays with our friend Turgenev. The memory of these conversations, at which I was present rather as an outsider, but most certainly an admirer, suggests to me that you will have the same goodwill for the very distinguished personage who will give you this letter—Lord Houghton—the statesman and writer in England, a devotee of all that is new and striking now written in France. He would indeed be flattered if you would allow him to make your acquaintance and would be happy if he could meet, at your place, the little circle of Sunday habitués I often had the pleasure of encountering: *messieurs* Daudet, Zola, de Goncourt, etc. Lord Houghton has a lively interest in Émile Zola's writings and would willingly be spokesman for him to his large and attentive English public. I'm very happy for myself, to find an occasion as fitting as this one, to give you a reminder of myself, and to thank you once more for the warm circumstances during which you allowed me to call you friend. A man of Lord Houghton's value is introduced simply by being named. I wanted above all to ask him to express to you my friendly greetings and sincere best wishes for your personal prosperity and your work. This is my second winter in London, but I promise myself next year the pleasure of a return to Paris at the time when you will be there, to knock very discreetly at your door. All the best, dear Monsieur Flaubert, with admiration and gratitude.

Henry James Jr.

47 · To William James

Ms Harvard

Reform Club,
Pall Mall. S.W.
15 July [1878]

Dear William:

I have just heard from mother that you had decided to be married on the 10th ult: and as I was divorced from you by an untimely fate on this unique occasion, let me at least repair the injury by giving you, in the most earnest words that my clumsy pen can shape, a tender bridal benediction.[1] I am very glad indeed to hear that you have ceased to find occasion for delay, and that you were to repair to the happy Adirondacks under hymeneal influences. I should think you would look forward, in effect, to next winter's work more freely and fruitfully by getting your matrimonial start thus much earlier. May you keep along at a pace of steady felicity. The abruptness of your union has prevented me from a becoming punctuality in sending Alice a small material emblem of my good wishes; and now I shall wait till next autumn and the beginning of your winter life. I thank her meanwhile extremely for the little note—a charming note—that she sent me in answer to my own—and I feel most agreeably conscious of my intensification of kinship. I envy you your mountains and lakes—your deep, free nature. May it do you both—weary workers—all the good you deserve.

Ever your fond and faithful brother
H.J. Jr.

1. WJ had married Alice Howe Gibbens, who had recently returned with her widowed mother and two younger sisters from a five-years' residence in Europe. She was teaching in a girls' school in Boston when she and WJ met.

48 · To Mrs. F. H. Hill

Ms Taylor

3 Bolton Street,
March 21st [1879]

My dear Mrs. Hill[1]—

I must thank you without delay for the little notice of *Daisy Miller* and the "Three Meetings," in this morning's Daily News, in which you say so many kind things so gracefully.[2] You possess in great perfection that amiable art. But, shall I confess it? (you will perhaps guess it,) my eagerness to thank you for your civilities to two of my tales, is slightly increased by my impatience to deprecate your strictures with regard to the third. I am distressed by the evident disfavour with which you view the "International Episode;" and meditating on the matter as humbly as I can, I really think you have been unjust to it. No, my dear Mrs. Hill, *bien non,* my two Englishmen are not represented as "Arries"; it was perhaps the fond weakness of a creator, but I even took to myself some credit for the portrait of Lord Lambeth, who was intended to be the image of a loveable, sympathetic, excellent-natured young personage, full of good feelings and of all possible delicacies of conduct. That he says "I say" rather too many times is very probable (I thought so, quite, myself, in reading over the thing as a book): but that strikes me as a rather venial flaw. I differ from you in thinking that he would, in fact, have been likely to say it with considerable frequency. I used the words because I remembered that when I was fresh to England and first began to "go out," I was struck with the way in which they flourished among the younger generation, especially when the younger generation was of the idle and opulent and pleasure-loving type. Depend upon it, it is not only "Arry" who says "I say." There are gentlemen and gentlemen—those who are constantly particular about what they say, and those who go in greatly for amusement and who say anything, almost, that comes into their heads. It has always seemed to me that in this latter racketing, pleasure-loving "golden-youth" section of English society, the very atmosphere was impregnated with slang. A year ago I went for six months to the St. James's Club, where (to my small contentment, personally) the golden youth of every description used largely to congregate, and during this period, being the rapacious and shameless observer that you know, I really made studies in London colloquialisms. I certainly heard more "I says" than I had ever done before; and I suppose that nineteen out of twenty of the young men in the place had been to a public school. However, this detail is not of much importance; what I meant to indicate is the (I think) incontestable fact that certain people in English society talk in a very offhand, informal, irregular manner, and use a great many roughnesses and crudities. It didn't seem to me that one was bound to handle their idiosyncrasies of speech so very tenderly as to weigh one idiom very long against another. In a word the Lord Lambeths of the English world are, I think, distinctly liable, in the turn of their phrases, just as they are in the gratification of their tastes—or of some of them—to strike quiet conservative people like your humble servant as vulgar. I meant to do no more than just rapidly indicate this liability—I meant it to be by no means the last impression that he would leave. It doesn't in the least seem to have been so, with most people, and if it didn't sound fatuous I should say that I had been congratulated by several people whom I suppose to be of an observing turn upon the verisimilitude of his conversation.—If it didn't seem fatuous, too, or unmannerly, to inflict upon you so very bulky a bundle of exposition as this letter has grown into, I should go on to say that I don't think you have been liberal to the poor little women-folk of my narrative. (That liberal, by the way, is but a conciliatory substitute for some more rigid epithet—say *fair,* or *just.*) I want at any rate to remonstrate with you for your apparent assumption that in the two English ladies, I meant to make a resumé of my view of English manners. My dear Mrs. Hill—the idea is fantastic! The two ladies are a picture of a special case, and they are certainly not an over-charged one. They were very determined their manners should not be nicer; it would have quite defeated the point they wished to make, which was that it didn't at all suit them that a little unknown American girl should marry their coveted young kinsman. Such a consummation certainly does not suit English duchesses and countesses in general—it would be quite legitimate to draw from the story an induction as to my conviction on that point. The story was among other things an attempt at a sketch of this state of mind, and, given what I wished to represent, I thought the touches by which the attitude of the duchess and her daughter is set forth, were rather light and discreet than otherwise. A man in my position, and writing the sort of things I do, feels the need of protesting against this extension of his idea in which, in many cases, many readers are certain to indulge. One may make figures and figures without intending generalizations—generalizations of which I have a horror. I make a couple of English ladies doing a disagreeable thing—*cela c'est vu:* excuse me!—and forthwith I find myself responsible for a representation of English manners! Nothing is my *last word* about anything—I am interminably supersubtle and analytic—and with the blessing of heaven, I shall live to make all sorts of representations of all sorts of things. It will take a much cleverer person than myself to discover my last impression—among all these things—of anything. And then, in such a matter, the bother of being an American! Trollope, Thackeray, Dickens, even with their big authoritative talents, were free to draw all sorts of unflattering English pictures, by the thousand. But if I make a single one, I am forthwith in danger of being confronted with a criminal conclusion—and sinister rumours reach me as to what I think of English society. I think more things than I can undertake to tell in forty pages of the *Cornhill.* Perhaps some day I shall take more pages, and attempt to tell some of these things; in that case, I hope, there will be a little, of every sort, for every one! Meanwhile I shall draw plenty of pictures of disagreeable Americans, as I have done already, and the friendly Briton will see no harm in that!—it will seem to him a part of the natural fitness!—Since I am in for it—with this hideously egotistic document— I do just want to add that I am sorry you didn't find a little word of appreciation for the two other women's figures in the *I.E.*, which I really think a success. (You will smile at the artless crudity of my vanity!) The thing was the study—a very sincere, careful, intendedly minute one—of the state of mind of a couple of American women pressed upon by English circumstances—and I had a faith that the picture would seem life-like and comprehensible. In the case of the heroine I had a fancy it would even seem charming. In that of the elder sister, no, I hadn't such a faith: she is too garrulous, and, on the whole, too silly;—it is for a silly woman that she is offered. But I should have said it was obvious that her portrait is purely objective—

she is not in the least intended to throw light upon the objects she criticizes (English life and manners etc.); she is intended to throw light on the American mind alone, and its way of taking things. When I attempt to deal with English manners, I shall approach them through a very different portal than that of Mrs. Westgate's intelligence. I was at particular pains to mark the limitations of this organ —by some of the speeches I have put into her mouth—such as the grotesque story about the Duke who cuts the Butterworths. In a word she is, throughout, an ironical creation!—Forgive this inordinate and abominable scrawl—I certainly didn't mean to reward you for your friendly zeal in reading so many of my volumes by despatching you another in the innocent guise of a note. But your own frankness has made me expansive—and there goes with this only a grain of protest to a hundredweight of gratitude. Believe me, dear Mrs. Hill, very faithfully yours

H. James Jr.

1. Mrs. Frank H. Hill, wife of the editor of the London *Daily News*.
2. The review was of *Daisy Miller and Other Stories*. HJ makes an interesting slip in referring to his story of "Four Meetings" as "Three Meetings," the latter being the title of a tale by Turgenev.

49 · To Grace Norton

Ms Harvard

3, Bolton Street
Sunday A.M. June 8th [1879]

My dear Grace—

I have lying before me a letter of yours of which I will on no account mention the date, as I think there may be some slight chance of your having forgotten it. The paper is yellow and the ink faded with time; but as the sentiment which prompted it has I am sure by no means undergone a similar disfigurement I may allude with a certain boldness to its antiquity and trust you to believe that if *this* contemporary document is my first response to it, there are all sorts of excellent London reasons for the fact. And what can be better than a London reason? Nothing, surely, unless it be a London folly. In truth the follies here, half the time *are* the reasons; by the follies I mean the interruptions, the accidents, the innumerable engagements, the delusive and distracting social entanglements which interpose between one's bewildered vision and one's oldest friends all sorts of vaguely-grinning phantoms of acquaintances who demand for the time to be treated as realities, and yet who are so hollow and transparent that through their very substance one sees the images of the said old friends sitting afar off, neglected, patient, a little reproachful and divinely forgiving! But this morning, dear Grace, I am happy to say that I see you through no interposing British medium—it seems to me that I behold you in the highest relief and the most vivid distinctness, across an interval of the clear bright air that belongs to your customary summer habitation. I have settled in my mind that you have gone to Ashfield—or that if you have not you ought to have! I don't know why I say that—it's a strange world in which I pretend to talk to you even in jest about what you ought to have done!—I will go so far as to say that your letter came to me in the midst of the dark and dreadful winter from which even yet we can hardly be said to have emerged. It has been the most ingeniously detestable one I have ever known, and yet in spite of its horrors it has passed very quickly and left me with some pleasant impressions. It is difficult to talk to you about my impressions—it takes a great deal of space to generalise; and (when one is talking of London), it takes even more to specify! I am afraid also, in truth, that I am living here too long to be an observer—I am losing my sense of peculiarities and differences—I am sinking into dull British acceptance and conformity. The other day I was talking to a very clever foreigner—a German (if you can admit the "clever")—who had lived a long time in England and of whom I had asked some opinion. "Oh, I know nothing of the English," he said, "I have lived here too long—twenty years. The first year I really knew a great deal. But I have lost it!" That is getting to be my state of mind, and I am sometimes really appalled at the matter of course way of looking at the indigenous life and manners into which I am gradually dropping! I am losing my standard—my charming little standard that I used to think so high; my standard of wit, of grace, of good manners, of vivacity, of urbanity, of intelligence, of what makes an easy and natural style of intercourse! And this in consequence, of my having dined out during the past winter 107 times![1] When I come home you will think me a sad barbarian—I may not even, just at first, appreciate your fine points!—You must take that speech about my standard with a grain of salt—but excuse me; I am treating you—a proof of the accusation I have brought against myself—as if you were also a dull-eyed Briton. The truth is I am so fond of London that I can afford to abuse it—and London is on the whole such a fine thing that it can afford to be abused! It has all sorts of superior qualities, but it has also, and English life, generally, and the English character have, a certain number of great plump flourishing uglinesses and drearinesses which offer themselves irresistibly as *pincushions* to criticism and irony. The British mind is so totally unironical in relation to itself that this is a perpetual temptation. You will know the things I mean—you will remember them—let that suffice. *Non ragioniam di lor!*—I don't suppose you will envy me for having dined out 107 times—you will simply wonder what can have induced me to perpetrate such a folly, and how I have survived to tell the tale! I admit that it is enough for the present, and for the rest of the summer I shall take in sail. When the warm weather comes I find London evenings very detestable, and I marvel at the powers of endurance of my fellow "factors", as it is now the fashion to call human beings. (Actors—poor blundering unapplauded Comedians would be a better name.) Would you like a little gossip? I am afraid I have nothing very lively in hand; but I take what comes uppermost. I am to dine tonight at Sir Frederick Pollock's, to meet one or two of the (more genteel) members of the Comédie Française, who are here just now, playing with immense success and supplying the London world with that invaluable boon, a topic. I mean the whole Comédie is here *en masse* for six weeks. I have been to see them two or three times and I find their artistic perfection gives one an immense lift out of British air. I took with me one night Mrs. Kemble, who is a great friend of mine and to my sense one of the most delightful and interesting of women. I have a sort of notion you don't like her; but you would if you knew her better. She is to my mind the first woman in London, and is moreover one of the consolations of my life. Another night I had with me a person whom it would divert you to know—a certain Mrs. Greville[2] (a cousin, by marriage, of the Greville papers): the queerest creature living, but a mixture of the ridiculous and the amiable in which the amiable preponderates. She is crazy, stage-struck, scatterbrained, what the French call an *extravagante*; but I can't praise her better than by saying that though she is on the whole the greatest fool I have ever known, I like her very much and get on with her most easily. But why should I analyse poor Mrs. Greville to you? She is worth mentioning however as one of a family who form a positive *bou-*

quet of fools. Her mother, Mrs. Thélusson, who is one of the nicest women I have seen, is a simply delicious and exquisite goose, and her sister Lady Probyn is touchingly devoid of common sense. "They are all geese, but Mrs. G. is a *mad* goose!" That remark was made to me the other day by a dear friend of Mrs. G's and may serve you as a specimen—as a reminder—of the amenities of London conversation.— What shall I say more? (Don't bruit the above, by the way, abroad at Ashfield!) I dined last night in a sort of American circle—at the house of C. Godfrey Leland,[3] who has lived here many years and is (if you don't know it) a distinguished American author. I grieve to say that the occasion was not absolutely enlivening though after dinner there was one of those grotesque literary parties so common here, in which people are pointed out to you as having written the "most delightful" papers on the Icelandic dialects etc. The day before this I dined at the house of Mrs. Sutherland Orr, who is a very nice woman who writes in the *Nineteenth Century* against the "emancipation" of women (sensible creature) and has the further merit of being the sister of Frederic Leighton the painter (and new president of the Royal Academy) who is, in turn, the pleasantest (for simple pleasantness) man in London. The day before that I dined with three or four young men at a club, notably with young Arnold, a very intelligent clever fellow, a nephew of the sympathetic Matthew. I find young England often very pleasant—very ingenuous and intelligent. The day before that I dined with Mme du Quaire, where there were rather "smartish" people; and *ainsi de suite!*—I have seen a little this winter of your friend the John Clarks, but not as much as I should have liked. You know I am by way, as they say here, of liking them—"old black cat" and all. They have been a good deal bored this winter by having undertaken the guardianship of a couple of young girls (the Miss Van de Weyers) who have lately lost their mother, and have undertaken furthermore with these young ladies one of those common households which seem with the English a peculiar impossibility. It has ended in affliction and the poor Clarks have taken refuge again at Tillypronie, where if I remain in England I shall go once more and see them. But I shall not remain in England (you will perhaps be glad to hear that); I shall go abroad if possible, to breathe a little foreign (I hope a little Italian) air. But of course I shall return to London next year—I am a hopeless and helpless cockney, as I have told you before. Is that gossip enough, dear Grace? It is at least egotism enough. But I will add another egotistic item. I am just finishing a short novel which will presently appear in six numbers of Scribner.[4] This is to say please don't read it in that puerile periodical (where its appearance is due to—what you will be glad to hear—large pecuniary inducements); but wait till it comes out as book. It is worth being read in that shape.—I have asked you no questions—yet I have finished my letter. Let my blessing, my tender good wishes and affectionate assurances of every kind stand instead of them. Divide these with Charles, with your mother, with the children, and believe me, dear Grace, always very faithfully yours,

H. James Jr.

1. HJ wrote "some 107 times" but then crossed out the word "some." However, William Hoppin, first secretary of the American legation in London, recorded in his diary that HJ told him he dined out 140 times during the winter of 1878–79.

2. Mrs. Richard Greville (Sabine Matilda Thellusson) and her idiosyncrasies were further pictured by HJ in his account of how she took him to Tennyson's Milford cottage to hear the Bard read "Locksley Hall."

3. Charles Godfrey Leland (1824–1903), Philadelphia author and editor, best known for his German-dialect poems.

4. *Confidence* appeared in *Scribner's* XVIII and XIX (August–December 1879).

50 · To Alice James

Ms Harvard

Florence
April 25*th* [1880]

Dearest sister.

I think I announced in my last letter home that the next time I should write, you should be the object of my favours, and as this declaration has probably thrown you into a fever of expectation and impatience, I will prolong no further a silence of which I am already much ashamed. I am well aware that an abominable interval has elapsed since I last gave you news of me; but I on my side also have been waiting for a token from Quincy Street,—a token which however arrived three days since in the shape of a letter from mother, with date of March 28th (it had been delayed some days in London, where my letters during a temporary uncertainty as to address had at my request been retained). Thank our dearest mammy effusively—it is the letter in which she speaks of William's beginning to build his house, of the death of Wilky's father-in-law, etc., enclosing the letter from Bob describing Mr. Cary's funeral. I hope these events are having comfortable consequences; i.e. that William has chosen a happy model for his dwelling, and is seeing it rise to the skies with magic swiftness; and that Wilky's wife and children will be eased off, financially, by the demise of their relative. I got a characteristically quaint letter from Wilky about a month ago (telling me that something I had sent him had "identified me to his memory," and speaking in the highest terms of the conjugal and domestic virtues of his wife). In Bob's letter, enclosed by mother, he (Bob) sent me a graceful message (*à propos* of Hawthorne,)[1] but I can't make out whether or no he had received quite a long letter I wrote him before leaving London. If so I trust he will answer it—and will mother kindly mention it to him?—I wrote home last from Florence, and in Florence behold me still. In the interval, however, I took a short run down to Rome and Naples, spending in the latter place (or rather at Posilippo) three days with Joukowsky, who is the same impracticable and indeed ridiculous mixture of Nihilism and bric à brac as before, and who is living in great intimacy with Richard Wagner, the composer, who is spending some months at Naples, and whom Joukowsky thinks the greatest and wisest of men.[2] He endeavoured to *m'attirer chez lui* (that is J. did); but I kept away because Wagner speaks no French and I no German, as you are probably aware. Jouk.'s present plan—it will probably last about six months— is to go and live at Bayreuth "*afin de prendre part au grand œuvre*": that is to paint decorations for Wagner's operas. But as he believes that the Nihilists will presently overturn every human institution and make *place nette,* in order to begin afresh, he may not put this project into execution. He is always under somebody's influence: first (since I have known him) under Turgénieff's, then under the Princess Ourousoff's, whom he now detests, and who despises him, then under H.J. Jr. (!!) then under that of a certain disagreeable Onéguin (the original of Turgenieff's Neshdanoff, in *Virgin Soil*), now under that of Wagner, and apparently in the near future under that of Mme W., who is the daughter of the Abbé Liszt and Daniel Stern (Mme d'Agoult) and the divorced wife of Von Bülow, the pianist.—Naples, as regards her nature, seemed to me enchanting; but the vileness of her humanity took the edge from my enjoyment of the outlines of Vesuvius and Capri, and the classic blue of the Bay—all of which things I would give fifty times over for an hour of Rome, where I spent, very happily, five or six days. The pleasantest of these I went out and passed with Somerset Beaumont (a man you may have heard me speak of in England) who is living at an enchanting old Villa at Frascati, one of the loveliest places on earth. This day, which was in itself most charming, derived an extra merit from the contrast of Beaumont's admirable, honest, reasonable, wholesome English nature with the fantastic immoralities and aesthetics of the circle I had left at Naples, and which contained three or four other members I have not mentioned. At Rome I dined one day at the Storys', who were very friendly and *adulatory*, and another at Eugene Schuyler's, in company with the Waddingtons and their brother-in-law M. de Bunsen.—Florence just now is very lovely, and fairly favourable for work. I see more or less of the gentle and pure-minded Bootts; but less than I should do if they did not live up upon their hill top (to which they sometimes since removed again); the labour of scaling which under an Italian sun offers terrors to an individual prone to liquefaction. The simplicity of Boott's mental constitution only increases with age, but as it does so becomes easier to accept. Lizzie is also ever more acceptable than ever. I see no one else of importance here, though it is a place where one is liable to tea-parties; I have to call, for instance, on Constance Fenimore Woolson, who has been pursuing me through Europe with a letter of introduction from (of all people in the world!) Henrietta Pell-Clark. Constance is amiable, but deaf, and asks me questions about my works to which she can't hear the answers.[3] I shall probably remain absent from England till June 1st, my state of mind being divided between relief and regret at being away from London now. It is an excellent thing for me to be away, but my homesickness is keen, and I blush to confess that I have arrived at that prosaic maturity when the picturesqueness of Italy seems at times to but half console me for the lack of my club and my London habits. Love to father and mother and aunt. (I hope the latter sometimes sees my letters.) I greet you dearest sister on both cheeks.

Your fondest
H. James Jr.

1. HJ's critical study of Hawthorne, published four months earlier, had a hostile reception in the United States as seeming critical of America.

2. HJ seems to have been perturbed to find his Parisian friend Paul Joukowsky (Zhukovski) living in a veritable nest of homosexuals. HJ never met Wagner.

3. Miss Woolson (1840–1894), a popular American novelist, was a grand-niece of James Fenimore Cooper. She lived abroad after 1879, and became a close friend of HJ's. Her privately printed diaries and journals, edited by Clare Benedict, show that HJ called often and took her to galleries and museums in Florence. These meetings are recounted (in light disguise) in her tale "A Florentine Experiment." See Edel, *Henry James: A Life* (1985), pp. 155–157.

51 · To J. W. Cross

Ms Private

Florence
May 14*th* 1880

My dear Cross.

I have just heard of your marriage, and I must give myself the satisfaction of sending you a word of very friendly sympathy on the occasion—which I beg you to communicate, in the most deferential form, to your illustrious wife.[1] Receive my heartiest congratulations and good wishes, and try and fancy that they have hovering about them the perfume and promise of a Florentine Maytime. I have congratulated friends before on their approaching, or accomplished, nuptials; but I have never had the privilege of doing so in a case in which I felt (as today) all the cordiality of mankind mingling with my individual voice. Don't let the mighty murmur drown my feeble note, by the way; but remember that I am what the newspapers call a "distinct factor" in any sense of the good-will of your fellow-mortals that you may now enjoy. Don't on the other hand dream of answering this hasty note—you have probably so many letters to write. I am on the point of returning to England and I shall see you then. I wish I could fold into this sheet a glimpse of the yellow Arno, the blue-grey hills, the old brown city which your wife knows so well and which she has helped to make me know.—But I will only attempt to insert, again, a friendly handshake from yours very faithfully

Henry James Jr.

1. Cross had married George Eliot.

52 · *To Eliza Lynn Linton*

Ms Unknown[1]

[August 1880]

My dear Mrs. Linton.

I will answer you as concisely as possible—and with great pleasure—premising that I feel very guilty at having excited such ire in celestial minds, and painfully responsible at the present moment.

Poor little Daisy Miller was, as I understand her, above all things *innocent.* It was not to make a scandal, or because she took pleasure in a scandal, that she 'went on' with Giovanelli. She never took the measure really of the scandal she produced, and had no means of doing so: she was too ignorant, too irreflective, too little versed in the proportions of things. She intended infinitely less with G. than she appeared to intend—and he himself was quite at sea as to how far she was going. She was a flirt, a perfectly superficial and unmalicious one, and she was very fond, as she announced at the outset of 'gentlemen's society.' In Giovanelli she got a gentleman—who, to her uncultivated perception, was a very brilliant one—all to herself, and she enjoyed his society in the largest possible measure. When she found that this measure was thought too large by other people—especially by Winterbourne—she was wounded; she became conscious that she was accused of something of which her very comprehension was vague. This consciousness she endeavoured to throw off; she tried not to think of what people meant, and easily succeeded in doing so; but to my perception she never really tried to take her revenge upon public opinion—to outrage it and irritate it. In this sense I fear I must declare that she was not *defiant,* in the sense you mean. If I recollect rightly, the word 'defiant' is used in the tale—but it is not intended in that large sense; it is descriptive of the state of her poor little heart, which felt that a fuss was being made about her and didn't wish to hear anything more about it. She only wished to be left alone—being herself quite unaggressive. The keynote of her *character* is her innocence— that of her *conduct* is, of course, that she has a little sentiment about Winterbourne, that she believes to be quite unreciprocated—conscious as she was only of his protesting attitude. But, even here, I did not mean to suggest that she was playing off Giovanelli against Winterbourne—for she was too innocent even for that. She didn't try to provoke and stimulate W. by flirting overtly with G.—she never believed that Winterbourne was provokable. She would have liked him to think well of her—but had an idea from the first that he cared only for higher game, so she smothered this feeling to the best of her ability (though at the end a glimpse of it is given), and tried to help herself to do so by a good deal of lively movement with Giovanelli. The whole idea of the story is the little tragedy of a light, thin, natural, unsuspecting creature being sacrificed as it were to a social rumpus that went on quite over her head and to which she stood in no measurable relation. To deepen the effect, I have made it go over her mother's head as well. She never had a thought of scandalising anybody—the most she ever had was a regret for Winterbourne.

This is the only witchcraft I have used—and I must leave you to extract what satisfaction you can from it. Again I must say that I feel 'real badly,' as D.M. would have said, at having supplied the occasion for a breach of cordiality. May the breach be healed herewith! . . . Believe in the very good will of yours faithfully,

H. James

1. The text given here is reprinted from the biography of Mrs. Linton by George Somes Layard, *Mrs. Lynn Linton: Her Life, Letters, and Opinions* (1901). A Victorian bluestocking, Eliza Lynn Linton (1822–1898) wrote fiction, pioneered on "the woman question," and practiced spiritualism. She had written HJ to ask him whether Daisy Miller was "obstinate and defying, or superficial and careless," and told him that an argument over the story had lost her "the most valuable intellectual friend I ever had."

53 · *To Mrs. Henry James, Sr.*

Ms Harvard

Mentmore
Leighton Buzzard
Nov. 28*th* [1880]

Dearest mammy.

I received a good letter from you a few days ago, and as I have more leisure at this moment than I may have for some days to come, I will address you a few affectionate lines. (I have forgotten the date of your letter; but it was the one which enclosed that touching communication from poor Bob describing his health etc.) I wrote yesterday, briefly, to William, and he will, I suppose, give you the benefit, such as it is, of my note. This is a pleasant Sunday, and I have been spending it (from yesterday evening) in a very pleasant place. "Pleasant" is indeed rather an odd term to apply to this gorgeous residence, and the manner of life which prevails in it; but it is that as well as other things beside. Lady Rosebery (it is her enviable dwelling) asked me down here a week ago, and I stop till tomorrow A.M. There are several people here, but no one very important, save John Bright[1] and Lord Northbrook, the last Liberal Viceroy of India. Millais the painter has been here for a part of the day, and I took a walk with him this afternoon back from the stables, where we had been to see three winners of the Derby[2] trotted out in succession. This will give you an idea of the scale of Mentmore, where everything is magnificent. The house is a huge modern palace, filled with wonderful objects accumulated by the late Sir Meyer de Rothschild, Lady R.'s father. All of them are precious and many are exquisite, and their general Rothschildish splendour is only equalled by their profusion. Lady R. is large, fat, ugly, good-natured, sensible and kind; and Lord R. remarkably charming— "so *simpatico* and swell," as the young lady in Florence said: that is, *simpatico* as well as swell.

I have spent a good part of the time in listening to the conversation of John Bright, whom, though I constantly see him at the Reform Club, I had never met before. He has the repute of being often "grumpy"; but on this occasion he has been in extremely good form and has discoursed uninterruptedly and pleasantly. He gives one an impression of sturdy, honest, vigorous, English middle-class liberalism, accompanied by a certain infusion of genius, which helps one to understand how his name has become the great rallying-point of that sentiment. He reminds me a good deal of a superior New Englander— with a fatter, damper nature, however, than theirs. There are no ladies save a little Mrs. Godley, the *effacée* wife of a wonderful universal-information and high-sense-of-duty private Secretary of Gladstone, with whom (Godley himself) I also walked this afternoon;[3] and a graceful Lady Emma Baring, daughter of Lord Northbrook, whose prettiness, as is so often the misfortune of the British damsel, is impaired by protruding teeth. They are at afternoon tea downstairs in a vast, gorgeous hall, where an upper gallery looks down like the colonnade in Paul Veronese's pictures, and the chairs are all golden thrones, belonging to ancient Doges of Venice. I have retired from the glittering scene to meditate by my bedroom fire on the fleeting character of earthly possessions, and to commune with my mammy, until a supreme being in the shape of a dumb footman arrives, to ventilate my shirt and turn my stockings inside out (the beautiful red ones imparted by Alice—which he must admire so much, though he doesn't venture to show it), preparatory to my dressing for dinner. Tomorrow I return to London and to my personal occupation, always doubly valued after forty eight hours passed among *ces gens-ci,* whose chief effect upon me is to sharpen my desire to distinguish myself by personal achievement, of however limited a character. It is the only answer one can make to their atrocious good fortune. Lord Rosebery, however, with youth, cleverness, a delightful face, a happy character, a Rothschild wife of numberless millions to distinguish and to demoralize him, wears them with such tact and bonhomie, that you almost forgive him.[4] He is extremely nice with Bright, draws him out, defers to him etc., with a delicacy rare in an Englishman. But, after all, there is much to say—more than can be said in a letter—about one's relations with these people. You may be interested, by the way, to know that Lord R. said this morning at lunch that his ideal of the happy life was that of Cambridge, Mass., "living like Longfellow." You may imagine that at this the company looked awfully vague, and I thought of proposing to him to exchange Mentmore for 20 Quincy Street.—I have little other personal news than this, which I have given you in some detail, for entertainment's sake. I am very glad you sent me Bob's letter, which gives me a sense, most affecting, both of his trials and his advantages—I mean his good spirit, the esteem in which the railway people hold him, and his capacity for work. I hope the latter will soon return to him, but that, also, he may not again have to tax it so hard. I wish he had a little more of the Rothschild[5] element in his existence, and that I could do something to help him. Perhaps some day I may.—I spent last Sunday (from Saturday to Monday) at Sara Darwin's, whom I found apparently very well and bright—as lovable and natural as ever. I also beheld little Lily Norton and her grotesque resemblance to Charles. She seems to flourish, in a rather colourless way, under an amiable and talkative French governess. While I think of it, *àpropos* of nothing, *please send me a good photograph of Garfield*—I want to see his face. I hope the house is quiet and happy. I wrote a short note to father the other day, and will soon send him a longer one. (My note enclosed some cheques, and I hope came safely.)—I trust Alice's oral regimen is still a resource. I am sending her presently another hat, which I will write her more about, when I know the exact day it leaves, so that she may get it from Mrs. Mason, who takes it. I embrace you dearest mother, and also your two companions.

Ever your fondest
H. James Jr.

1. John Bright (1811–1889), son of a miller, was a leading opponent of the Corn Laws. He served in various posts in Gladstone governments from 1868 onward.

2. Between 1875 and 1928 Lord Rosebery's horses "won every great race with the exception of the Ascot Gold Cup." See Robert James, *Rosebery* (1963).

3. John Arthur Godley (1847–1932), first Baron Kilbracken, was Gladstone's principal private secretary.

4. Archibald Philip Primrose (1847–1929), fifth earl of Rosebery, was to be foreign secretary and, in 1894–95, prime minister.

5. HJ wrote "Mentmorish" but crossed it out and substituted "Rothschild."

3 · Conquests
1880–1890

With the publication in 1878 of "Daisy Miller," his short story about a young flirt from Schenectady, New York, Henry James achieved considerable international fame. Magazines in the United States and in Britain wanted his work, and he applied himself to reaping as large a harvest as possible. This was the period when, in tale after tale, and in a series of short novels, James exploited the "international"—indeed made it his own. He dealt with young Americans, bringing their liveliness and alertness, brashness and ignorance into citadels of European tradition. His general readers enjoyed his contrasts of manners and national traits and the brilliant comedy of his social situations. Critics perceived in James's work high moral values and an extraordinary grasp of how an environment functions through character. His humor was ironic and satirical, created with delicacy and instinctive charm.

James's conquest of London was sudden and thorough. He was promptly in demand in all the great houses as well as with the members of his own craft. In the annals of American letters no literary-social triumph was greater or more complete. To this time belong James's tales of "the chase for the husband"—the titled British pursuing American beauties, or the beauties in turn pursuing British titles. James was the original historian of the interplay that would ultimately lead to the marriage of an American divorcée with a British ex-king. The sense of confidence reflected in James's work, his intellectual power and wit, his observation and close study of character culminated in the masterpiece of his literary prime, *The Portrait of a Lady*, which tells the story of an intellectual young woman from Albany and her fateful marriage to an American expatriate in Italy.

After completing *The Portrait of a Lady*, HJ revisited the United

States, where his fame was recognized. He saw Washington for the first time and met President Chester Arthur; he visited his parents in Cambridge, and spent some time in Manhattan, his birth-city. He had been away for the greater part of a decade. The detailed record of his stay may be read in his first American journal (*Complete Notebooks*, 213–233) and in some of the ensuing letters.

The letters of these years show James at his epistolary best. They are in effect a chronicle of the American writer taking, in his thirties, the measure of Europe and understanding with extraordinary wisdom the eruption upon the European scene of the newly rich Americans, as well as the artists in search of a career, and the social climbers in search of European *cachet*. We see James in his letters moving with ease among the British and Scottish nobility; he is taken up by Sir Charles Dilke; he converses with Gladstone and John Bright; he meets his literary coevals, Trollope and Meredith, Tennyson and Browning; he visits all the great painters in their studios. It is a fascinating and easy life led outside his long lonely hours at his writing desk in Bolton Street and later in front of the large west window in De Vere Gardens, from which HJ looked out at flushed London sunsets and the great British metropolis—at Britain's late nineteenth century—and recorded it in his copious letters as well as in his works.

54 · To Sir John Clark

Ms Barrett

Metropolitan Club
Washington, D.C.
Jan. 8*th* [1882]

My dear Sir John.[1]

This is the fag-end of a rather busy morning, but I shall not let it pass without sending you a greeting. I meant to do so on New Year's day, but one isn't an American in America for nothing. It isn't the land of leisure, my dear Sir John, though it is doubtless to a certain extent that of pleasure. In the good old world one's mornings are sacred—and that is my letter-writing time. But here, as you know, we have abolished a good many of the sanctities, and the busy world

marks you for its own before you have left the matutinal couch. It is
not too late, however, to wish you a happy New Year, and a long con-
tinuity of the same. (By *you*, whenever I say anything pleasant, I always mean her Ladyship as well.) I want to give you a few *de mes
nouvelles*, and to ask for as many as possible of your own. If, however,
I should undertake to relate you my adventures and impressions in full,
I should scarcely know where to begin. My adventures indeed have
chiefly been impressions, for I have not been travelling extensively—I
have only been seeing people and things in Boston and New York. I
have spent a month in either place, and shall probably pass the rest of
the winter here, which is probably the most entertaining (on the
whole) of the three. I find here our good little friends the Adamses,
whose extremely agreeable house may be said to be one of the features
of Washington.[2] They receive a great deal and in their native air they
bloom, expand, emit a genial fragrance. They don't pretend to conceal (as why should they?) their preference of America to Europe, and
they rather rub it into me, as they think it a wholesome discipline for
my demoralized spirit. One excellent reason for their liking Washington better than London is that they are, vulgarly speaking, "someone"
here, and that they are nothing in your complicated Kingdom. They
have the friendliest recollection of you and Lady Clark, and you were
the first Europeans they asked me about when I arrived. I am spending
my time very pleasantly, seeing a great many people and finding every
one most genial and friendly. I too am "someone" here, and it will be at
a terrible sacrifice of vanity that I return to England and walk in to dinner after every one, alone, instead of marching with the hostess or the
prettiest woman present! But I love my London better than my vanity,
and expect to turn up there about the month of May. I should like to
put America into a nutshell for you; but like Carlyle's Mirabeau, it has
"swallowed all formulas." Things go very fast here, and the change
that has taken place in the last ten years is almost incredible. The increase of civilization, of wealth, luxury, knowledge, taste, of all the
arts and usages of life, is extremely striking, and all this means the
increase of the agreeable. I won't answer for what the country may
have become in this way a hundred years hence. New York today is a
very brilliant city—but it takes a great fortune to enjoy it, nothing
under a million (sterling) is called a great fortune there now. On the

other hand I believe that Washington is the place in the world where money—or the absence of it, matters least. It is very queer and yet extremely pleasant: informal, familiar, heterogeneous, good-natured, essentially social and conversational, enormously big and yet extremely provincial, indefinably ridiculous and yet eminently agreeable. It is the only place in America where there is no business, where an air of leisure hangs over the enormous streets, where every one walks slowly and doesn't look keen and preoccupied. The sky is blue, the sun is warm, the women are charming, and at dinners the talk is always general. Having been here but for a few days I haven't yet seen our British Minister, Sackville-West; but he appears to be much liked, and he has a most attractive little ingénue of a daughter, the *bâtarde* of a Spanish ballerina, brought up in a Paris convent, and presented to the world for the first time here.[3]—But while I sit scribbling here, where are you, my dear Laird? for I have not forgotten your dread scheme of sailing to the Cape. Are you rubbing shoulders with Kaffirs or tossing upon the Southern ocean? I won't take space in conjecture; but shall send this to Tillypronie to be forwarded. I shall write my name on the outside, so that if it falls into Lady Clark's hands she may perhaps have the gracious impulse to open it and see in it a sign of my attachment. I trust, however, that she is not at Tillypronie, but at the more genial Bournemouth, where I remember it was a part of your plan that she should winter. Wherever either of you are I hope you are decently well and *vraisemblablement* happy. I am deadly homesick for the chimney-pots of London, and shall behold them again, I devoutly trust, about the middle of May; for after all, my sojourn here is an exile mitigated by optimism! Tell me about the Boers and the Kaffirs, and tell me too that poor Arthur Coltman, to whom I send my friendly remembrance, is the better for his rough remedy. I hope *you* are not the worse for it. 3 *Bolton Street* will always reach me—or my father's—*Cambridge, Mass., United States.* But address rather Bolton Street, as the British mind has an indefeasible tendency to misdirect over here. It is the only fault I see in it.

Ever very affectionately yours
H. James Jr.

1. Sir John Forbes Clark, Bt. (1821–1910), and Lady Clark owned what HJ described as "the highest placed laird's house in Scotland" in Tillypronie.

2. Henry Adams (1838–1918) and his wife, the former Marion (Clover) Hooper, were HJ's principal hosts in Washington.

3. This was Victoria, illegitimate daughter of Sir Lionel Sackville-West and Pepita, a Spanish gypsy dancer. She married her half-cousin, who fell heir to the Sackville title, thus becoming Lady Sackville-West. Her daughter, Vita Sackville-West (Lady Nicolson), wrote a biography of Pepita.

55 · *To Isabella Stewart Gardner*

Ms Gardner

> Metropolitan Club
> 723 15th St.
> Washington, D.C.
> January 23rd [1882]

Dear Mrs. Gardner,[1]

Why shouldn't I put into execution today that very definite intention of writing to you from Washington? I have been here nearly three weeks and I ought to have a good many impressions. I have indeed a certain number, but when I write to you these generalities somehow grow vague and pointless. Everything sifts itself down to *one* impression—which I leave to your delicate imagination. I shall not betray it if I can help it—but perhaps I shan't be able to help it.—Washington is on the whole as pleasant as you told me I should find it—or at least that you had found it. I try to find everything that you do, as that is a step toward being near you. I went last night to the Loring's where you told me you had flung down your *sortie de bal* in the dusky entry, where it looked like a bunch of hyacinths,—and found there the repulsive and fatuous Oscar Wilde, whom, I am happy to say, no one was looking at.[2]—Washington is really very good; too much of a village materially, but socially and conversationally bigger and more varied, I think, than anything we have. I shouldn't care to live here—it is too rustic and familiar; but I should certainly come here for a part of every winter if I lived in the United States. I have seen a good many people, dined out more or less, and tried to make myself agreeable. The Adamses tell me I succeed—that I am better than I was in London. I don't know whether you would think that. I have not fallen in love nor contracted an eternal friendship, though the women, as a general thing, are pleasing. The most of a personage among them is Mrs. Robeson;[3] but she is fifty years old and fundamentally coarse. Very charming, however, with a *désinvolture* rather rare *chez nous.* There are also some charming girls—not rosebuds, e.g. Miss Bayard and Miss Frelinghuysen, who are happy specimens of the *finished* American girl—the American Girl who has profited by the sort of social education that Washington gives. Plenty of men, of course, more than elsewhere, and a good many energetic types; but few "accomplished gentlemen." I met the President the other day (at dinner at Mr. Blaine's) and thought him a good fellow—even attractive.[4] He is a gentleman and evidently has that amiable quality, a desire to please; he also had a well-made coat and well-cut whiskers. But he told me none of the secrets of state and I couldn't judge of him as a ruler of men. He seemed so genial however that I was much disposed to ask him for a foreign mission. Where would you prefer to have me? I wish the States over here would send each other ambassadors—I should like so much to be at the head of a New York legation in Boston—I see a good deal of our excellent Adamses, who have a very pretty little life here. Mrs. A. has perennial afternoon tea—two or three times a day—and frequent dinners at a little round table.[5]

I remain here till the middle of February, and after that I go back to New York for a fortnight. Then I go to make a little tour in the South, etc.; and *then*—and *then*—I should tell you if I were not afraid of betraying that emotion I spoke of in beginning. I hope you will be very amiable during the month of April, which I expect to spend in the neighborhood of Boston. I almost betray it there, and I must control myself. I hope you are having a genial winter—I should be delighted to hear a little about it. I venture to take for granted that your husband is completely recovered, and that you have never failed to be well. I remain

Very faithfully yours
H. James Jr.

1. Isabella Stewart Gardner (Mrs. J. L. Gardner, 1840–1924) commonly called "Mrs. Jack," Boston hostess and art collector, who built the Gardner Museum in the Fenway.

2. Wilde had just begun his celebrated American tour.

3. The wife of Congressman George Maxwell Robeson of New Jersey.

4. President Chester A. Arthur.

5. In "Pandora" (1884), a story about a "self-made girl," the American heroine obtains a foreign post for her fiancé from the U.S. president during a party at the home of the Bonnycastles, who can be recognized as the Henry Adamses.

56 · *To Lord Rosebery*

Ms Scotland

Boston
February 27th 1882

My dear Rosebery.[1]

Ever since I heard a few weeks ago that you had become the father of an heir to your greatness—and your goodness—I have wished to let you know that in this distant land I put candles into my window in honour of the event. This modest illumination was but the symbol of my sympathy and good wishes—fortunate father of a fortunate son! May the latter young man emulate your amiability and profit by your wisdom! He inherits at the outset a fund of good will which ought to make his little life a success even before other things arrive to confirm the tendency. I should have said this to you long ago, but that I have lately had a personal sorrow which has given me much occupation. My mother died suddenly a month ago, and the event has given me much to think of and to attend to. It will not however, probably, cause me to alter my original plan of returning to England in May. I spent the early part of the winter in seeing something of America—an extensive (and expansive) country, with many idiosyncrasies. It is not so much a country as a world—but you know all that better than I.—I am desperately homesick for London, and the intestinal convulsions of the British Empire only increase my tender interest in it, and my desire to be near the sick-room, as it were, to get the last news of the illustrious invalid. I am proud to think of the doctors—or nurses—I number among my friends—and I entreat you to use all your skill! I make my best obeisance to Lady Rosebery and I remain of your dear lordship, the very devoted

Henry James

1. See Letter 53.

57 · To William James

Ms Harvard

131 Mt. Vernon St. [Boston]
Jan 1st 1883

Dear William

I received this A.M. your note of the 20th, written after you had seen the news of Father's death in the *Standard*. I can imagine how sadly it must have presented itself, as you sit alone in those dark far-away rooms of mine. But it would have been sadder still if you also had arrived only to hear that after those miserable eight days at sea he was lost forever and ever to our eyes. Thank God we haven't another parent to lose; though all Aunt Kate's sweetness and devotion makes me feel, in advance, that it will be scarcely less a pang when *she* goes! Such is the consequence of cherishing our "natural ties!" After a little, Father's departure will begin to seem a simple and natural fact, however, as it has begun to appear to us here. I went out yesterday (Sunday) morning, to the Cambridge cemetery (I had not been able to start early enough on Saturday afternoon, as I wrote you I meant to do)—and stood beside his grave a long time and read him your letter of farewell[1]—which I am sure he heard somewhere out of the depths of the still, bright winter air. He lies extraordinarily close to Mother, and as I stood there and looked at this last expression of so many years of mortal union, it was difficult not to believe that they were not united again in some consciousness of my belief. On my way back I stopped to see Alice[2] and sat with her for an hour and admired the lovely babe, who is a most loving little mortal. Then I went to see F. J. Child,[3] because I had been told that he has been beyond every one full of kindness and sympathy since the first of father's illness, and had appeared to feel his death more than anyone outside the family. Every one, however, has been full of kindness—absolutely *tender* does this poor old Boston appear to have shown itself. Among others Wendell Holmes (who is now a Judge of the Supreme Court)[4] has shone—perhaps a little unexpectedly, in this respect. Alice has been ill this last twenty four hours—but not with any nervousness; only from nausea produced apparently from the doses of salvic soda that Beach has been giving her. She is at present much better. Your letter makes me nervous in regard to your dispositions of coming home. *Don't for the world think of this, I beseech you*—it would be a very idle step. There is *nothing* here for you to do, not a place even for you to live, and there is every reason why you should remain abroad till the summer. Your wishing to come is a mere vague, uneasy sentiment, not unnatural under the circumstances, but corresponding to no real fitness. Let it subside as soon as possible, we all beg you. I wrote you two days ago everything that there is to be told you as yet as regards Father's will.[5] Wait quietly till you hear more from me. I am going as soon as I can get away, to Milwaukee, and I will write you more as soon as I have been there. Aunt Kate is still here. Make the most of London.

Ever yours
H. James Jr.

1. The eloquent letter written by WJ from London, where he was staying in HJ's rooms, arrived too late to be read by his father. The full text is printed in Henry James, ed., *Letters of William James* (1920), I, 218–220.

2. WJ's wife, to be distinguished from Alice, his sister, mentioned elsewhere in this letter.

3. F. J. Child (1825–1896), professor of English at Harvard, best known for his five-volume edition of English and Scottish popular ballads.

4. Holmes was at this time a member of the Supreme Court of Massachusetts.

5. HJ was named executor of his father's estate.

58 · To George Du Maurier

Ms Harvard

115 East 25th Street,
New York
April 17th, 1883

My dear Du Maurier,

I send you by this post the sheets of that little tribute to your genius which I spoke of to you so many months ago and which appears in the *Century* for May.[1] The magazine is not yet out, or I would send you that, and the long delay makes my article, so slight in itself, rather an impotent conclusion. Let me hasten to assure you that the "London Society," tacked to the title, is none of my doing, but that of the editors of the Magazine, who put in an urgent plea for it. Such as my poor remarks are, I hope you will find in them nothing disagreeable, but only the expression of an exceeding friendliness. May my blessing go with them and a multitude of good wishes!

I should have been to see you again long ago if I had not suddenly been called to America (by the death of my father) in December last. The autumn, before that, I spent altogether abroad, and have scarcely been in England since I bade you good-bye, after that very delightful walk and talk we had together last July—an episode of which I have the happiest, tenderest memory. Romantic Hampstead seems very far away from East 25th St: though East 25th St. has some good points. I have been spending the winter in Boston and am here only on a visit to a friend,[2] and though I am *New-Yorkais d'origine* I never return to this wonderful city without being entertained and impressed afresh. New York is full of types and figures and curious social idiosyncrasies, and I only wish we had some one here, to hold up the mirror, with a fifteenth part of your talent. It is altogether an extraordinary growing, swarming, glittering, pushing, chattering, good-natured, cosmopolitan place, and perhaps in some ways the best imitation of Paris that can be found (yet with a great originality of its own.) But I didn't mean to be so geographical; I only meant to shake hands, and to remind myself again that if my dear old London life is interrupted, it isn't, heaven be praised, finished, and that therefore there is a use—a delightful and superior use—in "keeping up" my relations. I am talking a good deal like Mrs. Ponsonby de Tomkyns, but when you reflect that you are not Sir Gorgius Midas,[3] you will acquit me. I have a fair prospect of returning to England late in the summer, and that will be for a long day. I hope your winter has used you kindly and that Mrs. Du Maurier is well, and also the other ornaments of your home, including the Great St. Bernard. I greet them all most kindly and am ever very faithfully yours,

Henry James

P.S. I don't know whether your pen-and-ink is all for pictures; but if it ever takes the form of a short note, such a genial missive would find me at 131 Mount Vernon St. Boston, Mass. U.S.A.; or be punctually forwarded from my London rooms—3 Bolton Street, Piccadilly.

1. "Du Maurier and London Society," *Century* XXVI (May 1883), 48–65. HJ had met Du Maurier (1834–1896), the French-born *Punch* cartoonist (and later author of *Trilby*), in 1877; they became close friends.

2. HJ was visiting E. L. Godkin, editor of the *Nation*.

3. Caricature personalities in Du Maurier's *Punch* cartoons.

59 · *To Emma Lazarus*

Ms *Columbia*

131 Mt. Vernon Street
May 9th [1883]

Dear Miss Lazarus,[1]

I congratulate you heartily on your definite purpose of promising yourself of the other half (as it were) of our little world-ball, and send you with great pleasure a note to Mrs. Procter,[2] who is a most delightful and wonderful old person, and a great friend of mine. She doesn't "entertain" in the usual sense of the word—i.e. give dinners etc.; but she receives, eagerly, every Tuesday and every Sunday afternoons. She lives in a "flat," on the top of a high apartment-house, as her address. Send her my note by post, and send a word with it, saying that you will present yourself on the nearest Sunday or the nearest Tuesday, as the case may be, *without waiting to be* "asked." On Sunday afternoons you will be sure to find Browning there; go as often as you can. I will write to Mrs. P myself and ask her to make you acquainted with Lady Goldsmid, whom I think you will find it pleasant to know. Kindly send me your prospective London (bankers'?) address, that I may send you one or two notes more, in case I don't find time to do so before the 15th which I probably shall. Take everything "easy," amuse yourself largely and discreetly and believe me ever, very truly yours

Henry James

1. Emma Lazarus (1849–1887), whose verses are inscribed on the Statue of Liberty, had expressed to HJ a wish to meet certain poets abroad, notably Browning. HJ probably met her through her connections with the *Century*.

2. For Mrs. Procter see Letter 45, note 6.

3. Lady Goldsmid is described in Letter 45.

60 · *To Lady Rosebery*
Ms Scotland

Boston, U.S.A.
131 Mount Vernon St.
June 16th [1883]

Dear Lady Rosebery.

I have just inflicted on you one of those injuries which require an instant apology. I have given a note of introduction to you—and I hasten to notify you of this audacious assault on your liberty and leisure. Perhaps you will forgive me when I tell you that the bearer is a very discreet, intelligent and amiable young man, who will neither bother you, nor bore you, and who is incapable of rash insistence. His name—rather an odd one—is Lawrence Godkin, and he is the son of one of my oldest and best friends, a man of much distinction here, and one of our first—or I should rather say our first—journalists, Edwin Lawrence Godkin, Editor of the *Nation*, New York. The youth goes to Europe for the summer, and when his father asked me the other day for a few introductions for him I bethought myself that I might perhaps appeal to your benevolence. I ought, I know, to minimize the crudity of this appeal by specifying something that you might do for him; but specifying is under the circumstances rather a delicate matter. However, I will risk the suggestion that if you should be spending a Sunday at Mentmore and should have an interstice for a very slender young New Yorker, he would drop into it gratefully and I should be very grateful for him. Perhaps this, after all, only makes my proceeding more crude—so, in my uncertainty, I will drop the question and leave my modest *protégé* to one of those happy accidents by which—when they are not still happier intuitions—your friends so often profit. This at any rate is another pretext for writing to you;—I had one already, but two are better (for my incorrigible modesty) than one. My letter has been hanging over your head for some weeks past, and if it has not descended it is because even from here I have seen you buried beneath those whitening drifts which the London heavens—if there be a heaven above London—discharge at this season of the year, and I was unwilling to contribute a particle of postal matter to the deluge. Then I reflect that it is very likely that after all you won't answer me (before I next have the honour of seeing you) and that my letter therefore will not greatly make you feel its weight. After many detentions I have at last the prospect of sailing for England toward the last of August. That is not immediate, but it is definite; and it is a great improvement in the prospects I have had all winter which were (on account of interminable family matters) a departure incalculably postponed. I must not however speak to even so sympathetic a Briton as yourself, as if my attitude toward my native land were that of constantly attempted flight! It isn't that I love it less, but that I love London more, and that being of a nature eminently constructed for homesickness my positive and negative poles have by a fatal (yet delightful) accident got turned upside-down. But I am (through my veil of my homesickness) enjoying our American summer, which is a revelation of light and heat such as I haven't had for ten years—upwards of that time having elapsed since I last spent these months here. Your English June is, like your roastbeef (I don't mean that of Mentmore, where the golden mean prevails), under-done; whereas ours is cooked beyond the possibility of any further cookery. I feel like a well-selected joint, slowly revolving on the spit, under the eye of the great chef who presides over our destinies—and our temperature. Excuse these irreverent pleasantries and remember that hot weather is relaxing. My sister, who is in the country, has lent me a little house which she has in this place, and I am leading an existence which I fondly try to flatter myself is productive. That is I am trying to scribble, and if I succeed I shall have the honour of sending you what I produce. Boston becomes about the 10th of June a social desolation; every one is in *villeggiatura* and remains so till the autumn. I am under various promises to various friends to participate with them in this mode of existence, but I relinquish with regret the lonely town, where I wear the minimum of clothing, take many baths a day and dine mainly on lemonade and ices. American life in summer is however very pleasant, and, given our climate, people understand it very well—people, that is, who cultivate the breezy verandah and dine as much as possible in the open air, where the viands can by no possibility grow cold. There are in this part of the country various centres of *villeggiatura*—Lenox, Beverly, Nahant, Newport etc.—of which the fame may in some degree have reached your ears, and which are very charming and original. Newport indeed is given up to billionaires and "dudes" (I will explain the dude when I see you next); but the others are a very pleasant mixture of carnal comfort and sweet simplicity. I won't however undertake to write the natural history of the American "summer resort"; perhaps some day your enlightened curiosity will lead you to come and look into the subject. Of topics I am afraid that we have none to speak of here just now—now that we have all read Mrs. Carlyle, and "Mr. Isaacs,"[1] and even Ernest Renan's *Souvenirs de Jeunesse*.[2] We find Mrs. Carlyle rather squalid, but a great one for saying things well, and we thirst, generally, for the blood of J. A. Froude.[3] *Apropos* of saying things well, you will find some tremendously well said in the volume of Renan I just mentioned. "Des gens d'esprit vivent en Amérique, à la condition de n'être pas trop exigeants!" that is one of them, though of course it is insufferably impertinent. I won't bother you with vain conjectures about your family and your way of life—as I hope the former, and believe the latter, are all that can possibly be desired. I fix my eyes on your husband, through interposing newspapers, and the vision is always inspiring. Please to give him my friendliest—my very friendliest—regards. I feel very far away from English politics here, and I won't deny that there is a sweet repose in the feeling; all the more that I have them with such confidence in Rosebery, Smalley and Mr. Gladstone. I hope Rosebery is in good spirits and good health, and venture to believe in the former as I see he has been winning races—though I don't know that he does that for elation. Be so good, at any rate, as to congratulate him on anything that may have happened to him lately that he may happen to care about. I hope your little posterity flourishes, and shall return to England much agitated by conjecture as to whether your eldest daughter will remember me. I trust your season has been to your taste—neither too mild nor too wild! I have two excellent memories of about this moment—or a little later—of last summer. One is a breakfast—which I may perhaps be allowed to call *intime*—of which I partook in that dear little cylindrical room at Lansdowne House: the other is of a drive with Rosebery, the length of the Thames Embankment, late in the nocturnal hours. Each of these episodes, looked at across the Atlantic and from amid the vacancies of Boston, seems deeply romantic. I wish you a comfortable summer—many cylindrical breakfasts and also nocturnal drives, if you like them, and remain, dear Lady Rosebery, very faithfully yours

Henry James

1. *Mr. Isaacs: A Tale of Modern India*, a novel by F. Marion Crawford.

2. Renan's *Souvenirs d'Enfance et de Jeunesse* (1883) contains his celebrated invocation to Athena on his first view of the Acropolis.

3. J. A. Froude, as Carlyle's literary executor, had been publishing the biographical materials of Carlyle and his wife; his frankness disturbed and outraged the Victorian traditions of privacy and of respectful homage to the dead.

61 · To George Pellew

Ms Princeton

131 Mt. Vernon St.

June 23d [1883]

My dear Pellew:[1]

I found your thin red book on my table when I came in late last night, and read it this morning before I left my pillow—read it with much entertainment and profit. It contains many suggestive things very happily said, and I thank you much for your friendly thought in sending it to me. It is interesting as an attempt at scientific criticism of the delightful Jane—though when I read the first page or two I trembled lest you should overdo the science. But you don't overdo anything—you are indeed, I think, a little too discreet, too mild. I could have found it in me to speak more of her genius—of the extraordinary vividness with which she saw what she did see, and of her narrow unconscious perfection of form. But you point out very well all that she didn't see, and especially what I remember not to have seen indicated before, the want of moral illumination on the part of her heroines, who had undoubtedly small and second-rate minds and were perfect little she-Philistines. But I think that is partly what makes them interesting today. All that there was of them was feeling—a sort of simple undistracted concentrated feeling which we scarcely find any more. In of course an infinitely less explicit way, Emma Woodhouse and Anne Eliot give us as great an impression of "passion"—that celebrated quality—as the ladies of G. Sand and Balzac. Their small gentility and front parlour existence doesn't suppress it, but only modifies the outward form of it. You do very well when you allude to the narrowness of Miss Austen's social horizon—of the young Martin in *Emma* being kept at a distance, etc; all that is excellent. Also in what you say of her apparent want of consciousness of nature. A friend of mine in England went to see the "Cobb" at Lyme because in *Persuasion* it had inspired Miss A. with the unprecedented impulse of several lines of description. He said to himself that it must be wonderful, and he found it so, so that he bought a house there and remained. Do write another little red essay describing and tracing the growth of the esti-mate of local colour in fiction—the development of the realistic de-scription of nature—the consciousness of places being part of the story, etc. You will do it excellently. The quotation (by "Mr. Murch") you mention on p. 26, is simply the closing sentence of Macaulay's essay on Mme d'Arblay![2]—I shall be much interested in what you do next, and remain very faithfully yours,

Henry James

1. George Pellew (1860–1892) received the Bowdoin Prize at Harvard in 1883 for his dissertation on Jane Austen's novels. The letter contains one of James's rare comments on Miss Austen, over and above his ironies on the Austen cult in "The Lesson of Balzac."

2. The closing sentence of Macaulay's essay on Madame d'Arblay reads: "But the fact that she has been surpassed gives her additional claim to our respect and gratitude; for in truth, we owe to her not only Evelina, Cecilia and Camilla, but also *Mansfield Park* and the Absentee."

62 · To Grace Norton

Ms Harvard

131 Mount Vernon St.,
Boston
July 28*th* [1883]

My dear Grace,

Before the sufferings of others I am always utterly powerless, and the letter you gave me reveals such depths of suffering that I hardly know what to say to you. This indeed is not my last word—but it must be my first. You are not isolated, verily, in such states of feeling as this—that is, in the sense that you appear to make all the misery of mankind your own; only I have a terrible sense that you give all and receive nothing—that there is no reciprocity in your sympathy—that you have all the affliction of it and none of the returns. However—I am determined not to speak to you except with the voice of stoicism. I don't know *why* we live—the gift of life comes to us from I don't know what source or for what purpose; but I believe we can go on living for the reason that (always of course up to a certain point) life is the most valuable thing we know anything about and it is therefore presump-tively a great mistake to surrender it while there is any yet left in the cup. In other words consciousness is an illimitable power, and though at times it may seem to be all consciousness of misery, yet in the way it propagates itself from wave to wave, so that we never cease to feel, though at moments we appear to, try to, pray to, there is something that holds one in one's place, makes it a standpoint in the universe which it is probably good not to forsake. You are right in your con-sciousness that we are all echoes and reverberations of the *same,* and you are noble when your interest and pity as to everything that sur-rounds you, appears to have a sustaining and harmonizing power. Only don't, I beseech you, *generalize* too much in these sympathies and tendernesses—remember that every life is a special problem which is not yours but another's and content yourself with the terrible algebra of your own. Don't melt too much into the universe, but be as solid and dense and fixed as you can. We all live together, and those of us who love and know, live so most. We help each other—even un-consciously, each in our own effort, we lighten the effort of others, we contribute to the sum of success, make it possible for others to live. Sorrow comes in great waves—no one can know that better than you—but it rolls over us, and though it may almost smother us it leaves us on the spot and we know that if it is strong we are stronger, inasmuch as it passes and we remain. It wears us, uses us, but we wear it and use it in return; and it is blind, whereas we after a manner see. My dear Grace, you are passing through a darkness in which I myself in my ignorance see nothing but that you have been made wretchedly ill by it; but it is only a darkness it is not an end, or *the* end. Don't think, don't feel, any more than you can help, don't conclude or de-cide—don't do anything but *wait.* Everything will pass, and serenity and *accepted* mysteries and disillusionments, and the tenderness of a few good people, and new opportunities and ever so much of life, in a word, will remain. You will do all sorts of things yet, and I will help you. The only thing is not to *melt* in the meanwhile. I insist upon the necessity of a sort of mechanical condensation—so that however fast the horse may run away there will, when he pulls up, be a somewhat agitated but perfectly identical G.N. left in the saddle. Try not to be ill—that is all; for in that there is a future. You are marked out for success, and you must not fail. You have my tenderest affection and all my confidence.

Ever your faithful friend—
Henry James

63 · *To Theodore E. Child*

Ms Barrett

3 Bolton St. Piccadilly
Oct. 10*th* [1883]

My dear Child.

What a dear little note from Alphonse, and how I thank you for so fully transmitting it! My heart warms to him and I am most grateful to him for the rank he assigns me in the animal kingdom.[1] It seemed to me that in all these be-Britished years my French had become quite that of Stratford-atte-Bowe. I found your other note but last night on my return from Scotland, and the second came in this A.M. Thank you kindly; I shall be delighted to go to break bread with you somewhere, *aussitôt l'arrivée* in the city of sense, if not of the soul. My dream is to go over to Paris about Christmas time, and I anticipate the greatest pleasure from seeing Daudet, as I beg you to tell him, with many thanks. How charmingly he says whatever he has to say—*craquelé comme une figure*[2] is the happiest possible description of sunburn. I value you his compliment, but it is a terrible thing to have to live up to!—your account of Huntington is very interesting—there is something very humorous in the idea of his moving, after thirty years, five doors off! I am only very sorry to hear of his illness—I suppose you mean that he has one of the miserable incidents of an honoured old age, an affection of the *vessie*[3] or thereabouts. I hope the doctor will ease him off. Can't his friend Clemenceau[4] do something for him; or is Clemenceau occupied exclusively with the national bladder? Give

Huntington many good wishes from me, and tell him that I hope he not only collects the Great but recollects the small. I trust he will be still *dans son quartier* (not in Florence, I mean, if he still goes there) at Christmastide. I am sorry to have missed you when you were in this place—I only got back from America, where I had been since last December, on September 1st. I appreciate fully what you say about one's always remaining a foreigner and outsider in Paris; and it is because one is so much less so here that I cling to my London. Apropos of Paris and the foreign, how beautifully the French are conducting their relations with their neighbours! If only nothing will happen before Christmas.

Ever yours,
Henry James

1. Child sent a note from HJ to Daudet, who replied: "Remerciez Henry James de sa charmante et affectueuse lettre. S'il se tire de sa langue comme de la nôtre, c'est un rude lapin. J'aimerais bien le connaître. Amenez-le moi, je vous en prie, à son premier voyage; que nous déjeunions longuement et affectueusement." This may be translated: "Thank Henry James for his charming and affectionate letter. If he handles his own tongue in the way he handles ours he's a formidable guy [literally "a rough rabbit"]. I'd like to know him. Bring him along as soon as he comes so we may lunch leisurely and affectionately." Daudet had actually met HJ at Flaubert's in 1876.

2. Literally "crackle like a face."

3. The bladder.

4. Georges Clemenceau (1841–1929), a friend of Daudet and Zola, later premier of France, called "The Tiger" during the First World War.

64 · To Elizabeth Boott

Ms Harvard

3 Bolton St. Piccadilly
Dec. 11th [1883]

Dear Lizzie.

I must thank you tenderly for your copious and charming letter which came in this morning. The promptness of my answer must be the measure of my appreciation. Excuse me if I am rather brief—my correspondence, coming on top with my other scribbling, and always keeping pace with it, is so large and exacting. It is especially valuable to me to get news of Alice from one who sees her frequently—even though that news is condemned to be but indifferently good. She writes to me whenever she can, but I think I have no illusions about her condition. Her loneliness is of course a drawback; she is very fond of her independence and that is in itself an advantage to her. There are few people she would care to live with or to have live with her. It is my belief that in the course of time her health will mend; but I am prepared for many more delays and obstacles. She fortunately has great pluck, and in certain ways much freedom. I do not wonder she should not wish to come abroad while she is still so great an invalid; yet I confess I tremble when I think of Katharine Loring's absence. But time will help us all. It helped poor Wilky at last, and his death, which was an unmitigated release, lifts a great load off my mind. I am completely re-domiciled here—though not in St. John's Wood—having at the last moment changed my mind about that move and given up the house. It was a perfect little residence, with a pretty garden and a most commodious and agreeable interior—it had once belonged to a painter and the studio had become the dining room, a really noble apartment; but the place was too far from the centre of things and it was revealed to me in a dream that I should spend half the time on the roads. So that, *per ora,* having resisted that temptation I shall remain in these after all very comfortable and central rooms. They have many advantages. Sooner or later, I suppose, I shall take a house, but there is no hurry, and when I do a conjugal Mrs. H. is not among the articles of furniture that I shall put into it. I think, my dear Lizzie, that the human race is going crazy and am sorry to see that the madness has touched your gentle and luminous brain as well. Twenty people have spoken to me of late about renouncing my happy state—all save three or four taking upon themselves to urge it. Those three or four—the only wiseheads—have remarked "Don't—don't—for heavens sake!" and I never shall, my dear Lizzie, for I find life quite interesting enough as it is, without such complicated and complicating appendages. What strikes me most in the affaire is the want of application on the part of society of the useful, beneficent, and civilizing part played in it by the occasional unmarried man of a certain age. He keeps up the tone of humanity—he stands for a thousand agreeable and delightful things. People ought really to be ashamed not to feel better than that what one is doing for it. *Dunque, cara Lisa, non mi sposarò mai—mai!* The Rensellina is much improved—writes no more notes, cultivates reserve and discretion etc.; but even for this—*mai, mai.* The lady just mentioned is here still, having many social ties now, apparently in England. She has always her German maid and her little dog; but she has not as yet anything else. I heard the other day that she was engaged to Hamilton Aïdé: but the tale is not confirmed.— The Littératrice is also here, and is really an angel of quiet virtue; *ma non prenderò neppure lei!*[1] These ladies don't meet, fortunately, and both are behaving very well. Their stay in the British capital appears to be of indefinite duration.—I hope you won't doubt of my sincerity if I remark even in a sentence immediately following the above statement that I wish you were here too! I do indeed, for I think you would enjoy the artistic world of London, and find it intelligent, and cultivated—find it, that is, above all, sociable and entertaining. I went only last night to a pleasant artistic function: to see Leighton,[2] as president of the R[oyal] A[cademy], deliver the annual prizes to the students of that Institution. Boughton took me, who is a very good fellow, if a weak painter, and before it we dined together with dear little Abbey, the American, and Alfred Parsons,[3] the landscapist, his *fidus achates.* Leighton is wonderful for such an occasion as that—he *represents* admirably—and the thing was interesting. I often see Tadema,[4] and also Du Maurier, who has something in him singularly intelligent and sympathetic and satisfactory and whom I like exceedingly. Burne-Jones[5] I have become quite intimate with, and he sends me photos of his works, marked with assurances of his "affection." A few days hence I dine with Richmond, the younger, and also with Frank Dicey; so you see that, if you come, I am prepared to show you round among the British studios, despise them though you will, and Philistine though they be. Burne-Jones is really interesting, and is (privately) a most delightful caricaturist and pencil-satirist, little as you might suspect it. I hear with interest of your own exhibits and of your life and manners this winter. Give this to your father and tell him to read between the lines how I cherish and remember him. I shall write to him ultimately—or rather, I mean, proximately. I fear Lady Rose's[6] death will have checked your Newport visit. Poor Aunt Mary will feel it much. Ever dear Lizzie very faithfully yours

H. James

1. HJ is indulging here in considerable private wit concerning the rumors of his planning to marry. In coupling the bouncing "Rensellina" (probably Mrs. Philip Livingstone Van Rensselaer, whom HJ had met in London: see Letter 45) with Charles Hamilton Aïdé, the inveterate party-goer and aesthete of London society (see Letter 45, note 5), HJ is creating a highly incongruous couple. As for the "Littératrice" who is "an angel of quiet virtue," HJ affirms in his Italian phrase "but I will take not even her." She is probably Miss Woolson.

2. Frederick, later Lord Leighton (1830–1896), a neoclassical painter of immense prestige in his day. He had served as president of the Royal Academy since 1878.

3. George Henry Boughton (1833–1905) and Edwin Austin Abbey (1852–1911) were American painters residing in London; Alfred Parsons (1847–1920) was a British landscape painter and book illustrator.

4. Lawrence Alma-Tadema (1836–1912), a Dutch painter of the neoclassical school, who had settled in England. He was at this time at the height of his fame.

5. Edward Coley Burne-Jones (1833–1898), eminent Pre-Raphaelite painter, who portrayed women as willowy beauties.

6. Lady Rose, an aunt of HJ's Temple cousins. See Letter 45, note 2.

65 · To John Addington Symonds

Ts Lubbock

Paris
Jan. [Feb.] 22nd 1884

My dear J. A. Symonds.

Your good letter came to me just as I was leaving London (for a month in this place—to return there in a few days), and the distractions and interruptions incidental to a short stay in Paris must account for my not having immediately answered it, as the spirit moved me to do. I thank you for it very kindly, and am much touched by your telling me that a communication from me should in any degree, and for a moment, have lighted up the horizon of the Alpine crevice in which I can well believe you find it hard, and even cruel, to be condemned to pass your life. To condole with you on a fate so stern must seem at the best but a hollow business; I will therefore only wish you a continuance of the courage of which your abundant and delightful work gives such evidence, and take pleasure in thinking that there may be entertainment for you in any of my small effusions.—I *did* send you the Century more than a year ago, with my paper on Venice,[1] not having then the prevision of my reprinting it with some other things.

I sent it you because it was a constructive way of expressing the good will I felt for you in consequence of what you have written about the land of Italy—and of intimating to you, somewhat dumbly, that I am an attentive and sympathetic reader. I nourish for the said Italy an unspeakably tender passion, and your pages always seemed to say to me that you were one of a small number of people who love it as much as I do—in addition to your knowing it immeasurably better. I wanted to recognize this (to your knowledge); for it seemed to me that the victims of a common passion should sometimes exchange a look, and I sent you off the magazine at a venture, in spite of its containing an article (*à mon adresse*) of painfully overcharged appreciation from my dear friend Howells and a horrible effigy of my countenance; to neither of which did I wish to give circulation. I spent last winter in the United States and while I was there another old and excellent friend of mine, Sergeant Perry, the most lettered American almost, and most unsuccessful writer that I know, read me a portion of a note he had had from you, in which you were so good as to speak (in a friendly— very friendly way) of the little paper in the *Century*. The memory of this led me, when *Portraits of Places* came out, to wish to put you in possession of the article in a more decent form. I thank you very sincerely for the good-natured things you say of its companions. It is all very light work indeed, and the only merit I should dream of any one finding in it would be that it is "prettily turned." I thank you still further for your offer to send me the Tauchnitz volumes of your Italian local sketches. I know them already well, as I have said, and possess them in the English issue; but I shall welcome them warmly, directly from you—especially as I gather that they have occasional retouchings.

I lately spent a number of months in America, after a long absence, but I live in London and have put my constant address at the top of my letter. I imagine that it is scarcely ever in your power to come to England, but do take note of my whereabouts, for this happy (and possibly, to you, ideal) contingency. I should like very much to see you— but I go little, nowadays, to Switzerland in summer (though at one time I was there a good deal). I think it possible moreover that at that season you get out of your Alps. I certainly should, in your place, for the Alps are easily too many for me.—I can well imagine the innumerable things you miss at Davos—year after year—and (I will say it) I think of you with exceeding sympathy. As a sign of that I shall send you everything I publish.[2]

I shake hands with me [you], and am very truly yours

Henry James

1. "Venice" appeared in the Century XXV (November 1882), 3–23, and was reprinted in *Portraits of Places* (1883) and in *Italian Hours* (1909).

2. This is apparently the only extant letter from HJ to Symonds.

66 · *To Francis Parkman*

Ms Mass. Historical

(3 Bolton St. Piccadilly W.)
15 Esplanade
Dover
August 24th [1884]

My dear Parkman.

This is only three lines, because I cannot hold my hand from telling you, as other people must have done to your final weariness, with what high appreciation and genuine gratitude I have been reading your Wolfe and Montcalm. (You see I am still so overturned by emotion that I can't even write the name straight.)[1] I have found the right time to read it only during the last fortnight, and it has fascinated me from the first page to the last. You know, of course, much better than any one else how good it is, but it may not be absolutely intolerable to you to learn how good still another reader thinks it. The manner in which you have treated the prodigious theme is worthy of the theme itself, and that says everything. It is truly a noble book, my dear Parkman, and you must let me congratulate you, with the heartiest friendliness, on having given it to the world. Do be as proud as possible of being the author of it, and let your friends be almost as proud of possessing his acquaintance. Reading it here by the summer-smooth channel, with the gleaming French coast, from my windows, looking on some clear days only five miles distant, and the guns of old England pointed seaward, from the rumbling, historic castle perched above me on the downs; reading it, as I say, among these influences, it has stirred all sorts of feelings—none of them, however, incompatible with the great satisfaction that the American land should have the credit of a production so solid and so artistic. There was three or four days ago a review of it in the *Times,* very complimentary, but without evidence of the writer's knowing much of the subject, as the article was a mere mechanical evisceration of the book. I didn't send it to you, because I thought it wouldn't strike you as valuable—but I will do so, after all, by this same post; though it is very likely you will have seen this already.

I am spending the month of August at this rather dingy and cockneyfied resort—or rather no-resort—where I find white cliffs and a very amusing sea (crowded with all the sails of the channel), leisure for work and a blessed immunity from any social encounters. In a week or two I shall cross to Paris, there to spend the greater part of the autumn. I hope, wherever this finds you, that it will descend upon a happy scene. The scene I figure is that delightful back verandah of yours at Jamaica Plain, from which the world seems all festooned with wisteria. I have been disappointed, this year, of a general expectation and hope that in London, the summer would bring you forth. Aren't you coming soon again, and haven't you any more papers or cabinets to dive into? I shall be very glad when there are signs of your reappearance. This will be a very interesting autumn for dwellers on these shores—thanks to the spectacle of a general election, with a new and immensely democratized electorate. Neither party seems to me rich in ideas just now, but the Tories are pitifully poor, and poorer still in men. They must transform themselves or perish, and it will be curious to see their contortions, in the effort. The Liberals have only one word to conjure with: Gladstone, and they use it to satiety. It is still tolerably potent, but it won't last forever, and we shall see. Come and see too! unless you are too fascinated by the spectacle of Cleveland.[2] Do give my kindest remembrance to your sisters and believe in the personal gratitude of yours ever very faithfully

H. James

1. Francis Parkman (1823–1893), the American historian, published in 1884 the volume *Montcalm and Wolfe* in his series depicting the conflict for domination of the New World.

2. Grover Cleveland loomed as the Democrat likely to upset twenty-three years of Republican power in the United States. He was elected President in the autumn of 1884.

67 · To Francis Boott

Ms Harvard

Adelphi Hotel
Liverpool
Nov. 13th [1884]

My dear Francis.

As I wrote on Tuesday to Lizzie you will know of my being for the moment in durance here. Alice was so extenuated by her voyage that she is resting here till Saturday or Sunday. K. P. Loring has gone to Bournemouth and Alice will go there next week.[1] I sympathise with your discomfiture and uncertainty in Paris, and can imagine that you should look about you and think of another *séjour*. But, my dear Francis, I cannot advise you on the subject of coming to London, beyond saying that I should be very glad to see you there. Lizzie would like it, and you wouldn't—that is my impression—and Lizzie's liking would depend upon her remaining there long enough to settle down to some regular life and interest. I am afraid that as a simple transient even she would not get into the proper swing, swim or rhythm. We shall of course have the cholera there too—but I somehow don't dread it much in this "tubbing" country. I know of course nothing about the letting of studios. There are many in London, and I have no doubt that Pennington could give her much information about them. I should be happy—delighted—I needn't say—to help you in any way in my power. Clarges Street and Half Moon Street are *full* of apartments—and all the streets about Hanover Square, etc., Cavendish Square, etc. I know of no special ones, as having had my own quarters the last eight years, I have had no need of going elsewhere. I recommend you, if you come to London, to come first to an hotel and look about you for rooms. All the places have the notice, in the door or window, of "apartments." E. Jackson probably goes to 40 Clarges Street, where I have known many people to stay and be happy. Thank you for hoping I shall see him; I hope I shall not! He is a bore and I don't care about him. It is exactly against such people, in London, that one must defend one's life and one's time. I hope you won't— after a little—find sufficient ground for leaving Paris; I shrink from the responsibility of positively drawing you to London. *You* might give me some bad moments if I were to be the cause of your being miserable there. Here is a table: for and against a London winter.

AGAINST	FOR
Darkness.	Good fires.
Fog—bad climate etc.	Good lodgings.
Necessity of being sometime in the place to get going.	Good cabs.
Absence of foreign and American customs.	Chance of seeing people if you stay long enough.
General fact that Italians hate it, and most strangers who are there (in winter) on a mere temporary footing.	General interest and richness of the biggest city in the world.
	Good service—the best—good prices!
Presence of H. James etc.	Presence of H. James.

Give my love to Lizzie and tell her I pray your path may be lighted.

Ever yours affectionately
H. James

1. Illness now made HJ's sister a permanent expatriate. Her intimate friend Katharine P. Loring (1849–1943) was her companion throughout her long invalidism.

68 · To William James

Ms Harvard

3 Bolton St. W.
Feb. 14th [1885]

Dear William.

I am quite appalled by your note of the 2d, in which you assault me on the subject of my having painted a "portrait from life" of Miss Peabody![1] I was in some measure prepared for it by Lowell's (as I found the other day) taking for granted that she had been my model, and an allusion to the same effect in a note from Aunt Kate. Still, I didn't expect the charge to come from you. I hold, that I have done nothing to deserve it, and think your tone on the subject singularly harsh and unfair. I care not a straw what people in general may say about Miss Birdseye—they can say nothing more idiotic and insulting than they have already said about all my books in which there has been any attempt to represent things or persons in America; but I should be very sorry—in fact deadly sick, or fatally ill—if I thought Miss Peabody *herself* supposed I intended to represent her. I absolutely had no shadow of such an intention. I have not seen Miss Peabody for twenty years, I never had but the most casual observation of her, I didn't know whether she was alive or dead, and she was not in the smallest degree my starting-point or example. Miss Birdseye was evolved entirely from my moral consciousness, like every person I have ever drawn, and originated in my desire to make a figure who should embody in a sympathetic, pathetic, picturesque, and at the same time grotesque way, the humanitary and *ci-devant* transcendental tendencies which I thought it highly probable I should be accused of treating in a contemptuous manner in so far as they were otherwise represented in the tale. I wished to make this figure a woman, because so it would be more touching, and an old, weary, battered and simple-minded woman because that deepened the same effect. I elaborated her in my mind's eye—and after I had got going reminded myself that my creation would perhaps be identified with Miss Peabody—*that* I freely admit. So I bore in mind the need of being careful, at the same time that I didn't see what I could do but go my way, according to my own fancy, and make my image as living as I saw it. The one definite thing about which I had a scruple was some touch about Miss Birdseye's spectacles—I remembered that Miss P.'s were always in the wrong place; but I didn't see, really, why I should deprive myself of an effect (as regards this point) which is common to a thousand old people. So I thought no more about Miss Peabody *at all,* but simply strove to realize my vision. If I have made my old woman *live* it is my misfortune, and the thing is doubtless a rendering—a vivid rendering, of my idea. If it is at the same time a rendering of Miss Peabody I am absolutely irresponsible—and extremely sorry for the accident. If there is any chance of its being represented to *her* that I have undertaken to reproduce her in a novel I will immediately write to her, in the most respectful manner, to say that I have done nothing of the kind, that an old survivor of the New England Reform period was an indispensable personage in my story, that my paucity of data and not my repletion is the faulty side of the whole picture, that, as I went, I had no sight or thought of her, but only of an imaginary figure which was much nearer to me, and that in short I have the vanity to claim that Miss Birdseye is a creation. You may think I protest too much: but I am alarmed by the sentence in your letter—"It is really a pretty bad business," and haunted by the idea that this may apply to some rumour you have heard of Miss Peabody's feeling *atteinte*. I can imagine no other reason why you should call the picture of Miss Birdseye a "bad business," or indeed any business at all. I would write to Miss P. on this chance—only I don't like to *assume* that she feels touched, when it is possible that she may not, and know nothing about the matter. If you can ascertain whether or no she does and will let me know, I will, should there be need or fitness, immediately write to her. Miss Birdseye is a subordinate figure in the *Bostonians,* and after appearing in the first and second numbers, vanishes till toward the end, where she reenters, briefly, and pathetically and honourably dies. But though subordinate, she is, I think, the best figure in the book, she is treated with respect throughout, and every virtue of heroism and disinterestedness is attributed to her. She is represented as the embodiment of pure, the purest philanthropy. The story is, I think, the best fiction I have written, and I expected you, if you said anything about it, would intimate that you thought as much—so that I find this charge on the subject of Miss P. a very cold douche indeed.—

I shall be very willing to let little Howard James[2] have $25, to be taken by you out [of] the money you say you owe me—by which I think you mean the money you had *prélevé* (or borrowed) from my share of the Syracuse rents to pay for Father's book (that is, for your half of the costs). I'm writing to B. Temple to tell him I withheld the $100, I enclosed him a ten dollar greenback.—About Alice I have written to Aunt Kate two or three times quite lately, and there ought to be an agreement between you that she always forwards you my notes. I sent her a word this A.M. with a very short note of Alice's, and one of K. Loring's, both just received by me from Bournemouth enclosed. Alice is evidently now rather stationary, but not *bad.* She has been a month at Bournemouth but has not yet left her room. Her *legs* seem always a serious question. K. Loring and Louisa will probably remain at B. till the end of April, and then go elsewhere. I shall then go to Alice, who, however, may subsequently rejoin the Lorings in the place they go to. They spend the summer in Europe. I don't think the climate has anything at all to do with Alice's state. She isn't in the least in touch with it, always indoors, with the same profuse fires, never reached by the outer air. I am sorry—very—for your botherations about your house.

Ever yours,
H. James

1. HJ included in *The Bostonians* (which dealt with reform movements in Boston) the character of an elderly former abolitionist whom he called Miss Birdseye. In Boston, his readers identified this fictional personage with the real-life Elizabeth Palmer Peabody (1804–1894), sister-in-law of Hawthorne, friend of Margaret Fuller, and a leading Transcendentalist and reformer. Miss Peabody, in 1860, had founded the first kindergarten in the United States. There seems to have been an unconscious element in HJ's choice of a name for his character: "Birdseye" suggests the equivalent of a "Pea-body."

2. Howard James (1866–1920), a cousin.

69 · To Violet Paget (Vernon Lee)

Ms Colby

St. Alban's Cliff
Bournemouth
May 10*th* [1885]

My dear Miss Paget.

I take up my pen, as we used to say in our infancy; but who shall say what I can possibly do with it—in such a case? The difficulty is increased by the fact that I am on my knees, prostrate, humble, abject, in the dust. That is an awkward position for articulate and intelligible speech, and yet I can't hold up my head, or rise to manly stature again, till I have caught some glimpse of a hint of a hope—even from the mere tremor of one of your eyelids—that there lurks in your generous nature, some slight capacity to pardon my disgusting conduct, my odious, unmannerly and inconceivable delay in writing to you. It is more inconceivable to me than to you, I assure you, and I haven't the slightest hesitation in saying that it is the most discreditable act (if *act* it can be called!) of an otherwise tolerably decent and virtuous life. Don't judge me by it, or if so, leave room for an appeal; for I hereby declare to you that the rest of my days shall be devoted to removing from your mind the vile implication my ignoble silence must have produced upon it. I am really not a bad person to be indebted to for compensation, and compensation you shall have, my dear Miss Paget, if I leave every other future duty and pleasure unregarded. There, I shall sit up again, and even with supplicating eyes, venture to look you in the face; not because I precipitately and fatuously assume that I have been forgiven, but because I do respectfully hope that you have listened. This has been for me a winter of infinite domestic worry, preoccupation and anxiety, and my correspondence and many other social duties have been woefully neglected in consequence. After I had allowed myself to be prevented a certain time from writing to you, the simple *shame* of my situation, I assure you, settled upon me like a spell and paralyzed me quite. Every week that—by a detestable fatality—I didn't write, the redemptory step became more difficult, till at last I began to feel that any interest you may have had in hearing from me had completely died out and that if I were at last to address you, you would merely return my letter, as a document that had fallen below its opportunities and had no intelligible message for you. This of course is nonsense; you have tolerance for all aberrations that are not of purpose, but only of hapless and accidental form. I am down at this dull place looking after my poor sister, who is wretchedly ill, and who has been for me, these last six months, a great anxiety and occupation. She came from America just at the time *Miss B.*[1] came out, in very bad case, and I grieve to say, has steadily been getting worse. I am remaining with her for the present, and for I know not how much longer. My preoccupations on her account have had much to do with the *demoralized* state I sank into (there is no other word than that) on this subject of writing to you.

I read *Miss B.* with eagerness, of course, as soon as I received the volumes, and have lately read a large part of them over again. It is to me an imperfect, but a very interesting book. As regards the *idea* of it, the conception and presentation of the character of the heroine, I think it a very fine one. The girl is really a very noble and remarkable vision, and she is sustained with singular evenness, in the key in which you have pitched her—except, I think at the end, in regard to the last fact that you have to relate of her. Making every allowance for a kind of grand rigidity and mournful, dismal, heroism that you have attributed to her—her offering to marry Hamlin strikes me as false, really unimaginable. Besides, *he* wouldn't, I think: he must at last have been immensely afraid of her, and his fear would have been deeper than his vanity. But Anne lives in the mind (outside of that point) as a creature projected (from *your* intelligence) in all her strange, original, tragic substance and form, with real imaginative and moral superiority. The imperfection of the book seems to me to reside (apart from, occasionally, a kind of intellectualized rowdyism of style) in a certain ferocity. It will probably already have been repeated to you to satiety that you take the aesthetic business too seriously, too tragically, and above all with too great an implication of sexual motives. There is a certain want of perspective and proportion. You are really too savage with your painters and poets and dilettanti; *life* is less criminal, less obnoxious, less objectionable, less crude, more *bon enfant*, more mixed and casual, and even in its most offensive manifestations, more *pardonable*, than the unholy circle with which you have surrounded your heroine. And then you have impregnated all those people too much with the sexual, the basely erotic preoccupation: your hand has been violent, the touch of life is lighter. This however is a secondary fact, with regard to the book; the primary one (for me) is that it's after my own heart in this sense: that it is bravely and richly, and continuously psychological—that, for you, *life* seems to mean moral and intellectual and spiritual life, and not the everlasting vulgar chapters of accidents, the dead rattle and rumble, which rise from the mere surface of things. I find the *donnée* of *Miss Brown* exceedingly in the right direction—a real subject, in the full sense of the word; carrying with it the revelation of character which is the base of all things and finding its *perspective* in that; appealing too to the intelligence, the moral sense and experience of the reader. You have appealed—indeed, too much to that sense; and too little to two or three others—the plastic, visual, formal—perhaps. You have proposed to yourself too little to make a firm, compact work—and you have been too much in a moral passion! That has put certain exaggerations, overstatements, *grossissements*, insistences wanting in tact, into your head. Cool first—write afterwards. Morality is hot—but art is icy! Excuse my dogmatic and dictatorial tone, and believe it is only an extreme indication of interest and sympathy in what you do. I regard *Miss Brown* as a most interesting and (if the word didn't sound so patronizing I should say *promising*) experiment. It has, in this age of thinnest levity and claptrap, the signal merit of being serious. Write another novel; you owe it to yourself, and to me—to give me a chance to show how prompt I shall be on *that* occasion! Be, in it, more piously plastic, more devoted to *composition*—and less moral: for in that last way you will seem (if you care) to your probable readers less *im*moral than they appear to have found *Miss B.* Dear Miss Paget—I shall write you again—for my spirit is greatly friendly to you. I shall also soon send you a book. I hope you are well and are coming this summer to England. I don't venture to breathe a word of the hope of hearing from you: that would be much happiness for yours most faithfully

Henry James

1. Violet Paget (1856–1935), better known by her pen name, Vernon Lee, dedicated *Miss Brown* as follows: "To Henry James I dedicate for good luck my first attempt at a novel."

70 · To James Russell Lowell

Ts Lubbock

St. Alban's Cliff
Bournemouth
May 29th [1885]

My dear Lowell.

My hope of coming up to town again has been defeated, and it comes over me that your departure is terribly near.[1] Therefore I write you a line of hearty and affectionate farewell—mitigated by the sense that after all it is only for a few months that we are to lose you. I trust, serenely, to your own conviction of this fact, but for extra safety just remark that if you don't return to London next winter I shall hurl myself across the ocean at you like a lasso. As I look back upon the years of your mission my heart swells and almost breaks again (as it did when I heard you were superseded) at the thought that anything so perfect should be gratuitously destroyed. But there is a part of your function which can go on again, indefinitely, whenever you take it up—and that, I repeat, I hope you will do soon rather than late. I think with the tenderest pleasure of the many fire-side talks I have had with you, from the first—and with a pleasure dimmed with sadness of so many of our more recent ones. You are tied to London now by innumerable cords and fibres, and I should be glad to think that you ever felt me, ever so lightly, pulling at one of them. It is a great disappointment to me not to see you again, but I am kept here fast and shall not be in town till the end of June. I give you my blessing and every good wish for a happy voyage. I wish I could receive you over there—and assist at your arrival and impressions—little as I want you to go back. Don't forget that you have produced a relation between England and the U.S. which is really a gain to civilization and that you must come back to look after your work. You can't look after it there: that is the function of an Englishman—and if *you* do it there they will call you one. The only way you can be a good American is to return to our dear old stupid, satisfactory London, and to yours ever affectionately and faithfully,

Henry James

1. With the coming of a new president in Washington, Lowell ended his ministry in London and returned to his old home in Cambridge.

71 · To Grace Norton

Ms Harvard

15 Esplanade, Dover
August 23d [1885]

My dear Grace.

It is absurd to pretend at this distance of time that this is an "answer" to your good letter of—I won't tell you when; but as an independent and irrelevant utterance it carries you my love, and every friendly wish that my heart can feel or my pen can form. My imagination (perched close here on the edge of the sea) traverses that unprofitable element and figures you, though without enthusiasm, sitting in the bowery porch of your window and listening to the crickets shriek as they do in Cambridge on summer nights. I say without enthusiasm, because this is not the best position I could wish for you: I would rather believe you are in fresh fields, or even frivolous places, like Newport or Lenox, interposing a little absence, distance or even alienation, from the usual Kirkland Street. For me, I am spending a delightfully quiet month of August at this convenient though not intrinsically dazzling place, which I have at various times resorted to before, when I have wanted rest and retirement, and of which the

principal merit is that it is salubrious and destitute of any possible social encounter. I returned from Bournemouth on July 10th, spent the
rest of that month (worrying and panting through the hideous fag-end
of the season) in London; escaped hither three weeks ago, and am
meditating at the end of a fortnight a further escape, consisting of a
visit to Paris, from September 10th to November 10th. Alice has been
spending the summer at Hampstead Heath, with Katharine Loring to
minister to her; and is very considerably better, though still an extreme invalid. K.P.L. stays with her till December (probably); and
Alice spends the winter in London, not because it is an ideal place for
an invalid, but because she has no strength for foreign journeys. Such,
dear Grace, is a rapid sketch of my domestic situation. Add to it that I
am pegging away to finish the *Princess* (a long-winded novel which has
just begun in the *Atlantic*), and that I have various other literary (ulterior) projects, and you will know almost all about me that is worth
knowing. I went up to town the other day to attend the service for
Grant[1] in the Abbey (hoping my name, as an eager assistant, would be
in all the American papers: was it!). The service *per se* was fine and
impressive and the number of English "illustrious" present creditable
to international courtesy; but Archdeacon Farrar's address, or sermon
(much praised) was, to my sense, so vulgar, so cheap and fifth rate, as
to make the occasion rather a torture to me. I gave poor old Lord
Houghton[2] my arm to come out, and that was the last I saw of him. I
liked him (in spite of some of his little objectionableness), and he was
always only kind to me. A great deal of the past disappears with him. I
am *dying*, literally *dying*, to know something about Lowell: how he appears, gets on, comports himself, and how and where he intends to
live—if he does so intend—in his native latitudes. Surely, he will
come back: he ought to. Perhaps you will not think that; and if you
don't perhaps you will tell me what you think he *"had"* ought to do? I
can't make it out; but should be very thankful to you for news of him,
or any personal impression. Mrs. Kemble returns on September 1st
from her annual Switzerland with her monumental punctuality: she
has never failed of that day for forty years!—and I, as soon as possible
afterwards, go up to town to embrace her—as one embraces a monument. (She lands at Folkestone—also for forty years!—or our embrace
would take place on a plank of the vessel here.) I am spending the
most *unsocial* summer—to my great delight—that has rolled over me

since I came to England: having almost entirely succeeded in keeping out of engagements to pay "staying" visits—a process for which the small faculty I ever had is rapidly quite deserting me. They don't pay, compared with the inordinate amount of time they consume, and I, at the age I have reached, have purposes far too precious to put the rest of my few years to, to be able to devote long days to sitting about and twaddling in even the most luxurious country houses. I spent five days at Ferdinand de Rothschild's[3] the last thing before coming down here, and the gilded bondage of that gorgeous place will last me for a long time. Don't breathe it to a soul, but I am rather weary and sick of London. However, it is, on the whole, the best place for me to live, and the solution of the problem will be in learning to live there differently from what I have done hitherto. The London mind is now absorbed in the great "Dilke Scandal"[4]—no very edifying chapter of social history. It is, however, by no means without a certain rather low interest if one happens to know (and I have the sorry privilege) most of the people concerned, nearly and remotely, in it. Donald Crawford has applied for a divorce from his wife on account of her relations with Dilke, the lady being the sister of Mrs. Ashton Dilke, C.D.'s late brother's wife. Hearing of this, Mrs. Mark Pattison,[5] in India (staying at Madras with the Grant Duffs), heroically makes it known that she is engaged to be married to Dilke (by way of comfort to him), and the news is in all the papers. Meanwhile another London lady whom I won't name,[6] with whom for years his relations have been concomitant with his relations with Mrs. Pattison, and whose husband died (strangely enough) just at the moment as the Rector of Lincoln, has had every expectation that he was on the point of marrying *her!* This is a very brief sketch of the situation, which is queer and dramatic and disagreeable. Dilke's private life won't (I imagine) bear looking into, and the vengeful Crawford will do his best to lay it bare. He will probably not succeed, and Dilke's political reputation, with the "great middle class," will weather the storm.[7] But he will have been frightened almost to death. For a man who has had such a passion for keeping up appearances and appealing to the said middle class, he has, in reality, been strangely, incredibly reckless. His long, double liaison with Mrs. Pattison and the other lady, of a nature to make it a duty of honour to marry *both* (!!) when they should become free, and the death of each husband at the same time—with the public watching to see *which* he *would* marry—

and he meanwhile "going on" with poor little Mrs. Crawford, who is a kind of infant—the whole thing is a theme for the novelist—or at least for *a* novelist. I, however, am not the one, though you might think it, from the length at which I have treated the topic! It will perhaps refresh you among New England bowers. Where are you, dear Grace, how are you, and what sort of life are you leading? Do give me some news of Shady Hill and what time brings forth there. I haven't seen Sara Darwin[8] since she came home, though she kindly asked me to Basset, at a moment when it was impossible to go. Your Montaigne, in the *Nation*, is delightful. Believe ever in the interest and friendship of yours most faithfully

Henry James

1. Ulysses S. Grant had died on 23 July 1885.

2. The literary Lord Houghton had in earlier years been very hospitable to HJ. See Letter 40, note 1.

3. The patron of the arts had just completed Waddesdon Manor, his French chateau set into the English countryside, and HJ had visited it for the first time.

4. Sir Charles Dilke, described by HJ as very skillful and very ambitious, had compromised his successful political career by his various liaisons.

5. Widow of the Rector of Lincoln College, Oxford. HJ had met her in 1869 (see Letter 8) and described her then as "highly emancipated."

6. This lady was named soon enough during the court proceedings. She was Mrs. James (Christina) Rogerson, another friend of HJ's.

7. HJ was wrong. Dilke married Mrs. Pattison and retired from public life.

8. The former Sara Sedgwick.

72 · To Edward Tyas Cook

Ms British Library

3 Bolton Street W.
January 23*d* [1886]

Dear Sir.

I must request you very earnestly and explicitly *not* to publish the note I was so reckless as to write you a couple of days since and which you have sent me, to my great alarm and surprise, in proof. It was a strictly private communication, intended simply to mitigate the dryness of my declining to comply with your invitation (to discourse upon the 100 books), and I have the best reasons in the world for wishing it not to appear in the columns of the *Pall Mall Gazette*. I depend upon your fine sense of honour not to let it figure there and remain truly yours

Henry James

73 · *To Mr. and Mrs. William James*

Ms Harvard

Villa Bricchière
Bellosguardo, Florence
December 23d [1886]

Dear William and Dear Alice.

I address you thus unitedly because I last heard from you both together—that is a week ago, when a letter from each of you, of December 2d, came in—William's containing a post office order for the books I sent him from London. I am very sorry you deemed it necessary to refund me for the same, as it has spoiled all my fun in sending them. You say (William) that your not doing so will establish the habit of my expecting to pay for the things you ask to be got for you. Precisely—it is just the habit I wish to establish; I grieve that you won't permit it. I intended the books for a Christmas present, with the simple—and very fortunate—irregularity of knowing in advance what you wanted. *Basta!* I sent both of your letters off to Alice—but though they are not before me they are pretty well graven on the tablets of my mind. It appeased my solicitude at last to learn from you (Alice) some of the facts about your mother's disembarkation—or rather about her unpacking. Woeful and sickening must this have been—and please assure her and Margaret again that I have mingled my tears with theirs— and with the salt horrors of their trunks. I am much touched by your mother's kind intention about the Afghan. I should have been delighted with it, and its bright American tints would have thrown a glamour over the already rather Londonish tone of my apartment— but I feel the loss of it to be the least of the disaster. I left London on the 3d of the month and have been here since the 8th. I have taken a three weeks' "let" of this furnished villa (that is of an apartment in it) from the proprietress (of the apartment), my old and excellent friend Miss Constance Fenimore Woolson—the gifted authoress. She has taken it for two years, and being in another villa is not ready to come into it till January 1st. I get it for the interval and meanwhile enjoy the space, the views, and the big wood fires. It is close to the Bootts' old villa (where Miss W. has a temporary apartment) but it has much finer views—and my perch on this hilltop lifted out of Florentine interruptions, has given me capital quiet hours for work. The Bootts are in Florence proper, and I suppose you will already have heard that Lizzie gave birth, six days ago, very quickly and quietly, to a robust male. She has been doing remarkably well ever since, and so has the child, and the whole affair has gone off much better than was feared. Her marriage, on a nearer view, doesn't seem any less "queer"—save that it seems always to have existed.[1] Duveneck is a good frank fellow, without any small or nasty qualities—but it is impossible to converse with him for more than two minutes and he will be a weight for her to carry for the rest of her life—I mean socially, and in the world. He is only half civilized—though he is very "civil." Boott's acceptance of him, personally, *à toute heure de la journée,* is pathetic and heroic, and might have been made the subject of a little tale by Turgénieff. Duveneck's painting appears to have picked up since his marriage (it had languished much, before) but he has very few specimens in Florence. I go to Rome about a fortnight hence, for a week or two, and then proceed northward, with a stop in Venice and one in Paris. Alice was in excellent form when I left London—and her notes show that she continues so. My impression is that she more or less expects Katharine, for a month, about three weeks hence. If K. *should* come I may stay abroad longer. I congratulate you on Chocorua[2] (is that the name?) I hope it will bring you all rest and peace and joy; especially in the way of having it always awaiting you. I wish there were more of "that side" in my own existence. This is the ninth letter I have written this A.M. (though it is not A.M. but 4 in the afternoon and I have been at my table since 9.30). Therefore I will embrace you both and wipe my pen. I embrace the infants as well. I haven't seen the review of Edmund Gurney's book in the *Saturday,* but I can well believe it was "infamous." The latter is today a simply ignoble sheet—so ignoble for every kind of stupidity and malevolence as to be a discredit to the British mind. I bought Gurney's big volumes[3] just before leaving London—for Gurney's sake, but they were too big to bring along and I haven't read a word of them. Ever your affectionate Brother.

1. Lizzie Boott had married, the previous winter, Frank Duveneck (1848–1919), a highly gifted Kentucky-born painter with whom she had studied earlier in Munich.
2. William James had purchased a large tract of land in Chocorua, New Hampshire; he used the summer house there for the rest of his life.
3. Edmund Gurney's best-known work on psychical research, *Phantasms of the Living* (1886).

74 · To Katherine De Kay Bronson

Ms Private

Hotel du Sud [Florence]
Saturday [15 January? 1887]

Dear Mrs. Bronson.

I called yesterday on the McClellans,[1] which I have been meaning to do from day to day—since dining with them some time ago. Mrs. McC., whom I found alone, broached the subject of the Venetian letter, and what she said about her daughter's distress and remorse, and about the general confusion and mortification of the family, was of a nature to suggest to me that I had better repeat it to you—as it may enable you to let them down more easily. They are evidently much ashamed of the matter—though she had nothing but this profession of regret and dismay (at the thing having come back to Venice) to say in exoneration. Evidently the thing was very thoughtlessly and above all *youthfully* done (though that last is no excuse for the mother), but it was done in perfect good faith as regards their utterly failing to realize that Venice would ever hear of it. As if everyone didn't hear of everything to-day! However, that was their naïveté—added of course to the daughter's flippancy. They have lived (as poor Mrs. M. herself said) as the great McClellan's family (though why so great I know not) in such an atmosphere of newspaper publicity and reporterism that they have lost all sense of perspective and proportion—though evidently they have not lost the sense of mortification when pulled up, and are very capable of learning a lesson. I am only very sorry they have learnt it at the expense of the poor little Montenegros.[2] I gave no sign whatever, of course, that you had written to me—and professed ignorance of the whole phenomenon. Mrs. M. thought your first letter "too impulsive"—but appeared to have derived satisfaction from the second. They despair of being able to go back to Venice—and want to be assured that they may *eventually* do so without finding every back turned to them. You will doubtless not be able to give them this assurance, but I took upon myself to say (for the mother's account of the girl's compunction rather touched me) that the breeze would blow over and that people would hold out the hand to her on feeling, after a while, that the thing had been a *péché de jeunesse* much repented of. All the same I think they ought to go back—they ought to take that penalty as their punishment. But I wanted to mention to you that the mother had *sfogatoed* to me and that humiliation reigns in their house—so that it will be rather humane of you to try and pour a little oil on the waters both here and in Venice if you have a chance. But good heavens, what a superfluous product is the smart, forward, over-encouraged, thinking-she-can-write-and-that-her-writing-has-any-business-to-exist American girl! *Basta!*—I am happy to say that I received this A.M. (sooner than I expected) a letter from my sister, telling me that she takes me at my word and that she will remain in my house as long as I see fit to stay abroad. That is all I want and it makes the difference that I can now look forward definitely to spending a good many weeks to come in this land of every charm. It also makes the difference, dearest lady, that I now *shall* decide to put in my three weeks in Rome. As I have settled, as I mentioned, to stay here till about February 5th, that will bring me to Venice only in the first days of March—a date which I fear will seem to you rudely distant. *Per contra,* when I do come it will be for a long time. If no odious inconvenient and unpleasant thing occurs in the meanwhile, I shall spend the *whole* of the spring there. For intrinsic reasons as well—I mean the sweetness of the place at that time, it will be much better for me to take those months—all the same, the more I think of your benevolence the more I wonder that I am anywhere but flat on my face before you. It is indeed almost in this attitude that I subscribe myself ever affectionately yours

Henry James

1. May Marcy McClellan, daughter of the Civil War general, had been introduced into Venetian society the previous winter and had written a gossipy letter to the New York *World* about Italian social life, ridiculing certain members of the nobility. Published on 14 November 1886, it created considerable scandal. See HJ's *Complete Notebooks*, 40–43.

2. The Montenegro family were among the nobility lampooned by Miss McClellan.

75 · To Grace Norton

Ms Harvard

34 De Vere Gardens W.
July 23rd, 1887

My dear Grace

I am ashamed to find myself back in England without having fulfilled the inward vow I took when I received your last good and generous letter—that of writing to you before my long stay on the continent was over. But I *almost* don't fail of that vow—inasmuch as I returned only day before yesterday. My eight months' escape into the happy immunities of foreign life is over and the stern realities of London surround me; in the shape of stuffy midsummer heat (that of this metropolis has a truly British ponderosity—it's as dull as an article in a Quarterly), smoke, circulars, invitations, *bills*, the one sauce that Talleyrand commemorated, and reverberations of the grotesque Jubilee. On the other hand my small home seems most pleasant and peculiar (in the sense of being my own), and my servants are as punctual as they are prim—which is saying much. But I enjoyed my absence, and I shall endeavour to repeat it every year, for the future, on a smaller scale: that is, to leave London, not at the beginning of the winter but at the end, by the mid-April, and take the period of the insufferable Season regularly in Italy. It was a great satisfaction to me to find that I am as fond of that dear country as I ever was—and that its infinite charm and interest are one of the things in life to be most relied upon. I was afraid that the dryness of age—which drains us of so many sentiments—had reduced my old *tendresse* to a mere memory. But no—it is really so much in my pocket, as it were, to feel that Italy is always there. It is rather rude, my dear Grace, to say all this to you—for whom it is there to so little purpose. But if I should observe this scruple about all the places that you don't go to, or are not in, when I write to you, my writing would go very much on one leg. I was back again in Venice—where I paid a second visit late in the season (from the middle of May to July 1st)—when I got your last letter. I was staying at the Palazzo Barbaro, with the Daniel Curtises—the happy owners, to-day, of that magnificent house—a place of which the full charm only sinks into your spirit as you go on living there, seeing it in all its hours and phases. I went for ten days, and, they clinging to me, I staid five weeks: the longest visit I ever paid a "private family." The Curtises are very private—and a most singular, original and entertaining couple. If I were lolling in one of your arm-chairs I could tell you more—but I can't describe them as I scribble here without the disloyalty of *incompleteness*—so it is better to reserve them for the great occasion of the future, whenever it may come, when I shall *talk* everything my pen hasn't been able to manage. They were most friendly and hospitable—but I don't *think* I shall stay with them again—if I can avoid it without rudeness. They can't keep their hands off their native land, which they loathe—and their perpetual digs at it fanned (if a dig can fan) my patriotism to a fever. In the interval between my two visits to Venice I took again some rooms at the Villa Brichieri at Bellosguardo—the one just below your old Ombrellino—where I had stayed for three December weeks on my arrival in Florence. The springtime there was enchanting, and you know what a thing that incomparable view is to live with. I really *did* live with it, and rejoiced in it every minute, holding it to be (to my sensibilities) positively the most beautiful and interesting in the world. Florence was given over to fêtes during most of those weeks—the fêtes of the completion of the façade of the Duomo—which by the way (the new façade) isn't "half bad." It is of a very splendiferous effect—there is doubtless too much of it. But it does great honour to the contemporary (as well as to the departed) Italian—and I don't believe such work could have been produced elsewhere than in that country of the delicate hand and the insinuating chisel. I stepped down into the fêtes from my hill top—and even put on a crimson *lucco* and a beautiful black velvet headgear and disported myself at the great *ballo storico* that was given at the Palazzo Vecchio to the King and Queen. This had the defect of its class—a profusion of magnificent costumes but a want of *entrain*; and the success of the whole episode was much more a certain really splendid procession of the old time, with all the Strozzis, Guicciardinis, Rucellais, etc., mounted on magnificent horses and wearing admirable dresses with the childlike gallantry and glee with which only Italians can wear them, riding through the brown old streets and followed by an immense train of citizens all in the carefullest quattro-cento garb. This was really a noble picture and testified to the latent love of splendour which is still in those dear people and which only asks for a favouring chance to shine out even at the cost of ruining them. Before leaving Italy I spent a week with Mrs. Kemble on Lago Maggiore—she having dipped over there, in spite of torrid heat. She is a very (or at least a partly) extinct volcano today, and very easy and delightful to dwell with, in her aged resignations and *adoucissements*. But she did suggest to me—on seeing her again after so long an interval, that it is rather a melancholy mistake, in this uncertain life of ours, to have founded oneself on so many rigidities and rules—so many siftings and sortings. Mrs. Kemble is *toute d'une pièce*, more than any one, probably, that ever lived; she moves in a mass, and if she does so little as to button her glove it is the whole of her "personality" that does it.—Let us be flexible, dear Grace; let us be flexible! and even if we don't reach the sun we shall at least have been up in a balloon.—I left Stresa on the 15th of this month, had a glorious day on the Simplon amid mountain streams and mountain flowers, and came quickly home. I found here a note from Eliot [Norton] and immediately sent to him to come and lunch with me—but as I have had no answer he evidently has left town. I depend on seeing him later. And I depend also on seeing Lily [Norton]—probably I shall spend a Sunday at Basset next month. To prepare myself, perfidiously, for that incident, let me echo your judgment of the mistress of "Ridgemount." She has indeed a plentiful inanimacy and a strange absence of predictable qualities. But she is very ill—and very nice! Verily also, I think, very "near."—Lowell is the only person I have seen since I came back—he very kindly knocked at my door the morning after my return. He continues to be the simplest person in London, as well as one of the cleverest—and seems well and "gay" (!!) and as much as ever of a diner-out. He has lapsed (most wisely) into more modest quarters than he has hitherto occupied in London, and is now separated by a comfortable interval from his ambassadorship. Mrs. Smalley watches over him tenderly and is a most useful and devoted friend; she is a woman of a very fine nature and a very gentle presence. I dined with him yesterday—and she was there—in red velvet—and not her husband. But it is all right and most excellent for both of them. Don't keep this page which looks (accidentally) like silly gossip—but is mere friendly history. I wrote a good many (short) things while I was abroad—but they are buried in the bosom of the *Century, Harper, Atlantic* etc., who keep them, annoyingly, for what they suppose to be the mystic hour. *Pazienza* (that sounds conceited), and they will come. I am just beginning a novel about half as long (thank God!) as the *Princess*—and which will probably appear, at no very distant day, as a volume, without preliminary publication in a magazine. It will be called (probably) *The Tragic Muse;* but don't tell of it. I haven't answered your letter in the least, as you see—in the sense of taking it up piece by piece and making appropriate remarks and responses. But you will know none the less that I have digested it all. If you get a chance to give the friendliest of possible messages from me to poor Frank Parkman, please do so. Tell him I hold him in the highest sympathy and honour.—I go tomorrow A.M. to spend a day with Alice at Leamington—not having seen her, to speak of, for a year. She was there all last summer, from May, and directly after she came to town, late in the autumn, I went abroad. I got her to occupy my rooms a part of the time that I was abroad, to keep my servants from suicide, but she departed a month ago. I shall be here for the rest of the summer—save for little blotches of absence—and I look forward to some quiet months of work. I am trying, not without success, to get out of society—as hard as some people try to get in. I want to be dropped and cut and consummately ignored. This only demands a little patience, and I hope eventually to elbow my way down to the bottom of the wave—to achieve an obscurity. This would sound fatuous if I didn't add that success is *easily* within my grasp. I know it all—all that one sees by "going out"—today, as if I had made it. But if I had, I would have made it better! I think of you on your porch—amid all your creepers and tendrils; and wherever you are, dear Grace, I am your very faithful and much remembering friend,

Henry James

76 · *To Laura Wagnière*

Ms Unknown

[34 De Vere Gardens W.]
March 10*th* 1888

Dear Madame Wagnière.[1]

I don't think I know! Your curiosity is communicative and it makes me wish immensely I did.

But that isn't part of the story—what Mrs. Pallant said to the young man.[2] It was something pretty bad of course to make him give up, but the particular thing is a secondary affair whether it were true or whether it were false. The primary affair is that she told him something, no matter what—which *did* make him give up. The primary affair is also the nature and the behaviour of the lovely and inscrutable Linda. She thought Linda a monster of secret worldliness and in a fit of exaltation and penitence over her own former shabby conduct, wished to do something heroic and sacrificial to repair her reputation with her old lover. Therefore she abused the girl affectionately to his amorous nephew, but I have no light on what she said. She may have told him that she had been not as young ladies should be, but if she did I incline to think the statement was false. Linda was too careful of her future to have sacrificed to that extent to the present, and too little likely to have got into a mess that didn't pay—of course as you suggest (so sagaciously) it *might* have paid, and they were hard up etc.—But it wouldn't have paid in comparison with keeping straight and marry-ing—with patience—a lord or a millionaire. Yet I admit they were very hard up and that the thing *was* possible.

If it *had* happened, however, I think Mrs. P. would not, even in her exaltation, have mentioned it: whereas she might have done so if it were false. Do you understand? You see, I have in the story told you all I can for the money. I am as ignorant as you, and yet not as supposing!

It was charming to hear from you. I wish it were sight as well as sound. I shall pray for that and am ever faithfully yours

Henry James

I shall myself thank your mother for her delightful and generous letter.

1. Mme Wagnière, née Laura Huntington of Boston, a niece of Horatio Greenough, had married a Swiss-Italian banker.

2. Mme Wagnière had just read James's "Louisa Pallant," in which the mother of the young girl is so horrified by her daughter's calculating coldness that she warns a suitor against her. James did not relate what the woman had said about her daughter; in his characteristic way he avoided "vain specifications."

77 · To Frederick Macmillan

Ms British Library

34 De Vere Gardens W.
March 21st [1888]

Dear Macmillan.

I am just sending back the last proofs of my volume to Clark.[1] Therefore don't you think the enclosed title-page would perhaps do? I have thought of twenty things (Portraits Reduced, Figures Reduced, Faces and Figures, Smaller than Life, Essays in Portraiture, Likenesses, Appreciations etc. etc.—somehow they all sound—don't they?—like advertisements or *signs*); and this seems on the whole, the least objectionable.[2] It preserves the idea of the portrait, which is necessary, and conveys in a graceful and not obtrusive double meaning, both that the picture is *not* down to the feet, as it were, and that the appreciation is favourable—which in every case it happens to be. If however you should take a wild fancy to "Smaller than Life," I would give place to it. I think this improbable. If the title satisfies you will you please cause the note to Edinburgh to be posted. The sooner the book comes out the better, for I have an ardent wish that at as early a subsequent period as possible certain accumulated tales, which are panting to see the light in volumes, should be collected together. There will be by that time eight or nine of them—some of them rather long—and they will all have come out in periodicals by the time the last *Reverberator* (July 1st) is published in *Macmillan.* Therefore one might be getting them ready.

Yours ever
Henry James

P.S. I have left out six or seven of the original papers—and still the volume makes 408 pages!

1. The printers R. & R. Clark, Edinburgh.
2. The title *Partial Portraits.*

78 · *To Henrietta Reubell*

Ms Harvard

Aston Clinton,
Tring
April 1st 1888

Dear Miss Reubell.[1]

I wonder if you can give me any news of our poor desolate friend Boott—and of the helpless Duveneck as well? Have you seen them?— Have you heard from them or anything about them? I have heard from him of course but briefly and he is so simple and inexpressive that it is in [his] power to tell one very little about himself. I wonder much about him—in his hideously sad bereavement,[2] and if there were not great material obstacles and above all if one's *talk* with him would not be quite over at the end of the first three minutes—I would go over and see him. I wrote to him instantly that I would come if it would be a satisfaction or service to him, to see me, but he didn't take it up.

Lizzie's sudden death was an unspeakable shock to me—and I scarcely *see* it, scarcely believe in it yet. It was the last thing I ever thought of as possible—I mean before poor Boott's own surrender of his earthly burden. And the unnatural and most unhappy situation she has left behind her—those two poor uncongenial men tied together by that helpless baby—is something of which I don't see the solution. (I am writing in a room full of people talking—and they make me write erratically.) I have only wanted to ask you to send me three words when you *do* see Boott (whenever that is) and tell me what impression he makes on you—what he intends to do—what relation appears to exist between Duveneck and himself? Had you seen poor Lizzie long— or shortly?—before her death? What a strange fate—to have lived long enough simply to tie those two men with nothing in common together by that miserable infant and then vanish into space leaving them face to face! I shall miss her greatly. I had known her for twenty-three or four years—seen her for longish periods together—very familiarly, and I had a great affection for her. She was a dear little quiet, gentle, intelligent laborious lady. And the future looks dark for poor F.B.—one can only hope that it won't be long. The child is the complication—without it he and Duveneck could go their ways respectively—Duveneck to marry again in the fulness of time, and he to return to his Bostonian relationships and kindnesses, where he would be tenderly looked after to the end of his days. Have you seen any of

D's work this winter—and especially the portrait of Lizzie? Is it good or interesting? I came down here yesterday (it is the house of the sweet and motherly little old Lady de Rothschild and her daughter and son-in-law, the Cyril Flowers)³ to spend these two days of the Easter holidays. The house is full of people—Mr. and Mrs. Gladstone among others. So life goes on even when death, close beside one, punches black holes in it. This house is charming friendly and natural—by far the most cosy and homey of all the Rothschild houses.—I have seen the two great portraits which Sargent has sent over to go into the Academy—a month hence: Mrs. Marquand and Mrs. Boit. They are both full of talent life and style and as he only could have painted them, but very different from each other. Mrs. M. will do him great good with the public—they will want to be painted like that—respectfully honourably, dignement. It is a noble portrait of an old lady. Our dear Iza won't do him good—though she is wonderful and of a living! But she not only speaks—she *winks*—and the philistine will find her vulgar. Poor dear Iza!⁴ I hope you are in good form and am ever your *tout dévoué*

Henry James

1. Henrietta Reubell (1840–1924), child of an international marriage, that of the French Frederic Reubell and the American Julia C. Coster, maintained a successful salon at her home at 42 avenue Gabriel; she was the original for HJ's Miss Barrace in *The Ambassadors*. Her middle name is usually given as Talletta, which may have been a nickname; HJ once characterized her as "the tall Etta, who has so much *cachet.*"

2. Elizabeth Boott Duveneck had died of pneumonia in Paris on 22 March 1888.

3. Cyril Flower, later Lord Battersea, married Constance, granddaughter of Nathan Mayer Rothschild and daughter of Sir Anthony de Roy Rothschild.

4. Both portraits were a success; that of Mrs. Boit, the former Mary Louisa (Iza) Cushing, is now in the Boston Museum of Fine Arts.

79 · To Robert Louis Stevenson

Ms Yale

34 De Vere Gardens W.
July 31st [1888]

My dear Louis.

You are too far away—you are too absent—too invisible, inaudible, inconceivable.¹ Life is too short a business and friendship too delicate a matter for such tricks—for cutting great gory masses out of 'em by the year at a time. Therefore come back. Hang it all—sink it all and come back. A little more and I shall cease to believe in you: I don't mean (in the usual implied phrase) in your veracity, but literally and more fatally in your relevancy—your objective reality. You have become a beautiful myth—a kind of unnatural uncomfortable unburied *mort.* You put forth a beautiful monthly voice, with such happy notes in it—but it comes from too far away, from the other side of the globe, while I vaguely know that you are crawling like a fly on the nether surface of my chair. Your adventures, no doubt, are wonderful, but I don't successfully evoke them, understand them, believe in them. I do in those you write, heaven knows—but I don't in those you perform, though the latter, I know, are to lead to new revelations of the former and your capacity for them is certainly wonderful enough. This is a selfish personal cry: I wish you back; for literature is lonely and Bournemouth is barren without you. Your place in my affection has not been usurped by another—for there is not the least little scrap of another to usurp it. If there were I would perversely try to care for him. But there isn't—I repeat, and I literally care for nothing but your return. I haven't even your novel to stay my stomach withal. The wan wet months elapse and I see no sign of it. The beautiful portrait of your wife shimmers at me from my chimney-piece—brought some months ago by the natural McClure[2]—but seems to refer to one as dim and distant and delightful as a "toast" of the last century. I wish I could make you homesick—I wish I could spoil your fun. It is a very featureless time. The summer is rank with rheumatism—a dark, drowned, unprecedented season. The town is empty but I am not going away. I have no money, but I have a little work. I have lately written several short fictions—but you may not see them unless you come home. I have just begun a novel which is to run through the *Atlantic* from January 1st and which I aspire to finish by the end of this year. In reality I suppose I shall not be fully delivered of it before the middle of next.[3] After that, with God's help, I propose, for a longish period, to do nothing but short lengths. I want to leave a multitude of pictures of my time, projecting my small circular frame upon as many different spots as possible and going in for number as well as quality, so that the number may constitute a total having a certain value as observation and testimony. But there isn't so much as a creature here even to whisper such an intention to. Nothing lifts its hand in these islands save blackguard party politics. Criticism is of an abject density and puerility—it doesn't exist—it writes the intellect of our race too low. Lang,[4] in the D[aily] N[ews], every morning, and I believe in a hundred other places, uses his beautiful thin facility to write everything down to the lowest level of Philistine twaddle—the view of the old lady round the corner or the clever person at the dinner party. The incorporated society of authors (I belong to it, and so do you, I think, but I don't know what it is) gave a dinner the other night to American literati to thank them for praying for international copyright. I carefully forbore to go, thinking the gratulation premature, and I see by this morning's *Times* that the banquetted boon is further off than ever. Edmund Gosse has sent me his clever little life of Congreve, just out, and I have read it—but it isn't so good as his Raleigh.[5] But no more of the insufferable subject. I see—or have lately seen—Colvin[6] in the mazes of the town—defeated of his friends' hope for him of the headship of the museum—but bearing the scarcely-doubted-of loss with a gallantry which still marks him out for honourable preferment. I believe he has had domestic annoyances of a grave order—some embroilment in the City, of his feckless brother and consequent loss of income to his Mother etc.—Of all this however, I have only vague knowledge—only enough to be struck with the fine way he is not worsted by it. We always talk of you—but more and more as a fact not incontestable. "Some say he is going to such and such a place—there is a legend in another quarter that he was last heard of—or that it is generally supposed—" But it is weak, disheartened stuff. Come, my dear Louis, grow not too thin. I can't question you—because, as I say, I don't conjure you up. You have killed the imagination in me—that part of it which formed your element and in which you sat vivid and near. Your wife and Mother and Mr. Lloyd suffer also—I must confess it—by this failure of breath, of faith. Of course I have your letter— from Manasquan (is that the idiotic name?) of the—ingenuous me, to think there was a date! It was terribly impersonal—it did me little good. A little more and I shan't believe in you enough to bless you. Take this, therefore, as your last chance. I follow all with an aching wing, an inadequate geography and an ineradicable hope. Ever, my dear Louis, yours, to the last snub—

Henry James

1. Stevenson had gone to the South Seas, never to return. He and HJ had been warm friends since their meetings in 1885 at Bournemouth, where HJ had gone to be near his sister Alice. They continued their highly styled correspondence until Stevenson's death. Many of their letters were published in Janet Adam Smith, ed., *Henry James and Robert Louis Stevenson* (1948).

2. S. S. McClure (1857–1949) had founded a literary syndicate in New York, purchasing short stories from writers and selling them at low prices to newspapers. Stevenson sold serial rights of *St. Ives* to McClure, and then a series of South Sea letters. McClure, while in England, had called on HJ with an introduction from Stevenson. In his memoirs, *My Autobiography* (written for him by Willa Cather), McClure says that James "questioned me minutely about everything pertaining to Stevenson. His interest was keen, sympathetic, personal."

3. *The Tragic Muse* ran from January 1889 to May 1890 in the *Atlantic*.

4. For Andrew Lang, see Letter 40, note 2.

5. Gosse's *Congreve* had just been published; his *Raleigh* had appeared in 1886.

6. Sidney Colvin (1845–1927) had been Slade Professor of Fine Art at Cambridge and was now keeper of the prints and drawings at the British Museum. He was an intimate friend of Stevenson's and later the editor of Stevenson's letters.

80 · To The Deerfield Summer School

Ms Unknown

Summer 1889

I am afraid I can do little more than thank you for your courteous invitation to be present at the sittings of your delightfully sounding school of romance,[1] which ought to inherit happiness and honour from such a name. I am so very far away from you that I am afraid I can't participate very intelligently in your discussions, but I can only give them the furtherance of a dimly discriminating sympathy. I am not sure that I apprehend very well your apparent premise, "the materialism of our present tendencies," and I suspect that this would require some clearing up before I should be able (if even then) to contribute any suggestive or helpful word. To tell the truth, I can't help thinking that we already talk too much about the novel, about and around it, in proportion to the quantity of it having any importance that we produce. What I should say to the nymphs and swains who propose to converse about it under the great trees at Deerfield is: "Oh, do something from your point of view; an ounce of example is worth a ton of generalities; do something with the great art and the great form; do something with life. Any point of view is interesting that is a direct impression of life.

You each have an impression colored by your individual conditions; make that into a picture, a picture framed by your own personal wisdom, your glimpse of the American world. The field is vast for freedom, for study, for observation, for satire, for truth." I don't think I really do know what you mean by "materializing tendencies" any more than I should by "spiritualizing" or "etherealizing." There are no tendencies worth anything but to see the actual or the imaginative, which is just as visible, and to paint it. I have only two little words for the matter remotely approaching to rule or doctrine; one is life and the other freedom. Tell the ladies and gentlemen, the ingenious inquirers, to consider life directly and closely, and not to be put off with mean and puerile falsities, and be conscientious about it. It is infinitely large, various and comprehensive. Every sort of mind will find what it looks for in it, whereby the novel becomes truly multifarious and illustrative. That is what I mean by liberty; give it its head and let it range. If it is in a bad way, and the English novel is, I think, nothing but absolute freedom can refresh it and restore its self-respect. Excuse these raw brevities and please convey to your companions, my dear sir, the cordial good wishes of yours and theirs,

Henry James

1. In 1889 HJ was invited to attend the Summer School at Deerfield, Massachusetts, for a discussion of the art of the novel. He sent, instead, this letter, which was read during the proceedings and later published in the New York *Tribune*, 4 August 1889.

81 · To William James

Ms Harvard

Hotel de Hollande
r. de la Paix
Paris: Nov. 28th [1889]

My dear William.

Don't curse me for sending you the young Leonard Huxley,[1] who has written me the enclosed appeal; and to whom I have, after anxious searchings, ventured to give a note to you. I don't think you *will* objurgate me; in the first place because his plan in the U.S. seems respectable, useful and interesting, and in the second because he is such a charming fresh, manly, cleanly type of young English master at a great school. He is a son, of course, of the great Thomas—and is highly esteemed at Charterhouse. He is married, *of course,* to a "niece of Matt. Arnold"—sister of Mrs. Humphry Ward! I have the pleasantest recollection of him—of his face, type and speech.—I pray he be not an utterly inacceptable burden—and am pretty sure he won't.—I send you this from Paris, where I have been for the last five weeks. Toward the end I relented in regard to the exhibition[2] and came over in time for the last fortnight of it. It was despoiled of its freshness and invaded by hordes of furious Franks and fiery Huns—but it was a great impression and I'm glad I sacrificed to it. So I've remained on—I go back December 1st. It happens that I have been working very hard all this month—almost harder than ever in my life before—having on top of other pressing and unfinished tasks undertaken, for the bribe of large lucre, to translate Daudet's new *Tartarin* novel for the Harpers—whereby the proof sheets (the thing is the delightful work of a slowly dying man—he has motorataxia),[3] hot from his pen of genius have been pouring in upon me and have had to be attended to even in the midst of matters still more urgent. I had a talk of an hour and a half with him the other day—about "our work"(!!) and his own queer, deplorable condition, which he intensely converts into *art*, profession, success, copy, etc.—taking perpetual notes about his constant suffering (terrible in degree), which are to make a book called *La Douleur,* the most detailed and pessimistic notation of pain *qui fût jamais.* He is doing, in the midst of this, his new, gay, lovely "Tartarin" for the Harpers *en premier lieu;* that is, they are to publish it serially with wonderfully "processed" drawings before it comes out as a book in France—and I am to represent him, in English (a difficult, but with ingenuity a pleasant and amusing task) while this serial period lasts. I have seen a good deal of Bourget, and as I have breakfasted with Coppée[4] and twice dined in company with Meilhac, Sarcey, Albert Wolff, Goncourt, Ganderax, Blowitz,[5] etc., you will judge that I am pretty well saturated and ought to have the last word about *ces gens-ci.* That last word hasn't a grain of subjection, or of mystery, left in it: it is simply, "Chinese, Chinese, Chinese!" They are finished, besotted mandarins, and their Paris is their celestial Empire. With that, such a Paris as it sometimes seems! Nevertheless I've enjoyed it, and though I am very tired, too tired to write to you properly, I shall have been much refreshed by my stay here, and have taken aboard some light and heat for the black London winter. I shall see Alice on December 4th or 5th—I haven't seen her (through the sufficiency of Katharine's long visit) since the day I stopped with you on your way to Liverpool. I suppose the house has been the great cinder in your eye, though not, I trust, to producing tears all the autumn. I hope you are all sifting down and that your life seems larger for it. I am afraid, however, Alice can't be anything but very tired—and I send her much love. Did Millet ever write to you? I wrote to him urgently, but had no answer. I hope that above house and college and life and everything, you still hold up an undemented head, and are not in a seedy way.

Ever your affectionate
Henry

1. Leonard Huxley (1860–1933), son of the scientist Thomas Henry Huxley and future father of Aldous Huxley.
2. The Paris Exhibition of 1889.
3. Daudet did not die until 1897.
4. François Coppée (1842–1908), poet and dramatist, whose stories of drab existences and humble people had considerable appeal.
5. Henri Meilhac (1831–1897) was librettist for Offenbach and a well-known playwright, collaborator with Ludovic Halévy in drawing-room comedies; Francisque Sarcey (1827–1899) was drama critic of *Le Temps*. Henri de Blowitz (1825–1903) was the special Paris correspondent of the *Times*.

4 · Defeats
1890–1895

After two decades of "a reasonable show of fame," Henry James found the particular public he had created for his work turning away from him. It had responded during the 1870s and early 1880s to his discovery of the "international" theme—his tales about young Americans and their European adventures. After *The Portrait of a Lady* (1881) he attempted new subjects. But his reformers and feminists in *The Bostonians,* his revolutionaries in *The Princess Casamassima,* and the struggles of performing artists and painters with society in *The Tragic Muse* did not have the same appeal. These were solid novels but they had neither the brilliance nor the ironic spirit of his earlier works. The fairy-tale element had disappeared. Editors still bought his short stories for the magazines, but even this market had undergone a change. One new element was illustration; and James was unhappy that his work had to play, as it seemed, second fiddle to the illustrators and wait while they drew their pictures.

As he surveyed his position in the literary world and its market-place, and pondered his earlier successes, James began to feel a certain melancholy and self-doubt—even though he never for a moment stopped writing. Today we would say that he had arrived at a kind of "mid-life crisis." He had a sense of shrinking opportunities. In his 1893 tale "The Middle Years," his aging novelist finds that "the infinite of life had gone" and that "he should never again, as at one or two great moments of the Past, be better than himself."

What took over now was an old ambition to succeed in the theatre. He was aware of his gift for dialogue; and he had studied the French "well-made" plays closely. "My books don't sell," he wrote to Robert Louis Stevenson, "and it looks as if my plays might. Therefore I am going with a brazen front, to write half a dozen." And this was what he did. He stopped writing novels; he supported himself by producing short stories and gave the greater part of his time to wooing actors and stage managers. What he did not recognize sufficiently was the chasm that exists between literature and "theatre." James had always been a man of the study. He was accustomed to dealing with editors, not with temperamental actors and actresses or the powerful actor-managers who dominated the British stage. The proscenium fettered his imagination; he felt imprisoned behind the footlights. His language tells us this. The theatre was a "straitjacket." He was indulging in circus-life—he called it "the sawdust and orange peel" phase of his creativity.

Between 1890 and 1895 James wrote half a dozen plays, tailored (he thought) to the immediate stage conditions he really did not understand. Two were produced. He had wild dreams of the gold that would pour in at the box office. But he had more difficulty than he knew getting actors and actresses on and off the stage; what seemed to him ingenuity was simply clumsiness. He relied too much on his verbal power. He began by being blind to Ibsen's economy of stage effect; only later did he realize how "the Northern Henry" was a great gift to the actors' art. It was one thing to imitate French comedies and farces, but it was another to get Ibsen's kind of play on paper. James tried to do the seemingly easy comedy of Oscar Wilde, but he lacked Wilde's common touch, his ability to reach the audience across the footlights.

The letters of this time reflect, behind their lively facade of boldness and energy, an inner despair. They show also that he had reached a time of personal loss—his sister died in 1892, his friend Miss Woolson in 1894, and Robert Louis Stevenson shortly after. He mourned them but kept at his theatricals. Finally he had a play accepted for production by London's matinee idol, George Alexander. It was a costume play, highly romantic and delicately written. The best critics—the emerging Bernard Shaw, A. B. Walkley, William Archer—praised its language and literary qualities, but on its first night it proved a historic flop. James was booed by the audience. This personal drama can be read in his letters.

82 · *To Frederick Macmillan*

Ms British Library

34 De Vere Gardens W.
March 28*th* 1890

My dear Macmillan.

I thank you for your note and the offer of £70.0.0.[1] Don't, however, think my pretensions monstrous if I say that, in spite of what you tell me of the poor success of my recent books, I still do desire to get a larger sum, and have determined to take what steps I can in this direction. These steps I know will carry me away from you, but it comes over me that this is after all better, even with a due and grateful recognition of the readiness you express to go on with me, unprofitable as I am. I say it is "better" because I had far rather that in those circumstances you should *not* go on with me. I would rather not be published at all than be published and not pay—other people at least. The latter alternative makes me uncomfortable and the former makes me, of the two, feel least like a failure; the failure that, at this time of day, it is too humiliating to consent to be without trying, at least, as they say in America, to "know more about it." Unless I can put the matter on a more remunerative footing all round I shall give up my English "market"—heaven save the market!—and confine myself to my American. But I must experiment a bit first—and to experiment is of course to say farewell to you. Farewell then, my dear Macmillan, with great regret—but with the sustaining cheer of all the links in the chain that remain still unbroken.

Yours ever
Henry James

P.S. I am not unaware or oblivious that I am actually in your debt to the extent of whatever fraction of £200 on account (which you paid me July 9th 1888) is represented by the third of the books then covenanted for here and in the U.S.—the *Aspern Papers* and *A London Life* being the two others. I will engage that this last member of the batch (about five short tales) shall appear in the autumn—if that will suit you.—H.J.

1. On completion of serial publication of HJ's long novel *The Tragic Muse* in the *Atlantic Monthly* (it ran to seventeen installments) the novelist as usual offered the hardcover

rights to Macmillan. He was shocked at the advance proposed, much less than for his earlier works. In his Olympian way with publishers, HJ bade farewell to Macmillan, who however compromised by taking a five-year lease on the work and giving HJ an advance of £250. Sales of the book were poor; at the end of the five years HJ still owed Macmillan £170.

83 · *To Alice James*

Ms Harvard

Palazzo Barbaro [Venice]
June 6*th* [1890]

Dearest Sister,

I am ravished by your letter after reading the play[1] (keep it locked up, safe and secret, though there are three or four copies in existence) which makes me feel as if there had been a triumphant première and I had received overtures from every managerial quarter and had only to count my gold. At any rate I am delighted that you have been struck with it exactly as I have *tried* to strike and that the pure *practical* character of the effort has worked its calculated spell upon you. For what encourages me in the whole business is that, as the piece stands, there is not, in its felicitous form, the ghost of a "fluke" or a mere chance: it is all "art" and an absolute address of means to the end—the end, viz., of meeting *exactly* the immediate, actual, intense British conditions, both subjective and objective, and of acting in (to a minute, including entr'actes) two hours and three-quarters. Ergo, I can do a dozen more infinitely better; and I am excited to think how much, since the writing of this one piece has been an education to me, a little further experience will do for me. Also I am sustained by the sense, on the whole, that though really superior acting would help it immensely, yet mediocrity of handling (which is all, at the best, I am pretty sure, that it will get) won't and can't *kill* it, and that there may be even something sufficiently general and human about it, to make it (given its eminent actability) "keep the stage," even after any first vogue it may have has passed away. *That* fate—in the poverty-stricken condition of the English repertory—would mean profit indeed, and an income to my descendants. But one mustn't talk of this kind of thing yet. However, since you have been already so deeply initiated, I think I will enclose (keep it sacredly for me) an admirable letter I have just received from the precious *Balestier*[2] in whose hands, as I wrote you, I placed the settlement of the money-question, the terms of the written agreement with Compton.[3] Compton saw him on Monday last—and I send the letter mainly to illustrate the capital intelligence and competence and benevolence of Balestier and show you in what good hands I am. He will probably strike you, as he strikes me, as the perfection of an "agent"—especially when you consider that he has undertaken this particular job out of pure friendship. Everything, evidently, will be well settled—on the basis, of course, which can't be helped, of production in *London* only about the middle of next year. But by that time I hope to have done a good bit more work—and I shall be beguiled by beginning to follow, in the autumn, the rehearsals for the country production. Keep Balestier's letter till I come back—I shall get another one from him in a day or two with the agreement to sign. You will see how much he confirms my good personal impression of Compton. If Compton's maximum in the country is £100 (gross-receipts) a night it ought to be taken (always assuming, of course, the play to be successful) as his *average* in a London theatre, where prices are higher—twice as high—and seats, above all, stalls, more numerous. Therefore with weekly matinées my ten per cent would certainly bring me upwards of £80 a week—and this, going on steadily for some time, would make up a sum very well worth while. But, further, a nightly "take" in London of only £100 for a *successful* play, is moderate—and I might probably look for £350 a month: which, as a steady thing, would seem to me a fortune. But the *real* fact is that any play, in *London*, which should bring me £350 a month, would so soon get into swing in America that the larger (simultaneous) profits would come from there—to say nothing (vide Balestier letter) of the simultaneous country company and of Australia! These castles in Spain are at least exhilarating. In a certain sense I should like you very much to communicate to William your good impression of the drama—but on the whole I think you had better not, for the simple reason that it is very important it shouldn't be talked about (especially so long) in advance—and it wouldn't be *safe*, inasmuch as every whisper gets into the papers—and in some fearfully vulgarized and perverted form. You *might* hint to William that you have read the piece under seal of secrecy to me and think so-and-so of it—but are so bound (to me) not to give a sign that *he* must bury what you tell him in tenfold mystery. But

I doubt if even *this* would be secure—it would be in the *Transcript* the next week.—Venice continues adorable and the Curtises the soul of benevolence.[4] Their upstairs apartment (empty and still unoffered—at forty pounds a year—to any one but me) beckons me so, as a foot-in-the-water here, that if my dramatic ship had begun to come in, I should probably be tempted to take it at a venture—for all it would matter. But for the present I resist perfectly—especially as Venice isn't *all* advantageous. The great charm of such an idea is the having in Italy, a little cheap and private refuge independent of hotels etc., which every year grow more disagreeable and German and tiresome to face—not to say dearer too. But it won't be for this year—and the Curtises won't let it. What Pen Browning[5] has done here, through his American wife's dollars, with the splendid Palazzo Rezzonico, transcends description for the beauty, and, as Ruskin would say, "wisdom and rightness" of it. It is altogether royal and imperial—but "Pen" isn't kingly and the *train de vie* remains to be seen. Gondoliers ushering in friends from pensions won't fill it out. The Rodgerses[6] have turned up but are not oppressive—seeming mainly to be occupied with being constantly ill. That is Katie appears everywhere to collapse badly and expensively, and I judge she has something gravely the matter with her. She has "doctors" at every place they go—is in bed for days etc.—and yet they go everywhere. I don't encourage them (I have indeed seen them but once—when I took them on the water by moonlight) to talk about "the will"—as it's disagreeable and they really know nothing about it. I am thinking, after all, of joining the Curtises in the evidently most beautiful *drive* (of upwards of a week, with rests) they are starting upon on the 14th, from a place called Vittorio, in the Venetian Alps, two hours' rail from here, through Cadore, Titian's country, the Dolomites etc., toward Oberammergau. They offer me, pressingly, the fourth seat in the carriage that awaits them when they leave the train—and also an extra ticket they have taken for the play at Oberammergau if I choose to go so far. This I shall scarcely do, but I *shall* probably leave with them, drive four or five days and come *back,* via Verona, by rail—leaving my luggage here. Continue to address here—unless, before that, I give you one other address while I am gone. I shall find all letters here, on my return, if I do go, in the keeping of the excellent *maestro di casa*—the Venetian Smith. I should be back, at the *latest,* by the 25th—probably by the 20th. In this case I shall presumably go back to Florence to spend four or five days with Baldwin[7] (going to Siena or Perugia); after which I have a dream of going up to Vallombrosa (nearly 4000 feet above the sea—but of a softness!) for two or three weeks—till I have to leave Italy on my way home. I am writing to Edith Peruzzi,[8] who has got a summer-lodge there, and is already there, for information about the inn. If I don't go there I shall perhaps try Camaldoli or San Marcello—all high in the violet Apennines, within three or four hours, and mainly by a little carriage, of Florence. But I *want* to compass Vallombrosa, which I have never seen and have always dreamed of and which I am assured is divine—infinitely salubrious and softly cool. The idea of lingering in Italy a few weeks longer on these terms is very delightful to me—it does me, as yet, nothing but good. But I shall see. I put B[alestier]'s letter in another envelope. I rejoice in your eight gallops—they may be the dozen now.

Ever your
Henry

1. The dramatized version of HJ's novel *The American*.
2. Wolcott Balestier (1861–1891), an American publisher's representative in England.
3. Edward Compton (1854–1918), head of the Compton Comedy Company, produced *The American*.
4. Daniel and Ariana Curtis of Boston, who lived in the Palazzo Barbaro.
5. The son of Robert and Elizabeth Barrett Browning.
6. Maternal relatives traveling abroad.
7. Dr. William Wilberforce Baldwin (1850–1910), an American physician who practiced in Florence.
8. The former Edith Story, daughter of the sculptor W. W. Story, had married a descendant of the Medici, Simone Peruzzi di Medici.

84 · To William Archer

Ms British Library

34 De Vere Gardens W.
Dec. 27th 1890

Dear Sir.

I am much obliged to you for your interest in an obscure and tremulous venture.[1] It *is* true that a play of mine is to be produced at a mysterious place called Southport, which I have never seen, a week from tonight, and it is further true that the production is one to which I myself, and every one concerned, have, and has, contributed as seriously as the particular conditions would allow. The performance is *not* a "scratch" one, to establish copyright, but a carefully prepared one to which I have lent a zealous hand and in which the performers, wholly deficient in celebrity, but inflamed, I think, with something of the same zeal, will do their individual best. I won't deny that I should be glad to know that the piece was seen by a serious critic, and by yourself in particular, but I shrink from *every* responsibility in the way of recommending such a critic to attempt so heroic a feat. The place is far, the season inclement, the interpretation, *extremely* limited, different enough, as you may suppose, from what I should count on for representation in London. The circumstances *may* be definitely uncomfortable. I have carefully followed rehearsals, but the whole thing is a leap in the dark, and my hope is greater than my confidence. On the other hand it is apparently to be months before the play comes to town—as I accepted at the outset the essence of the proposal made me (and of which the general attempt was the direct result): the proviso, namely, that the piece should be produced (and only *occasionally!*) in the provinces for upwards of a year before being brought out in London. England, Scotland and Ireland therefore will behold it before the starved metropolis. But it will come—I believe—before long, considerably nearer town than Southport, and probably in more seductive weather. At any rate I have hopes that I may be represented otherwise in London before the drama in question is revealed here; for if I have made up my mind to make a resolute theatrical attempt, I am far from considering that one makes it with a single play. I mean to go at it again and again—and shall do so none the worse for knowing that you may give some heed to the undiscourageable flounderings of yours very truly

Henry James

1. William Archer (1856–1924), a leading Victorian drama critic, had asked HJ's permission to review the out-of-town opening of *The American*, which took place in Southport, near Liverpool, on 3 January 1891.

85 · *To Alice James and Katharine P. Loring*

Ms Harvard

Prince of Wales Hotel
Southport
[4 January 1891]

My dear Children.

I wired you an half hour ago a most veracious and historical account of yesterday's beautiful evening.[1] It was really *beautiful*—the splendid success of the whole thing, reflected as large as the surface presented by a Southport audience (and the audience was very big indeed) could permit. The attention, the interest, the outbursts of applause and appreciation hushed quickly for fear of losing (especially with the very bad acoustic properties of the house) what was to follow, the final plaudits, and recalls (I mean after each act) and the big universal outbreak at the end for "author, *author*, AUTHOR!" in duly *delayed* response to which, with the whole company grinning delight and sympathy (behind the curtain) I was led before by Compton to receive the first "ovation," but I trust not the last, of my life—all this would have cured you (both) right up if you could only have witnessed it. The great feature of the evening was the surprising way Compton "came out," beyond anything he had done, or shown, at rehearsal,— acting really exceedingly well and putting more force, ability and above all art and charm and *character* into his part than I had at all ventured to expect of him. He will improve it greatly, ripen and *tone* it, as he plays it more, and end, I am sure, by making it a *celebrated* modern creation. He *may* even become right enough in it to do it in America—though as to that one must see. The Comptons of course are intensely happy, and their supper with me here, with Balestier[2] for a fourth, was wildly joyous, as you may infer when I tell you it lasted from 11 to 1.45 A.M. Mrs. Compton was "cured right up" by our success—she acted, in her own Mrs. Comptonish way, *very* neatly and gracefully, for a lady who had been ill in bed for a week. She was exceedingly well-dressed—all Liberty, but very good Liberty. Every one, in fact, worked his and her hardest and did his and her best; and though some of them, notably Valentin, who made himself very handsome, were much impaired by extreme nervousness, there was no real flaw on the extreme smoothness of the performance, which "went" as if it were a fiftieth. On the other hand, of course, I felt freshly the importance of a change of Mme de B[ellegarde] and Mrs. Bread, of Lord Deepmere and perhaps, or probably, even of Valentin and the Marquis for the London production. As for Newman, Compton simply *adores* the part and will, I feel sure, make it universally beloved. Well, he *may* like it, for though I say it who shouldn't, I was freshly struck, in my little "cubby" beside the curtain in the right wing (where I stuck all the evening, save to dash out and embrace every one in the entractes), I was more than ever impressed, I say, with its being *magnificent*—all the keyboard, the potential fortune of an actor. The wondrous Balestier dashed out between the third and fourth acts and cabled to the *New York Times* fifty vivid words which will *already* have been laid on every breakfast table (as it were) in that city. I strongly suspect they will bring in prompt applications for the "American rights." I will tell you a droll anecdote of William Archer's behaviour and attitude.[3] I go part of the way to Cheltenham[4] tonight, sleep at Birmingham and spend tomorrow at C. Expect to see you Tuesday evening. If Katharine could send me a word—telegraphic—about how you are—to 4 Promenade Terrace C.—I should be glad. I am writing to William, but you might send him on this letter just as it stands.

Ever yours
Henry James

P.S. *Sunday noon.* Compton has just come in to tell me that he has already seen a number of people present last night who were *unanimous* about the success of the piece, the great hit he has made it—and ergo—the large fortune that opens to it. His own high spirits indeed tell everything.

1. The telegram read: "Unqualified triumphant magnificent success universal congratulations great ovation for author great future for play Comptons radiant and his acting admirable writing Henry."
2. HJ had invited Balestier as his guest at the first night.
3. Alice James recorded in her diary 7 January 1891 that Archer told HJ "I think it's a play that would be much more likely to have success in the Provinces than in London." She added that "these uncalled for and depressing amenities from an entire stranger seemed highly grotesque." *The Diary of Alice James*, ed. Edel (1964).
4. At Cheltenham HJ visited his close friend Constance Fenimore Woolson (see Letter 50, note 3).

86 · *To Robert Louis Stevenson*

Ms Yale

34 De Vere Gardens W.
January 12*th* 1891

My dear Louis.

I have owed you a letter too shamefully long—and now that I have taken my pen in hand, as we used to say, I feel how much I burn to communicate with you. As your magnanimity will probably have forgotten how long ago it was that you addressed me, from Sydney, the tragic statement of your permanent secession, I won't remind you of so detested a date. That statement, indeed, smote me to the silence I have so long preserved: I couldn't—I didn't—protest; I even mechanically and grimly assented; but I couldn't *talk* about it—even to you and your wife. Missing you always is a perpetual ache—and aches are disqualifying for gymnastic feats. In short we forgive you (the Muses and the soft Passions forgive *us!*) but we can't quite *treat* you as if we did. However, all this while I have many things to thank you for. In the first place for Lloyd.[1] He was delightful, we loved him—*nous nous l'arrachâmes.* He is a most sympathetic youth, and we revelled in his rich conversation and exclaimed on his courtly manners. How vulgar you'll think us all when you come back (there is malice in that "when"). Then for the beautiful strange things you sent me and which make for ever in my sky-parlour a sort of dim rumble as of the Pacific surf. My heart beats over them—my imagination throbs—my eyes fill. I have covered a blank wall of my bedroom with an acre of painted cloth and feel as if I lived in a Samoan tent—and I have placed the sad sepia-drawing just where, fifty times a day, it most transports and reminds me. To-day what I am grateful for is your new ballad-book,[2] which has just reached me by your command. I have had time only to read the first few things—but I shall absorb the rest and give you my impression of them before I close this. As I turn the pages I seem to see that they are full of charm and of your "Protean" imaginative life—but above all of your terrible far-off-ness. My state of mind about that is the strangest—a sort of delight at having you poised there in the inconceivable; and a miserable feeling, at the same time, that I am in too wretched a back seat to assist properly at the performance. I don't want to lose *any* of your vibrations; and, as it is, I feel that I only

241

catch a few of them—and that is a constant woe. I read with un-restrictive relish the first chapters of your prose volume[3] (kindly vouch-safed me in the little copyright-catching red volume), and I loved 'em and blessed them quite. But I *did* make one restriction—I missed the *visible* in them—I mean as regards people, things, objects, faces, bod-ies, costumes, features, gestures, manners, the introductory, the *per-sonal* painter-touch. It struck me that you either didn't feel—through some accident—your responsibility on this article quite enough; or, on some theory of your own, had declined it. No theory is kind to us that cheats us of *seeing*. However, no doubt we shall rub our eyes for satiety before we have done. Of course the pictures—Lloyd's blessed photographs—*y sont pour beaucoup*; but I wanted more the note of portraiture. Doubtless I am greedy—but one *is* when one dines at the Maison d'or. I have an idea you take but a qualified interest in "Beau Austin"[4]—or I should tell you how religiously I was present at that memorable première. Lloyd and your wonderful and delightful mother will have given you the agreeable facts of the occasion. I found it—not the occasion, so much, but the work—full of *quality*, and stamped with a charm; but on the other hand seeming to shrug its shoulders a little too much at scenic precautions. I have an idea, however, you don't care about the matter, and I won't bore you with it further than to say that the piece has been repeatedly played, that it has been the only honourable theatrical affair transacted *dans notre sale tripot* for many a day—and that Wm. Archer *en raffole* periodically in the "World." Don't despise me too much if I confess that *anch' io son pit-tore. Je fais aussi du théâtre, moi;* and am doing it, to begin with, for reasons too numerous to burden you with, but all excellent and prac-tical. In the provinces I had the other night, at Southport, Lan-cashire, with the dramatization of an early novel—*The American*—a success *dont je rougis encore*. This thing is to be played in London only after several months—and to make the tour of the British Islands first. Don't be hard on me—simplifying and chastening necessity has laid its brutal hand on me and I have had to try to make somehow or other the money I don't make by literature. My books don't sell, and it looks as if my plays might. Therefore I am going with a brazen front to write half a dozen. I have, in fact, already written two others than the one just performed—and the success of the latter pronounced—really *pro-nounced*—will probably precipitate them. I am glad for all this that you are not here. Literature is out of it. I miss no occasion of talking of you. Colvin I tolerably often see: I expect to do so for instance to-night, at a decidedly too starched dining-club to which we both be-long, of which Lord Coleridge is president and too many persons of the type of Sir Theodore Martin[5] are members. Happy islanders— with no Sir Theodore Martin. On Mrs. Sitwell[6] I called the other day, in a charming new habitat; all clean paint and fresh chintz. We always go on at a great rate about you—celebrate rites as faithful as the early Christians in the catacombs. Gosse has just published a singularly clever, skilful, vivid, well-done biography of his father—the fanatic and naturalist—very happy in proportion, tact and talent. Filial pity *lui a porté bonheur*—it is one of the good biographies. He is altogether prosperous and productive—concerning himself, however, I think, too much with the "odd jobs" of literature and too little with the finer opportunities. But I find him one of the very few intelligent and, on such matters, conversible creatures here.

January 13*th.*—I met Colvin last night, after writing the above—in the company of Sir James Stephen, Sir Theo. Martin, Sir Douglas Galton, Sir James Paget, Sir Alfred Lyall, Canon Ainger, and George Du Maurier. How this will make you lick your chops over Ori and Rahiro and Tamatia and Taheia—or whatever *ces messieurs et ces dames*, your present visiting list, are called. He told me of a copious diary-letter he has just got from you, bless you, and we are discussing a day on which I shall soon come to meat or drink with him and listen to the same. Since yesterday I have also read the ballad book—with the ad-miration that I always feel as a helplessly verseless creature (it's a senti-ment worth nothing as a testimony) for all performances in rhyme and metre—especially on the part of producers of fine prose.

January 19*th.*—I stopped this more than a week ago, and since then I have lacked time to go on with it—having been out of town for sev-eral days on a base theatrical errand[7]—to see my tribute to the vul-garest of the muses a little further on its way over the provincial circuit and re-rehearse two or three portions of it that want more effective playing. Thank heaven I shall have now no more direct contact with it till it is produced in London next October.—I broke off in the act of speaking to you about your ballad-book. The production of ringing and lilting verse (by a superior proser) always does *bribe* me a little— and I envy you in that degree yours; but apart from this I grudge your writing the like of these ballads. They show your "cleverness," but they don't show your genius. I should say more if it were not odious to a man of my refinement to write to you—so expectantly far away—in remonstrance. I don't find, either, that the cannibalism, the savagery *se prête,* as it were—one wants either less of it, on the ground of suggestion—or more, on the ground of statement; and one wants more of the high impeccable (as distinguished from the awfully jolly), on the ground of poetry. Behold I *am* launching across the black seas a page that may turn nasty—but my dear Louis, it's only because I love so your divine prose and want the comfort of it. Things are various because we do 'em. We mustn't do 'em because they're various. The only news in literature here—such is the virtuous vacancy of our consciousness—continues to be the infant monster of a Kipling. I enclose, in this, for your entertainment a few pages I have lately written about him, to serve as the preface to an (of course authorized) American *recueil* of some of his tales.[8] I may add that he has just put forth his longest story yet—a thing in Lippincott which I also send you herewith—which cuts the ground somewhat from under my feet, inasmuch as I find it the most youthfully infirm of his productions (in spite of great "life"), much wanting in composition and in narrative and explicative, or even implicative, art.[9]

Please tell your wife, with my love, that all this is constantly addressed also to her. I try to see you all, in what I fear is your absence of habits, as you live, grouped around what I also fear is in no sense the domestic hearth. Where do you go when you want to be "cosy"?—or what at least do you *do?* You think a little, I hope, of the faithful forsaken on whose powers of evocation, as well as of attachment, you impose such a strain. I wish I could send a man from Fortnum and Mason's out to you with a chunk of *mortadella.* I am trying to do a series of "short things" and will send you the least bad. I mean to write to Lloyd. Please congratulate your heroic mother for me very cordially when she leaps upon your strand, and believe that I hold you all in the tenderest remembrance of yours ever, my dear Louis,

Henry James

1. Lloyd Osbourne, Stevenson's stepson.
2. *Ballads* (1891).
3. Fifteen of the thirty-five letters Stevenson had written him from the South Seas were

gathered into the privately printed volume *The South Seas* (1890) and were published serially during 1891 in the New York *Sun*.

4. A play Stevenson had written in collaboration with W. E. Henley.

5. Sir Theodore Martin (1816–1909), a Scottish man of letters who wrote for the theatre and prepared for Queen Victoria a five-volume life of the Prince Consort.

6. Frances Sitwell (1839–1924), a friend of Stevenson's, later married Sidney Colvin.

7. HJ continued to attend performances of *The American* in country towns.

8. A preface to the American edition of *Mine Own People* (1891).

9. The *Lippincott* issue of January 1891 contained an installment of Kipling's *The Light That Failed*.

87 · To Edmund Gosse

Ms Leeds

34 De Vere Gardens W.
Apr. 28*th* [1891]

My dear Gosse.

I return the Ibsenite volume[1] with many thanks—especially for the opportunity to read your charming preface which is really *en somme* and between ourselves (I wouldn't say it to Lang) more interesting than Ibsen himself. That is I think you make him out a richer phenomenon than he is. The perusal of the dreary *Rosmersholm* and even the reperusal of *Ghosts* has been rather a shock to me—they have let me down, down. Surely the former isn't *good?*—any more than the tedious *Lady from the Sea* is? *Must* I think these things works of skill? If I must I will—save to you alone: to whom I confide that they seem to be of a grey mediocrity—in the case of "Rosmersholm" *jusqu'à en être bête*. They don't seem to me dramatic, or dramas at all—but (I am speaking of those two particularly) moral tales in dialogue—without the objectivity, the visibility of the drama. They suggest curious reflections as to the Scandinavian stage and audience. Of course they have a serious—a terribly serious, "feeling for life," and always an idea—but they come off so little, in general, as plays; and I can't think that a man who is at odds with his form is ever a first-rate man. But I may be grossly blind, and at any rate don't *tell* it of yours tremulously

Henry James

1. Gosse (1849–1928), a specialist in Scandinavian languages and a translator at the Board of Trade, had long championed Ibsen. The preface to which James refers appeared in

Volume I of the Lovell's Series of Foreign Literature edition of Ibsen's works (1890). On the flap of the envelope of this letter HJ wrote: "Your preface perfect, granting premises."

88 · *To Robert Louis Stevenson*

Ms Yale

34 De Vere Gardens W.
Oct. 30th 1891

My dear Louis.

My silences are hideous, but somehow I feel as if you were inaccessible to sound. Moreover it appears that my last letter, despatched many months ago, I admit, never reached you. But Colvin tells me that a post leaves tomorrow via San Francisco, and the effect of diminished remoteness from you is increased by the fact that I dined last night with Henry Adams, who told me of his visits to you months and months ago.[1] He re-created you, and your wife, for me a little, as living persons, and fanned thereby the flame of my desire not to be forgotten of you and not to appear to forget you. He lately arrived—in Paris—via New Zealand and Marseilles and has just come to London to learn that he can't go to China, as he had planned, through the closure, newly enacted and inexorable, of all but its outermost parts. He now talks of Central Asia, but can't find anyone to go with him— least of all, alas, me. He is about to ship La Farge home—now in Brittany with his French relations (and whom I have not seen). I feel as if I ought to make my letter a smoking porridge of news; but it's a bewilderment where to begin. Nothing, however, seems more foremost than that Colvin is really in a state of substantially recovered health. I dined with him a few days since at the Athenaeum and he gave me a better impression than he had done for years. He has passed through black darkness—and much prolonged; but I think he sees daylight and hears the birds sing. That little black demon of a Kipling will have perhaps leaped upon your silver strand by the time this reaches you— he publicly left England to embrace you many weeks ago—carrying literary genius out of the country with him in his pocket. As you will quarrel with him at an early day, for yourself, it is therefore not needful I should say more of him than that nature languishes since his departure and art grunts and turns in her sleep. I am told you and Lloyd

are waking them both up in *The Wrecker*,[2] but I have had the fortitude
not to begin the Wrecker yet. I *can't* read you in snippets and between
the vulgar covers of magazines; but I am only biding my time and
smacking my lips. I am a baser cockney even than you left me, inasmuch as now I don't even go to Bournemouth. I have made, in a
whole year, but two absences from London—one of six weeks, last
spring, in Paris, and another of the same duration, in the summer, in
Ireland, which has a shabby foreign charm that touches me. Yet I'm
afraid I have little to show for such an adhesion to my chair—unless it
be holes in the seat of my trousers. I have written and am still to write
a goodish many short tales—but you are not to be troubled with them
till they prop each other up in volumes. I mean never to write another
novel; I mean I have solemnly dedicated myself to a masterly brevity. I
have come back to it as to an early love. "La première politesse de
l'écrivain" says lately the exquisite Anatole France, "n'est-ce point
d'être bref? La nouvelle suffit à tous. [That word is nouvelle.][3] On peut
y renfermer beaucoup de sens en peu de mots. Une nouvelle bien faite
est le régal des connoisseurs et le contentement des difficiles. C'est
l'élixir et la quintessence. C'est l'onguent précieux." I quote him because il dit si bien. But you can ask Kipling. Excuse me for seeming to
imply that one who has distilled the ointment as you have needs to ask
anyone. I am too sceptical even to mention that I sent you ages ago
The Tragic Muse[4]—so presumable is it that she never reached you. I
lately produced here a play—a dramatization of my old novel *The
American* (the thing was played last spring in various places in the
country), with circumstances of public humiliation which make it
mainly count as an heroic beginning. The papers slated it without
mercy, and it was—by several of its interpreters—wretchedly ill-
played; also it betrays doubtless the inexperience of its author and suffers damnably from the straightjacket of the unscenic book. But if I
hadn't done, on solicitation, this particular thing I shouldn't have begun ever at all; and if I hadn't begun I shouldn't have the set purpose
to show, henceforth, what flower of perfection I presume to think I
can pick from the dusty brambles—ah meagre vegetation!—of the
dramatic form. The play is in its fifth week—and will probably trav-
erse a goodish many others; but it has been a time (the first, God
knows!) when I have been on the whole glad you are not in England.
Adams has made me see you a little—both, and I look to John LaFarge

247

to do so a little more. (He comes in a few days.) Colvin has read me your letters when he discreetly could, and my life has been a burden from fearing to unfold the *Times* every morning to a perusal of Samoan convulsions. But apparently you survive, little good as I get of it. We are all under water here—it has rained hard for five months—and the British land is a waste of waters, as in the first pages of geologies. I am consumed with catarrh and rheumatism and lumbago—and when Adams talked to me last night of the tropics I could have howled with baffled desire. My poor sister—slowly and serenely dying—is too ill for me to leave England at present: she has a house in London now. I don't know whom to tell you about more that you would care to hear of. Edmund Gosse has written a novel—as yet unpublished—which I wot little of. Hall Caine[5] has put forth *A Scapegoat* to the enrichment, I believe, of all concerned—but I am not concerned. I will send you the work as soon as it is reduced in bulk. The Frenchmen are passing away—Maupassant dying of locomotor paralysis, the fruit of fabulous habits, I am told. *Je n'en sais rien;* but I shall miss him. Bourget is married and will do good things yet—I send you by this post his (to me very exquisite, as perception and as expression—that is as literature) *Sensations d'Italie.*[6] I saw Daudet last winter, more or less in Paris, who is also *atteint de la moelle épinière* and writing about it in the shape of a novel called *La Douleur,* which will console him by its sale. I greet your wife, my dear Louis, most affectionately—I speak to you too, dear Mrs. Louis, in every word I write. I desire to express the very friendliest remembrance of your heroic mother—who accounts for her son, and still more wonderfully for her daughter-in-law and grand young stepson. My love to the gallant Lloyd. Vouchsafe me a page of prose and believe in the joy that a statement that you bloom with a tropic luxuriance, will, if made in your own hand, convey to your flaccid old friend

Henry James

1. Adams and John La Farge had traveled together in the South Seas.

2. *The Wrecker* (1892), written in collaboration with Lloyd Osbourne.

3. Anatole France, pseudonym of Jacques-Anatole-François Thibault (1844–1924). The brackets are HJ's. He had probably been reading France's *Causeries* in *Le Temps,* published as *La Vie littéraire* (1888–1892).

4. *The Tragic Muse,* a novel about an actress and a painter, was published by Macmillan in June 1890.

5. Henry Hall Caine (1853–1931), author of romantic-sentimental novels, had just published *The Scapegoat.*

6. HJ had known the conservative French novelist Paul Bourget (1852–1935) since 1884. The anti-Semitic Bourget had just married the Jewish Minnie David, a Catholic convert.

89 · To Edmund Gosse

Ms Leeds

34 De Vere Gardens W.
November 17th 1891

My dear Gosse.

Please have patience with me a little longer. I am very susceptible to the friendliness of your note, but I have been not only infinitely occupied, but moody, misanthropic, melancholy, morbid, morose, and utterly unfit for human converse or genial scenes.[1] I continue, frankly speaking, painfully and perversely unsociable—and shall, as the phrase is, never be the same man again. When a relative light breaks it will guide me to your door; but in the meanwhile I must grope in solitude and blush (for my involuntary rigours), in seclusion. I must throw myself on your charity, which I know to be liberal, and on your wife's, in which I have a still larger confidence, and I am, my dear Gosse, with every appreciation of your sympathy, yours, with every impulse of conciliation but every instinct of retirement, most faithfully

Henry James

1. The alliterative sentence suggests how much HJ was upset by the reviews and stage problems during the short-lived London run of his dramatization of *The American*.

90 · To Edmund Gosse

Ms Congress

Europaeischer Hof
Dresden. Thursday
[10 December 1891]

My dear Gosse.

I delay as little as possible to tell you *où nous en sommes*. We arrived at 9 last (Wednesday) night after a deadly, dreary journey and a miserable delay on Monday night at Dover. The funeral,[1] most happily— if I may use so strange a word—had been successfully delayed till this

A.M.; when it took place most conveniently and even picturesquely according to arrangements already made by the excellent Heinemann ladies and the American consul Mr. Knoop. The English chaplain read the service with sufficient yet not offensive sonority and the arrangements were of an admirable, decorously grave German kind which gives one, really, a higher idea of German civilization. The three ladies came, insistently, to the grave—the others were Heinemann, his mother and I, and the excellent Mr. Knoop. The little cemetery is suburbanly dreary, but I have seen worse. The mother and sister are altogether wonderful, and so absolutely composed—that is Mrs. B. and Josephine—that there is scarcely any *visible* tragedy in it. By far the most interesting is poor little concentrated, passionate Carrie,[2] with whom I came back from the cemetery alone in one of the big black and silver coaches, with its black and silver footmen perched behind (she wanted to talk to me), and who is remarkable in her force, acuteness, capacity and courage—and in the intense—almost manly—nature of her emotion. She is a worthy sister of poor dear big-spirited, only-by-death-quenchable Wolcott, and if we judged her—in speaking of a certain matter lately—"unattractive," her little vivid, clear-talking, clear-*seeing* black robed image today (and last evening) considerably—in a certain way—to my vision—modifies that judgment. What is clear, at any rate, is that she can do and face and more than face and do, for all three of them, anything and everything that they will have to meet now. They are going home (to the U.S.) as soon as they can—and they are going to London first: I suppose about a week hence. One thing, I believe, the poor girl would *not* meet—but God grant (and the complexity of "genius" grant) that she may not have to meet it—as there is no reason to suppose that she will. What this tribulation is—or would be, rather, I can indicate better when I see you. Please tell your wife that gladly and piously I carried her pot of English flowers to the poor women—and Josephine had them in her hand during all the service this morning. When the clergyman had said his last words at the grave—they were the first flowers dropped into the horrid abyss—poor Josephine tottered to the edge and let them fall. Strange enough it seemed to stand there and perform these monstrous rites for the poor yesterday-so-much-living boy—in this far-away, alien city. Even after them, and at this hour—it all seems like some deadly clever game or invention—to beat Tauchnitz[3] of his own. I stay three or four days and rest—see the Museum, etc.—and then I go back, the same way—by Cologne, Brussels, etc.—but not so fatiguingly fast. There seems little appearance that I shall travel with them—or wait for them—the three women: they are now perfectly capable themselves. They will probably write your wife their plans. They have plenty of present money. I am very tired—*auf Wiedersehen* to both of you.

Yours always—
Henry James

1. HJ's young friend Balestier (see Letter 83) died of typhoid fever in Dresden.

2. Balestier's sister, Caroline Starr Balestier (1865–1939), who married Rudyard Kipling in 1892.

3. Balestier, in partnership with Heinemann, had organized a new softcover publishing house to compete with the continental Tauchnitz editions.

91 · To W. Morton Fullerton

Ms Harvard

34 De Vere Gardens W.
Jan. 18*th* 1892

It is always charming, *mon cher enfant*,[1] to see a scrap of your predestined publicity perverted toward me and to consume in private what was meant for mankind. I echo almost hysterically your sage animadversions about the bards of the breakfast. Vulgarer crudities never usurped a vulgarer chance. The floods of verbiage of your personal organ and of all the others bow me down with unassuagable melancholy. We have—over here—the genius of frumpy hypocrisy and clumsy cant. The *Times* would be worse without you—that is all I can say. *I* am worse without you (than I was with you), so that the induction is justified. London is pestilential and I am seedy. You asked me some time ago sometimes to send you something I write—so I risk the January *Atlantic* with a paper on Lowell[2] which you perhaps won't have seen. I *have* a sick sorethroat or I would pour forth a profuse strain. *Soignez-vous*, my dear child, and *soignez bien* any sympathy that you may continue to entertain for yours always

Henry James

P.S. I today, at All Souls', Langham Place, "gave away" Carolyn Balestier to Rudyard Kipling[3]—a queer office for *me* to perform—but it's done—and an odd little marriage.

1. Son of a Congregationalist clergyman, the Connecticut-born Fullerton (1865–1952) was a contemporary of Santayana and Berenson at Harvard and in the late 1880s worked as a literary journalist in Boston. In 1890 he was appointed to the London *Times*. He was welcomed from the first by HJ, but moved also in the homosexual world of Oscar Wilde and Lord Ronald Sutherland Gower, the sculptor.

2. HJ's memorial essay, "James Russell Lowell," *Atlantic* LXIX (January 1892), 35–50, reprinted in *Essays in London and Elsewhere* (1893).

3. See Letter 90.

92 · To Mrs. Hugh Bell

Ms Private

34 De Vere Gardens W.
Tuesday
[23 February 1892]

Dear Mrs. Bell.[1]

I am very sorry you are *not* here to mingle with these things—it would make them so much more interesting. In your absence they are, honestly, scarcely enough so to kindle in me the flame of the valued reporter. Still, I have seen them as through a glass darkly and you are welcome to the faint repercussion. Oscar's play (I was there on Saturday)[2] strikes me as a mixture that will run (I feel as if I were talking as a laundress), though infantine to my sense, both in subject and in form. As a drama it is of a candid and primitive simplicity, with a perfectly reminiscential air about it—as of things *qui ont traîné*, that one has always seen in plays. In short it doesn't, from that point of view, bear analysis or discussion. But there is so much drollery—that is, "cheeky" paradoxical wit of dialogue, and the pit and gallery are so pleased at finding themselves clever enough to "catch on" to four or five of the ingenious—too ingenious—*mots* in the dozen, that it makes them feel quite *"décadent"* and *raffiné* and they enjoy the sensation as a change from the stodgy. Moreover they think they are hearing the talk of the *grand monde* (poor old *grand monde*), and altogether feel privileged and modern. There is a perpetual attempt at *mots* and many of them *râter*: but those that hit are very good indeed. This will make, I think, a success—possibly a really long run (I mean through the Season) for the play. There is of course absolutely no characterization and all the people talk equally strained Oscar—but there is a "situation" (at the end of Act III) that one has seen from the cradle, and the thing is conveniently acted. The "impudent" speech[3] at the end was simply inevitable mechanical Oscar—I mean the usual trick of saying the unusual—complimenting himself and his play. It was what he was there for and I can't conceive the density of those who seriously reprobate it. The tone of the virtuous journals makes me despair of our stupid humanity. Everything Oscar does is a deliberate trap for the literalist, and to see the literalist walk straight up to it, look straight at it and step straight into it, makes one freshly avert a discouraged gaze from this unspeakable animal. The Mitchell-Lea affair[4] was naturally, yesterday afternoon before a fatally female and but languidly *empoignée* house, a very different pair of sleeves. It is a perfectly respectable and creditable effort, with no gross awkwardness or absurdity in it, nothing in the least calculated to make the producers redden in the watches of the night. But it is too long, too talky, too thin and too colourless, rather flat and rather grey. I should think that it was capable of compressibility into a quite practicable three-act drama (there are *five*, just heaven) which would produce an effect. Marian Lea was clever and pretty.—But come up to town and stir up the pot yourself. Miss Robins spoke a prologue, very well save that one couldn't hear her. I'm delighted the gallant boy is disrubescent. May he soon release you to your natural duties. Thanks for your kind attention to *Nona V.*[5]—a very small and simple *fantaisie* of which the end is soon. I greet all your house and am yours, dear Mrs. Bell, most truly

Henry James

1. Florence Bell (née Olliffe, 1852–1930) had married a wealthy Yorkshire colliery owner; a minor dramatist herself, she became a strong supporter and confidante of HJ in his stage endeavors.

2. HJ attended the opening of Oscar Wilde's *Lady Windermere's Fan* at the St. James's Theatre on 20 February 1892. The cast included George Alexander as Lord Windermere and Marion Terry as Mrs. Erlynne.

3. Wilde appeared before the audience wearing a metallic carnation in his buttonhole and holding a lighted cigarette in his hand.

4. Marion Lea and Langdon Mitchell were a producing team in London and friends of the Kentucky-born actress Elizabeth Robins (1863–1952), who was very much involved in Ibsen.

5. The first of two installments of HJ's short story "Nona Vincent" in the *English Illustrated Magazine,* in which Mrs. Bell may have recognized herself as the gifted "theatrical" woman whom HJ called Mrs. Alsager.

93 · *To William James*

Ms Harvard

34 De Vere Gardens
March 8*th* 1892

My dear William.[1]

Alice died at exactly four o'clock on Sunday afternoon (about the same hour of the same day as mother), and it is now Tuesday morning. But, even now the earliest moment my letter can go, or could have gone, to you is tomorrow P.M.—and there were innumerable things yesterday to do. Yesterday afternoon came your cable. You wouldn't have thought your warning necessary if you had been with us, or were with us now. Of course the event comes to you out of the comparative vague and unexplained, for you won't get our letters of Wednesday last and of Saturday for some days yet, alas. I wrote you as fully as I could on both of these days. On Saturday the end seemed near—yet also as if her strange power to *last* might still, for a few days, assert itself. The great sign of change on Saturday A.M. and, as I wrote you, the inexpressibly touching one, was the sudden cessation of all suffering and distress, which, up to Friday night, had been constant and dreadful. The pleuritic pain, the cough, the fever, all the sudden complications of the previous few days which came, so unmistakably, as *the* determining accident at the mercy of which we had felt her to be (and without which she might still have lived on for some weeks—even possibly,—though this I greatly doubt—some months): all these things which, added to the suffering they already found, were pitiful to see, passed from her in the course of a few hours, fell away blissfully and left her consciously and oh, longingly, close to the end. As I wrote you on Saturday, the deathly look in her poor face, added to this simplification, and which, in its new intensity, had come on all together in the night, made me feel that the end *might* come at any moment. I came away on Saturday afternoon, not to break the intense stillness which Katharine wished to create near in order that she might sleep— for though she was quiet she didn't sleep. Lloyd Tuckey[2] saw her, that evening, for the second time that day, and I was back there for the hours before 10. I wanted to stay the night—but Katharine thought I had better not—and it turned out better. For I couldn't have been in the room or done anything. She became restless again—but without pain—said a few barely audible things—(one of which was that she *couldn't*, oh, she COULDN'T and begged it mightn't be exacted of her, live *another* day), had two or three mouthfuls of nourishment at 1 or 2 and then, towards 6, sank into a perfectly gentle sleep. From that sleep she never woke—but after an hour or two it changed its character and became a loud, deep, breathing—almost stertorous, and this was her condition when I got to the house at 9. From that hour till 4 P.M. Katharine and Nurse and I sat by her bed. The doctor (who had doubted of the need of his returning, and judged that she would *not* live till morning) came at 11.30—but on Katharine's going down to him and describing exactly Alice's then condition, asked leave *not* to come into the room, as he preferred not to, in the last hour before death, when there was nothing to do or to suggest, unless it was insisted on. For about seven hours this deep difficult and almost automatic breathing continued—with *no* look of pain in the face—only more and more utterly the look of death. They were infinitely pathetic and, to me, most unspeakable hours. They would have been intolerable if it had not been so evident that all the hideous burden of suffering consciousness was utterly gone. As it is, they were the most appealing and pitiful thing I ever saw. But I have seen, happily, but little death immediately. Toward the end, for about an hour, the breathing became a constant sort of smothered whistle in the lung. The pulse flickered, came and went, ceased and revived a little again, and then with all perceptible action of the heart, altogether ceased to be sensible for some time before the breathing ceased. At three o'clock a blessed change took place—she seemed to sleep—I mean to breathe— without effort, gently, peacefully and naturally, like a child. This lasted an hour, till the respirations, still distinct, paused, intermitted and became rarer—at the last, for seven or eight minutes, only one a minute, by the watch. Her face then seemed in a strange, dim, touching way, to become clearer. I went to the window to let in a little more of the afternoon light upon it (it was a bright, kind, soundless Sunday), and when I came back to the bed she had drawn the breath[3] that was not succeeded by another.

I went out and cabled you about half an hour later—I knew you would be in great suspense every hour after her cable of the day before. Since then I have sat many hours in the still little room in which so many months of her final suffering were compressed, and in which she lies as the very perfection of the image of what she had longed for years, and at the last with pathetic intensity, to be. She looks most beautiful and noble—with *all* of the august expression that you can imagine—and with less, than before, of the almost ghastly emaciation of those last days. Only last night (I have not yet been at the house today) had a little look of change begun. We have made all the arrangements—they have been on the whole simple and easy—with the Cremation Society, for a service tomorrow afternoon (early) at Woking. Of course you know her absolute decision on this point—and she had gone into all the details. For myself I rejoice, as you doubtless will, and Katharine does, that we are not to lay her, far off from the others, in this damp, black alien English earth. Her ashes shall go home and be placed beside Father's and Mother's. She wished we should be simply four—Katharine and I, her Nurse, and Annie Richards,[4] who, though almost never seeing her, has shown devoted friendship to her ever since she (Annie) has been in England. I will try and send you a line tomorrow after it is over. Katharine is the *un*broken reed, in all this, that you can imagine, and I rejoice, unspeakably in the rest and liberation that have come to her. The tension—the strain and wear— of these last months has been more serious than any before—and I hope she won't go back immediately to new claims and responsibilities. She has, practically, a large margin of convenience here, as Alice's lease of that pleasant little house runs on till May 1st. She will probably stay yet a month. She considers that there were almost unmistakable signs, in the last weeks of Alice's life, of the existence of the *internal* tumour (the second one), which Baldwin last summer pronounced probable. The final "accident"—brought on (though at a moment when her strength was at the last ebb and her distress from the tumour in the breast and all her nervous condition and her perpetual gout and rheumatism was absolutely unbearable from day to day, and she was simply living from day to day, and night to night, on the last desperate resources of morphia and hypnotism)—this strange complication which simply *made* a sudden collapse of everything was ostensibly a mysterious cold, communicated by nurse (who had a bad one) and producing all the appearance of pleurisy—with a sharp pain in the side (she lived only in perpetual poultices the last three or four days—up to Saturday night when she wished everything off) and a dreadful cough which shook her to pieces and made impossible the quiet which was the only escape from the ever-present addition of "nervousness." But Katharine thinks that an internal tumour close to the lung, where Baldwin placed it, was accountable for much of this last disorganization. However, she will tell you, later, of all these things—perhaps you will think I try to tell too much. I shall write by this post briefly to Bob, but won't you please immediately send him this. I hope he got a prompt echo of my cable.—Katharine will probably also tell you immediately that Alice very wisely under the circumstances, I think, in an alteration made *lately* in her will, after your plan of coming abroad this summer for a year came home to her, named her (K.P.L.) and J. B. Warner[5] her executors. She had first named you and me—but she came later to think it probable that she would die this summer—live *till* then—during the months you would probably be in Europe—which would be for the execution of the will on your part a burdensome delay. Besides, with all the load upon you, she wished to spare you all trouble. But I *must* close this endlessness— even if I send you more of it by the same post. Ever yours, and your Alice's, and Bob's affectionate

Henry James

1. This letter, and those of the next few weeks, are written on mourning stationery, with a half-inch black border.

2. Dr. Charles Lloyd Tuckey, author of *Psycho-Therapeutics, or Treatment by Hypnotism and Suggestion,* treated AJ on the recommendation of WJ.

3. At this point HJ wrote the words "last breath," then crossed out the word "last" and added "that was not succeeded by another."

4. Annie Ashburner Richards (1846–1909), a close friend of AJ's, daughter of Samuel Ashburner of Cambridge and a cousin of the Sedgwicks.

5. Alice's lawyer.

94 · To Isabella Stewart Gardner

Ms Gardner

34, De Vere Gardens W.
Aug [September] 3d 1892

Dear Donna Isabel.[1]

I don't know where this will find you, but I hope it will find you with your hair not quite "up"—neither up nor down, as it were, in a gauze dressing-gown, on a seagreen (so different from pea-green!) chair, beneath a glorious gilded ceiling, receiving the matutinal tea from a Venetian slave. I never answered the delightful letter you were so good as to write me on the eve of your departure from Venice because I thought it only fair to leave you alone a month—to reward, in a word, by an effort of abnegation, the patience with which, during so many weeks, you harmonised our conflicting claims.[2] Now, however, that you have fallen back into your incorrigible hospitalities, you expose yourself to the outrage of friendship and I have—comparatively speaking—no scruple in peeping into your dim saloon. Don't tell me that you are *not* seated there in the attitude and costume which it was apparently my sole privilege to admire—I mean only *my* not my *only* privilege. I was haunted by vague apprehensions that you may be fidgetted by visions of cholera and quarantine—begotten indeed by the solitary, foolish little circumstance that an American youth (Richard Norton)[3] whom I was thinking of "sending" to you and who was at any rate to spend September in Venice, writes me that he has given it up at the behest of "the doctors." He was a fool to *ask* the doctors—one would know what they would say. I hope you have done nothing of the kind and indeed I don't see you. Therefore if the interlude is over, your light tread is again on the marble floors. I wish I could patter along that polished perfection of the library again.[4] I would give all the tin watering-pots I possess to see the big Tita come in, in the morning, on diffident tiptoes with my bath in a coffee-vessel. I should like greatly to hear your late adventures, and all about the Engadine and Bayreuth and the rest. Did you go to Vienna? I hope not—to be cooked over, like something underdone, which you surely are not. Did Bayreuth come off and did the Ranee[5] come on?

My own history has been mortally dull. After romance the sternest reality. I spent a fortnight near my brother on the Lake of Geneva—as "near" as was possible to a brother who started for Engadine and Chamounix as soon as I arrived—the inevitable reward of virtuous sacrifice.[6] *N'en faites jamais!* If it was to be done over—how I would have waited for the regatta! Delightful was your picture of this scene with the casual recompense of Mrs. Mason's[7] gondolier. I can see the gesture with which she shied at him! But I wish I had been there to see all the rest!—Do tell me how the dear old place looks and feels—only not how it smells—again! Are the little white papers on *my* clean shutters still? Probably not—and my pink chairs and my lemon sofa have also been snatched up. But tell me what chances survive—what *occasions* wait. I haven't seen the Curtises yet—they are still in Norfolk. But I believe they come up from one day to another. I am supposed to be at Brighton, but I came back yesterday under stress of

deplorable weather! I am in and out, but I have my eye on the pro-
prietors of the topmost floor. Tell me something about Asolo and the
unspeakable Goldona. Do go there; take a drive—and a walk—and a
sit for me.[8] Tell me about the court at tea-time and if there is any
jeunesse left to come to it. My brother and his wife and children spent
the winter in Florence and I fear I can't go to Italy again till I go to see
them. But I shall go as soon as I can. I shall, however, take intense
pains to be here when you come.—Is little Smith still in the field?[9]
Give my love to him if he is. I send *tanti saluti* to the padrone, and am
dear Donna Isabel, ever the padrona's devotissimo

Henry James

1. See Letter 55.

2. HJ is referring back to his visit to the Palazzo Barbaro during July 1892, when Mrs.
Gardner, who had rented the palace from the Curtises, was his hostess.

3. Charles Eliot Norton's son, later a director of the School of Classical Studies in
Rome.

4. With her overflow of guests, Mrs. Gardner converted the long rectangular library in
the Barbaro into a bedroom for HJ during his stay.

5. Margaret Brooke, Ranee of Sarawak (b. 1849), wife of the second "white rajah" in
Borneo, Charles Vyner Brooke, moved in Anglo-American circles in London and on the
Continent. HJ found her an affectionate and loyal friend. In the 1890s she had a love affair
with W. Morton Fullerton (see Letter 91).

6. WJ, on sabbatical, had brought his family to Europe.

7. See Letter 24, note 3.

8. Katharine De Kay Bronson, HJ's old Venetian friend, spent her summers at La Mura
in Asolo.

9. Joseph Lindon Smith, a Boston painter and a protégé of Mrs. Gardner's, who taught
decorative arts classes at the Museum of Fine Arts.

95 · To Sarah Butler Wister

Ms Congress

34 De Vere Gardens W.
January 20*th* 1893

Dear Mrs. Wister.

I have just written to Mrs. Leigh, and she may send you my letter—
but I must speak to you a direct, and very old friend's, word. I stood
by your mother's grave[1] this morning—a soft, kind, balmy day, with
your brother-in-law and tall pale handsome Alice, and a few of those

of her friends who have survived her, and were in town—and were not ill—as all the world lately has been. The number is inevitably small—for of her generation she is the last, and she had made no new friends, naturally, for these last years. She was laid in the same earth as her father—and buried under a mountain of flowers—which *I* don't like—but which many people, most people do. It was all bright, somehow, and public and slightly pompous. I thought of you and Mrs. Leigh "far away on the billow," as it were—and hoped you felt, with us here, the great beneficence and good fortune of your mother's instantaneous and painless extinction. Everything of the condition at the last, that she had longed for was there—and nothing that she had dreaded was. And the devotion of her old restored maid, Mrs. Brianzoni, appears to have been absolute—of every moment and of every hour. She stood there this morning with a very white face and her hands full of flowers. Your mother looked, after death, extraordinarily like her sister. Indeed the resemblance to Leighton's last drawing of Mrs. Sartoris[2] was *complete*. I mention these things—to bring everything a little nearer to you. I am conscious of a strange bareness and a kind of evening chill, as it were, in the air, as if some great object that had filled it for long had left an emptiness—from displacement—to all the senses. It seemed—this morning—her laying to rest—not but that I think, I must frankly say, the act of *burial* anything but inacceptably horrible, a hideous old imposition of the church—it seemed quite like the end of some reign or the fall of some empire. But she wanted to go—and she went when she could, at last, without a pang. She was very touching in her infirmity all these last months—and yet with her wonderful air of smouldering embers under ashes. She leaves a great image—a great memory.—I have greatly regretted to hear lately that you have not been well. Please receive, dear Mrs. Wister, all my sympathy—all my participation, which though far is not faint, in everything which touches you closely—and believe me when I say that I hope you will look upon me ever as your very constant old friend

Henry James

1. Mrs. Wister (1835–1908) and her sister Mrs. Leigh were daughters of the eminent Victorian actress Francis (Fanny) Anne Kemble and her American husband, the southern plantation owner Pierce Butler.
2. The former Adelaide Kemble, Mrs. Kemble's sister.

96 · To Edward Compton

Ms Texas

Hotel Westminster
rue de la Paix
Tuesday [2 May 1893]

My dear Compton.

I answer your note immediately, as it contains some words about a point, in the play,[1] which should be cleared up without loss of time. Of course I never dreamed of looking to you for any "criticisms"—and to tell the truth wouldn't have *wanted* any, this time, as they mainly disturb and disconcert while the work is under way and one's nerves are in tension. I only expected—what you have *given* me—a voice, on the question of whether or no you *liked* the act—as a spectator, an irresponsible outsider in your stall—thought it interesting as a *beginning,* the first chapter of a story etc. This hope you have answered very agreeably and I have been delighted that you and your wife have been able to say so emphatically that, sitting there in your box, you *are* interested. It was all that was to be expected or desired that you *should* say. But—Oh, monstrous *but!*—it behoves me to let you know without even a day's delay that the "ending" that you express a dread of *is* the only ending I have ever dreamed of giving the play. I oughtn't to talk of "giving" it to the play—it *is* the play, the very essence and meaning of the subject—which is what I meant by telling you (as I recall that I did) that the subject was a case of "magnanimity." The idea of it is that Domville throwing up the priesthood to take possession of his place in the world etc. finds, in fact, that he comes into the world only to make himself happy at the *expense* of others—a woman in one case (act 2), a man in the other (act 3); and in the face of this reality—ugly and cruel—turns back again to his old ideal, renounces his personal worldly chance, sacrifices himself and makes the others happy. *That* subject seemed to me simple, charming, touching—very pretty. To make him come out (of his old ideal) simply to *marry* Mrs. Peverel is, for me, not only no subject at all, but a very ugly and displeasing (as well as flat and undramatic) substitute for one. To make a Catholic priest, or a youth who is next door to one (the interest of the play is that he is just all *but* one) *marry,* really, when it comes to the point, *at all,* is to do, to spectators—a disagreeable and uncomfortable thing: the utmost length one may go to is represent him as thinking, as dreaming, for an hour, that he innocently and blissfully *may*. The subject, as I have entertained it, appears to me *charming*—picturesque, tender, human, dramatic, and with the pathos of it not too grave to injure the pretty comedy atmosphere. But of course if your public is such a public that it can't see any of that charm, and wants such a *bêtise* instead, we are engaged in a blind-alley—and the sooner we recognise it the better. My *dénouement* is my very *starting-point*—and my subject is my subject, to take or to leave. If your conviction is that the piece won't *go* unless Guy marries Mrs. Peverel (for he *doesn't* of course marry the other female), then it is a blessing (though mingled with bitterness) that the words of your letter have revealed it to me without a further prolongation of our illusion. They have caused the pen to drop from my hand this morning and my work is suspended till I hear from you again. I can't work of course straight *into* the thing (with my eyes open) that is going to prove an objection. What I want to hear from you is that—or *whether*—you, *after reflection,* are still strongly convinced that Domville's return (after his misleading erratic episode) to the holy place he had forsaken, will be fatal for an audience. You *seem* to feel it very strongly—you allude to it as an impossibility. But I ask you to look at it as a *possibility*—and *then* to tell me what you think. If you are still then of the same mind we must simply drop Guy Domville. (I shall in that case probably go on with him *myself*—I am so fond of him; addressing him to other conditions.) What happens in II and III is in three words that he finds (discovers) on the very eve of marriage, that Mary Brasier is being *sacrificed* to him, and then, in dismay and remorse, throws up, on the spot, all the advantages and prospects, her fortune, her young beauty, the pleasures of the life he has been introduced to [through] her, and *ensures*—brings about—her union to the man she really loves. Yearning still, after this, for the fuller taste of life that has been dashed from him, he swings back to Porches—only to realise that his happiness there will, if realised, be on the ruins of that of his old friend—and he determines to bring about the union of Humber and Mrs. Peverel—and then to steal beneficently back to the cloister. He *does* this and ends in beauty and glory, as it were. This is a bald account of the matter and I only write the meagre words because as I just definitely *sound* you on the subject of the dénouement I thought it not fair not to add a few sentences that will show you a little more what I mean by it. *Do* I mean something that your audience won't understand? It is a *complete* surprise to me to suppose so, for I have been going on with a great sense of security. Your note of alarm is a blight that comes now far better than later, but such as it is it has cast such a shade over the future that I shall not be able to recover myself before I hear from you again—and time, alas, is precious. Be absolutely frank, on this point, and as clear as you can *see.* I feel that I must, moreover, add this: that my plan, such as it is, is an absolutely *final* one. I can make another (which will be another play), but I can't touch *this* one. Above all don't if you *are* distinctly sceptical try to persuade yourself that you *do* believe. I'll take hold—as soon as I can *get* hold—of another subject—but this effort is wasted.

Yours ever
Henry James

1. HJ had sent Edward Compton the first act and a scenario for the remaining two acts of a play titled *Guy Domville.* He considered it suitable for the Compton Comedy Company, which specialized in romantic plays. The Comptons liked the first act and the scenario, but (as with their production of *The American*) asked for a "happy ending." To give the earlier play that kind of ending, HJ had written a new fourth act. This letter, one of a series of long letters to Compton, expresses HJ's bewilderment—as he said in an earlier letter written three days before this one: "I have a general strong impression of my constitutional inability to (even in spite of intense and really abject effort) *realise* the sort of simplicity that the promiscuous British public finds its interest in—much more, after this indispensable realisation, to *achieve* it. Even when I think I am dropping most diplomatically to the very rudiments and stooping, with a vengeance, to conquer, I am as much 'out of it' as ever, and far above their unimaginable heads" (29 April 1893, Ms Texas).

97 · *To George Alexander*

    Ms Unknown

2 Wellington Crescent,
Ramsgate
Sunday [2 July 1893]

Dear Mr. Alexander.[1]

I counted fully when I last saw you on sending a *part* of what I spoke of to you, the other day, before so many days had elapsed. But I counted without a good many complications—in fact an unprecedented number of domestic hindrances—from which, finally, how-ever, I have fled, and shall not return—remaining out of town—"in spite of all temptations"—for the present. At the same time I wanted to wait to send you *with* the finished first act (of one of the subjects I alluded to) the scenario, as detailed as possible, of the other two acts. But, not to delay longer, I have determined to dispatch by the same post as this note, in another cover, a fresh type-copy of the said first act, which has just come in and which I have been waiting for. A de-tailed Scenario of Act Second goes this evening to the copyist—who will quickly return it, so that you shall have it in three or four days. A statement of Act III will come to you two or three days later. In the meanwhile you will perhaps find time to read the complete first act. These things will constitute "exhibit" No. I.—In the group of three subjects I spoke to you of.

"Exhibit" No. II is the scenario of a three-act comedy pure and simple, on an intensely contemporary subject,[2] which you shall re-ceive in the course of a small number of days after getting the state-ment of Act III of this first thing. The Scenario in question was drawn up two months ago—but I want to recopy it and send it to be type-copied. This will take but little time.

Exhibit No. III is a three-act contemporary play, less purely a comedy,[3] but on a subject very beautiful to my sense—of which the complete Scenario is yet to write. Now that I have quiet conditions, however, I can promise you that you shall not have to wait for it very long. These three subjects have of course in common that they are essentially subjects with a hero—dealing with a *man's* situation. In the second the man is scarcely ever off the stage.—It occurs to me that I may perhaps have some difficulty this Sunday afternoon in getting my big first-act book in a Ramsgate letter-box. Please understand therefore that if it doesn't reach you with this tomorrow morning it will in the evening.

Yours very truly,
Henry James

1. The actor-manager George Alexander (1856–1918) was at the height of his career when HJ sent him his play *Guy Domville*, originally intended for Compton (see Letter 96).

2. It is difficult to say which scenario this was; it might have been the one based on his short story "The Chaperon." See HJ, *Complete Plays*, ed. Edel (1949), 457–462.

3. From HJ's description this would probably have been his scenario for *The Reprobate*, published in *Theatricals: Second Series* (1895).

98 · *To W. Morton Fullerton*

Ms Harvard

2 Wellington Crescent
Ramsgate, July 14*th* [1893]

My dear Fullerton.

No, I'm not a brute for having failed so long to thank you for the good offices, proffered at least, of your last letter, and for the touching two words you had the friendly thought of sending me when the indignity that life had heaped upon poor Maupassant found itself stayed.[1] I wanted moreover to applaud your energy and vivacity during the *journées de juin* and the art with which you brought internecine warfare home to us.[2] But not till this hour, as ever is, have I been sufficiently my master to thank you for these luxuries. The detail of my servitude would not interest you; but knowing my feeble powers of resistance you will believe in the fact. I don't know what prevented my wiring you a crystalline tear to drop on Maupassant's grave. Or rather, I do. Everything prevented it, including the fact that my tears had been already wept; even though the image of that history had been too *hard* for such droppings. I have taken refuge from the abominations and over-populations of London in this refined retreat, where there is no one I know—no one but 'Arry and his female, who don't know me— or at least pretend they don't, a delicacy of which Mayfair is incapable. *J'y suis, j'y reste.* It was very good of you to offer to send me the last distillation of Bourget and the last chunk of Zola.[3] They lie at present on my intellectual board. What *won't* the French write about next? Strange are the loves of a sick sexagenarian and his niece. Yet I love my Zola. Also my Fullerton and am his ever

Henry James

1. Guy de Maupassant died on 6 July 1893 in an insane asylum in Paris, his insanity a consequence of syphilis.
2. Fullerton had written a series of dispatches for the *Times* on France's political situation.

3. The Bourget novel was *Un Scrupule*; Zola's novel was *Le Docteur Pascal*, in the Rougon-Macquart series.

99 · *To Elizabeth Robins*

Ms Texas

The Athenaeum,
Wednesday 2 P.M.
[6 December 1893]

Dear Miss Robins.[1]

Only a word to say that the result (for your very sympathetic ear) of the ghastly—yes, it's the word!—two hours I have just brought to a close at Daly's is that I write to him to-night to withdraw my piece.[2] The "rehearsal" left me in such a state of nervous exasperation that I judged it best—or rather I could only control myself and trust myself enough—to say, simply, to him, after the last word was spoken: "I shall take some hours to become perfectly clear to myself as to the reflections which this occasion—taken in connection with your note of Saturday, causes me to make. And then I will write to you—" and then to walk out of the theatre. To Ada Rehan (white, haggard, ill-looking almost in *anguish*) I couldn't bring myself to *speak*. I know Bourchier[3] and said good-bye to him—but I was not given a single *second's* opportunity of having the least contact or word with any other member of the company; who began and stammeringly *read* their parts the instant I came in, and vanished the instant the third act ended. Don't pity me too much—rather rejoice with

Yours always
Henry James

1. Elizabeth Robins, the actress who helped introduce Ibsen into England. She played the role of Madame de Cintré in HJ's *The American*.

2. Augustin Daly (1838–1899), the American producer, had accepted HJ's play *Mrs. Jasper*, later renamed *Disengaged*, for his star Ada Rehan (1860–1916) and scheduled it for his London season.

3. Arthur Bourchier (1863–1927), actor-manager and a founder of the Oxford University Dramatic Society.

100 · *To Dr. W. W. Baldwin*

Ms Morgan

34 De Vere Gardens W.

January 26*th* [1894]

My dear Baldwin.[1]

I write you in much embarrassment and perplexity. Mrs. Benedict's cable was the first news I have had of poor Miss Woolson's being— having been—even ill,[2] and it was accompanied with the expression of the wish that I should go to Venice. In my horror and distress I began to make preparations to get off as soon as possible—but a sec- ond cable from her a few hours later, mentioning, or implying, that Miss [Grace] Carter had come, combined with your own two most kind telegrams—these things have made me delay and ask myself if what can be done is not being done so effectually by Miss C. and the American consul (whose immediate and adequate action I have taken for granted,) that, reaching there on Tuesday or Wednesday (the earli- est moment I *can*,) I should probably find myself confronted with mere accomplished facts. Her (Miss Carter's) wiring you not to come even from Florence seems to me to suggest all this. But I wired her yesterday afternoon asking her to tell me if she *desired* me—and getting no an- swer, I have again repeated the inquiry. I know you are deadly busy, and infinitely worried, but if you can find time to tell me *something* of what has so strangely and sadly happened I shall be very very grateful. To me it is all ghastly amazement and distress. I hadn't even heard Miss Woolson was ill. Hadn't she sent for *you?* I have a dismal, dread- ful image of her being alone and unfriended at the last. But what sud- den disaster overtook her—pneumonia supervening on influenza? That her funeral is to be in Rome—where she would have wished—is in some degree a comfort. But poor isolated and fundamentally tragic being! She was intrinsically one of the saddest and least happy natures I have ever met; and when I ask myself what I *feel* about her death the only answer that comes to me is from what I felt about the melan- choly, the limitations and the touching loneliness of her life. I was greatly attached to her and valued exceedingly her friendship. She had no dread of death and no aversion to it—rather a desire and even a passion for it; and infinite courage and a certain kind of fortitude. Eternal peace be her portion! *Can* you write to me—no matter how briefly? This won't reach you for two or three days—but even then if I can do any good by coming I will do so. I expect at any rate to come about April first—at least I fondly hope it. I have written to Miss Carter and told her what I tell you. I take it, however, the funeral can be delayed a very small number of days, and that I should now, with whatever speed it would be at all possible to make, miss it. Do tell me about it—it must have been difficult to arrange. Your last letter to me is still unacknowledged. You have my tenderest compassion in your hideous, your cruel loss of money. What burdens you carry and what blows you get! Very sad indeed, and very characteristic of a dreadful American type of life and character, your brother's dreadfully painful story. I can well believe how it has overdarkened you. But I hope it is all growing less bad. Meanwhile I rejoice that you have struck a vein of such terrible interest in your poor infinitely to be helped and pitied *contadini*.[3] The Sicilians have profoundly one's sympathy. Poor Italy— but how I want to see it! *Poveri noi!* Excuse my haste and incoherency. Yours, my dear Baldwin, evermore

Henry James

1. See Letter 83, note 6.

2. Constance Fenimore Woolson had been a close friend of HJ's since the early 1880s (see Letter 50). Her letters to him, published in Edel, ed., *Henry James, Letters* III (1980), reveal a strong affection for him. See also Edel, *Henry James, A Life* (1985). Mrs. Clara Benedict, Fenimore's sister, first informed HJ of her death; and Grace Carter, a cousin, who happened to be in Munich, went to Italy to make the funeral arrangements.

3. Dr. Baldwin devoted much time to the health of the Tuscan peasants in the Abruzzi.

101 · To John Hay

Ms Brown

34 De Vere Gardens W.
January 28*th* 1894

My dear Hay.

Your telegram, and Nevin's[1] share in it, last night, lifted a terrible weight off my spirit, and I can scarcely express to you the comfort I take in the knowledge that you are in Rome and that poor Miss Carter, with her burden of dreadful exertion and responsibility, has been able to look to your sympathy and cooperation. Up to five o'clock yesterday afternoon I expected to start this morning for Rome, arriving, if I should make my connections, at 6 on Tuesday morning—in order, simply, to stand, that day, by that most unhappy woman's grave. But coming in—from Cook's office—with my preparations made—I found on my table a note from Miss Fletcher[2] (of Venice—who is now in London), enclosing a cutting from a Venetian newspaper which gave me the first shocking knowledge of *what* it was that had happened. Before the horror and pity of it I have utterly collapsed—I have let everything go, and last night I wired to Miss Carter that my dismal journey was impossible to me.[3] I have, this morning, looked it more in the face, but I can't attempt it. I shall wire you tomorrow morning—one can do nothing here to-day; but meanwhile I must repeat to you that with the dreadful *image* before me I feel a real personal indebtedness to you in the assurance I have of your beneficent action and tenderness—in regard to offices that you will scarcely know how to make soothing and pitying enough. Will you very kindly express to Nevin my appreciation (as an old friend of his as well as of hers) of every consoling honour that he may pay? Miss Woolson was so valued and close a friend of mine and had been so for so many years that I feel an intense nearness of participation in every circumstance of her tragic end and in every detail of the sequel. But it is just this nearness of emotion that has made—since yesterday—the immediate horrified rush to personally *meet* these things impossible to me. I can't *think* of Venice for the present—nor of any other inevitable vain contacts in Rome (apart from the immense satisfaction of seeing you and your wife); from the moment there is nothing of value for me to *do*. She had always been, to my sense (and I think must have been to that of almost all her friends—those who were not too stupid), a woman so little formed for positive happiness that half one's affection for her was, in its essence, a kind of anxiety; but the worst sensibility to suffering or exposure to disaster that I ever apprehended for her was far enough from this brutal summarized tragedy. I have, as yet, no understanding of it or of its monstrous suddenness—and can only, till I know something, take refuge in a dim supposition of the ill (spoken in this hideous Venetian paragraph) that always haunted her—some misery of insomnia pushed to nervous momentary frenzy. But what a picture of lonely unassisted suffering! It is too horrible for thought! The only image I can evoke that interposes at all is that of the blest Roman cemetery that she positively *desired*—I mean in her extreme love of it—and of her intensely consenting and more than reconciled rest under the Roman sky. *Requiescat.* I shall wire you tomorrow asking you to kindly see that some flowers with my name attached are laid beside her there. Will there not be, for kindness' sake, and that of her so extremely honourable literary position, a few Americans (having known her or not) to stand with you there? I should be grateful to you if you would express to Miss Carter for me (though I have already done it myself and shall do it again) my sense of what all Miss Woolson's friends owe to her devotion in surmounting the added difficulties of burial in Rome.—I didn't know, my dear Hay, till last night, that you were in Rome, or at all where you were; beyond the general supposition that you were still in Europe. When you were in London last summer I was abroad, and I have had no chance—until this so somber one—to find myself in relation with you since. But there was an occasion—almost equally somber—a couple of months ago when only the constant over-pressure that one's life seems never to cease to bring with it prevented me from writing to you. Indeed the intention to write has remained all the while at the back of my head. Miss Woolson, in a letter from Venice, briefly mentioned to me the startling fact of Clarence King's mental illness—without any details.[4] I was infinitely shocked; you were the first person I thought of and I had the most cordial impulse to write to you. But I didn't know in the least where you were; other occupations and pre-occupations overbore it, and I daresay you were conscious of my silence. But please believe that there was a sympathy for you in it. The fact itself is tragic enough—but I don't know what the real truth may be—for better or worse. What a history—what a denouement! Won't you, my dear Hay, write to me now—(with something of yourselves too, and of your movements and whereabouts these next weeks and months?) You have my heartiest wish for your own exemption from ills. It has been a real balm to talk with you this morning, and I am yours more than ever

Henry James

1. John Hay (1838–1905), who had been one of Lincoln's secretaries and would later become secretary of state, was a friend of HJ's from the early 1870s. He was also an old friend of Miss Woolson's. Robert Jenkins Nevin was for many years rector of St. Paul's American Church in Rome.

2. Constance Fletcher (1858–1938), who wrote under the name of George Fleming, was an old friend of HJ's and a long-time resident of Venice. Among her popular works was *Kismet.*

3. Miss Woolson's death was reported as a suicide by newspapers in Venice, London, and New York. Her family claimed that she had fallen from a small window into the little Venetian street behind the palace in which she had her apartment. HJ seems from the first to have accepted the idea of suicide. Miss Woolson was buried 31 January in the non-Catholic (commonly called the Protestant) cemetery in Rome near the graves of Keats and Shelley.

4. Clarence King (1842–1901), first head of the U.S. Geological Survey and a close friend of John Hay and Henry Adams.

102 · To Francis Boott

Ms Harvard

34 De Vere Gardens W.
Jan. 31st [1894]

My dear Francis.[1]

I had a letter from you a fortnight ago which about this time I should be answering—thanking you for. It is not for that I write you now, however, but because I feel how, like myself, you must be sitting horror stricken at the last tragic act of poor C.F.W. I can't *explain* it to you—it is with my present knowledge, too dreadfully obscure—and I am tired with the writing and telegraphing to which I have had to give myself up in consequence—especially with the exhaustion of a second long letter to poor Mrs. Benedict (258 Fourth Avenue, New York). Besides, I am still too sickened with the news—too haunted with the image of the act—and too much, generally, in darkness. For three days I only knew (by a cable from Mrs. Benedict) that she was dead—and I was almost in the very act of starting for Rome—to be present at her funeral (she is buried *there* today—Mrs. B. had asked me to go to Venice, and I hadn't been able to get off), when the evening papers here told the rest of the dreadful story. (She had had influenza and I simply supposed at first that it had quickly taken some fatal form.) The event seems to me absolutely to demand the hypothesis of sudden *dementia* and to admit of none other. Pitiful victim of chronic melancholy as she was (so that half one's friendship for her was always anxiety), nothing is more possible than that, in illness, this obsession should abruptly have deepened into suicidal mania. There was nothing *whatever*, that I know of, in her immediate circumstances, to explain it—save indeed the sadness of her lonely Venetian winter. *After* such a dire event, it is true, one sees symptoms, indications in the past; and some of these portents seem to me now not to be wanting. But it's all unspeakably wretched and obscure. She was not, she was never, wholly sane—I mean her liability to suffering was like the *doom* of mental disease. On the other hand she was the gentlest and kindest of women—and to me an admirable friend. She wished to be buried in Rome. Her cousin Miss Carter came instantly from Munich and did everything. I will write you more of it all when I know more. You will be immensely touched and compassionate. What a world!—and life what a "treat"! Yours, dear Francis, always

Henry James

1. See Letter 16, note 3.

103 · To Mr. and Mrs. William James

Ms Harvard

Grand Hotel, Rome
May 28th 1894

My dear William—my dear Alice—

I wrote you a scrappy note from Ravenna a few days since—but I must follow it up, without delay, with something better. I came on here an hour afterwards, and shall remain till June 1st or 2d. I find Rome deliciously cool and empty and still very pleasing in spite of the "ruining" which has been going on so long and of which one has heard so much—i.e., the redemption and cocknefication of the ruins. It is "changed" immensely—as everyone says; but I find myself, I am afraid, so much *more* changed—since I first knew and rhapsodised over it, that I am bound in justice to hold Rome the less criminal of the two. I am thinking a little about going down—if the coolness lasts—for three or four days to Naples; but I haven't decided. I feel rather hard and heartless to be prattling about these touristries to you, with the sad picture I have had these last weeks of your—William's—state of suffering. But it is only a way of saying that that state makes me feel it to be the greater duty for me to be as well as I can. *Absit omen!* Your so interesting letter of the 6th, dictated to Alice, speaks of the possibility of your abscess continuing not to heal—but I trust the event has long ere this reassured, comforted and liberated you. Meanwhile may Alice have smoothed your pillow as even she has never smoothed it before. I turn quite sick when I hear from you that on top of this tribulation you have had to undergo another of Bob's fits of madness. This time it seems to me really a little too strong—too strong and too cruel—and I don't know what to say or to do to help you. Is the state produced in him by a difficulty in re-investing his capital? What else had he before him, for months, but this question of the *suites* of his withdrawal? Alas, alas, I bleed. Apropos of these things I have just received from Warner (from London) the legal paper to have executed in regard to my participation in the Wyckoff compromise[1]—he asking me to do this before a U.S. consul. But the paper is all drawn explicitly up to be put through before the consul in *London*—so that I am afraid I must wait till I get back there to have the thing done. Warner's note makes no allusion to this point—from which I judge he takes for granted I will do it simply on my return. I will go to see the consul here or in Florence and ask him if *he* can be substituted for the London one; but I am afraid he will say no—so that, as I have been desiring not to get back to De Vere Gardens before August 1st, I fear I may entail on you and Bob the wait of these intervening weeks—unless I go home sooner. Such delay as I may inflict upon you (making you *tarder* to come into your share of the $3000), I beg you both to forgive me. You speak of the question of the sending of the fourth copy of Alice's Diary to Bob (in his present profane state), as if it were a matter still under discussion—whereas I have been assuming that action was taken by Katharine in the sense in which I immediately wrote you that I had written her (in the 1st days of April), on hearing from you that the book had *not* been sent, and on hearing from Katharine that you judged it ought to be.[2] I had instantly judged likewise, and as Katharine had written to me that she was only waiting for my voice in the matter, I immediately expressed to her that I begged her without delay to transmit the copy to Bob. This seemed to me the only safe, and normal course, the only one putting us *à l'abri* from some violent resentment on his part. But it shows what "safety" is in dealing with a madman—that *now* the danger, the resentment, may be in his *having* it. At any rate is not his having it a *fait accompli*? I don't know for sure—for I haven't heard from Katharine since then. When I wrote to her (to send the book), I hadn't yet received my copy—delayed in London; and it only came a few days later—on which I wrote her again a letter which (discreet—on the subject of her editing—as it was) she may not have liked—perhaps; though this idea may be groundless on my part. At any rate I haven't as yet heard from her again—and am therefore in the dark as to Bob's possession or non-possession. As soon as I had *seen* the Diary the question began greatly to worry me—though I still hold that—given the fact that it *exists*, in the (to me!) regrettable form it does—the only thing that didn't put us (practically) too much in the wrong was to make him an equal inheritor of it with us. In other words—as I mentioned to you in my note from Ravenna—the printedness-*en-toutes-lettres* of so many names, personalities, hearsays (usually, on Alice's part, through *me!*) about people etc. has, through making me intensely nervous and almost sick with terror about possible publicity, possible accidents, reverberation etc., poisoned as yet a good deal of my *enjoyment* of the wonderful character of the thing—though it has not in the least dimmed my perception of that character. This has been above all really why (in addition to a peculiar pressure of occupation) I haven't written to you sooner on the subject. I was too depressed to face it! The other day, in Venice, Miss Wormeley,[3] who is with the Curtises, said to me, as if she knew all about it, "I hear your sister's *letters* have just been published, and are so delightful": which made me almost jump out of my skin. It will probably seem to you that I exaggerate; in fact I am sure it will, as neither of your letters makes any allusion to this disturbing feature—which to me was almost all (as it were) that I could *first* see. At any rate what I am *now* full of, as regards Bob's possession of the book, is the possible angry, irresponsible *communication* of it in his hands—or the equally irresponsible well-meaning but very dreadful-to-me-to-think-of adventures it may have in those of the two Marys.[4] I seem to see them showing it about Concord—and talking about it—with the fearful American newspaper lying in wait for every whisper, every echo. I take this side of the matter hard, as you see—but I bow my head to fate, and am prepared for the worst. *All* my sense of danger would have been averted if Katharine had only had a little more—had in about *twenty places* put blanks or initials for names. When I see that *I* say that Augustine Birrell[5] has a self-satisfied smirk after he speaks—and see that Katharine felt no prompting to exercise a discretion about the name—I feel very unhappy, and wonder at the strangeness of destiny. I used to say everything to Alice (on system) that could *égayer* her bedside and many things in utter confidence. I didn't dream she wrote them down—but this wouldn't have mattered—the idea of her doing so would only have interested me. It is the printing of these privacies *telles quelles* that distresses me, when a very few merely superficial discriminations (leaving her *text,* sacredly, really untouched) would have made all the difference! It is a "surprise" that is too much of a surprise, though meant so well. My observations about Birrell ("coloured" a little too to divert Alice!) were for instance made at a dining-club of which we both are members and about which I gossiped to the sister—on my principle of always bringing in the world to her and telling her in her sick solitude everything I could scrape together. As regards the life, the power, the temper, the humour and beauty and expressiveness of the Diary in itself—these things were partly "discounted" to me in advance by so much of Alice's talk during her last years—and my constant association with her—which led me often to reflect about her extraordinary force of mind and character, her whole way of taking life—and death—in very much the manner in which the book does. I find in its pages, for instance, many things I heard her say. None the less I have been immensely impressed with the thing as a revelation of a moral and personal picture. It is heroic in its individuality, its independence—its face-to-face with the universe for-and-by herself—and the beauty and eloquence with which she often expresses this, let alone the rich irony and humour, constitute (I wholly agree with you) a new claim for the family renown. This last element—her style, her power to write—are indeed to me a delight—for I never had many letters from her. Also it brings back to me all sorts of things I am glad to keep—I mean things that happened, hours, occasions, conversations—brings them back with a strange, living richness. But it also puts before me what I was tremendously conscious of in her lifetime— that the extraordinary intensity of her will and personality really would have made the equal, the reciprocal life of a "well" person—in the usual world—almost impossible to her—so that her disastrous, her tragic health was in a manner the only solution for her of the practical problem of life—as it suppressed the element of equality, reciprocity, etc. The violence of her reaction against her British *ambiente,* against everything English, engenders some of her most admirable and delightful passages—but I feel in reading them, as I always felt in talking with her, that inevitably she simplified too much, shut up in her sick room, exercised her wondrous vigour of judgment on too small a scrap of what really surrounded her. It would have been modified in many ways if she had *lived* with them (the English) more—seen more of the men, etc. But doubtless it is fortunate for the fun and humour of the thing that it wasn't modified—as surely the critical emotion (about them), the essence of much of their nature, was never more beautifully expressed. As for her allusions to H.—they fill me with tears and cover me with blushes. What I should *like* to do *en temps et lieu* would be, should no catastrophe meanwhile occur—or even if it should!—to *edit* the volume with a few eliminations of text and dissimulations of names, give it to the world and then carefully burn with fire our own four copies. I find an immense eloquence in her passionate "radicalism"—her most distinguishing feature almost—which, in her, was absolutely direct and original (like everything that was in her); unreflected, uncaught from entourage or example. It would really have made her, had she lived in the world, a feminine "political force." But had she lived in the world and seen things nearer she would have had disgusts and disillusions. However, what comes out in the book—as it came out to me in fact—is that she was really an Irishwoman!—transplanted, transfigured—but none the less fundamentally national—in spite of her so much larger and finer than Irish intelligence. She felt the Home Rule question absolutely as only an Irishwoman (not anglicised) could. It was a tremendous emotion with her—inexplicable in any other way—and perfectly explicable by "atavism." What a pity she wasn't born there—and had her health for it. She would have been (if, always, she had not fallen a victim to disgust—a large "if") a national glory!—But I am writing too much—and my late hindrances have left me with tremendous arrears of correspondence. I thank you, dear Alice, *caramente*, for your sweet letter received two or three weeks before William's. I crudely hope you won't let your house—so as to have it to go [to] in the summer. Otherwise what will become of you? I dig my nose into the fleshiest parts of the young Francis. Tell Peggy I cling to her—and Harry too, and Billy not less.—Thanks for the allusion to the Jones-Alexander situation. I judge, in fact, however, it is *not* a fiasco (*The Masqueraders*) but a success with a certain quantity of run in it—that will take it through the summer. The question of the rehearsals of my piece will probably loom before me early in the autumn. However I know nothing till I get back—and the unspeakable Jones, even for one of his minor achieve-

ments, may have months and months *dans le ventre.*—I haven't sent
you "The Yellow Book"—on purpose; and indeed I have been weeks
and weeks receiving a copy of it myself. I say on purpose because although my little tale which ushers it in ("The Death of the Lion")[6]
appears to have had, for a thing of mine, an unusual success, I hate too
much the horrid aspect and company of the whole publication. And
yet I am again to be intimately—conspicuously—associated with the
second number. It is for gold and to oblige the worshipful Harland (the
editor).[7] Wait and read the two tales in a volume—with two or three
others. Above all be *debout,* and forgive the long reticence of your
affectionate

Henry

1. Joseph Banges Warner (1848–1923) was the lawyer of members of the James family
including HJ. He was executor of AJ's estate and had just helped settle the estate of the
novelist's Wyckoff cousin.

2. See *The Diary of Alice James,* ed. Edel (1964). HJ's youngest brother, Robertson
(Bob), now lived in Concord, Massachusetts. AJ's friend Katharine Loring (see Letter 67)
printed four copies of the diary in 1894, for herself and the three surviving brothers of AJ.

3. Katherine Prescott Wormeley (1830–1908), American translator of Balzac's *Comédie Humaine.* She was a sister of Ariana Curtis.

4. The two Marys were Mary Holton James, Robertson's wife, and their daughter, later
Mary James Vaux, who did indeed publish portions of the diary in 1934.

5. Augustine Birrell (1850–1933) would later be president of the Board of Education and also chief secretary for Ireland. He was an essayist whose "Obiter Dicta" were
widely read.

6. "The Death of the Lion" appeared in the *Yellow Book,* I (April 1894), 7–52, and was
reprinted in *Terminations* (1895).

7. Henry Harland (1861–1905), expatriate American novelist and first editor of the
Yellow Book.

104 · To William James

Ms Harvard

34, De Vere Gardens W.
Aug. 10th '94

My dear William.

I have accidentally delayed to acknowledge your last remittance—
the $100 you lately sent from the June rents and for which many

thanks. I won't make this the occasion for a real letter—as I am pressed with occupation and my record is an empty one. London is empty, too, thank heaven—and we are having a dark, cold, wet summer—as different as possible from the last—that of *your* perspirations and problems. I go tomorrow for two or three weeks to St. Ives, Cornwall, where Mrs. Leslie Stephen[1] has kindly engaged me quarters. I have never been there—but I believe it is highly picturesque and very mild. And it is far from London—ten hours—and there is to be, to the best of my belief, no one I know there but the Stephens. I fear however the raininess of it. Leslie is writing his brother Fitzjames's Life[2] at the widow's instance and much *à contre coeur*—through having had no agreement with him, and no intercourse, on *any* one subject. He finds it therefore "difficult"—and no wonder. It is not thus that you will write mine.

I hope the promise of your early summer has been kept—I mean that the pigless Chocorua etc. has yielded compensations. I pray all be well with you. I think it is since I last wrote that I spent a night and morning with the Rudyard Kiplings in the country. He spouted to me many admirable poems—but all violent, as it were—and all about steamers and lighthouses. The best, however, are quite magnificent—they will all shortly be published and gathered together. I expect nothing more from him in any mature prose—save some beast-stories. Have you read the Jungle-book? So thrilling, but so bloody. His marriage is evidently most happy—but his American domicile half a mystery and half a misfortune.[3] *Basta.* I embrace you *all.* I hope your ameliorations hold.

Ever your
Henry

1. HJ's visit to the Stephens in Cornwall brought him into the landscape and domesticity later treated by Virginia Stephen (Woolf) in her novel *To the Lighthouse.*

2. *The Life of Sir James Fitzjames Stephen* (1895).

3. Rudyard Kipling, after his marriage to Caroline Balestier, resided for several years in Brattleboro, Vermont.

105 · To Marion Terry

Ms Colby

Reform Club, Pall Mall, S.W.
Saturday noon [5 January 1895]

Dear Miss Terry.[1]

I don't want to worry you—on the contrary; so this is only a mere word on the chance I didn't say a couple of nights ago *distinctly* enough that your business of the end of Act I—your going and leaning your face against the pillar of the porch—couldn't possibly be improved. Please believe from me that it is perfectly beautiful and *right*—like, indeed, your whole performance, which will do you great honour. Rest quiet, this weary day, at least about *that*.

Yours most truly
Henry James

1. Marion Terry, sister of Ellen Terry and an accomplished actress, played the leading role of Mrs. Peverel opposite George Alexander's Guy Domville.

106 · To William James

Ms Harvard

34 De Vere Gardens W.
Jan. 9th 1895

My dear William.

I never cabled to you on Sunday 6th (about the first night of my play) because, as I daresay you will have gathered from some despatches to newspapers (if there have been any, and you have seen them), the case was too complicated. Even now it's a sore trial to me to have to write about it—weary, bruised, sickened, disgusted as one is left by the intense, the cruel ordeal of a first night that—after the immense labour of preparation and the unspeakable tension of suspense—has, in a few brutal moments, not gone well. In three words the delicate, picturesque, extremely human and extremely artistic little play, was taken profanely by a brutal and ill-disposed gallery which had shown signs of malice prepense from the first and which, held in hand till the end, kicked up an infernal row at the fall of the curtain. There followed an abominable quarter of an hour during which all the forces of civilization in the house waged a battle of the most gallant, prolonged and sustained applause with the hoots and jeers and catcalls of the roughs, whose *roars* (like those of a cage of beasts at some infernal "zoo") were only exacerbated (as it were!) by the conflict. It was a cheering scene, as you may imagine, for a nervous, sensitive, exhausted author to face—and you must spare my going over again the horrid hour, or those of disappointment and depression that have followed it; from which last, however, I am rapidly and resolutely, thank God, emerging. The "papers" have into the bargain, been mainly ill-natured and densely stupid and vulgar; but the only two dramatic critics * who count have done one mere justice. Meanwhile all *private* opinion is apparently one of extreme admiration—I have been flooded with letters of the warmest protest and assurance. The horridest thing about the odious scene was that Alexander lost his head and made a speech of a dozen words in which (in his nervous bewilderment) he had the air of deferring to the rumpus as to the "opinion of the public," an accident that excited, outside of the obstreperous gallery, universal reprobation and of which he has since been, I think, signally ashamed. It is what Archer alludes to in the provisional few words in the *World*, which, with Clement Scott's article in the *Telegraph*, I send you by this post. I add two or three letters that will show you the "key" of the aforesaid "private" opinion. Every one who was there has either written to me or come to see me—I mean every one I know and many people I don't. Obviously the little play, which I strove to make as broad, as gross, as simple, as clear, as British, in a word, as possible, is over the heads of the *usual* vulgar theatre-going London public—and the chance of its going for a while (which it is too early to measure) will depend wholly on its holding on long enough to attract the *unusual*. I was there the second night (Monday, 7th) when, before a full house—a remarkably good "money" house Alexander told me—it went singularly well. But it's soon to see or to say, and I'm prepared for the worst. The thing fills me with horror for the abysmal vulgarity and brutality of the theatre and its regular public * *—which God knows I have had intensely even when working (from motives as "pure" as pecuniary motives *can* be) against it; and I feel as if the simple freedom of mind thus begotten to return to one's legitimate form would be simply by itself a divine solace for everything. Don't worry about me: I'm a Rock. If the play has no life on the stage I shall publish it; it's altogether the best thing I've done. You would understand better the elements of the case if you had seen the thing it followed (*The Masqueraders*) and the thing that is now succeeding at the Haymarket—the thing of Oscar Wilde's.[1] On the basis of *their* being plays, or successes, my thing is necessarily neither. Doubtless, moreover, the want of a roaring actuality, simplified to a few big *familiar* effects, in my subject—an episode in the history of an old English Catholic family in the last century—militates against it, with all *usual* theatrical people, who don't want plays (from variety and nimbleness of fancy) of different *kinds,* like books and stories, but only of *one* kind, which their stiff, rudimentary, clumsily-working vision recognizes as the kind they've had before. And yet I had tried so to meet them! But you can't make a sow's ear out of a silk purse.—I can't write more—and don't ask for details. This week will probably determine the fate of the piece. If there is increased advance-booking it will go on. If there isn't, it will be withdrawn, and with it all my little hope of profit. The time one has given to such an affair from the very first to the very last represents in all—so inconceivably great, to the uninitiated, is the amount—a pitiful, tragic bankruptcy of hours that might have been rendered retroactively golden. But I am not plangent—one must take the thick with the thin—and I have such possibilities of another and better sort before me. I am only sorry for your and Alice's having to be so sorry for yours forever,

Henry

P.S. I can't find the letter I wanted most to send you—it was so singularly eloquent and strong from (on the part of her husband too) Mrs. Frank Hill, wife of the ex-editor of the *Daily News*—both very old friends of mine. I have stupidly lost it somehow. But I stick in a little one from the dramatic critic of the *St. James's Gazette.* Clement Scott's article in the *Telegraph*—is the work of a man crudely awfully vulgar and Philistine—but I only mention it to show how he has been "drawn." But their standard of "subtlety"!—God help us! With one's i's all dotted as with pumpkins!—

* W. Archer and Clement Scott. I will send you Archer's next week notice.

* * I mean as represented by most of the Newspaper people—a really squalid crew.

1. *The Masqueraders* by Henry Arthur Jones (1851–1929). HJ had attended, on the first night of his own play, Oscar Wilde's new play at the Haymarket, *An Ideal Husband.*

107 · *To W. Morton Fullerton*

Ms Harvard

34 De Vere Gardens W.

January 9*th* 1895

My dear Fullerton.

Your sympathy enters into the soul of a man singularly accessible to affection and with whom sensibility to certain manifestations of it is a pleasure akin in its quality—almost to pain.—The vulgar, the altogether brutish rumpus the other night over my harmless and ingenious little play was the abomination of an hour—and an hour only. Deep and dark is the abyss of the theatre. Even in the full consciousness of the purity and lucidity of one's motives (mine are worthy of Benjamin Franklin) one asks one's self what one is doing in that *galère*. However, nothing matters but one's honour and one's sanity. The little play in question presents to the uncivilized the unpardonable anomaly of not belonging to the kind which is the only kind they know—a roaring actuality of intention united to a "bloody" crudity of execution. In the presence of that howling mob I felt once for all what an utter nonconductor such an atmosphere, even when comparatively cleared, must ever be to even the most simplified ingenuity and the most studied Britishness of which I am capable. You *can't*, after all make a sow's ear out of a silk purse—which is what I have been too heroically trying. The future is exquisitely rosy to me with the invitation to purge myself of that heroism and return to the exercise of diviner functions. I am purged—the other night purged me. Anderson's[1] part of the work was exquisite. I have innumerable notes to answer. I *have* been deluged with reassurance and admiration. But the play is wounded, probably to death. Fortunately it is not a vital member of yours, my dear Fullerton, very exhaustedly, preoccupiedly and responsively,

Henry James

P.S. If the thing comes off I shall probably publish it, and then you shall have a copy.

1. Percy Anderson, the stage designer.

5 · Discoveries
1895–1901

The letters written by Henry James during the five years after the failure of *Guy Domville*—the watershed of his creative life—tell us very little about his private feelings, although there are abundant indications in his notebooks and elsewhere that he went through a period of profound depression. The painful rejection by a London audience, addressed to him personally as he appeared on stage expecting to receive applause, had the effect of drawing him into a desire to try new themes and new techniques, to experiment in various ways that would take him away from earlier directions. It is in the subject matter of his novels and tales during this time that we can read how troubled his spirit was and how, beneath his brave show of activity and energy, a kind of chronic melancholy had set in. The works show some kind of psychological regression to earlier phases of his juvenile and adolescent being and helplessness. I have dealt with these psychological complexities in my biography of James. The stories James wrote on a series of themes new to his imagination eloquently put us into his preconscious and unconscious fantasies: stories about unsuccessful authors who are "too good" for their public and seem to die of their goodness, as if the *Guy Domville* episode had been a kind of death and rebirth; stories about psychologically abused children, little girls who muddle through to adult life, and little boys who die fighting for their manhood. This is the period too in which he produces his greatest and most important ghostly tales, as if he had crossed a boundary into the eerie world of Poe and the Ingoldsby Legends of Canon Barham. It is precisely at this juncture that he writes "The Turn of the Screw," which incorporates all three elements: the doomed little boy, the struggling little girl, and the regressed adolescent—the governess in whose charge the children are placed.

The postdramatic fiction from *The Spoils of Poynton* through *What Maisie Knew*, "In the Cage," and *The Awkward Age*—all placed in childhood and adolescence where his earlier novels dealt exclusively with adults—terminates in a strange novel, *The Sacred Fount*, which deals with the predatory war of the sexes. Read in sequence, these revelatory works show us Henry James in a full-blown "midlife crisis" triggered by his playwriting *débacle*. In the experimental novels we can discern his anxieties and his buried and long-suppressed sexual feelings.

We must remind ourselves that in his letters James speaks of his work only seldom and then usually tangentially—mainly about problems of getting it published. The letters I have selected are filled with peripheral hints of the turmoil within, well hidden behind his outward calm and pursuit of new modes of fiction and new techniques of narration—techniques that would filter into the innovations of Joyce and Virginia Woolf.

Termination of James's "dramatic years" brought an understandable desire to get away from London. He sought escape from the pressures of society and urban stress; he felt a need for a "great good place" (as he put it in a revealing story) where he could regain possession of his thwarted Selfhood. This resulted in his leasing Lamb House, a small but charming eighteenth-century house at Rye, in Sussex. What James overlooked at this juncture was his huge appetite for social life, and the ease with which he could escape loneliness—the loneliness of an aging bachelor—in Britain's metropolis. If his years of country life (with generous and frequent excursions to London) enabled him to commune with himself, and to work strenuously, they showed also, and as never before, the depth of his anchorite solitude. He had a good deal of country social life, and formed friendships with the little nest of novelists settled in this part of Sussex—Conrad and Hueffer, H. G. Wells and Kipling—but the great winter storms and the rainy weather often confined him to his fireside. He might figure himself as a country squire, but this did not suffice. And in his outpourings to younger men to come and stay with him, the long visits he received from the crippled Jonathan Sturges and his appeals to the attractive Morton Fullerton and Hendrik Andersen, we may see a bachelor whose life had been without love, and the apparently latent homoeroticism that was surfacing more and more in James.

His work continued to be "sacred," and this period saw a series of discoveries in narrative fiction of great importance later to the "modern movement." It was also a time of discoveries of the self in its new rural environment. In London he had longed for the peace of the countryside. In the countryside he longed for the bustle and variousness of London. The transition period led him, as he turned the corner into the Edwardian years, to his final major novels and the theme of "live all you can," which is at the heart of his turn-of-century *The Ambassadors*. That novel tells us that the depression of the late 1890s has been overcome, that James is ready for his final work.

108 · To William Edward Norris

Ms Yale

34, De Vere Gardens W.
January 10*th* 1895

My dear Norris.

I must indeed, my dear Norris, in spite of your prohibition, shake hands back—very firmly, very responsively. Your letter makes me too glad for me to hold my tongue over it—and I am touched even to tears at the image it gives me of your sitting there writing it in your so consecrated study, by the near-heaving sea and under the midnight lamp. It takes a load off my mind—the load of the sense of your having made the devoted journey, half across the wintry England, only to come in for *that*[1]—and then to have the dark mechanic return from the blighted pilgrimage. But I quite agree with you that no experience is wasted that has any really human vibration, and I can assure you that what your fidelity certainly did was to bring us nearer together. I shall never forget your kind, tenderly-embarrassed face when you came in to see me; nor how conscious I was that I couldn't bear up under the mere *sentiment* of what I felt. For I was in truth physically most seedy not having slept for several nights, and becoming at last aware of what a strain of fatigue the but just-ceased five weeks' high-pressure rehearsals had been. This made me mingle but poorly in the fine, rich gossip of some of my guests—but I was much better—after a better night—on the morrow. And now, thank God, that sorry business seems quite behind, or below, or at any rate, away from me. I don't know anything about the play save that on Monday, to a very full house, it went as at a highly successful *première*—beautifully, admirably. It has, however, *du plomb dans l'aile*—and a good deal, at any rate; and I am wholly prepared for the very worst. Thank heaven, indeed, there is *another* art—and that you *do* have a corner for me, however small, in the C.L. Beside the black abyss of the theatre the C.L. seems a chamber of the gods.—I must write you specifically about the best clause in your letter. I shall certainly see you again at Torquay and meanwhile I bless your sympathy, your hospitality and your daughter, and am, my dear Norris, affectionately yours

Henry James

1. William Edward Norris (1847–1925), minor Victorian novelist, described by HJ as "tremendously old-fashioned at 45." Norris had come from his home in Devonshire to attend the opening of *Guy Domville* and was among the guests invited to lunch with James the next day.

109 · *To Ariana Curtis*

Ms Dartmouth

34, De Vere Gardens, W.
Friday March 1st '95

Dear Mrs. Curtis.

Your proposal about my doing an article on Symonds would be most inspiring if ever so many things—or several, at least, were different. I have written to Horatio B. [1]—at the prompting of your letter—but I have had absolutely to say to him that exceedingly as his book interested me, and admirable, in many ways, as the subject of liberal review as it would be—and J.A.S. in general would be—it is impossible *I* should tackle the task. There are numerous reasons (of extreme present occupation with other work); but a more cogent reason than any other is that the job would be quite too difficult. The difficulty indeed would be (to my sense), insurmountable. There was in Symonds a whole side—*tout un côté*—that was strangely morbid and hysterical and which toward the end of his life coloured all his work and utterance. To write of him without dealing with it, or at least looking at it, would be an affectation; and yet to deal with it either ironically or ex-plicitly would be a Problem[2]—a problem beyond me. And then I didn't know him—I never saw him; and that, I think, would have to have been, for a critic of him, a corrective, a guide. In short I beg off, though H.B.'s two volumes have made the man much more interesting than he was to me before, and quickened greatly my sense of his ex-traordinary gifts. These were in their extent and variety, and in the really heroic vitality with which they were accompanied, most re-markable, I think. Yet there are also in him—in his work—there *were* in him—things I utterly don't understand; and a need of taking the public into his *intimissima* confidence which seems to me to have been almost insane.—All thanks for the new lights on the Edith-Cosimo story.[3] *Che vuole?* it all disappoints and depresses me. Edith seems to me to be wanting in dignity. That dear Mrs. B[ronson] hasn't a "proper pride" one has too much, always, felt; but my theory has always been that Edith *had.* But what becomes of even the properest when the pas-sion yclept "divine" undermines the dignity? If she is madly in love I'll excuse her. Otherwise not. I hate her going to shop and "wait on" the Rucellais in Florence almost as much as if she were my cousin. A per-son here who has been long (always) in Italy and much in Florence, tells me the Rucellais have no title *at all*—count or other, in their family. They are of the oldest *un*titled Florentine stock, like the Peruz-zis. The "count" is an invention (says she); for Edith?—But you will forget this frippery in the Singhalese jungle. Brave and wonderful you. I? *Jamais de la vie!* I hail your Ceylon plan, however, as a delightful sign of health and energy. However, *c'a tempo.* Angelo[4] as a father both in law and in equity is delightful. *Tanti saluti affetuose.*

Henry James

1. Mrs. Curtis urged HJ to review Horatio F. Brown's two-volume biography of the late John Addington Symonds (1840–1893), just published.

2. HJ alludes here to two "Problem" pamphlets written by Symonds, one dealing with Greek homosexuality and the other, "A Problem in Modern Ethics," with modern homo-sexuality. Symonds distributed the latter pamphlet to fifty of his friends, describing it as intended for "medical psychologists and jurists." His friends persuaded him not to circulate these works further, since this would have ruined his career and reputation, as the Oscar Wilde case soon showed. HJ had written a story about Symonds a decade earlier, "The Author of 'Beltraffio,'" the plan for which is in his notebooks under date of 26 March 1884.

3. HJ alludes here to Edith Bronson, the daughter of his old Venetian friend Katherine De Kay Bronson, who was being wooed by Cosimo Rucellai. The novelist later used this

courtship for his story "Miss Gunton of Poughkeepsie" (1900). The plan is recorded in the notebooks for 27 February 1895.

4. The Curtises' gondolier.

110 · To Mr. and Mrs. William James

Ms Harvard

34 De Vere Gardens W.
March 28*th* 1895

Dear Alice and dear William.

I have had within a few days a sweet letter from each of you. Yours, Alice, came to me the other day in Dublin; from which place I returned last night (after a stay of more than a fortnight), to find William's awaiting me here. I rejoice in the good news of your (Wm's) alleviated duties, easier work for the rest of the year. I hope the months will now ebb in a smooth current. I am much interested in your projected summer on the Cape and William's ulterior lectures in Colorado. How large your life swings compared to mine, and how much—beside the lone bachelor's—it takes in! I trust indeed, if these things depend upon it, that you may let the gentle Chocorua. I should think there would always be American families wanting such a "summer-home." But what I wish you most is comparative quiet—I mean immunity from the human deluge which seems to roll over you. But I fear that, with so many nets out and raking the waters, this is the boon that will be ever unattainable to you. Every glimpse you give me of your domestic life is a picture of heroic sacrifices, romantic charities, and acceptances of everyone else's burdens. It is magnificent—if it doesn't kill you. It almost kills *me* to think of it. My Irish episode,[1] thank heaven, is over, though the second phase of it, my visit to the sweet, really angelic (as host and hostess) Wolseleys, was as delightful as any experience of wasteful and expensive social idleness *can* be to a preoccupied and hindered worker. My six days at the Castle were a gorgeous bore, and the little viceregal "court" a weariness alike to flesh and spirit. Young Lord Houghton, the Viceroy, "does it," as they say here, very handsomely and sumptuously (having inherited just in time his uncle, Lord Crewe's, great property); but he takes himself much too seriously as a representative of royalty, and his complete Home

Rule—or rather hate—Home Rule boycotting by the whole landlord and "nobility and gentry" class (including all Trinity College, Dublin) leaves his materials for a "court," and for entertaining generally, in a beggarly condition. He had four balls in the six days I was there and a gorgeous banquet every night—but the bare official and military class peopled them, with the aid of a very dull and second-rate, though large, house-party from England. His English friends fail him—won't come because they know to what he is reduced; and altogether he is quite a pathetic and desolate and impossible young man—from the constant standing—in a cloud of aide-de-camps—on one's hind-legs—to [from] whom I was devoutly thankful to retire. He means well—but he doesn't matter; and the sense of the lavish extravagance of the castle, with the beggary and squalor of Ireland at the very gates, was a most depressing, haunting discomfort.—On the other hand the Royal Hospital (Lord W.'s residence as Commander of the Forces) was a very delightful episode. *They* do, really, all that poor Lord H. fails to do, and the military *milieu* and types were very amusing and suggestive to me. Lord W. is a singularly and *studiously*, delightful Person and my acquaintance of seventeen years with them has made our relations of the easiest, as it has made their kindness, really, of the greatest. They *dragged* me to them, quite; but if they did so they most sweetly made it up to me. The Royal Hospital—a kind of Irish Chelsea ditto, or Invalides for 150 old Irish soldiers (founded by Charles II), is a most picturesque and stately thing—out of which the residence of the Commander has been liberally carved. It contains one of the finest great halls in the British islands, in which, on the 14th (while I was still at the Castle), Lady W. gave a remarkably beautiful fancy-ball. The ladies were each a special Gainsborough, Sir Joshua or Romney portrait, and the men (save H.J.) in uniform, court dress or (most picturesque) hunt evening dress—the prettiest of all the fopperies of the English foppish class. I was, by special license, the sole black coat. But it is a blessing to have returned to one's own little workaday world and to begin to hoe again one's little garden. This is the last of my social episodes, for months to come; and I positively pine and languish for a long stretch of operose *complete* detachment, such as I can only get by leaving London. I shall probably have to wait for this to the first of May—but then I shall go for several months. I have, thank heaven, absorbing and magnificent work cut out—the best I have ever done; and I have also my eye on the right little place (not Ramsgate!) whose

name I won't yet reveal. I go down to see it, probably, next week—
even as you two will have gone, fruitfully, I trust, to reconnoiter at
Cape Cod. Is Harry[2] preparing to enter Harvard next autumn?—
Something in your letter seemed to suggest it. My love and blessing to
him if he is. Your anecdotes of Boott's[3] little tenacities and fidelities
are very touching. I owe him a letter which he shall soon have.

Your constant
Henry

1. This "episode" was HJ's visit to the Lord Lieutenant of Ireland, Robert Offley Ashburton Crewe-Milnes, 2d Baron Houghton (1855–1945), son of his old friend Richard
Monckton Milnes, the 1st Baron. He also visited Lord Wolseley (1833–1913), then
commander-in-chief in Ireland.

2. WJ's oldest son, Henry (1879–1947), called Harry to distinguish him from his
novelist-uncle.

3. Francis Boott (see Letter 16, note 3), after many years in Europe, was now living in
Cambridge, Massachusetts.

111 · To Edmund Gosse

Ms Leeds

34 De Vere Gardens W.
Monday [8 April] 1895

My dear Gosse.

Yes, I will come with pleasure to-morrow, Tuesday. Yes, too, it has
been, it is, hideously, atrociously dramatic and really interesting—so
far as one can say that of a thing of which the interest is qualified by
such a sickening horribility.[1] It is the squalid gratuitousness of it all—
of the mere exposure—that blurs the spectacle. But the *fall*—from
nearly twenty years of a really unique kind of "brilliant" conspicuity
(wit, "art," conversation—"one of our two or three dramatists, etc.")
to that sordid prison-cell and this gulf of obscenity over which the
ghoulish public hangs and gloats—it is beyond any utterance of irony
or any pang of compassion! He was never in the smallest degree interesting to me—but this hideous human history has made him so—in a
manner.[2] À demain—

Yours ever,
Henry James

1. Oscar Wilde had been charged two days earlier with offenses under Section 11 of the Criminal Law Amendment Act of 1885 (homosexuality). Bail was refused, and Wilde went to Holloway Jail.

2. On the envelope flap HJ scrawled, after he sealed the letter, "Quel dommage—mais quel Bonheur—que J.A.S. ne soit plus de ce monde." The allusion was to Symonds (see Letter 109).

112 · To Edmund Gosse

Ms Leeds

34 De Vere Gardens W.
Sunday [28 April 1895]

My dear Gosse.

Thanks—of a troubled kind, for your defense of my modesty in the *Realm*.[1] The article is brilliantly clever—but I have almost the same anguish (that is my modesty has) when defended as when violated. You have, however, doubtless done it great good, which I hereby formally recognise. These are days in which one's modesty is, in every direction, much exposed, and one should be thankful for every veil that one can hastily snatch up or that a friendly hand precipitately muffles one withal. It is strictly congruous with these remarks that I should mention that there go to you tomorrow A.M. in two registered envelopes, at 1 Whitehall, the fond outpourings of poor J.A.S.[2] I put them into two because I haven't one big enough to hold all—and it so happens that of that size I have only registered ones. I'm afraid I shan't see you—so preoccupied do the evenings seem—till the formidable 9th.[3] Our guest (you might have mentioned it in the *Realm*) has a malady of the bladder, which makes him desire strange precautions—and I see—I foresee singular complications—the flow of something more than either soul or champagne at dinner.—Did you see in last evening's halfpenny papers that the wretched O.W. seems to have a gleam of light before him (if it really counts for that), in the fearful exposure of his (of the prosecution's) little beasts of witnesses?[4] What a nest of almost infant blackmailers!

Yours ever
Henry James

1. This article dealt with Alphonse Daudet's impending visit to London; it was later included in Gosse's *French Profiles* (1904).

2. Gosse had apparently sent HJ Symonds' autobiography, later locked away in the London Library until its recent publication as *The Memoirs of John Addington Symonds*, ed. Grosskurth (1984).

3. The 9th was the date of HJ's dinner at the Reform Club in honor of Daudet.

4. An allusion to some of the Crown witnesses in the first trial of Oscar Wilde, one of whom was characterized by the judge as "a most reckless, unreliable, unscrupulous and untruthful witness." See *The Letters of Oscar Wilde*, ed. Hart-Davis (1962), 452.

113 · To Leslie Stephen

Ms Berg

34 De Vere Gardens W.
May 6th 1895

My dear Stephen.

I feel unable to approach such a sorrow as yours[1]—and yet I can't forbear to hold out my hand to you. I think of you with inexpressible participation, and only take refuge from this sharp pain of sympathy in trying to call up the image of all the perfect happiness that you drew and that you gave. I pray for you that there are moments when the sense of that rushes over you like a possession that you still hold. There is no happiness in this horrible world but the happiness we have *had*—the very present is ever in the jaws of fate. *I* think, in the presence of the loss of so beautiful and noble and generous a friend, of the admirable picture of her perfect union with you, and that for her, at any rate, with all its fatigues and sacrifices, life didn't pass without the deep and clear felicity—the best it can give. She leaves no image but that of the high enjoyment of affections and devotions—the beauty and the good she wrought and the tenderness that came back to her. Unquenchable seems to me such a presence. But why do I presume to say these things to you, my dear Stephen? Only because I want you to hear in them the sound of the voice and feel the pressure of the hand of your affectionate old friend

Henry James

1. Leslie Stephen had just lost his wife, the former Julia (Jackson) Duckworth, mother of Virginia Woolf and Vanessa Bell.

114 · *To Francis Boott*

Ms Harvard

[Osborne Hotel] Torquay
Oct. 11*th* [1895]

My dear Francis.

This is but a small p.s. of three lines to the letter I posted to you yesterday: after doing which I became aware that I hadn't alluded to poor W. W. Story's death the news of which I had just seen in the *Times.*[1] I make up the omission rather on general grounds of aesthetic decorum than on that of supposing his departure affects you much— for I believe you didn't like him, or any feature of *casa* Story. I feel a certain sense of historic mutation in the thought that *casa* Story is no more: it had been for so long, and went back so far: it had seen so much and so many come and go. You it had seen go, hadn't it?—But not very often come! I saw poor W.W. in Rome sixteen months ago and he was the ghost, only of his old clownship—very silent and vague and gentle. It was very sad and the Barberini very empty and shabby. What will become of that great unsettled population of statues, which his children don't love nor covet? There were hundreds of them in his studio, and they will be loose upon the world. Well—he had had fifty years of Rome; and that is something.—I also forgot to mention to you that Mrs. Benedict and her daughter[2] lately passed through London on their way back to the U.S.—very futile and foolish, poor things, and exclusively taken up with a dog C.F.W. had acquired, in Venice, the last weeks of her life, and had scarcely lived with, as he was mainly in the hands of her gondoliers. He occupies the forefront of poor Mrs. B.'s existence and all her talk and—especially to those for whom he has no shadow of association with C.F.W. he is a weariness to the spirit and a stumbling block to the feet. Mrs. B. is very considerably mad. But she is much better of her great prostration, and the little girl is gentleness incarnate. I receive the news of Kitty Emmet's[3] death—I suppose you never retouched her. But you do retouch Tweedy?[4] How it must improve them! How ghostly must Newport be! But I see ghosts everywhere. You are the only solid substance. Yours, my dear Francis, *da capo.*

Henry James

1. For W. W. Story, see Letter 7, note 9.
2. Sister and niece of Miss Woolson. See Letter 100.

3. Katherine Temple Emmet (1843–1895), HJ's cousin and an older sister of Minnie Temple.

4. Edmund Tweedy. See Letter 17, note 7.

115 · To John Lane

Ms Texas

34, De Vere Gardens W.
February 2d 1896

Dear Mr. Lane.

Thanks for your note and for the two books—I am sorry that you have been unwell. I must thank you also for your statement of what you are disposed to do for anything of mine publishable in the *Yellow Book*[1]—thank you, that is, as making the matter definite. There is no use, however, in our discussing the question on any such basis as you propose, for it is impossible to me to contribute another story to the *Yellow Book* at £35. I have only once, for many years, accepted that sum; viz: in the case of the tale published in the Y.B. last July. I did so, much against the grain, because Harland made me an appeal, on your behalf, as I understood him, to do so, for some special reason, for that occasion only. At all events, my customary fee is more than double that amount. I have received £87 for a tale in 20,000 words which has just appeared in the (February) *Atlantic Monthly*.[2] I have just given *Chapman's Magazine of Fiction* a story in 10,000 words[3] for £50 for the English rights alone—exclusive of what I shall get for the American. I mention these current instances to show you that I can't meet you in the matter of magazine—of Y.B.—publication; and this renders it superfluous that we should discuss the question of any *book*. I may just mention however, that I should *not* care to appear in the form of the *Pierrot*, or in any series or "library"—in any way but as a detached and independent volume. Believe me yours very truly

Henry James

1. HJ's tale "The Death of the Lion" had been given a leading place in the first issue of John Lane's periodical *The Yellow Book*, April 1894. HJ published two other tales in *The Yellow Book*: "The Coxon Fund" in July 1894 and "The Next Time" in July 1896.

2. This was "Glasses," *Atlantic Monthly*, February 1896.

3. "The Way It Came," later renamed "The Friends of the Friends," May 1896.

116 · *To William Edward Norris*

Ms Yale

34 De Vere Gardens W.
February 4*th* [1896]

My dear Norris.[1]

Your letter is as good as the chair by your study-table (betwixt it, as it were, and the tea-stand) used to be; and as that luxurious piece of furniture shall (D.V.) be again. Your news, your hand, your voice sprinkle me—most refreshingly—with the deep calm of Torquay. It is in short in every way good to hear from you, so that, behold, for your sweet sake, I perpetrate that intensest of my favourite immoralities—I snatch the epistolary, the disinterested pen before (at 10 A.M.) squaring my poor old shoulders over the painful instrument that I fondly try to believe to be lucrative. It *isn't*—but one must keep up the foolish fable to the end. I am having in these difficult conditions a very decent winter. It is mild, and it isn't wet—not here and now; and it is— for me—thanks to more than Machiavellian cunning, more dinnerless than it has, really, ever been. My fireside really knows me on some evenings. I forsake it too often—but a little less and less. So you bloom and smack your lips while I shrivel and tighten my waistband. In spite of my gain of private quiet I have suffered very acutely by my loss of public. The American outbreak[2] has darkened all my sky—and made me feel, among many things, how long I have lived away from my native land, how long I *shall* (D.V.!) live away from it and how little I understand it today. The explosion of jingoism there is the result of all sorts of more or less domestic and internal conditions—and what is *most* indicated, on the whole, as coming out of it, is a vast new split or cleavage in American national feeling—politics and parties— a split almost, roughly speaking, between the West and the East. There are really two civilisations there side by side—in one yoke; or rather one civilisation and a barbarism. All the expressions of feeling *I* have received from the U.S. (since this hideous row) have been, intensely, of course, from the former. It is, on the whole, the stronger force; but only on condition of its fighting hard. But I think it *will* fight hard. Meanwhile the whole thing sickens me. That unfortunately, however, is not a reason for its not being odiously there. It's there all the while. But let it not be any more *here:* I mean in this scribblement. My admiration of Smalley[3] is boundless, and my appreciation and comfort and gratitude. He has really *done* something—and will do more—for peace and decency.

I went yesterday to Leighton's[4] funeral—a wonderful and slightly curious public demonstration—the streets all cleared and lined with police, the day magnificent (his characteristic good fortune to the end); and St. Paul's very fine to the eye and crammed with the *whole* London world—everyone except Gosse, whom I went afterwards to see (and comfort!) at the B[oard] of T[rade]. The music was fine and severe, but I thought wanting in volume and force—thin and meagre for the vast space. But what do I know?—No, my dear Norris, I *don't* go abroad—I go on May 1st into the depths (somewhere) of old England. A response to that proposal I spoke to you of (from Rome) is utterly impossible to me now. It says very little to me at best, but I can't now, at all—this year—give up unremunerated months to a job I'm not at all keen to undertake and for which I must desert work intensely pressing and unalterably promised.[5] I've two novels to write before I can *dream* of anything else; and to go abroad is to plunge into the fiery furnace of people. So either Devonshire or some other place will be my six months' lot. I must take a house, this time—a small and cheap one—and I must (deride me not) be somewhere where I can, without disaster, bicycle. Also I must be a little nearer town than last year. I'm afraid these things rather menace Torquay. But it's soon to say—I must wait. I shall decide in April—or by mid-March—only. Meanwhile things will clear up. I'm intensely, thank heaven, busy. I will, I think, send you the little magazine tale over which (I mean over whose number of words—infinite and awful) I struggled so, in September and October last, under your pitying eye and with your sane and helpful advice. It comes in to me this A.M.

I walk in Richmond Park on Saturday with the gallant Rhoda.[6] I have cut down Mrs. Henniker to almost nothing! I hope your daughter is laying up treasure corporeal in Ireland. I like *your* dinners—even I mean in the houses of the other hill-people; and I beg you to feel yourself clung to for ever by yours irrepressibly,

Henry James

1. See Letter 108.

2. President Cleveland's reassertion of the Monroe Doctrine during the boundary dispute between Venezuela and British Guiana.

3. The American correspondent G. W. Smalley. See Letter 40, note 3.

4. Frederick Lord Leighton, the neoclassical painter. HJ described the funeral in *Harper's Weekly* XLI (20 February 1896), 183.

5. The family of W. W. Story had asked HJ to write a life of the sculptor. See Letter 114.

6. Rhoda Broughton: see Letter 128.

117 · To Edward Holton James

Ms Vaux

34 De Vere Gardens W.
February 15*th* 1896

My dear Edward.[1]

I have valuable gifts from you to acknowledge—the more shame to me that day after day has lately elapsed without my catching the right and ready moment. It has come at last—in the still midnight—and I seize it with a desperate grasp. All thanks, my dear boy, for the friendly and familiar portrait which I have gracefully mounted in a vivid frame and on an eminence (of furniture), from which it fairly commands the scene of my existence. I like it very much—it is very natural and very resembling—to your papa. I therefore suppose that it looks like *you* and it, under the circumstances, ought to. It reminds me singularly, and oddly, of him—when he looked like that. You know what I mean. It reminds me also of yourself when you were here, so fleeting and un-assimilated an apparition—with a squashed hand, a dozen dogs and an engagement before the mast. For the two stories in the *Harvard Magazine* I am also gratefully indebted to you. I have read them with the searching of spirit (to begin with) inevitable to one who has in a manner set an example and who sees it (in his afternoon of life) inexorably and fatally followed. (By fatally I don't mean that you are dashing to your doom—but only that the happy poison is, to all appearance, distinctly in your blood.) I find your prose full of good intentions, and both the tales very bright and lively. I think *Cloistered* much the better of the two, and I think you will really write if you care enough to go through, for the purpose, the long grind of one's apprenticeship. I hope with all my heart you do, for the pleasure is worth the pain. You will however find out for yourself all sorts of things which will be the steps of your growth, and the joy probably, also, of your soul. Above all that one leaves quickly behind one's first experimentations—and that nothing that is worth doing is easy to do. Also that the more one gets *in*, the more one sees, and that for a long time, when one is young, one's successive stages and pleasures are at best provisional and momentary. One must take the business as seriously as possible—but one's success in it, *not* (for a long time, at least!) too much so. These "efforts" (excuse the patronizing term) seem to me to show a disposition which makes me want to give you all sorts of good advice. But that will come little by little, as occasion offers—it *can't* come all at once, like a recipe for a pudding. There is only one recipe—to care a great deal for the cookery. If you do all you can for this story-telling mystery, it will do a good deal for *you*. Live your life as your life comes to you; but, for your work, remember that an art is an art and that you must learn it with every sort of *help*, with the aid of all the implements. Read—read—read *much*. Read everything. You will always observe and live and feel; but for God's sake be as accomplished as you can. If you go in for literature be a man of letters. You have probably an heredity of *expression* in your blood (from your father through *his* father), and I see symptoms in your stories of the sense and gift for that. So gird your loins and store up your patience. Take the most important subjects you can, and write about the most human and manly things. We live in a frightfully vulgar age; and twaddle and chatter are much imposed upon us. Suspect them—detest them—despise them. Send me all you do—I shall always be delighted to see it. And I will send you *my* stuff—as soon as it becomes the final little book. I hope college still gives you some incitement and rewards. Get all you can out of it. I wrote lately to your mother and your sister. I hope you have a quiet little scribbling-hole in that charming Concord house. Receive, my dear nephew, the love and the blessing of your faithful old uncle

Henry James

1. Edward Holton James (1873–1954), eldest son of HJ's brother Robertson, was a student at Harvard at this time. A libertarian, E. H. James espoused both leftist and rightist causes in later years. HJ removed this nephew's name from his will for printing a pamphlet accusing George V of having contracted a morganatic marriage.

118 · To Clement K. Shorter

Ms *Private*

34 De Vere Gardens W.
February 24th 1896

Dear Mr. Shorter.[1]

I should be very glad to write you a story energetically designed to meet your requirement of a "love-story"—and to let you have it at the time and of the dimension that you mention—but the sum you name is less than that I am in the habit of receiving: it is, in fact, rating the instalments, individually, at my usual fee, a great deal less. I should however like to capture the public of the *Illustrated News,* and should be glad to surrender you the English serial rights of the work in question for £300, if you see your way to meeting me on that figure. The particular story I conceive Mrs. Clifford[2] to have spoken to you of is—must be—a plan I narrated to her more than a year ago and have carried for longer than that in my head: an idea that would, as I remember telling her, lend itself about equally well to a play—"of incident," or to a novel—of the same.[3] Two girls are indeed in the forefront of it. If you accept my amendment to your terms I should be able presently to fall to work on it. Believe me yours very truly

Henry James

1. Clement King Shorter (1857–1926), editor of the *Illustrated London News* from 1891 to 1900.
2. Mrs. W. K. Clifford (d. 1929), novelist and playwright.
3. The plan was recorded by HJ on 26 December 1893 at some length: see *Notebooks,* 138–141. It was then written as a play for Edward Compton (and probably Elizabeth Robins) titled *The Other House.* HJ converted an already completed script into the novel.

119 · To Edmund Gosse

Ms *Harvard*

The Vicarage, Rye
August 28th [1896]

My dear Edmund.

Don't think me a finished brute or a heartless fiend or a soulless ass, or any other unhappy thing with a happy name. I have pressed your letter to my bosom again and again, and if I've not sooner expressed to you how I've prized it, the reason has simply been that for the last month there has been no congruity between my nature and my manners—between my affections and my lame right hand. A crisis overtook me some three weeks ago from which I emerge only to hurl myself on this sheet of paper and consecrate it to *you*. I will reserve details—suffice it that in an evil hour I began to pay the penalty of having arranged to let a current serial begin[1] when I was too little ahead of it, and when it proved a much slower and more difficult job than I expected. The printers and illustrators overtook and denounced me, the fear of breaking down paralysed me, the combination of rheumatism and fatigue rendered my hand and arm a torture—and the total situation made my existence a nightmare, in which I answered not a single note, letting correspondence go to smash in order barely to save my honour. I've finished (day before yesterday), but I fear my honour—with *you*—lies buried in the ruins of all the rest. You will soon be coming home, and this will meet or reach you God only knows where. Let it take you the assurance that the most lurid thing in my dreams has been the glitter of your sarcastic spectacles. It was charming of you to write to me from dear little old devastated Vevey—as to which indeed you made me feel, in a few vivid touches, a faint nostalgic pang. I don't want to think of you as still in your horrid ice-world (for it is cold even here and I scribble by a morning fire); and yet it's in my interest to suppose you still feeling so all abroad that these embarrassed lines will have for you some of the charm of the bloated English post. That makes me, at the same time, doubly conscious that I've nothing to tell you that you will most languish for—news of the world and the devil—no throbs nor thrills from the great beating heart of the thick of things. I went up to town for a week on the 15th, to be nearer the devouring maw into which I had to pour belated copy; but I spent the whole time shut up in De Vere Gardens with an inkpot and a charwoman. The only thing that befell me was that I dined one night at the Savoy with F. Ortmans[2] and the P. Bourgets—and that the said Bourgets—but two days in London—dined with me one night at the Grosvenor club. But these occasions were not as rich in incident and emotion as poetic justice demanded—and your veal-fed table d'hôte will have nourished your intelligence quite as much. The only other thing I did was to read in the *Revue de Paris* of the 15th

August the wonderful article of A. Daudet on Goncourt's death—a little miracle of art, adroitness, demoniac tact and skill, and of taste so abysmal, judged by *our* fishlike sense, that there is no getting alongside of it at all. But I grieve to say I can't send you the magazine—I saw it only at a club. Doubtless you will have come across it. I have this ugly house till the end of September and don't expect to move from Rye even for a day till then. The date of your return is vague to me—but if it should be early in the month I wonder if you couldn't come down for another Sunday. I fear you will be too blasé, much. For comfort my Vicarage is distinctly superior to my eagle's nest[3]—but, alas, beauty isn't *in* it. The peace and prettiness of the whole land, here, however, has been good to me, and I stay on with unabated relish. But I stay in solitude. I don't see a creature. That, too, dreadful to relate, I like. You will have been living in a crowd, and I expect you to return all garlanded and odorous with anecdote and reminiscence. Mrs. Nelly's will all bear, I trust, on miraculous healings and feelings. I feel far from all access to the French volume you recommend. Are you crawling over the Dorn, or only standing at the bottom to catch Philip and Lady Edmund[4] as they drop? Pardon my poverty and my paucity. It is your absence that makes them. Yours, my dear Edmund, not inconstantly

Henry James

1. *The Other House*, in the *Illustrated London News*.
2. F. Ortmans, editor of *Cosmopolis*, an international journal, which printed in its January and February 1896 issues HJ's tale "The Figure in the Carpet" and in January and February 1898 "John Delavoy."
3. Point Hill, in Rye, where HJ had stayed earlier.
4. Gosse's wife and son.

120 · To Llewlyn Roberts

Ms Royal Literary Fund

34, De Vere Gardens W.
October 24th 1896

My dear Sir.

Permit me to express the desire to give my earnest support to the question of making an allowance from the Royal Literary Fund to Mrs.

Charles Dickens,[1] who has been left wholly unprovided for by the death of her husband. I feel as a man of letters—as I am sure we *all* must feel—the strength of the appeal residing in the urgent character of Mrs. Dickens's need and in the eloquent association of the illustrious name she bears.

Believe me yours very truly

Henry James

1. Roberts was the secretary of the Royal Literary Fund. Mrs. Dickens received, in due course, a Civil List pension.

121 · To W. Morton Fullerton

Dictated Ts Harvard

34 De Vere Gardens W.
25*th* February 1897

My dear Fullerton.

Forgive a communication, very shabby and superficial. It has come to this that I can address you only through an embroidered veil of sound. The sound is that of the admirable and expensive machine that I have just purchased for the purpose of bridging our silences. The hand that works it, however, is not the lame *patte* which, after inflicting on you for years its aberrations, I have now definitely relegated to the shelf, or at least to the hospital—that is, to permanent, bandaged, baffled, rheumatic, incompetent obscurity.[1] May you long retain, for yourself, the complete command that I judge you, that I almost see you, to possess, in perfection, of every one of your members. Your letter about my contribution to that flurry of old *romantique* dust[2] was as interesting to me as some of the sentiments it breathed couldn't fail to make it. All thanks for it—all thanks for everything; even for the unconscious stroke by which, in telling me how you have grown up since the day when her acquaintance (Mme. Sand's) was inevitable, you add to the burden of my years. Of course I knew you had; but I am cursed with a memory of my earlier time that beguiles me with associations at which I am able to see young friends, even the most "arrived," address a blank, uninfluenced stare. If I could wish you to be anything in any particular but what you are, I should wish you to have been young when *I* was. Then, don't you see, you would have known not only the mistress of *ces messieurs*, —you would almost, perhaps, have known *me*. And now you will never catch up! Neither shall I, however, my dear Fullerton—since it comes to that—if I give too much time to our gossip. I have so much less of that than you to do it in. Besides, it now begins to look definite that I *shall*, for a few days in April, have the pleasure of seeing you. I shall spend as many in Paris as possible—as many as the few—on my way then to three months in Italy.[3] Give me the benefit of your fine imagination to calculate exactly how few moments, with an eye to that, I can afford to take from the great business of arranging to be free. Let it answer your letter directly enough to assure you that no word of it was lost on yours, my dear Fullerton, always

Henry James

1. This letter to Fullerton is among the first HJ dictated. He began by using a shorthand stenographer, William MacAlpine; later he learned to dictate directly to a typist at the machine. HJ resorted to the typewriter at this time because of an acute attack of writer's cramp.

2. An article in the *Yellow Book*, January 1897, on George Sand and Alfred de Musset, entitled "She and He: Recent Documents."

3. HJ abandoned this plan and did not visit the Continent until 1899.

122 · *To James Abbott McNeill Whistler*

Dictated Ts Glasgow

34 De Vere Gardens W.
25 *th* February 1897

My dear Whistler.

Yes, even though it be an outrage to a man with your touch to address him in accents condemned to click into his ear—thanks to interposing machinery—a positive negation of every delicacy; yet nevertheless I *must* thank you over my hand and seal, and with nothing less than documentary force, for making me the possessor of your delightful little document of Monday. To have pleased you,[1] to have touched you, to have given you something of the impression of the decent little thing one attempted to do—this is for me, my dear Whistler, a rare and peculiar pleasure. For the arts are one, and with the artist the artist communicates. Therefore your good words come to me as from one who knows. You know, above all, better than anyone, how dreadfully few are such. One writes for one's self alone—one has accepted, once for all, the worst; so that such a sign as your letter makes me has all the beautiful cheer and comfort of the happy wind-fall—the something more, so much more, than was included in the beggarly bond. You have done too much of the exquisite not to have earned more despair than anything else; but don't doubt that some-thing vibrates back when that Exquisite takes the form of recognition of a not utterly indelicate brother. It was such a pleasure to see you again that I shall not neglect anything in the nature of the faintest further occasion. Yours, my dear Master, very constantly,

Henry James

1. HJ reciprocated Whistler's gift of an etching by sending him the just-published *The Spoils of Poynton.*

123 · To Mrs. William James

Dictated Ts Harvard

34 De Vere Gardens W.
1st December 1897

Dearest Alice.

It's too hideous and horrible, this long time that I have not written you and that your last beautiful letter, placed, for reminder, well within sight, has converted all my emotion on the subject into a con-stant, chronic blush. The reason has been that I have been driving very hard for another purpose this inestimable aid to expression, and that, as I have a greater loathing than ever for the mere manual act, I haven't, on the one side, seen my way to inflict on you a written letter, or on the other had the virtue to divert, till I should have finished my little book—to another stream—any of the valued and expensive industry of my amanuensis.[1] I *have*, at last, finished my little book—that is *a* little book, and so have two or three mornings of breathing-time before I begin another.[2] *Le plus clair* of this small inter-val "I consecrate to thee!"

I am settled in London these several weeks and making the most of

304

that part of the London year—the mild, quiet, grey stretch from the mid-October to Christmas—that I always find the pleasantest, with the single defect of its only not being long enough. We are having, moreover, a most creditable autumn; no cold to speak of and almost no rain, and a morning-room window at which, this December 1st, I sit with my scribe, admitting a radiance as adequate as that in which you must be actually bathed and probably more mildly golden. I have no positive plan save that of just ticking the winter swiftly away on this most secure basis. There are, however, little doors ajar into a possible brief absence. I fear I have just closed one of them rather ungraciously indeed, in pleading a "non possumus" to a most genial invitation from John Hay to accompany him and his family, shortly after the new year, upon a run to Egypt and a month up the Nile; he having a boat for that same—I mean for the Nile part—in which he offers me the said month's entertainment. It is a very charming opportunity, and I almost blush at not coming up to the scratch; especially as I shall probably never have the like again. But it isn't so simple as it sounds; one has on one's hands the journey to Cairo and back, with whatever seeing and doing by the way two or three irresistible other things, to which one would feel one might never again be so near, would amount to. (I mean, of course, then or never, on the return, Athens, Corfu, Sicily the never-seen, etc., etc.) It would all "amount" to too much this year, by reason of a particular little complication—most pleasant in itself, I hasten to add—that I haven't, all this time, mentioned to you. Don't be scared—I haven't accepted an "offer."[3] I have only taken, a couple of months ago, a little old house in the country—for the rest of my days!—on which, this winter, though it is, for such a commodity, in exceptionally good condition, I shall have to spend money enough to make me quite concentrate my resources. The little old house you will at no distant day, I hope, see for yourself and inhabit and even, I trust, temporarily and gratuitously possess—for half the fun of it, in the coming years, will be occasionally to lend it to you. I marked it for my own two years ago at Rye—so perfectly did it, the first instant I beheld it, offer the solution of my long-unassuaged desire for a calm retreat between May and November. It is the very calmest and yet cheerfullest that I could have dreamed—*in* the little old, cobble-stoned, grass-grown, red-roofed town, on the summit of its mildly pyramidal hill and close to its noble old church—

the chimes of which will sound sweet in my goodly old red-walled garden.

The little place is so rural and tranquil, and yet discreetly animated, that its being within the town is, for convenience and immediate accessibility, purely to the good; and the house itself, though modest and unelaborate, full of a charming little stamp and dignity of its period (about 1705) without as well as within. The next time I go down to see to its "doing up," I will try to have a photograph taken of the pleasant little old-world-town-angle into which its nice old red-bricked front, its high old Georgian doorway and a most delightful little old architectural garden-house, perched alongside of it on its high brick garden-wall—into which all these pleasant features together so happily "compose." Two years ago, after I had lost my heart to it—walking over from Point Hill to make sheep's eyes at it (the more so that it is called Lamb House!)—there was no appearance whatever that one could ever have it; either that its fond proprietor would give it up or that if he did it would come at all within one's means. So I simply sighed and renounced; tried to think no more about it; till at last, out of the blue, a note from the good local ironmonger, to whom I had whispered at the time my hopeless passion, informed me that by the sudden death of the owner and the preference (literal) of his son for Klondyke,[4] it might perhaps drop into my lap. Well, to make a long story short, it *did* immediately drop and, more miraculous still to say, on terms, for a long lease, well within one's means—terms quite deliciously moderate. The result of these is, naturally, that they will "do" nothing to it: but, on the other hand, it has been so well lived in and taken care of that the doing—off one's own bat—is reduced mainly to sanitation and furnishing—which latter includes the peeling off of old papers from several roomfuls of pleasant old top-to-toe wood panelling. There are two rooms of complete old oak—one of them a delightful little parlour, opening by one side into the little vista, church-ward, of the small old-world street, where not one of the half-dozen wheeled vehicles of Rye ever passes; and on the other straight into the garden and the approach, from that quarter, to the garden-house aforesaid, which is simply the making of a most commodious and picturesque detached study and workroom. Ten days ago Alfred Parsons,[5] best of men as well as best of landscape-painters-and-gardeners, went down with me and revealed to me the most charming possibilities for the treatment of the tiny out-of-door part—it amounts to about an acre of garden and lawn, all shut in by the peaceful old red wall aforesaid, on which the most flourishing old espaliers, apricots, pears, plums and figs, assiduously grow. It appears that it's a glorious little growing exposure, air, and soil—and all the things that were still flourishing out of doors (November 20th) were a joy to behold. There went with me also a good friend of mine, Edward Warren,[6] a very *distingué* architect and loyal spirit, who is taking charge of whatever is to be done. So I hope to get in, comfortably enough, early in May. In the meantime one must "pick up" a sufficient quantity of ancient mahogany-and-brass odds and ends—a task really the more amusing, here, where the resources are great, for having to be thriftily and cannily performed. The house is really quite charming enough in its particular character, and as to the stamp of its period, not to do violence to by rash modernities; and I am developing, under its influence and its inspiration, the most avid and gluttonous eye and most infernal watching patience, in respect of lurking "occasions" in not too-delusive Chippendale and Sheraton. The "King's Room" will be especially treated with a preoccupation of the comfort and aesthetic sense of cherished sisters-in-law; King's Room so-called by reason of George Second having passed a couple of nights there and so stamped it for ever. (He was forced ashore, at Rye, on a progress somewhere with some of his ships, by a tempest, and accommodated at Lamb House as at the place in the town then most consonant with his grandeur. It would, for that matter, quite correspond to this description still. Likewise the Mayors of Rye have usually lived there! Or the persons usually living there have usually *become* mayors! That was conspicuously the case with the late handsome old Mr. Bellingham whose son is my landlord. So you see the ineluctable dignity in store for me.) But enough of this swagger. I have been copious to copiously amuse you.

Your beautiful letter, which I have just read over again, is full of interest about you all; causing me special joy as to what it says of William's present and prospective easier conditions of work, relinquishment of laboratory, refusal of outside lectures, etc., and of the general fine performance, and promise, all round, of the children. What you say of each makes me want to see that particular one most. I rejoice with you, at any rate, over them all, and with William over what I hope *is* proving a simplified success. Most of all am I fondly *ému* in the prospect of the domestic relief that you are counting upon from your young German governess. May Peggy and Francis[7] twine about her even as the roses and jasmine clamber about the blushing walls of Lamb House! If she doesn't lift the labour you must just shunt the lot and come over here and live with *me*. I am delighted your sister Margaret gave you a good account of me. It was an immense pleasure to see her—and to see her so handsome and noble, and to find her such a complete *évocatrice*. May she have taken up the redomesticated sense with many interwoven coloured threads of memory. I almost feel that what I have most to thank you for is the deeply interesting letter you so kindly enclose to me from the magnificent and mysterious Milwaukeeite. I don't in the least know who he is and can't even quite make out his name (unless it be Ilsley) but he is surely a charming creature, and does the handsome thing, all round, with a vengeance. It makes me really feel as if we *were* a family!—Not that there is the least doubt, however, that we are. There are, unmistakably, few such. At all events I quite voluptuously revel in Mr. Ilsley and should be immensely glad if it would come in William's way to mention it to him. I don't know about whom of us all he is best. In short he is a pearl, and I venture to keep his letter.—I had a very great pleasure the other day in a visit, far too short—only just six hours—from dear old Howells, who did me a lot of good in an illuminating professional (i.e., commercial) way, and came, in fact, at quite a psychological moment. I hope you may happen to see him soon enough to get from him also some echo of *me*—such as it may be. But, my dear Alice, I must be less interminable. Please tell William that I have two Syracuse "advices,"[8] as yet gracelessly unacknowledged—I mean to *him*— to thank him for. It's a joy to find these particular months less barren than they used to be. I embrace you tenderly all round and am yours very constantly

Henry James

P.S. It may interest you to know that (I didn't want to put my scribe into the Secret)[9] I get Lamb House (for twenty-one years, with *my* option of surrender the seventh or the fourteenth) for £70 per annum—four quarterly payments of less than £18. And *they* do all the outer repairs, etc.!

1. William MacAlpine was an experienced stenographer who had worked largely in the record-keeping of various scientific societies.

2. The long ghost story "The Turn of the Screw" was serialized in *Collier's Weekly* from 27 January to 26 April 1898.

3. HJ's longstanding joke—an "offer" of marriage.

4. The gold rush to the Klondike in the Yukon Territory had been in the news since the previous year.

5. Alfred William Parsons (1847–1920), landscape gardener and artist.

6. Edward P. Warren (1856–1937), architect and friend, helped HJ find Lamb House.

7. WJ's youngest children.

8. HJ's share of the rents from the family real estate in Syracuse.

9. The postscript is in HJ's hand.

124 · To William James

Dictated Ts Harvard

34 De Vere Gardens W.
20 April 1898

My dear William.

There are all sorts of *intimes* and confidential things I want to say to you in acknowledgment of your so deeply interesting letter—of April 10th—received yesterday; but I must break the back of my response at least with this mechanical energy; not having much of any other—by which I mean simply too many odd moments—at my disposal just now. I do answer you, alas, almost to the foul music of the cannon.[1] It is this morning precisely that one feels the fat to be at last fairly in the fire. I confess that the blaze about to come leaves me woefully cold, thrilling with no glorious thrill or holy blood-thirst whatever. I see nothing but the madness, the passion, the hideous clumsiness of rage, or mechanical reverberation; and I echo with all my heart your denouncement of the foul criminality of the screeching newspapers. They have long since become, for me, the danger that overtops all others. That became clear to one, even here, two years ago, in the Venezuela time; when one felt that with a week of simple, enforced silence everything could be saved. If things *were* then saved without it, it is simply that they hadn't at that time got so bad as they are now in the U.S. My sympathy with you all is intense—the whole horror must so mix itself with all your consciousness. I am near enough to hate it, without being, as you are, near enough in some degree, perhaps, to understand. I am leading at present so quiet a life that I don't measure much the sentiment, the general attitude around me. Much of it can't possibly help being Spanish—and from the "European" standpoint in general Spain *must* appear savagely assaulted. She is so

309

quiet—publicly and politically—so decent and picturesque and harmless a member of the European family that I am bound to say it argues
an extraordinary illumination and a very predetermined radicalism
not to admire her pluck and pride. But publicly, of course, England
will do nothing whatever that is not more or less—negatively—for
our benefit. I scarcely know what the newspapers say—beyond the
Times, which I look at all for Smalley's cables:[2] so systematic is my
moral and intellectual need of ignoring them. One must save one's life
if one can. The next weeks will, however, in this particular, probably
not a little break me down. I must at least read the Bombardment of
Boston. May you but scantly suffer from it!

I have just come back from that monstrous rarity for *me,* a visit of
three or four days in the country—to G. O. Trevelyan,[3] who is extraordinarily rich and much-housed, and spends Easter at his huge (or
rather his wife's) modern mansion of Welcombe, near Stratford-on-
Avon. The Eastertide has been lovely; that country was full of spring
and of Shakespeare, besides its intrinsic sweetness; and I suppose I
ought to have been happy. Fortunately I've got, through protracted
and infernal cunning, almost altogether out of it. There was no one
there—they live only in a furnished wing of the huge, hereditary
white elephant of a house—but the Speaker and Speakeress of the
House of Commons, who are very amiable folk. Also deadly commemo-
rative Shakespeare trilogies at the Stratford theatre, to which we were
haled for two nights. Basta!

I rejoice with intense rejoicing in everything you tell me of your
own situation, plans, arrangements, honours, prospects—into all of
which I enter with an intimacy of participation. Your election to the
Institut[4] has, for me, a surpassing charm—I simply revel and, as it
were, wallow in it. *Je m'y vautre.* But oh, if it could only have come
soon enough for poor Alice to have known it—such a happy little nip
as it would have given her; or for the dear old susceptible Dad! But
things come as they can—and I am, in general, lost in the daily miracle of their coming at all: I mean so many of them—few as that many
may be: and I speak above all for myself. I am lost, moreover, just now,
in the wonder of what effect on American affairs, of every kind, the
shock of battle will have. Luckily it's of my nature—though not of my
pocket—always to be prepared for the worst and to expect the least.
Like you, with all my heart, I have "finance on the brain." At least I

try to have it—with a woeful lack of natural talent for the same. It is none too soon. But one arrives at dates, periods, corners of one's life: great changes, deep operations are begotten. This has more *portée* than I can fully go into. I shall certainly do my best to let my flat when I am ready to leave town; the difficulty, this year, however, will be that the time for "season" letting begins now, and that I can't depart for at least another month. Things are not ready at Rye, and won't be till then, with the limited local energy at work that I have very wisely contented myself with turning on there. It has been the right and much the best way in the long run, and for one's good little relations there; only the run has been a little longer. The remnant of the season here may be difficult to dispose of—to a sub-lessee; and my books— only a part of which I can house at Rye—are a complication. However, I shall do what I can this year; and for subsequent absences, so long as my present lease of De Vere Gardens runs I shall have the matter on a smooth, organised, working basis. I mean to arrange myself always to let—being, as such places go, distinctly lettable. And for my declining years I have already put my name down for one of the invaluable south-looking, Carlton-Gardens-sweeping bedrooms at the Reform Club, which are let by the year and are of admirable and convenient (with all the other resources of the place at one's elbow) *general* habitability. The only thing is they are so in demand that one has sometimes a long time to await one's turn. On the other hand there are accidents—"occasions."[5] Then—with this flat suppressed—I shall, with Lamb House but £70 a year and the Reform room but £50, I shall, in respect to *loyer*, have taken in a great deal of pecuniary sail. This business of making Lamb House sanitary and comfortable and very modestly furnishing is of course, as it came very suddenly, a considerable strain on my resources; but I shall securely outweather it— and this year, and next, thank heaven, my income will have been much larger than for any year of my existence.[6] My main drawback will be my sacrifice, on going to Rye, of my excellent Scotch amanuensis—whom I can't take with me, without too great an expense in making up to him the loss of his other—afternoon and evening—engagements here. Moreover he is not a desireable inmate—I couldn't again, as I did for eight weeks last summer, undertake his living with me. My pressing want is some sound, sane, irreproachable young typewriting and bicycling "secretary-companion," the expense of whom

would be practically a hundred-fold made up by increase and facili-
tation of paying work. But though I consider the post enviable it is
difficult to fill. The young typists are mainly barbarians—and the civilized, here, are not typists. But patience. I don't go into the Bob-
question more than to jubilate devoutly in your good news of him. I
don't *understand*, I fear, very clearly, your inquiry as to my assent (that
is the question itself) to your new Syracuse idea; but I *give*, that assent,
freely to what you think best—judging it to be in the interest of con-
servatism and prudence. I hope War will make no difference in the
advent of Harry and M.G. I shall be ready for H. by the mid-June. I
embrace you all—Alice longer than the rest—and am, with much actuality of emotion, ever your

Henry

1. The *Maine* had blown up in Havana harbor in February, and the Spanish-American
war had just begun. HJ had visions, fed by the war hysteria in the American press, of the
bombardment of Boston, and was "mainly glad Harvard College isn't—nor Irving Street—
the thing nearest Boston Bay" (letter to WJ, 22 April 1898).

2. G. W. Smalley. See Letter 40.

3. Sir George Otto Trevelyan (1838–1928), author of a history of the American
Revolution in six volumes (1899–1914).

4. WJ had just been elected a corresponding member of the Institut de France, the
French learned society. HJ addressed the envelope "William James, Esq., *Membre corre-
spondant de l'Institut (Académie des Sciences Morales et Politiques).*"

5. At this point HJ ceased dictating and completed the letter by hand.

6. Serialization of "The Turn of the Screw" and "The Awkward Age" and publication
of a large number of tales and articles, including regular contributions to the newly founded
journal *Literature*, gave HJ comfortable earnings at this time.

125 · To Guy Hoyer Millar

Ms Harvard

Rye [1898]

My dear Godson Guy.[1]

I learned from your mother, by pressing her hard, some time ago
that it would be a convenience to you and a great help in your career
to possess an Association football—whereupon, in my desire that you
should receive the precious object from no hand but mine I cast about
me for the proper place to procure it. But I am living for the present in

a tiny, simpleminded country town, where luxuries are few and football shops unheard of, so I was a long time getting a clue that would set me on the right road. Here at last, however, is the result of my terribly belated endeavour. It goes to you by parcel post—not, naturally, in this letter. I am awfully afraid I haven't got one of the right size: if so, and you will let me know, you shall have a better one next time. I am afraid I don't *know* much about the sorts and sizes since they've all been invented since I was of football age. I'm an awful muff, too, at games—except at times I am not a bad cyclist, I think—and I fear I am only rather decent at playing at godfather. Some day you must come down and see me here and I'll do in every way the best I can for you. You shall have lots of breakfast and dinner and tea—not to speak of lunch and anything you like in between—and I won't ask you a single question about a single one of your studies, but if you think that is because I can't—because I don't know enough—I *might* get up subjects on purpose.

Your most affectionate Godfather,
Henry James

1. Guy Millar was a grandson of George Du Maurier. HJ had known Guy's mother since her childhood.

126 · To H. G. Wells

Ms Bodleian

Lamb House, Rye
December 9*th* 1898

My dear H. G. Wells,[1]

Your so liberal and graceful letter is to my head like coals of fire—so repeatedly for all these weeks have I had feebly to suffer frustrations in the matter of trundling over the marsh to ask for your news and wish for your continued amendment. The shortening days and the deepening mud have been at the bottom of this affair. I never get out of the house till 3 o'clock, when night is quickly at one's heels. I would have taken a regular day—I mean started in the A.M.—but have been so ridden, myself, by the black care of an unfinished and *running* (galloping, leaping and bounding) serial[2] that parting with a day has been like parting with a pound of flesh. I am still a neck ahead, however, and *this* week will see me through: I accordingly hope very much to be able to turn up on one of the ensuing days. I will sound a horn, so that you yourself be not absent on the chase. Then I will express more articulately my appreciation of your various signs of critical interest, as well as assure you of my sympathy in your own martyrdom. What will you have? It's all a grind and a bloody battle—as well as a considerable lark, and the difficulty itself is the refuge from the vulgarity. Bless your heart, I think I could easily say worse of the T. of the S., the young woman, the spooks, the style, the everything, than the worst any one else could manage. One knows the *most* damning things about one's self. Of course I had, about my young woman, to take a very sharp line. The grotesque business I had to make her picture and the childish psychology I had to make her trace and present, were, for me at least, a very difficult job, in which absolute lucidity and logic, a singleness of effect, were imperative. Therefore I had to rule out subjective complications of her own—play of tone etc.; and keep her impersonal save for the most obvious and indispensable little note of neatness, firmness and courage—without which she wouldn't have had her data.[3] But the thing is essentially a pot-boiler and a *jeu d'esprit*.

With the little play, the absolute creature of its conditions, I had simply to make up a deficit and take a small *revanche*. For three mortal years had the actress for whom it was written (utterly to try to *fit*) persistently failed to produce it, and I couldn't wholly waste my labour. The B[ritish] P[ublic] won't read a play with the mere names of the speakers—so I simply paraphrased these and added such indications as might be the equivalent of decent acting—a history and an evolution that seem to me moreover explicatively and sufficiently smeared all over the thing. The moral is of course Don't write one-act plays.[4]

But I didn't mean thus to sprawl. I envy your hand your needle-pointed fingers. As you don't say that you're *not* better I prepare myself to be greatly struck with the same, and send kind regards to your wife. Believe me yours ever,

Henry James

P.S. What's this about something in some newspaper? I read least of all—from long and deep experience—what my friends write about me, and haven't read the things you mention. I suppose it's because they know I don't that they dare!

1. H. G. Wells (1866–1946) and HJ had met earlier that year when Wells moved into Spade House, across Romney Marsh from Rye. This was the beginning of their long and troubled friendship. See Edel and Ray, *Henry James and H. G. Wells* (1958).

2. *The Awkward Age* had begun to appear in *Harper's Weekly* in the October 1 issue.

3. James is explaining in this letter how he kept his character of the governess in "The Turn of the Screw" "impersonal"—so that she is not even named.

4. "Covering End," with which "The Turn of the Screw" made up the volume *The Two Magics.*

127 · To Henrietta Reubell

Ms Harvard

Lamb House, Rye
Sunday midnight
[12 November 1899]

Dear Etta Reubell.[1]

I have had great pleasure of your last good letter and this is a word of fairly prompt reconnaissance. Your bewilderment over *The Awkward Age*[2] doesn't on the whole surprise me—for that ingenious volume appears to have excited little *but* bewilderment—except indeed, *here*, thick-witted denunciation. A work of art that one has to *explain* fails in so far, I suppose, of its mission. I suppose I must at any rate mention that I had in view a certain special social (highly "modern" and actual) London group and type and tone, which seemed to me to se prêter à merveille to an ironic—lightly and simply ironic!—treatment, and that clever people at least would know who, in general, and what, one meant. But here, at least, it appears there are very few clever people! One must point with finger-posts—one must label with *pancartes*—one must explain with *conférences!* The *form*, doubtless, of my picture is against it—a form all dramatic and scenic—of presented episodes, architecturally combined and each making a piece of the building; with no going behind, no *telling about* the figures save by their own appearance and action and with explanation reduced to the explanation of everything by all the other things *in* the picture. Mais il parait qu'il ne faut pas faire comme ça: personne n'y comprend rien:

315

j'en suis pour mes frais—qui avaient été considérables, *très* considérables! Yet I seem to make out you were interested—and that consoles me. I think Mrs. Brook the best thing I've ever done—and Nanda also much *done.* Voilà! Mitchy marries Aggie by a calculation—in consequence of a state of mind—delicate and deep, but that I meant to show on his part as highly conceivable. It's *absolute* to him that N. will never have him—and she *appeals* to him for another girl, whom she sees him as "saving" (from things—realities she sees). If he does it (and she shows how she values him by wanting it), it is still a way of getting and keeping near her—of making for *her,* to him, a tie of gratitude. She becomes, as it were, to him, responsible for his happiness—they can't (*especially if the marriage goes ill*) *not* be—given the girl that Nanda is—more, rather than less, together. And the *finale* of the picture *justifies* him: it leaves Nanda, precisely, with his case on her hands. Far-fetched? Well, I daresay: but so are diamonds and pearls and the beautiful Reubell turquoises! So I scribble to you, to be sociable, by my loud-ticking clock, in this sleeping little town, at my usual more than midnight hour.—I'm so glad you saw and liked Mrs White: [3] she's far and away one of the most charming women I've ever known. Yet I see her rarely—one can't live in her world and do any work or save any money or retain control of three minutes of one's time. So a gulf separates us. I'm too poor to see her! She has extraordinary harmony and grace.—Well, also, I'm like you—I like growing (that is I like, for many reasons, *being*) old: 56! But I don't like growing *older.* I quite love my present age and the compensations, simplifications, freedom, independences, memories, advantages of it. But I don't keep it long enough—it passes too quickly. But it mustn't pass *all* (good as that is), in writing to *you!* There is nothing I shall like more to dream of than to be convoyed by you to the expositionist Kraals of the Savages and haunts of the cannibals. I surrender myself to you de confiance—in vision and hope—for that purpose. Jonathan Sturges lives, year in, year out, at Long's Hotel, Bond St., and promises to come down here and see me, but never does. He knows hordes of people, every one extraordinarily likes him, and he has tea-parties for pretty ladies: one at a time. Alas, he is three quarters of the time ill; but his little spirit is colossal. Sargent grows in weight, honour and interest—to *my* view. He does one fine thing after another—and his crucifixion (that is big Crucifié with Adam and Eve under each arm of cross catching drops of blood) for Boston Library is a most noble, grave and admirable thing. But it's already to-morrow and I am yours always,

Henry James

1. See Letter 78, note 1.
2. *The Awkward Age,* published in April 1899, was perhaps the most experimental of HJ's novels of the 1890s. It was a dialogue-novel, almost as if it were a play, and dealt with Anglo-French differences in the rearing of female adolescents.
3. Mrs. Henry White, née Margaret (Daisy) Stuyvesant Rutherford, wife of an American career diplomat, was a familiar figure in British and continental society.

128 · To Rhoda Broughton
Ms Chester

Lamb House, Rye
January 1st 1900

My dear Rhoda Broughton.[1]

I am sadly afraid that my silence and absence, so ungracefully persisted in, have well nigh cost me your esteem—or at least ranked me, for you, with those who appear perversely to *desire* to be forgotten: in which case you will, no doubt, unstintedly have obliged me! But I really haven't desired anything but to find myself again so placed that I might sometimes knock at your door and succeed in winning you for one of those walks and talks of which I cherish the impression as occasions fondly planned and plotted for, and not less fondly remembered. This dreadful gruesome New Year, so monstrously numbered, makes me turn back to the warm and coloured past and away from the big black avenue that gapes in front of us. So turning, I find myself, not wholly without trepidation, yet also with a generous confidence, face to face with your distinguished figure—which please don't consider me, rude rustic and benighted alien as I've become, unworthy to greet. The country has swallowed me up, for the time, as you foretold me that it would, but I haven't quite burnt my ships behind me, and I'm counting the months till I can resume possession, for at least half the year in future, of my London habitation. I've let it, for a longish time, but I haven't renounced it, and I'm so homesick for the blessed Kensington fields that I gloat over the prospect of treading them, finally, afresh. Meanwhile I've felt remote and unfriended and have lacked courage to write to you almost only (as it might look) to say: "See—from the way I keep it up—how I get on without you!" I get on without you very badly—and worse and worse the *more* I keep it up. I've been the victim, among other things, of an economic crisis, and since I came down here to take possession in June '98, haven't spent, at any possible period for finding people, three continuous days in town. This means, as you may suppose, that I *have*, pretty solidly, taken possession. But it isn't what I wanted to write to tell you. I want to make you a sign of faithful friendship and fond remembrance, to assure you of how poor a business I find it to be so deprived of your society, and to give you my fervent wishes for the dim twelvemonth to come. It looks to me full of goblins, to be deprecated by prayer and sacrifice—and my incense rises for your immunity, of every kind, not less than for my own. I've nothing to amuse you withal, or you should have it—not even another heavy book. I've done a good deal of work; but it's scattered and obscured—not yet collected. As soon as some of it is, I shall lay a copy at your feet. But I succumb to the sense of what a torment it is to talk with you thus onesidedly and imperfectly. How much I should like to ask you and to say to you! Heaven speed my chance. Think of me, please, meanwhile, as yours, dear Rhoda Broughton, always and always

Henry James

1. Rhoda Broughton (1840–1920), a Victorian novelist, whom HJ saw frequently and often accompanied to the theatre.

129 · To Mrs. William James

Ms Harvard

Lamb House, Rye
May 22d 1900

Dearest Alice.

Very gross my late silence. Your letter of the 16th, with a p.s. from William, and enclosing one of Harry's, has lately rejoiced my heart, and I have also a postcard from William. I am overjoyed at what I gather to be your reassured and re-enlightened state on the new information—i.e. Riegel's.[1] It does me far-reaching good. Right glad does it make me. I hope you have settled down to due moderation of care and due elation of consciousness. It is still but stingily summerish here—may *your* conditions be more *genialisch*—though I believe that's vile German. I was away from here last week three days (a long and dull story to tell), and along of Helena Gilder,[2] in town, met Mark Twain, who told me he is in correspondence with William and gave me a muddled and confused glimpse of Lord Kelvin, Albumen, Sweden and half a dozen other things (on which I was prevented from afterwards bringing him to book); the whole (most embroiled) hint of which makes me wonder if some such mixture as that is the "card" which William speaks of having up his sleeve. But though M.T. looked rosy as a babe, and said it was all "Albumen" and he was putting W. on it, I didn't know Lord Kelvin was a "Doctor" and don't understand "why *Sweden?*"[3] However, these things will doubtless transpire. Yet I heartily hope you will prove to be needing nothing but Nauheim. When the packet comes that William speaks of (for me to open) I will inspect and advise. A box of books *has* (to-day) come. Forgive my late-at-night rather weary brevity. My correspondence has got fearfully in arrears through Jonathan Sturges's long visit:[4] it is sad and strange that one of the most intelligent and *doué* mortals one knows should, inevitably, in fact, be the most (through his infirmity— which makes him *archi*-dependent) practically *draining*. I have a pile of letters chin-high before me—and am so working now, more and more, at fiction that, after my mornings, I feel quite depleted for even the most trivial forms of composition. And this grows as the fiction grows. So bear with my meagerness. All thanks for Harry's so interesting confidences. I greatly like to see them—though missing many of his allusions to people and not much knowing (and you will say caring!) who anyone is. But I greatly care who H. himself is. I hope Peggy keeps high and happy, and am always, dearest Alice, your affectionate

Henry

Thank you (P.S.) for telling me of Santayana's book (P. and R.)[5] which has come and which I find of an irresistible distraction. Charles Norton more or less due here—and the deadly Darwins expectant of a visit at Folkestone; I mean from me. And I must go!

1. Apparently one of WJ's doctors.
2. Helena De Kay Gilder, wife of Richard Watson Gilder, a New York editor.

3. Mark Twain had just returned from Sweden, where he had spent some time at the health establishment of Henrik Kellgren—and HJ heard the name as Kelvin, the British physicist, which accounts for his confusion.

4. Jonathan Sturges (1864–1909), a Princeton graduate, was crippled early by polio but led an active expatriate life in London, where he lived at Long's Hotel and had a circle of friends that included Whistler and Henry James. He often visited HJ in Lamb House for weeks at a time. It was Sturges whom Howells advised to "live all you can," a remark, made in Whistler's Paris garden, that led James to write *The Ambassadors*. After Sturges's death HJ's letters to Sturges were returned to the novelist and he destroyed them. This one survives thanks to a copy taken by Percy Lubbock.

5. This was George Santayana's *Interpretations of Poetry and Religion*, just published, which WJ recommended to his brother.

130 · To Cora Crane

Ms Columbia

Lamb House, Rye
June 5th 1900

Dear Mrs. Crane.

I have just seen the Moreton Frewens,[1] who, being at Brede, came in and found me, to my relief, at home, and who, I grieve to say, give me a bad account of their news from you of Crane. They speak of a telegram received today (Whitmonday) as unfavourable, and the effect of this is to make me regret I have not, as I fully intended any one of the last three or four days, got off sooner my response to the letter received from you while you were at Dover. Skinner[2] was to give me your new address, and twice have I been to ask for it without finding him. I have it now only from the Frewens. It is a shock to me that Crane is less well[3]—I was full of hope, and had been, in that hope, assuming that a good effect had come to him from his move: cheerful theories much disconcerted! I think of him with more sympathy and sorrow than I can say. I wish I could express this to him more closely and personally. On the Monday you were at Dover I was on the very point of going over to see you and had arranged for an absence of a day, domestically, the night before, but the A.M. brought with it a mass of proofs to be instantly attended to—I was under much pressure, and I lost the occasion, believing then that you were leaving—and leaving with all good omens—on the Tuesday. I learned afterwards that you had waited a day or two longer, but Skinner expressed doubts of Crane's having been able to see me even if I had gone—and that partly consoled me. I bicycled over to Brede with a couple of friends, a day or two after you had gone—to show them the face of the old house; but the melancholy of it was quite heartbreaking. So will it, I fear, always be to me. I won't pretend to utter hopes about Crane which may be vain—or seem to you to now, and thereby only irritating or, at least, distressing: but I constantly think of him and as it were pray for him. I feel that I am not taking too much for granted in believing that you may be in the midst of worries on the money-score which will perhaps make the cheque for Fifty Pounds, that I enclose, a convenience to you. Please view it as such and dedicate it to whatever service it may best render my stricken young friend. It meagrely represents my tender benediction to him. I write in haste—to catch the post. I needn't tell you how glad I shall be of any news that you are able to send me. I wish you all courage and as much hope as possible, and I am yours and his, in deep participation

Henry James

P.S. There must [be] a Banker at Badenweiler with whom you have dealings that will make the conversion of this cheque easy. So I trust.—H.J.

1. Moreton Frewen (1853–1924), an Englishman who traveled widely in the American West, had let Brede House to the Cranes. See Anita Leslie, *Mr. Frewen of England* (1966).

2. Dr. Ernest Skinner, the Rye general practitioner who was HJ's doctor.

3. Stephen Crane (1871–1900), author of *The Red Badge of Courage*, had been living with Cora Taylor for some time, and she had taken his name. They had rented Brede Place, a large Elizabethan manor house eight miles from Rye, settling in it in 1899. HJ had welcomed them as fellow Americans. Now Crane was dying at 29 of tuberculosis, and Cora had taken him to Germany in a special train in hope of a cure.

131 · To James B. Pinker

Ms Yale

Lamb House, Rye
July 25*th* 1900

Dear Mr. Pinker.[1]

I send you at last, today, the complete Ms of *The Sacred Fount*—as to the interminable delay of which I won't further expatiate. The reasons for this have been all of the best, and in the interest of the work itself—intrinsically speaking. It makes exactly 77,794 words—say, more roughly, about *seventy-eight* thousand. It won't do for serialisation—that is impossible, and it has the marks, I daresay, of a thing planned as a very short story, and growing on my hands, to a so much longer thing, by a force of its own—but a force controlled and directed, I believe, or hope, happily enough. It is fanciful, fantastic— but very close and sustained, and calculated to minister to curiosity. However, I can never descant on my own things. What I should like, as regards this, is almost any sum "down," that is *respectable,* for the English and American use of the book for any period short of surrender of copyright: three, five, seven years—in short whatever you can best do. The "down" is important.[2]—What goes to you today is *one* complete type-copy (327 pages), and another—the duplicate— goes to you tomorrow. I have then still another at your service should you desire it.

I hope you bear up—though I'm afraid "trade" doesn't—under this temperature,[3] and everything else.

Yours very truly,
Henry James

1. From 1898 on, HJ's literary agent was James Brand Pinker (1863–1922).
2. The book was published in both the United States and England, and HJ received about $5000 in advances from his publishers.
3. The Boer War.

132 · To W. Morton Fullerton

Ms Harvard

Lamb House, Rye
September 21st 1900

My dear Fullerton.[1]

It isn't—ne vous y trompez pas—your "handsome" telegram that makes me write; it isn't even—comparatively—the rich and solemn spaces of silence in which that missive floats like a lone Greek island in a blue Aegean: it is that I desire the sense of communication with you—and don't even desire it at your expense: depleting indeed though the little telegram must have been. I want *tout bonnement* to look at you and sign to you and sound to you—*show* to you, even, so far as may be: though, of course, if I could *see* you also by the same stroke this would be still better: and about that, indeed, I've a further word to say. Ages seem to me to have rolled by since I had any news of you— and it takes more than ages, as you see, to make me dull to that priva- tion. They have been rather full, for *me,* these ages, of preoccupations and pressures (as well as being, I ween, still fuller of the same for you); and, ever since the month of May in particular, waves and winds and surges, almost storms, of family-history, have spent themselves on my threshold and rattled my windows. Family-ties have tangled them- selves for me freely—even to cousinships feebly felt hitherto, but of a sudden practically to be reckoned with. This, however, is not a wail— I'm past all wailing: it's at most a *constatation:* save in so far as it be, my dear Fullerton, a handshake. Voyons, let me feel you *take* it for that; I mean for a handshake. I've sat as tight here, all the past year, as pos- sible—and that gives me, leaves me, little personal history save the blurred tablet of the immortal-subjective. I've done a great deal of work and am booked to do a great deal more: these things are actually in the lap of the gods—the infernal ones, the publishing and promul- gating crew. But they haven't crowded out visions of you, hopes of you, and still more *for* you. I've thought of your deeply-desirable *congé* and wondered if by chance you were again taking it in the form of a dash to America. I've a horrid fear that you may, that you *must,* have sacrificed on that altar most of your loose change of time. I want you here and I spin the fine web of the rare possibilities. It has been a lux- ury forbidden me for weeks, for months, by reason, exactly, of the constant occupancy of my pair of spare-rooms. (I've only two such, and an attic.) But at last I'm alone for the first time almost within my memory—or at least I *shall* be at any date after Friday, when I take my sister-in-law hence to Dover on her way to rejoin my poor brother who (and this time much the better for it), is about completing his third Nauheim cure. (They go together then to Italy.) *Have* you used up all your time?—Couldn't you, can't you, even if you have, squeeze out three or four golden days for me? Insidious magician, consider it well. This is a time of peace. September here has been, and still is, divine. There are grapes on the branch, and celery in the beds, and tomatoes on the tree (for we tree our tomatoes here—as the American humour- ists tree their coons). My amanuensis, daughty Scot, has just gone to flesh his virgin pilgrim's-staff, or I suppose I should say his rude clay-more, in Paris. The tick of the Remington is silent in my halls. All the little land is lovely roundabout. It's really an attaching, really in its quiet way, a quite adorable corner of the wicked earth. And the earth is *so* wicked just now. Only Lamb House is mild; only Lamb House is sane; only Lamb House is true. I've a pair of charming cousins[2]—ex-propriated and in a quaint old farmhouse—perched at two miles or so off, across the fields: a lovely walk for tea—and a still lovelier back, in the sunset for dinner. Save for that mild mitigation I'm alone. I'm alone and I think of you. I can't say fairer. I hope you are bearing up. I hope it's an easy year for you—*has* been one, I mean: in spite, I dare-say, of possibilities of incubus from the Exhibition. I've nourished the theory that the cyclone-centre *not* being, all these months, particu-larly rue Vignon,[3] you may have felt a little as if school were not keep-ing. However you felt, at any rate, assume my participation, and draw upon it—ah, freely! and *tachez donc* to come. I'd meet you at Dover—I'd do anything for you. Ever, my dear Fullerton, yours

Henry James

1. See Letter 91. Fullerton, in the Paris bureau of the *Times*, had acquired a certain reputation for his coverage of the Dreyfus case.
2. One of the cousins was Ellen (Bay) Emmet (1876–1941), who painted a portrait of HJ.
3. Where Fullerton then lived in Paris.

133 · To W. Morton Fullerton

Ms Harvard

Lamb House, Rye
September 26th 1900

My dear Fullerton.

I should have thanked you on the spot and at the hour for your ad-mirable and beautiful, your more than touching, your penetrating, letter of a few days since, had I not just so committed myself that sev-eral pages of unreserved (don't misread for undeserved) tribute to you had already winged their way from me and had practically crossed your own luminous track. I heard from you, in short, the day after writing to you—but you have left me nothing for it but to write you again. Yet

how, my dear Fullerton, *does* a man write in the teeth of so straight a
blast from—I scarce know what to call the quarter: the spice-scented
tropic isles of Eden—isles of gold—isles of superlative goodness? I
have told you before that the imposition of hands in a certain tender
way "finishes" me, simply—and behold me accordingly more finished
than the most *parachevé* of my own productions. I can only gasp—
gently, and thank you. You do with me what you will. You are terrifically intelligent; and I almost wish it were not *I* in question, that I
might, in a drier light, watch the beauty of your machinery. It *isn't* a
dry light for me—save as my pocket-handkerchief dries it. You're at
any rate the highest luxury I can conceive, and if it were not for a still
audible remnant of the golden chink of my deep, deep pocket, I
should wonder how the devil I can afford you. However, I shall persist
in you. I know but this life. I want in fact more of you, and how much
more my letter of the other day will have told you. How shall I tell
you, further, how it is that I can thus be conscious of your beneficence
and yet keep my head sufficiently to just clutch the situation not unin-
telligently myself too? The situation is that I want to be able to believe
better than I find myself believing—well, what? why, that you are giving a thought at all commensurate with your capacity for thought, to
my ponderous personal plea. You are dazzling, my dear Fullerton; you
are beautiful; you are more than tactful, you are tenderly, magically
tactile. But you're not kind. There it is. You *are* not Kind, save for the
lurid little glimpse of personal history in which you evoke for me the
withering, wallowing Walters, you tell me, after long months, not a
pitiful syllable about yourself. *That's* your inhumanity. I don't know
that it's calculated, but *le compte y est!* "What," you say, "you want,
insatiate archer, *that* also?" Yes; I want that also. I want five—you see
there's a method in my madness—little common, kind, correct words
that will hang somehow together as a Light on your Life. I can't help it
if that's the way I'm made. I sit here scribbling to you at my usual
hour—the minster-bell has sometime since struck twelve; the wind
has risen and it howls in my old chimneys; and in this position the
sense of things somehow seems to sit with me. Write me if you *must*
that it's impossible for you to come over for a few days—I shall as
frankly understand it as I shall deeply deplore it; but it will be, as it
were, a part of yourself on which I can put my hand, and it will
humour my own poor personal, mortal part. I absolutely know it's al-

most a monstrous proposition—so considerable a *déplacement* for you for so *single* a scant gain; but it was only on the ground of *miracle* that I sketched my fandango. Good-night and good rest. Please find in this everything in its order, and *in* everything that I am, my dear Fullerton, yours ever so gratefully and affectionately

Henry James

P.S. I am omitting what I most wanted to express: my deep satisfaction, my gross personal *comfort*, in your sacrificial—everything, to Walter.[1] I should like to see you, par exemple, *not* sacrifice! If ever you feel such a possibility of insanity breathing its breath upon you, *wire* me on the spot. I'll take you in hand.

1. Arthur Fraser Walter (1846–1910), the last member of more than a century of Walters who owned and controlled the London *Times*, which was founded by a Walter in 1789. The newspaper passed into the hands of Lord Northcliffe in 1908. Morton Fullerton was still working for the Paris bureau of the *Times*.

134 · To W. Morton Fullerton

Ms Barrett

Lamb House, Rye
October 2d 1900

My dear boy Fullerton.

How can I thank you kindly, tenderly enough for your so interesting, so touching letter? Let this question itself represent for you such elements of "reply" as, in our so frustrate conditions of intercourse, may temporarily serve. Read into my meagre and hurried words— well, read into them *everything*. I as perfectly understand and embrace your practical impossibilities of migration as I completely retain the consciousness of my original impressible vision of the spare, bare chance. Its very spareness and bareness endeared it to me, and I rocked its frail vitality in my arms as an anxious mother rocks the small creature of her entrails whose life is precarious. And now I have laid its shrivelled shape away to rest—as its little breathing-hour is over. Forgive this slightly gruesome image—which marks simply the moral that my absolute comprehension (ah, my hideous intelligence!) of your complex *asservissement* owes nothing to any attenuation of the sense that your not being able to be here leaves me face to face with it. I *am* face to face with it, as one is face to face, at my age, with every successive lost opportunity (wait till you've reached it!) and with the steady, swift movement of the ebb of the great tide—the great tide of which one will never see the turn. The grey years gather; the arid spaces lengthen, damn them—or at any rate don't shorten; what doesn't come doesn't, and what goes *does*.[1] I needn't ask you to believe that I don't say this to torment you, completely on your *side* as I am; I only say it to *feel*, myself, my loss; as I should have said it to feel my gain if you *had* been free. The next best thing to having you, in short, is thus to be *with* you *quand même. Don't* think, please, by the way, that I supposed you in any "oasis of calm" whatever. I saw the Paris of these months as a positive hell of worry and oppression for you—and that was why, was why . . . ! I only meant that, compared with some—so many other—past periods, your special *Times* tension was presumably less great. I figure your actual predicament luridly enough—and every jangle of your bell-rope vibrates in my own nerves. Sit as tight as you *can:* it's all we can ever do. I rejoice heartily that you got the three weeks in May you tell me of. I wish I might have got them *with* you—but this too apparently, was not, heaven help us, to have been thinkable. Let me the more beg you to put in order your record, your impressions—to give them a form in which I may have cognition of them. In this cognition I should delight. Don't be more difficult for me, in detail, than you *must*. (N.B. This *is* not a technical, but a general prayer!) Your letter exhales a complexity, an obscurity of trouble, which has for me but one light—the inevitableness, in relation to it, of my wondering if I mayn't hold out the conception of *help* to you; or rather of my absolutely *holding* out the assurance of it. Hold me then *you* with any squeeze; grip me with any grip; press me with any pressure; trust me with any trust. I wish I could help you, for instance, by satisfying your desire to know from "what port," as you say, I set out. And yet, though the enquiry is, somehow, of so large a synthesis, I think I *can* in a manner answer. The port from which I set out was, I think, that of the *essential loneliness of my life*— and it seems to be the port also, in sooth to which my course again finally directs itself! This loneliness, (since I mention it!)—what is it still but the deepest thing about one? Deeper about *me*, at any rate, than anything else: deeper than my "genius," deeper than my "discipline," deeper than my pride, deeper, above all, than the deep countermining of art. May that amount of information about it give you a lift! Take all this, at all events, my dear Fullerton, for the very soul of sympathy, and believe me always yours

Henry James

1. HJ echoes what he has just been writing in *The Ambassadors*—Strether's speech in the fifth part to Little Bilham about lost opportunities: "What one loses, one loses, make no mistake about that."

135 · To Ariana Curtis

Ms Taylor

105 Pall Mall S.W.
February 3d, 1901

Dear Mrs. Curtis.

I find it very hideous that I haven't written to you for so long, especially as, during these many past days in particular, I've so often thought of you. The sense of how you must be thinking of our fine historic drama and deep general emotion,[1] here has made me do that—and almost made me wish you might have been in London just now, gloomy and oppressed in an undefinable way, as London has really been. Yesterday, however, you might have had an impression that was worth the past rather pall-like state—so interesting and moving and picturesque and calculated to *give* impressions was the dear old Queen's funeral. I saw it decently enough from the windows of a friend at Buckingham Gate, and it was, with its cortège of Emperors, Kings and Princes, and its gun-carriage hearse (surmounted with the Crown—*the* crown, or rather crowns, the Scotch and Irish too) far-away the most imposing public function I've ever seen. The weather adjusted itself in a way positively *tender*, admirable altogether, and the attitude of the crowd (incredibly and immeasurably vast), was everything that could have been desired. It had no hitch, no anarchist bomb, no ugliness nor infelicity of any sort, and the principal actors in it must have drawn a deep and long breath after laying themselves down, last night, to rest. But strange is the feeling that the door is closed on the past sixty years and that we have faced about another way altogether, or if not quite perhaps altogether, enough to feed greatly, suspense and curiosity. The worst of the new Sovereign [Edward VII] is that he has *been* quite particularly *vulgar* for so many years, and can the Sovereign change his spots, especially when they have been so big? On the other hand he looked so remarkably well on horseback yesterday, and there is a general belief that he wants extremely to excel. I daresay he won't be worse than another. I shall be curious as to the composition of his entourage—but that, exactly, makes for interest. One hears that his hand is already felt, sharply and for good, at the War-office. And he has done since his mother's death several difficult things very well. *Speriamo dunque.* I miss however the good old Queen—of such beneficent duration. We all felt, publicly, at first, quite motherless. But to make up for it a little, we seem to have suddenly acquired a sort of unsuspected cousin in the person of mustachioed *William,*[2] who looked wonderful and sturdy in the cortège and who has done himself no end of good here by his long visit and visible filiality to the old Queen. The truthful account of her death appears to be that she died in his arms— he and Sir James Reid holding her and supporting her at the pillow, and the Prince and Princess of Wales having each a hand. At any rate he and the King are now more than ever close and intimate friends. May it make for peace!—In quite another order, I dined the other day, very happily, with dear little Miss [Jessie] Allen,[3] whose friendship knows no bounds, and who had, for her little dinner three of his wonderful Bertie and Bessie friends. Every one appears alike affected to her (I mean in the same way). I am afraid she has to "scrimp" a good deal, and her little—tiny—house was very cold, but her nature glows with a generous fire. I am delighted she goes to the south and to your sun and your kindness. She gave me of your recent news, and will give you of mine. I yearn for your golden life, but in vain, at present, in vain. I give you both much love and am yours ever and always

Henry James

1. Queen Victoria had died on 22 January 1901.
2. The German Kaiser.
3. HJ had originally met Elizabeth Jessie Jane Allen (1845–1918) at the Curtises' in Venice, and they had become close friends.

136 · *To Hendrik C. Andersen*

Ms Barrett

Lamb House, Rye
4 May 1901

My dearest Boy Hendrik.[1]

What an arch-Brute you must, for a long time past, have thought me! But I am not really half the monster I appear. Let me at least attenuate my ugly failure to thank you for certain valued and most interesting photographs. I spent the whole blessed winter—December to April—in London (save a week at Christmas), and returned here to take up my abode again but three or four weeks ago. It was only *then* that I found, amid a pile of postal matter unforwarded (as my servants, when I am away, have instructions only to forward *letters*), your tight little roll of views of your Lincoln. It had lain on my hall-table ever since it arrived (though I don't quite know when that had been); and my first impulse was [to] sit down and "acknowledge" it without a day's delay. Unfortunately—with arrears here, of many sorts, to be attended to after a long absence, the day's delay perversely imposed itself—and on the morrow my brother and his wife, whom you saw in Rome, arrived for a long stay, with their daughter in addition. They are with me still, and their presence accounts for many neglects—as each day, after work and immediate letters etc.—I have to give them much of my time. But here, my dear boy, I am at last, and I hold out to you, in remorse, remedy, regret, a pair of tightly-grasping, closely-drawing hands. I've lost your studio address—can't find it high or low; but I send this to Sebasti's bank—on the advice of my brother—as *they* (he and his wife) can't remember the thing either. I also enclose a letter which has just come to you here. May it all not fall short! My companions speak of you with the extremest tenderness, found you delightful and had the greatest pleasure in seeing you. My brother is also very interesting to me on the subject of your Lincoln—as, having seen it, he can control somewhat my impression based only on photographs. The latter show me how big a stride with it you have made in this short time and how stoutly you must have sweated over it; but I won't conceal from you that there are things about it that worry me a little. That comes, inevitably, partly from the fact of my being, alas, of a generation nearer to Lincoln than you (the younger generation of his lifetime, though I never saw him in the flesh); and having been drenched in youth with feeling about him, the sense of him, photographs, images, aspects of him. A *seated* Lincoln in itself shocks me a little—he was for us all, then, standing up very tall: though I perfectly recognise that that was a condition you may have *had*, absolutely, to accept. However, I like the head—think it on the whole very fine and right (though rather too smooth, ironed-out, simplified as to ruggedness, ugliness, *mouth* etc.); and it is the figure, especially as seen from the side, that somewhat troubles me. I don't feel the length of limb, leg, shanks, loose-jointedness, etc.—nor the thickness of the large body in the clothes—especially the presence of shoulders, big arms and big hands. It's in general a *softer*, smaller giant than we used to see—to see represented and to hear described. I do think he wants facially more light-and-shade, and more breaking-up, under his accursed clothing, more bone, more mass. He is, in general, more *placid* than one's own image of him, and than history and memory. Benevolent, but deeply troubled, and altogether tragic: that's how one thinks of him.—But forgive this groping criticism; far from your thing itself, I worry and fidget for the love of your glory and your gain; and I send you my blessing on your stiff problem and your, I am sure, whatever mistake one may make about it, far from superficial solution.—I hope you have had a winter void of any such botherations as to poison (in any degree) your work or trouble your brave serenity or disturb your youthful personal bloom; a winter of health, in short, and confidence and comfort. It has been a joy to me to be with any one who had lately seen you—and I wish that, without more delay, I could do the sweet same! There is much I want to say to you—but it's half past midnight, and I wax long-winded. So I bid you good night with my affectionate blessing. I count on seeing you here this summer. Give me some fresh assurance of the prospect. I have had a charming letter from Mrs. Elliott,[2] very happy over her Jack's finally-placed Boston show. *Meno male!* Yours, my dear Hans, always and ever

Henry James

1. Hendrik Christian Andersen (1872–1940), Norwegian-American sculptor, reared at Newport. HJ met him in Rome in 1899 and they formed an affectionate friendship, although the novelist was critical of Andersen's statues.

2. The former Maude Howe, wife of the American painter John Elliott, at whose home HJ met Andersen.

137 · To Sarah Orne Jewett

Ms Harvard

Lamb House, Rye
October 5th 1901

Dear Miss Jewett.

Let me not criminally, or at all events gracelessly, delay to thank you for your charming and generous present of *The Tory Lover.*[1] He has been but three or four days in the house, yet I have given him an earnest, a pensive, a liberal—yes, a benevolent attention, and the upshot is that I should like to write you a longer letter than I just now— (especially as it's past midnight) see my way to doing. For it would take me some time to disembroil the tangle of saying to you at once how I appreciate the charming touch, tact and taste of this ingenious exercise, and how little I am in sympathy with the experiments of its general (to my sense) misguided stamp. There I am!—yet I don't do you the outrage, as a fellow craftsman and a woman of genius and courage, to suppose you not as conscious as I am myself of all that, in these questions of art and truth and sincerity, is beyond the mere twaddle of graciousness. The "historic" novel is, for me, condemned, even in cases of labour as delicate as yours, to a fatal *cheapness,* for the simple reason that the difficulty of the job is inordinate and that a mere *escamotage,* in the interest of ease, and of the abysmal public *naiveté* becomes inevitable. You may multiply the little facts that can be got from pictures and documents, relics and prints, as much as you like—*the* real thing is almost impossible to do, and in its essence the whole effect is as nought: I mean the invention, the representation of the old CONSCIOUSNESS, the soul, the sense, the horizon, the vision of individuals in whose minds half the things that make ours, that make the modern world were non-existent. You have to *think* with your modern apparatus a man, a woman—or rather fifty—whose own thinking was intensely otherwise conditioned, you have to simplify back by an amazing *tour de force*—and even then it's all humbug. But there is a shade of the (even then) humbug that *may* amuse. The childish tricks that take the place of any such conception of the real job in the flood of Tales of the Past that seems of late to have been rolling over our devoted country—these ineptitudes have, on a few recent glances, struck me as creditable to no one concerned. You, I hasten to add, seem to me to have steered very clear of them—to have seen your work very bravely and handled it firmly; but even you court disaster by composing the whole thing so much by sequences of speeches. It's when the extinct soul talks, and the earlier consciousness airs itself, that the pitfalls multiply and the "cheap" way has to serve. I speak in general, I needn't keep insisting, and I speak grossly, summarily, by rude and provisional signs, in order to suggest my sentiment at all. I don't mean to say so much without saying more, and now I have douched you with cold water when I only meant just lightly and kindly to sprinkle you as for a new baptism—that is a *re*-dedication to altars but briefly, I trust, forsaken. Go back to the dear country of the *Pointed Firs, come* back to the palpable present-*intimate* that throbs responsive, and that wants, misses, needs you, God knows, and that suffers woefully in your absence. Then I shall feel perhaps—and do it if only *for* that—that you have magnanimously allowed for the want of gilt on the gingerbread of the but-on-this-occasion-*only* limited sympathy of yours very constantly,

Henry James

P.S. My tender benediction, please, to Mrs. Fields.

1. Miss Jewett (1849–1909), the American writer, had sent HJ her historical novel. This letter shows HJ explaining that he sometimes writes "the mere twaddle of graciousness," but refusing to do so for the author of *The Country of the Pointed Firs* (1896).

138 · To Rudyard Kipling
Ts Harvard

Lamb House, Rye
October 30th 1901

My dear Rudyard.

I can't lay down *Kim*[1] without wanting much to write to you: absolutely and most gratefully, coercive in that direction is, in fact, your magnificent book. And yet to write is to try to bridge such a dreadful interval of separation and silence that I almost feel as if I mightn't reach you—I mean as if the lapse in our commerce at the best so hindered (by the perversity that Rye isn't Rottingdean, nor Rottingdean Rye) were a thing of positive impenetrable thicknesses. I've a horrid sense that I've stupidly let these thicknesses grow (through a couple of crowded, complicated anxious summers etc., among other recent matters): though I shall in a moment assure you, properly, how little heart I've had to do that. I must in the first place simply *penetrate*, at any cost, so that here goes—and I beseech you to feel the silence in question crumble and send up a golden dust.

I overflow, I beg you to believe, with *Kim*, and I rejoice in such a saturation, such a splendid dose of you. That has been the great thing, I find; that one could sink deep and deep, could sit in you up to one's neck. Inevitably, at my age, and with the habits and arrears of my craft, I read with comment and challenge, in face of the material; in other words I have some small reserves and anxieties—as to your frequent *how* of performance. But these things haven't mattered. They floated away like upset boats and drowned sages in the current; and I've surrendered luxuriously to your genius. Don't scoff at me, nor let Mrs. Carrie scoff, nor your children (who must be pretty well up to scoffing age now), when I tell you that I take you as you are. It might be that I wished you were quite different—though I don't. I should still, after this, just fatalistically take you. You are too sublime—you are too big and there is too much of you. I don't think you've cut out your subject, in *Kim* with a sharp enough scissors, but with that one little nut cracked—so!—the beauty, the quantity, the prodigality, the Ganges-flood, leave me simply gaping as your procession passes. What a luxury to *possess* a big subject as you possess India; or, to pat you still more on the head, what a cause of just pride! I find the boy himself a dazzling conception, but I find the Lama more yet—a thing damnably and splendidly *done*. Bravo, bravo, Lama, from beginning to end, and bravo, bravo, the whole idea, the great many-coloured poem of their relation and their wild Odyssey—void of a false note and swarming with felicities that you can count much better than I. The way you make the general picture live and sound and shine, all by a myriad touches that are like the thing itself pricking through with a little snap—that makes me want to say to you: "Come, all else is folly—sell all you have and give to the poor!" By which I mean chuck public affairs,[2] which are an ignoble scene, and stick to your canvas and your paint-box. There are as good colours in the tubes as ever were laid on, and *there* is the only truth. The rest is base humbug. Ask the Lama.

Ask the Lama too, while you are about it, why you shouldn't come over to see me some merciful day when it would give me joy and support. Direct signals to this effect have long failed me: I've known of you, for half the year, nothing but that—these three winters, hideously, isn't it?—you've been overseas and beyond my imagination; and the other half, that is, for these three summers, I've known nothing of *anything* outside my anxiously-applied domestic consciousness, or in other words the walls of my house or garden, by reason of the constant pressure of my brother William and his fortunes, his ill condition, his wife and his, always, youngster or two (mainly a youngstress, Peggy). He has been long and wearily ill, and still isn't much other, and my existence has had that for pivot and centre. But he has lately returned to America, and I seem of late to have looked more over the wall. As I say, I wish I could pull *you* over it hitherward—you being, immediately, the largest animated object my searchlight rests upon. I only have a sinking sense that you accept no invitation for anything further than South Africa for the moment; also, I sit among the ruins of a smashed household—having had lately the pleasure of losing two servants, a man and wife; who had lived with me for sixteen years (and whom I finally dispensed with in sixteen hours); otherwise I would make my appeal straight to Mrs. Carrie. I go up to town after Christmas; to remain till May, and if so be it that you don't migrate again, this year, too headlong, I shall ask your leave to come down, one of the very first days, from the comparatively thinkable Victoria. Cross country journeys *hence*—save for return the following year—are superlatively unthinkable. Till Christmas I shall be occupied grinding my teeth and breaking my heart over the finish of a book[3] promised for January 1st, and on which my already oft-perjured life depends. Please take this ugly scrawl, meanwhile and plead with your wife to take it, as my issue from the longest tunnel in the world. I haven't, for months, looked at the serried row of the presentation copies, so richly bedight, that I owe you both, right and left—for I travel with the whole shelf, and in the tunnels they serve to read by—without feeling that, thus constantly and admirably addressed by you, I ought to be eternally, since I can't be anything like as eloquently—replying. I needn't tell you how much I hope you are both personally sound and scatheless, and that I involve you all in the affectionate interest of yours, my dear Rudyard, very constantly,

Henry James

1. *Kim* had just been published.
2. Kipling's patriotic verses about the Boer War.
3. *The Wings of the Dove.*

6 · Mastery
1902–1915

Henry James's last letters are informal, easier, more spontaneous, and less distancing than his earlier letters. They remain gracefully baroque, filled with delicate ironies and high, subtle humor. He still mints grand phrases and splendid periods—this was second nature to him—and he seems on much more relaxed terms with the world. His epistolary life has acquired two facets in his late years—the typewritten and the handwritten. The first involves the presence of a typist in his workroom, for he has acquired the habit of dictating directly to his typewriter. Private communion has given way to communion through an intermediary. He resorts to his old form only late at night, when he still takes white pages into his confidence—as he did with his notebooks of an earlier time—in his massive scrawl. The diaries of his last amanuensis, Theodora Bosanquet, give us glimpses of the workroom sociabilities: James chats, explains, gives the typist the background of his correspondents and then goes off into his long and woven sentences. The medium and the message have become mixed, and never more than when James forgets to go on with his prose and begins to dictate his ruminations, which resemble his late dictated notes for his novels.

From the turn of the century, the death of Queen Victoria, the Edwardian years, to the coming of war in 1914, we see an active productive literary master, accomplishing wonders of work in his old age. His aging is a kind of triumphal procession until illness overtakes him in 1910—and even then he still needs to dictate sentences and does so up to his dying moments. At the approach of his sixties he writes his three big novels, *The Ambassadors*, *The Wings of the Dove*, and *The Golden Bowl*. He then (in 1904) sails for the United States. He has stayed abroad twenty years. The trip is a triumph. He lectures and finds he can hold audiences. He tours parts of America never visited before: the Middle West, the South, California, and writes *The American Scene* (1907), an elegy for the America he had known, the old New York of his childhood and the New England of his young manhood. It is also a trenchant complaint to the new age, as he studies the evanescence that has become an American style and the sprouting arrogance of the new skyscrapers. He returns to England to write a batch of tales dealing with his rediscovered homeland. This "American phase" is the obsession of his late years: he revises his work for the "New York Edition" of twenty-four volumes—the name chosen as a tribute to the city of his birth. He shores up his travel writings in *English Hours* (1905) and *Italian Hours* (1910) and revises his much-loved *Little Tour in France*. He is no sooner convalescent after his 1910 illness, in the new era of George V, when he breaks new ground with his autobiographies, *A Small Boy and Others* (1913) and *Notes of a Son and Brother* (1914). These foreshadow Proustian subjectivity, and coincide with the publication of the French novelist's *Swann's Way*.

Fascinated though he is by his recovered America, Henry James feels that it has betrayed him. It is now a continent of exploitation, and he puts his peroration in *The American Scene* into the mouth of an American Indian. The United States preys on its environment and that of its neighbors; he dislikes the jingoism of Theodore Roosevelt, whom he visits in the White House. In his uncompleted novel, *The Ivory Tower*, he plans a kind of parable of a society ruled by the aggressive rich, and he wants to depict the money-greed and the amassing of great fortunes. In one of his long letters to the widowed Mrs. William James, who has urged him to settle, for his last years, in Cambridge, he replies in strong language: he talks about the "tentacles" of Cambridge, and with adverbial emphasis:

> Dearest Alice, I could come back to America (could be carried back on a stretcher) to *die*—but never, never to live. To say how the question affects me is dreadfully difficult because of its appearing so to make light of you and the children—but when I think of how little Boston and Cambridge were of old ever *my* affair, or anything but an accident, for me, of the parental life there to which I occasionally and painfully and losingly sacrificed, I have a superstitious terror of seeing them at the end of time again stretch out strange inevitable tentacles to draw me back and destroy me . . . I haven't a single other tie in America that means ten cents to

me—*really* means it. You see my capital—yielding all my income, intellectual, social, associational, on the old investment of so many years—my capital is *here,* and to let it all slide would be simply to become bankrupt. (Letter 176)

He is lonely during these last years, and his letters to the admiring young men around him, Hugh Walpole, Morton Fullerton, Jocelyn Persse, show him reaching out for their company and their youth. Rye becomes impossible to him; its winters are long and he has much depression. He goes increasingly back to London and finally to an apartment on the Thames. But there are moments when Edith Wharton, his newfound affluent friend, brings America to him—she constantly demands his company and provides the excitement of her motor car and expert chauffeur. Life becomes very lively in London and Paris when she is there. She also offers intimate confidences and all the excitement—and anguish—of her love affair with Morton Fullerton, the journalist whom James introduced to her. Fullerton is an old-fashioned "masher," a runner-after both women and men: he loves and leaves, swoops down and flies away, and Mrs. Wharton experiences much passion and anguish, a bitter mix. James entertains the confidences of both parties with the curiosity and empathy of his elderly bachelorhood. He had more or less described such an affair a few years earlier in *The Ambassadors*—Madame de Vionnet who cries for her lover, the light-hearted young American Chadwick Newsome.

The 1914 war catches James by surprise. He had accustomed himself to the nineteenth-century optimism that the world was evolving into a more enlightened and less aggressive age. The August guns become "a nightmare from which there is no waking save by sleep." His letters rise to new heights of eloquence and compassion as he contemplates human waste and ravaged lives. After the first shocks, he returns to his philosophy of stoicism: even war is a form of "life," and there is heroism all around him. Remembering how Whitman nursed the wounded during the Civil War (and recalling his own younger brothers as soldiers before they were out of their teens), James begins to visit hospitals and rest homes as well as refugee centers. His homoeroticism responds, as it always has, to the idea of the "young soldier" who lives with an image of courage and great deeds but also in the presence of death and annihilation.

When a group of Americans abroad organizes the American Volunteer Motor Ambulance Corps in France, the novelist gives it full support and becomes its honorary chairman, using his pen and name to make known its work. During these last months he writes—old and ailing and now suffering from chronic angina—the equivalent of a book (published after his death as *Within the Rim*) about the "long wards" in the hospitals, the refugees in Chelsea, and the grand alliance with France. Six months before his death, the novelist becomes a British subject, after keeping his American citizenship in England for forty years. Just before his death, when he has had a stroke, he receives from George V the Order of Merit—but he is in reality past the knowledge of this final honor. His quest was to awaken from the nightmare.

139 · To Hendrik C. Andersen

Ms Barrett

105 Pall Mall S.W.
February 9th 1902

My dear, dear dearest Hendrik.

Your news[1] fills me with horror and pity, and how can I express the tenderness with which it makes me think of you and the aching wish to be near you and put my arms round you? My heart fairly bleeds and breaks at the vision of you *alone,* in your wicked and indifferent old far-off Rome, with the haunting, blighting, unbearable sorrow. The sense that I can't *help* you, see you, talk to you, touch you, hold you close and long, or do anything to make you rest on me, and feel my participation—this torments me, dearest boy, makes me ache for you, and for myself; makes me gnash my teeth and groan at the bitterness of things. I can only take refuge in hoping you are *not* utterly alone, that some human tenderness of *some* sort, some kindly voice and hand *are* near you that may make a little the difference. What a dismal winter you must have had, with this staggering blow at the climax! I don't of course know *what* fragment of friendship there may be to draw near to you, and in my uncertainty my image of you is of the darkest, and my pity, as I say, feels so helpless. I wish I could go to Rome and put my hands on you (oh, how lovingly I should lay them!) but that, alas, is odiously impossible. (Not, moreover, that apart from *you,* I should so much as like to be there now.) I find myself thrown back on anxiously and doubtless vainly, wondering if there may not, after a while, [be] some possibility of your coming to England, of the current of your trouble inevitably carrying you here—so that I might take consoling, soothing, infinitely close and tender and affectionately-healing *possession* of you. This is the one thought that relieves me about you a little—and I wish you might fix your eyes on it for the idea, just of the possibility. I am in town for a few weeks but I return to Rye April 1st, and sooner or later to *have* you there and do for you, to put my arm round you and *make* you lean on me as on a brother and a lover, and keep you on and on, slowly comforted or at least relieved of the first bitterness of pain—this I try to imagine as thinkable, attainable, not wholly out of the question. There I am, at any rate, and there is my house and my garden and my table and my studio—such as it is!—and your room, and your welcome, and your place everywhere—and I press them upon you, oh so earnestly, dearest boy, if isolation and grief and the worries you are overdone with become intolerable to you. There they are, I say—to fall upon, to rest upon, to find whatever possible shade of oblivion in. I will *nurse* you through your dark passage. I wish I could do something *more*—something straighter and nearer and more immediate but such as it is please let it sink into you. Let all my tenderness, dearest boy, do *that*. This is all now. I wired you three words an hour ago. I can't *think* of your sister-in-law—I brush her vision away and your history with your father, as I've feared it, has haunted me all winter. I embrace you with almost a passion of pity.

Henry James

1. The death of Andersen's brother Andreas, a painter.

140 · To Ford Madox Hueffer

Ms Harvard

Lamb House, Rye
September 9th 1902

My dear Hueffer.

I thank you ever so kindly for your letter, which gives me extreme pleasure and almost for the moment makes me see the *Wings* myself, not as a mass of mistakes, with everything I had intended absent and everything present botched! Such is the contagion of your charming optimism. There is something, I suppose, by way of leaven in the lump; but I feel—have been feeling—mainly as if I had deposited in the market-place an object chiefly cognisable and evitable as a lump. Nothing, all the same, is ever more interesting to me than the consideration, with those who care and see, or want to, of these bottomless questions of How and Why and Whence and *What*—in connection with the mystery of one's craft. But they take one far, and, after all, it is the *doing* it that best meets and answers them.

The book had of course, to my sense, to be composed in a certain way,[1] in order to come into being at all, and the lines of composition, so to speak, determined and controlled its parts and account for what is and what isn't there; what isn't, e.g., like the "last interview" (Hall Caine[2] would have made it large as life and magnificent, wouldn't he?) of *Densher* and *Milly*.[3] I had to make up my mind as to what was my subject and what wasn't, and then to illustrate and embody the same logically. The subject was Densher's history with Kate Croy—hers with him, and Milly's history was but a thing involved and embroiled in that. But I fear I even then let my system betray me, and at any rate I feel I have welded my structure of rather too large and too heavy historic bricks. But we will talk of these things, and I think I have a plan of getting over to Winchelsea some day next week, when I shall no longer have three American cousins staying with me, and two others at the Mermaid![4] But I will consult you telegraphically first. I am hoping you *have* been able to pass the book on to Conrad.

Yours most truly,
Henry James

1. Hueffer (later Ford Madox Ford, 1873–1939) had asked HJ why he omitted the big confrontation scenes in *The Wings of the Dove*.

2. Sir Hall Caine (1853–1931), author of a series of best-selling sentimental novels such as *The Woman Thou Gavest Me* (1913).

3. Hueffer created the legend that he was the original of the passive-aggressive journalist character, Merton Densher. This does not fit the evidence. A more credible original would be Morton Fullerton.

4. Various Emmet relations. The Mermaid Inn at Rye is a short distance from Lamb House.

141 · To Manton Marble

Ms Houghton

> Reform Club
> Pall Mall S.W.
> December 5*th*, 1902

Dear Manton Marble.[1]

Your generous letter comes back to me here from Rye, after a delay—I having first stopped my letters, as I was to have returned home sooner. Coming hither on my way, I have been considerably detained. I learn with emotion—which is not, however, that of surprise, of the substantial new benefit you have conferred on me, and I sink almost, beneath the weight of your so multitudinous bounty. I seem to surmise that the book which has not scrupled, proceeding from the source of so much impunity, to swell the current in question, and which I shall find at L[amb] H[ouse]—I surmise that this valuable volume is the *Webb* volume of which we spoke—and I feel how I drop far below the argument in merely saying that I rejoice to possess it, and to be able to read it again in the light of your eulogy; also that I heartily thank you for it. Still, all the same, take my word for it, as a dabbler in fable and fiction, that the plays and the sonnets were never written but by a *Personal Poet*, a Poet and Nothing Else, a Poet, who, being Nothing Else, could never be a Bacon (the subject of 10 vols. from a Spedding),[2] into the bargain. I give you in fact my word of honour for it, and if that gift is not at least part payment for your incorrigible munificence, I don't know what may be. The difficulty with the divine William is that *he* isn't, wasn't the Personal Poet of the calibre and the conditions, any more than the learned, the ever so much *too* learned, Francis. However, we will talk of these things again in your halls of delight and by your vast ironic sea. I recall my Sunday in the presence of these things with a sense of the romantic already mellow and almost melancholy. I greet Mrs. Marble with all the tenderness of that sentiment, and I am yours and hers, both, more than ever,

> Henry James

1. Marble (1834–1917), proprietor and editor of the New York *World* (1862–1876) and a dedicated bimetallist, was often visited by HJ at his home near Brighton. Marble had sent HJ a new book attempting to prove Bacon wrote Shakespeare.
2. James Spedding (1808–1881) edited the works of Bacon in seven volumes as well as his letters, and wrote his life.

142 · *To Urbain Mengin*

Ms Harvard

Lamb House, Rye
January 1st 1903

My dear Urbain Mengin.[1]

Your letter, your beautiful book, your faithful remembrance, your shining magnanimity—all, all confound and overwhelm me, so that I approach you crawling *à quatre pattes* and with my forehead in the dust. I won't undertake to explain or attenuate my long and unmannerly silence—to which, moreover, I have again and again exposed your exemplary patience. You know me for the most execrable of correspondents, and there is nothing to add to that. Your great handsome wide-margined large-printed, yellow-covered *Italie des Romantiques* came to me safely more months ago than I have the courage to confess to in round numbers. Call it 100 and *n'en parlons plus*. I mean let us not speak of my base delay. Let us, on the contrary, speak—a little— of the volume itself; though, as I understand, it was for you a superimposed and inevitable task, you won't care to have it judged as you would an utterance of your heart—I have in any case attentively and appreciatively read it; finding in it much entertaining matter very succinctly and agreeably presented; especially liking your Lamartine, your Chateaubriand and your Mme de Staël. How little they all *saw* compared with *nous autres!* And to have had to become "romantique," and break a thousand window-panes, to see even that little! The only thing one can say is that they saw more—(more beauty) than the Pres[ident] de Brosses.[2] But we would kick their posteriors today for what they *didn't* see—especially that big yellow-satin *derrière* of Mme de Staël. What I regret is that you can have treated a poet of a vertiginous lyric *essor* like Shelley's without in any way indicating his quality and splendour—which I don't think *fair,* as we say. He is one of the great poets of the world, of the rarest, highest effulgence, the very genius and incarnation of poetry, the poet-type, as it were. But you speak only of the detail of his more or less irrelevant itinerary, and put in scarce a word for what he signifies and represents. I regret it for the reason that French readers have very rarely occasion to hear of him, so that when by chance they do I can't but be sorry that the case isn't stated for him more liberally as *poet.* He was the strangest of human beings, but he was *la poésie même*, the sense of Italy never melted into *anything (étranger)* I think, as into his "Lines in the Euganaean Hills" and *d'autres encore.* "Come where the vault of blue Italian day . . . !" is, for *me*, to *be* there *jusqu'au cou!* And *de même* for Keats, the child of the Gods! Read over again to yourself, but *aloud,* the stanzas of the *Adonais* (or I wish I could read them *to* you!) descriptive of the corner of Rome where they both lie buried,[3] and then weep bitter tears of remorse at having sacrificed them to the terrestrial *caquetage* of A. de Musset! Forgive my emphasis. I feel as if my poor friends had lost an opportunity in the doux pays de France. Mais il ne s'agit pas de ça. Il s'agit de vous y souhaiter pour vous-même mille douceurs pendant l'année qui commence. I hope you are happily adjusted to Melun and that Paris is well within your extended grasp. It appears to have ceased, alas, almost completely to be within mine. I am very much where you left me last—save that I am a great deal older and *plus gros* and *plus pesé* and *plus solitaire.* I spend eight months of the year in this place (favourable to work and health and poverty and much *too* favourable to thought) and four in London, for which place I presently depart. Travelling is less and less in my line, and except that I greatly yearn to go back, before I descend into the deep tomb, to dear old Italy for a year. There we must still meet. I foresee that you will never come again to England, and France, for me, is but an engaging dream.—The Paul Bourgets were here (in England), as you probably know, for a few weeks last summer; but I saw them but for a few hours, in London, and have had no news of them since. I don't know in what *île d'or* they are wintering—but you must be better informed. Goodnight—good-day; it is past midnight and I am, my dear Mengin, very faithfully yours

Henry James

1. Mengin (1864–1955) had arrived in England during the 1880s as French tutor to the future Duke of Sutherland, with an introduction to HJ from Paul Bourget. He had now received his doctorate from the University of Paris for a dissertation on the British romantics in Italy, a copy of which he sent to HJ. See Robert Mengin, *Monsieur Urbain* (Paris, 1984).

2. Charles de Brosses, known as the Président de Brosses, of Dijon, famous for a lengthy dispute with Voltaire. A series of his letters on Italy was published in 1836. See Letter 17, note 2.

3. The Protestant Cemetery in Rome, which figures in "Daisy Miller," and where Miss Woolson was buried not far from the graves of Keats and Shelley.

143 · To Jocelyn Persse

Ms Harvard

Lamb House, Rye
July 21st 1903

My dear Jocelyn.[1]

Coming back late last night from an absence of several days I found your photograph and note awaiting me: in which I so rejoiced that I presently asked myself what the "blow" would (or wouldn't) have been had the gift failed me, or had I been fool enough not to invite it—and for exactly that hour. It welcomed me (with Maximilien's aid)[2] home to my empty halls and made them seem for the moment less lonely. Your portrait is good enough to be a satisfaction, in spite of belonging to the vicious order of the "licked" and stippled—the elaborately re-touched: with its value of resemblance, however, not quite *all* pumice-stoned away. So, to cherish you the better, I have you already under glass and in a frame of modest richness—from which, to make room for you, I have evicted an old photograph of an old friend (of whom I have a later and much better one). I only regret that your brave young name, in your remarkable young fist, doesn't complete the present-ment. For you are one of those of whom the beholder asks Who you are. However, you are not for the staring crowd.—My absence, of which you gently inquire, dragged and seemed long to me, from day to day; but I did the things that were necessary, both in town and coun-try, and the rising tide of a more private existence now begins to cover the sandy space. From Friday P.M. to Monday morn, down close to Leith Hill in Surrey I had indeed rather a sense of peace in a lovely land and with some old American friends who have taken a house there. On Saturday I had quite a wondrous drive—in that miracu-lously rural, almost romantic Surrey country which is so absurdly near the dire South London. But these will seem pale adventures to *you*, luxurious youth, whom I seem to see launched on the huge (and agi-tating) wave of the King's visit, and into endless Irish junketting. May these things not float you too direfully far—far, I mean, from the vir-tuous *grind* of life and the sober realities that a homely friend can hope to share with you! The waters, here, verily, threaten to close a good deal over my own patient head [and][3] more shallow inkpot. It is meant to do nothing of the kind—it isn't a bombardment (though it looks so like one) to reduce you. Don't be reduced; keep your course and bide your time. Only have it present to you—and never doubt of it—that no small sign of your remembrance will ever fail even of its most meagre message to yours, my dear Jocelyn, always

Henry James

1. A Persse of Galway, and a nephew of Lady Gregory, Jocelyn (1873–1943) was a handsome young man-about-town, "hunting, social, extremely good-natured." HJ had recently met him and they had promptly become good friends. Persse to Leon Edel, 31 August 1937: "Henry James was the dearest human being I have ever known. Why he liked me so much I can't say." Hugh Walpole told Sir Rupert Hart-Davis, "believe it or not, Henry James was madly in love with him." See Edel, *Henry James: A Life*, 575–576.
2. Maximilien (Max) was HJ's dachshund.
3. The letter is torn here.

144 · To Manton Marble

Ms Houghton

Lamb House, Rye
Oct. 10*th*, 1903

Dear Manton Marble.

You have in your infinite mercy already permitted me this vulgar aid to survival (of an impaired sort) in the everlasting Struggle—so that I unblushingly presume upon past impunity. The real fact is moreover that you pile up your bounties and benefits into so massive a mountain that my onward path can bore through, or even arrive at some process of outflanking, only by a resort to that energetic blasting for which machinery is obviously required. Thus do I cause the very accumulations of your goodness to fly about your ears in the violent sound of my Remington. The beautiful Symonds volume,[1] too princely by half, reached me a day or two ago, seeming thereby to perch on [an] Apennine, on an Alp. I have stood staring at it for hours, almost with a sinking of the heart, and quite, at first, with an extinction of voice. And as yet, as you see, even, I can't quaver out a proper straightforward Thankyou. All I can do is to put the precious thing on one of my shelves, in the highest company prevailing there, and swagger up and down in front of it.

347

I can, however, bring out a thankyou for your intimation in respect to the little atrocity I mentioned remembering to have perpetrated (on W. W[hitman])[2] in the gross impudence of youth—yea, even a thankyou-very-much-indeed. But nothing would induce me to reveal the whereabouts of my disgrace, which I only recollect as deep and damning. The place I dimly remember, but the year is utterly vague to me—I only know that I haven't seen the accursed thing for more than thirty years, and that if it were to cross my path nothing would induce me to look at it. I am so far from "keeping" the abominations of my early innocence that I destroy them wherever I spy them—which, thank goodness, occurs rarely.

I hope you both were able really to take your ease at your inn, and that your forest of Arden worked, practically, as you liked it. I received your little pictorial reproach, and the shaft, so prettily feathered, pierced me; yet without wounding to the death, reserved as I was to be this summer for heavier and more crushing (though alas not fully liberating) projectiles. The very bad but very crowded little hotel that I had begun to keep, very hard, even when I last wrote you, has been my care, among other cares, up to this day, and the establishment still remains open, with its staff drawing wages, its omnibus meeting all trains, and its proprietor a broken and desperate man. I don't at least take my ease in *mine* inn! It's really but when the inn *isn't* one's own that ease can be predicated. However, only give me time, and if only just from the impulse of wild *general* vindictiveness, I shall, by driving up to your door, do my best to make of the pair of you again a landlord and landlady. Give me till later in the autumn—give me till I *can* leave home. I feel as if I were sticking fast in the middle of my Simplon tunnel, but I am there as everywhere very gratefully and constantly yours

Henry James

1. This may have been John Addington Symonds's study of Walt Whitman, published in 1893.

2. HJ alludes to his unsigned review of Whitman's *Drum-Taps*, published in the *Nation*, 16 November 1865 (when he was 21); the review has been reprinted in *Henry James: Literary Criticism (American)*, Library of America (1984).

145 · To Henry Adams

Ms Mass. Historical

Lamb House, Rye
November 19th 1903

My dear Adams.

I am so happy at hearing from you *at all* that the sense of the particular occasion of my doing so is almost submerged and smothered.[1] You did bravely well to write—make a note of the act, for your future career, as belonging to a class of impulses to be precipitately obeyed and, if possible, even tenderly nursed. Yet it has been interesting, exceedingly, in the narrower sense, as well as delightful in the larger, to have your letter, with its so ingenious expression of the effect on you of poor *W. W. S[tory]*—with whom, and the whole business of whom, there is (yes, I can see!) a kind of *inevitableness* in my having made you squirm—or whatever is the proper name for the sensation engendered in you! Very curious, and even rather terrible, this so far-reaching action of a little biographical vividness—which did indeed, in a manner, begin with me, myself, even as I put the stuff together—though pushing me to conclusions less grim, as I may call them, than in your case. The truth is that any retraced story of bourgeois lives (lives other than great lives of "action"—*et encore!*) throws a chill upon the scene, the time, the subject, the small mapped-out facts, and if you find "great men thin" it isn't really so much their fault (and least of all yours) as that the art of the biographer—devilish art!—is somehow practically *thinning*. It simplifies even while seeking to enrich—and even the Immortal are so helpless and passive in death. The proof is that I wanted to invest dear old Boston with a mellow, a golden glow—and that for those who know, like yourself, I only make it bleak—and weak! Luckily those who know are indeed but three or four—and they won't, I hope, too promiscuously tell. For the book, meanwhile, I seem to learn, is much acclaimed in the U.S.—a better fate than I hoped for the mere dissimulated-perfunctory. The Waldo Storys absolutely *thrust* the job upon me five, six, *seven* years ago— and I had been but dodging and delaying in despair at the meagreness of the material (*every*—documentary—scrap of which I have had thriftily to make use of). At last I seemed to see a *biais* of subjective amplification—by which something in the nature of a *book* might be made, and then I could with some promptness work my little oracle. Someone has just written to ask me if the family "like it," and I have replied that I think they don't know whether they like it or not! They are waiting to find out—and I am glad on the whole they haven't access to *you*. I wish I myself had—beyond *this*. But even this, as I tell you, has been a great pleasure to yours, my dear Adams, always and ever

Henry James

1. HJ's *William Wetmore Story and His Friends* had been published earlier that autumn by Blackwood in Edinburgh. Adams's long letter to HJ was written the preceding day from Paris. He told HJ, "You have written not Story's life, but your own and mine . . . I feel your knife in my ribs." His central argument was that HJ had demonstrated the provincialism of Boston in the half-century from 1820 to 1870. The text of Adams's letter appears in *Letters of Henry Adams 1892–1918*, ed. Ford (1938), 413–415.

146 · To Viscount Wolseley

Ms Harvard

Lamb House, Rye
December 7*th* 1903

Dear Lord Wolseley.

I feel I must absolutely not have passed these several last evenings in your so interesting and vivid society without thanking you almost as much as if you had personally given me the delightful hours or held me there with your voice. I have read your two volumes[1] from covers to covers and parted from you with a positive pang. They form a "human document" of a fascinating order, and I greatly rejoice that you were moved to produce them. Last winter, in London, when you once mentioned to me that you were doing this work, you said something a little sceptical, I remember, about the value of, or the warrant for, autobiography in general; to which I hadn't then the full and ready reply. This warrant is, for yours, that it renders your friends (even such old ones as me—to say nothing of your enemies, if you need ever, save in a campaign, have thought of *them*) the service of making them know you ever so much better still than they presumed to think they did. And you do this in such a naturally and inevitably gallant, familiar, unconscious way, that one's affection, if I may say so, is as much quickened as one's knowledge and admiration are enlarged. It's a beautiful, rich, *natural* book—and happy the man whose life and genius have been such that he has only to *talk*, veraciously, and let memory and his blessed temperament float him on, in order to make one live so with great things and breathe so the air of the high places (of character and fortitude). To a poor worm of peace and quiet like me—yet with some intelligence—the interest of communicating so with the military temper and type is irresistible—and of getting so close (comparatively!) to the qualities that make the brilliant man of action. Those are the qualities, unlike one's own, that are romantic and wonderful to one, and when I think that you have lived all your days by them and with them and for them, I feel as if I had never questioned you nor sounded you enough, nor (in spite of the charm of intercourse!) got half that one might "out of" you. However, men of genius never can explain their genius, and you have clearly been a soldier and a paladin, and understood that mystery, very much in the same manner as Paderewski plays[2] or as Mr. Treves[3] removes appendices; so that we have to make the best of you at that. But what, as a dabbler in the spectacle of life, I think I most envy you, is your infinite acquaintance, from the first, with superlative *men*, and your having been able so to gather them in, and make them pass before you, for you to handle and use them. They move through your book, all these forms of resolution and sacrifice, in a long, vivid, mostly tragical procession—and many of them must have half haunted you, while you wrote, in the quiet days of Glynde. You have led, at any rate, so many lives, and the book tells but half of them. It even now almost takes my breath away to see that when I first knew you, years ago, in exquisite Portman Square, you were almost fresh from the shambles of "Cadmassie" [Kumasi],[4] and yet you had so much other freshness too that you have had to wait till today to find them worth mentioning. What the book, meanwhile, does tell it tells admirably—with such good nature, spontaneity and juvenility. To have done and seen it all, and still be young and *write* young, and *read* young—well, that is to lead many lives, as I say. It has all been to me a piece of intimate (and rather humiliating) experience. I would give all I have (including Lamb House!) for an hour of your retrospective consciousness, one of your more crowded memories—that for instance of your watch, before your quarters, during the big fight in Ashantee, when the fellow was eyeing you to see if you wouldn't get out of it. All the Ashantee pages carry one immensely along. *But I feel like that fellow*—such is the effect of your style.—Well, the effect of mine will be to make you wish I would stop. Please don't dream, overloaded with letters as you must be, that this is susceptible of the slightest "acknowledgement." I scarcely dare, for common shame, let me add, to send Lady Wolseley any message save that I am conscious of the depths of my guilt to her and that I am preparing even now a full confession, for her private and particular eye. I haven't communicated with her for so long, in spite of urgent reasons why I should, that I should violate every law of proportion by tacking on mere "regards" to her, however affectionate, here. And yet I am with equal attachment and constancy hers and yours always and ever

Henry James

1. *The Story of a Soldier's Life* (1903), by Viscount Garnet Wolseley.
2. Ignacy Jan Paderewski (1860–1941), the Polish pianist, then at the height of his career.
3. Sir Frederick Treves (1853–1923) had removed Edward VII's appendix the previous year.
4. Wolseley commanded the expedition sent against King Koffee of Ashanti in 1873 and occupied Kumasi in 1874. Ashanti is the core of the old kingdom of Ghana annexed by Britain in 1902.

147 · To Louise Horstmann

Ms Taylor

Lamb House, Rye
August 12*th* 1904

Dear Miss Horstmann.[1]

Don't think I have forgotten that I promised a week ago to give you by letter, for the sake of distinctness, the principal heads of our little understanding about this house. I came back from Ascot and from London to rather a complication of calls upon my time, but have been meaning each day to make you a proper sign.

I give you up the house then on Saturday September 3rd, as it will be all ready for you on that date, and you can send things on, which will be duly taken care of, even if you should not yourselves arrive immediately. And I understand that you take the house for six months from the said Saturday, September 3rd—that is, say, as the best estimate, to the first Saturday in March—with option to you, certainly, of taking it on at the same rate for two or three months longer if you should feel so disposed.

You pay me Five Pounds a week for the same, and as I suggested the other day at Laleham you make three payments of two months each: the first on taking possession; the second at the end of two months; the third at the end of two months more. This includes everything, I paying the Servants' wages, and you being liable, naturally, for no Rates or Taxes: except always the Gas-bill contracted during your stay, as is customary in such cases.

I make the house over to you, practically, just as I have been living in it, and you will find it, I make bold to say, in very good and tidy condition. I leave all the Servants, who amount to five in number including the Gardener and the Houseboy. The latter has his meals in the house, but doesn't sleep, and the Gardener of course does neither, having his cottage close by the garden gate. You will find this functionary, George Gammon, an excellent, quiet, trustworthy fellow in all respects—a very good carpenter into the bargain and thoroughly handy at mending anything that gets broken in the house. I have endowed him with a small hand-cart, which is kept in the vault beneath the Garden-room, highly convenient to the House door, and which I find quite sufficient for the conveyance of my luggage, or that of visitors, to and from the Station for all comings and goings. The distance is so short that it means, save in some extraordinary rain, the complete suppression of flies—which is a great simplification.

The Cook-Housekeeper, Mrs. Paddington, is really, to my sense, a pearl of price; being an extremely good cook, an absolutely brilliant economist, a person of the greatest method, order, and respectability, and a very nice woman generally. If you will, when you let her see you, each morning, in the dining-room after breakfast, just also suffer her to take you into the confidence, a little, of her triumphs of thrift and her master-strokes of management, you will get on with her beautifully—all the more that she gets on thoroughly well with her fellow-servants, a thing that all "good" cooks don't do. She puts before me each week, with the Tradesmen's books, her own weekly book, by the existence of which the others are distinctly, I think, kept down. But these are matters that you will of course know all about.

The Parlour-maid, Alice Skinner, has lived with me for six years—
that is with an interval of no great length, and is a thoroughly respectable, well-disposed, and duly competent young woman. And the
Housemaid is very pretty and gentle—and not a very, *very* bad one.
The House-boy, Burgess Noakes, isn't very pretty, but is on the other
hand very gentle, punctual and desirous to please—and has been with
me three years. He helps the Parlour-maid, cleans shoes, knives, door-
steps, windows etc. and makes himself generally useful. Also takes
letters to the Post-Office and does any errands. Naturally he brushes
clothes and "calls," in the morning, those of his own sex who may
repose beneath the roof. Lastly, though of such diminutive stature, he
is, I believe, nineteen years old.

The Servants will of course tell you just what tradespeople I employ
and I should be glad if you could go on with the same. They are in fact
the inevitable ones of the place, and are all very decent, zealous, reasonable folk. I leave almost everything "out" save some books, of a
certain rarity and value, which I lock up; and there is, I think, a full
sufficiency of forks and spoons etc. as well as of all household linen.

Lastly, I take the liberty of confiding to your charity and humanity
the precious little person of my Dachshund Max, who is the best and
gentlest and most reasonable and well-mannered as well as most beautiful, small animal of his kind to be easily come across—so that I think
you will speedily find yourselves loving him for his own sweet sake.
The Servants, who are very fond of him and good to him, know what
he "has" and when he has it; and I shall take it kindly if he be not too
often gratified with tid-bits between meals. Of course what he most
intensely dreams of is being taken out on walks, and the more you are
able so to indulge him the more he will adore you and the more all the
latent beauty of his nature will come out. He is, I am happy to say, has
been from the first (he is about a year and a half old) in very good,
plain, straightforward health, and if he is not overfed and is sufficiently exercised, and adequately brushed (his brush being always in
one of the bowls on the hall-table—a convenient little currycomb)
and Burgess is allowed occasionally to wash him, I have no doubt he
will remain very fit. In the event, however, of his having anything at
all troublesome the matter with him, kindly remember that there is
an excellent "Vet" a dozen miles away, who already knows him, and
would come over to see him for a moderate fee on any sign made. This

person is "Mr. Percy Woodroffe Hill," Canine Specialist, St. Leonard's-on-Sea—a telegram would promptly reach him.

You may find it pleasant to belong to the little Golf Club out at Camber Links—to which a small and innocent steam tram jogs forth a number of times a day. I don't know that a six months' membership is worth a year's fee, moderate though the latter be; but it is sometimes a resource to have tea there of a Sunday afternoon, and if you will mention my name to the Secretary, Captain Dacre Vincent, he will gladly inscribe you on the easiest terms possible. There are lots of pretty late summer and early autumn walks—over field paths etc. and I wish I might both carry out my American destiny and be at hand to put you up to my own rambles. Perhaps, however, you are not like me, crimson ramblers—in which case you will walk about the garden!

Such is my simple showing—but I shan't scruple to add a postscript to this, later on, if any illuminating remark occurs to yours, your sister's, and John Boit's most truly

Henry James

1. Jessie Allen found tenants to occupy Lamb House during HJ's trip to America, and he got in touch with them. Louise Horstmann was about to marry John Boit, member of a family James had known in his early days in Rome.

148 · To Edmund Gosse

Ms Congress

The Mount
Lenox, Mass.
October 27th 1904

My dear Gosse.

The weeks have been many and crowded since I received, not very many days after my arrival,[1] your incisive letter from the depths of the so different world (from this here); but it's just because they have been so animated, peopled and pervaded, that they have rushed by like loud-puffing motor-cars, passing out of my sight before I could step back out of the dust and the noise long enough to dash you off such a response as I could fling after them to be carried to you. And during my first three or four here my postbag was enormously—appallingly—

heavy: I almost turned tail and reembarked at the sight of it. And then I wanted above all, before writing you, to make myself a notion of how, and where, and even *what*, I was. I have turned round now a good many times, though still, for two months, only in this corner of a corner of a corner, that is named New England; and the postbag has, happily, shrunken a good bit (though with liabilities, I fear, of re-expanding), and this exquisite Indian summer day sleeps upon these really admirable little Massachusetts mountains, lakes and woods in a way that lulls my perpetual sense of precipitation. I have moved from my own fireside for long years so little (have been abroad, till now, but once, for ten years previous) that the mere quantity of movement re-mains something of a terror and a paralysis to me—though I am get-ting to brave it etc., and to like it, as the sense of adventure, of holiday and romance, and above all of the great so visible and observ-able world that stretches before one more and more, comes through and makes the tone of one's days and the counterpoise of one's home-sickness. I am, at the back of my head and at the bottom of my heart, transcendently homesick, and with a sustaining private reference, all the while (at every moment verily), to the fact that I have a tight an-chorage, a definite little downward burrow, in the ancient world—a secret consciousness that I chink in my pocket as if it were a fortune in a handful of silver. But, with this, I am having a most charming and interesting time, and seeing, feeling, how agreeable it is, in the matu-rity of age to revisit the long-neglected and long unseen land of one's birth—especially when that land affects one as such a living and breathing and feeling and moving great monster as this one is. It is all very interesting and quite unexpectedly and almost uncannily de-lightful and sympathetic—partly, or largely, from my intense impres-sion (all this glorious golden autumn, with weather like tinkling crystal and colours like molten jewels) of the sweetness of the country itself, this New England rural vastness, which is all that I've seen. I have been only in the country—shamelessly visiting, and almost only old friends and scattered relations—but have found it far more beautiful and amiable than I ever dreamed, or than I ventured to remember, I had seen too little, in fact, of old *to* have anything, to speak of, to remember—so that seeing so many charming things for the first time I quite thrill with the romance of elderly and belated discovery. Of Boston I haven't even had a full day—of N.Y. but three hours, and I have seen nothing whatever, thank heaven, of the "littery" world. I have spent a few days at Cambridge, Mass., with my brother, and have been greatly struck with the way that in the last twenty-five years Harvard has come to mass so much larger and to have gathered about her such a swarm of distinguished specialists and such a big organization of learning. This impression is increased this year by the crowd of foreign experts of sorts (mainly philosophic etc.) who have been at the St. Louis congress and who appear to be turning up overwhelmingly under my brother's roof—but who will have vanished, I hope, when I go to spend the month of November with him—when I shall see something of the goodly Boston. The blot on my vision and the shadow on my path is that I have contracted to write a book of Notes—without which contraction I simply couldn't have come; and that the conditions of life, time, space, movement etc. (really to *see*, to get one's material) are such as to threaten utterly to frustrate for me any prospect of simultaneous work—which is the rock on which I may split altogether—wherefore my alarm is great and my project much disconcerted; for I have as yet scarce dipped into the great Basin at all. Only a large measure of Time can help me—to do anything as decent as I want: wherefore pray for me constantly; and all the more that if I can only arrive at a means of application (for I see, already, from here, my *Tone*) I shall do, verily, a lovely book. I am interested, up to my eyes—at least I think I am! But you will fear, at this rate, that I am trying the book on you already. I *may* have to return to England only as a saturated sponge and wring myself out there. I hope meanwhile that your own saturations, and Mrs. Nelly's, prosper, and that the Pyrenean, in particular, continued rich and ample. If you are having the easy part of your year now, I hope you are finding in it the lordliest, or rather the *un*lordliest leisure. I saw of course in Cambridge dear old C. E. Norton, very ancient and mellow now, àpropos of whose daughters and whose Dantesque fame this undergraduate pleasantry may, though irrelevant, interest you. The eldest of the three girls is much the prettiest, and they go declining, whereby they are known in college as Paradiso, Purgatorio and Inferno. The third is *very* plain. I commend you to all felicity and am, my dear Gosse, yours always,

Henry James

1. HJ arrived in the United States at the end of August 1904 for his long-planned American journey.

149 · *To Mary Cadwalader Jones*

Ms Harvard

1603 H. St.
Washington D.C.
January 13 1905

Dearest Benefactress![1]

A word of thanks, heaped up and flowing over, for everything you have lately surpassed yourself in doing for me—for the exquisite bounty which follows my steps and hangs about me like the soft music in some gilded and flowered Masque or fairytale. I am, briefly, doing as well here as I can do without your magic and your mercy, and I am, above all, abundantly justified of my yearning little Southward move. It's ever so much blander and softer an air, already, and everything human and social is in mild harmony with that. Henry Adams, dear man, is a philosophic father to us, and La Farge, Saint Gaudens[2] and even your unassuming Célimare[3] expand and gently extravagate in the large license of Liberty Hall. We went (without Henry) last night to a big and really quite pompous function at the White House—where, supper being (for the comparatively select few) served at small—or small-ish—tables, the President did St.-G. and H.J. the honour to put us at his—with Célimare next the lady who was at his right. If this is "royal favour" I suppose poor Célimare ought to bloom. Theodore Rex is at any rate a really extraordinary creature for native intensity, veracity and *bonhomie*—he plays his part with the best will in the world and I recognise his amusing likeability. McKim's[4] dinner was a big success and beautifully done—but the Eagle screamed in the speeches as I didn't know that that Fowl was still (after all these years and improvements) *permitted* to do. It was werry werry quaint and queer,—but so is *everything*, sans exception, and the sensitive Célimare absorbs it at every pore. His affair at Philadelphia, a (to *him*) dazzling success, a huge concourse, five or six hundred folk, a vast hall and perfect brazen assurance and audibility on Célimare's part.[5] *Il s'est révélé conférencier*, and on the strength of it is to sing his little song again (for a heavy fee) at Bryn Mawr, on the 19th. I come back then to Philadelphia (the *most*, the fantastically, kind) and stay three days with J. William White and three days at Butler Place;[6] after which I retrace again my steps southwards *straight*,—without stopping here. I go for two days to

Richmond and then for four or five down to Charleston to meet there Owen Wister, invalidical (nervously), but ever so amiable etc. This will make a *short* Washington—but a quite sufficient one (especially if I come back much later on for a few days). But farewell—my letters devour me; I have 390 still to write. I think I rather *did* make the point at suite 884[7] (at the last) that I *couldn't* come back there. A thousand thanks for the photographic service. Continue to be *invraisemblable,* give my love to Beatrix, the Earth-shaker, and believe in the affection of your clinging

Célimare

1. Mary Cadwalader Rawle had married Edith Wharton's brother, Frederick Rhinelander Jones. The marriage was later dissolved.

2. Augustus Saint-Gaudens (1848–1907), the American sculptor.

3. Mrs. Jones and her daughter Beatrix called HJ Célimare after a character in a Eugène Labiche farce, a man who remains the spoiled darling of his womenfolk in spite of his infidelities. HJ is describing the White House dinner he attended at the invitation of President Theodore Roosevelt.

4. Charles Follen McKim (1847–1909), leader of the neoclassical revival in architecture and member of the influential firm of McKim, Mead and White.

5. HJ's first American lecture, "The Lesson of Balzac," was delivered in Philadelphia on 9 January 1905.

6. Dr. J. William White (1850–1916), an eminent Philadelphia surgeon. Butler Place was the Wister home in Germantown.

7. Edith Wharton's New York home, 884 Park Avenue.

150 · To Edith Wharton

Ms Yale

1603 H St. Washington
January 16th 1905

Dear Mrs. Wharton.[1]

If I have delayed writing to you it is in order not to resemble too much certain friends of ours who *don't,* in similar situations, delay—who send back Parthian shots, after leaving you, from the very next *étape.* But there have again and again, under the pressure of events, been words on my lips for which your ear has seemed the only proper receptacle—and which for want of that receptacle, I fear, have mostly faltered and failed and lost themselves forever. Let me make it distinct, at any rate, that things have been very convenient and pleasant for me, "straight along"—the reading of *une petite cochonnerie,* as Jusserand says of his successive *oeuvres,* having constituted at the too amiable Philadelphia an almost brilliant scene—600 persons listening (and to *what, juste ciel!*) like one. I felt as if I had really *me révélé conférencier* (to myself at least); but too late, at last, and after having lived too long in the deep dark hole of silence. I repeat the thing, at any rate, on the 19th, at the earnest Bryn Mawr—quite like a mountebank "on tour." The only drawback is that the really touching friendliness and *bonhomie* of all those people, their positively fantastic *obligeance* (it is really very special and beautiful and boring) bury one under such a mountain of decent response that the *place,* the funny Philadelphia itself, taken as a subject to play with a little, melts away from one forever. And the same, a little, with this so oddly-ambiguous little Washington, which sits here saying, forever, to your private ear, from every door and window, as you pass, "I am nothing, I am nothing, nothing!" and whose charm, interest, amiability, *irresistibility,* you are yet perpetually making calls to commemorate and insist upon. One must hold up one's end of the plank, for heaven only knows where the other rests! But, withal, it's a very pleasant, soft, mild, spacious vacuum— peopled, immediately about me here, by Henry Adams, La Farge and St.-Gaudens,—and then, as to the middle distance, by Miss Tuckerman, Mrs. Lodge and Mrs. Kuhn; with the dome of the Capitol, the Corcoran Art Gallery and the presence of "Theodore"—Theodore I—as indispensable *fond.* I went to Court the other night, for the Diplomatic Reception, and he did me the honour to put me at his table and almost beside him—whereby I got a rich impression of him and of his being, verily, a wonderful little machine: destined to be overstrained, perhaps, but not as yet, truly, betraying the least creak. It functions astoundingly and is quite exciting to see. But it's really *like* something behind a great plate-glass window "on" Broadway. I lunch with the Lodges[2] today, I dine with the Jusserands tomorrow[3]—he really delightful and she much better, a little "marked," but perfectly adequate, and after Bryn Mawr I go to spend three or four Philadelphian days with my old friend Sarah Wister at Butler Place. To remount *vers le Nord* chills me in thought—this relative mansuetude of the Washington air and prettiness of the Washington light, have affected me as such a balm. But I then come back to overtake or join (probably) the G[eorge] Vanderbilts, and be personally conducted by them for three or four days at the formidable Biltmore. After that I possibly join Owen Wister (queerly, though I think but imaginatively and superficially blighted in health—only physical—and with a young medical attendant) at Charleston—or at any rate work down to Florida and New Orleans. Such is the only witchcraft I am being used with—for the present, though I *may* have roamed, delirious and flower-crowned, as far as the farthest West before I see you again. I seem to see patria nostra *simplify* as I go—see that the *main* impressions only count, and that these can be numbered on the fingers; which is truly a blessed vision. I hope meanwhile that the snow isn't too high by your doorstep, nor the doubt (of the immediate human scene) too heavy on your heart. How can you doubt of a scene capable of flowering at any moment into a Mrs. Toy.[4] By that sign you shall conquer. If you have seen Mrs. Chanler again she will have told you perhaps of the pilgrimage I made with her in the rain to the Washington Cemetery—for a chance *de nous soulager*, critically, unheard *que par les morts*. She was for those first days a resource—emotionally—that I greatly miss.[5] And, I miss, intensely, Walter Berry[6]—and fear I shall continue to do so, as I seem destined to retire, sated (with everything but *him*) about the moment he comes back. But I have had from him a charming note. I hope you have the same—that is, I mean news of cheer and comfort from Wharton. And I am wondering further what you may perhaps be learning *de plus funeste encore* from Minnie-Paul.[7] But never dream of writing to tell me, I shall hear, in time—for all the use I can be in the matter. Don't, I mean, begin to *croire* devils, "answer" this sprawling scribble which has really no dimensions at all—no more length than breadth or thickness. Only fight your own battle (like Prometheus—) with the elements (of civilization). We shall see them in due course somehow softened by springtime, and shall meet again under that benediction. Believe me yours very constantly

Henry James

1. HJ had met Mrs. Wharton (1862–1937) socially on two occasions in the past, but their first meeting as fellow writers was in London in December 1903.

2. Senator Henry Cabot Lodge and his wife, the former Anna Davis.

3. Jules Jusserand (1855–1932), French ambassador to Washington, whom HJ had known in London.

4. Mrs. William (Nancy) Toy.

5. HJ had known Margaret Terry Chanler (1862–1952), daughter of the painter Luther Terry, since his Roman days. He and Mrs. Chanler visited the grave of Mrs. Henry Adams to see the Saint-Gaudens statue of a veiled figure Henry Adams had placed there.

6. Walter Van Rensselaer Berry (1859–1927), international lawyer, friend of Proust, HJ, and Mrs. Wharton. See Edel, "Walter Berry and the Novelists," *Nineteenth Century Fiction* 38, no. 4 (March 1984), 514–528.

7. The Bourgets.

151 · *To Charles Scribner's Sons*

Ms Princeton

Memorandum [30 July 1905]

My idea has been to arrange for a handsome "definitive edition" of the greater number of my novels and tales—I say of the greater number because I prefer to omit several things, especially among the shorter stories. I should wish probably to retain all my principal novels—that is with the exception possibly of one.

My impression is that my shorter things will gain in significance and importance, very considerably, by a fresh grouping or classification, a placing together, from series to series, of those that will help each other, those that will conduce to something of a common effect. My notion is, at any rate, very rigidly to sift and select the things to be included, thereby reducing the number of volumes to an array that will not seem, for a collective edition, very formidable. My idea is, further, to revise everything carefully, and *to re-touch*, as to expression, turn of sentence, and the question of surface generally, wherever this may strike me as really required. Such a process, however, will find its application much more in the earlier, the earliest things than in those of my later or even of my middle period. It is called for in *Roderick Hudson* and *The American* for instance, to my sense, much more than anywhere else. The edition will thus divide itself into about ten volumes of regular novel length, into a few volumes of distinctively *short* novels, not more than two of which, or three at the most, would completely fill a moderate volume; and into a considerable number of short stories, six or eight of which are longer than the common magazine short-story, and the whole list of which is susceptible of an effect of revival by the re-classification that I have mentioned. A good many of these, which have all been collected in volumes, I shall wish, as I say, to drop; but the interest and value of the edition will, I think, rest not a little on the proper association and collocation of the others.

Lastly, I desire to furnish each book, whether consisting of a single fiction, or of several minor ones, with a freely colloquial and even, perhaps, as I may say, confidential preface or introduction, representing, in a manner, the history of the work or the group, representing more particularly, perhaps, a frank critical talk about its subject, its origin, its place in the whole artistic chain, and embodying, in short, whatever of interest there may be to be said about it. I have never committed myself in print in any way, even so much as by three lines to a newspaper, on the subject of anything I have written, and I feel as if I should come to this part of the business with a certain freshness of appetite and effect. My hope would be, at any rate, that it might count as a feature of a certain importance in any such new and more honorable presentation of my writings. I use that term honorable here because I am moved in the whole matter by something of the conviction that they will gain rather than lose by enjoying for the first time—though a few of the later ones have in some degree already partaken of that advantage—a form and appearance, a dignity and beauty of outward aspect, that may seem to bespeak consideration for them as a matter of course. Their being thus presented, in fine, as fair and shapely will contribute, to my mind, to their coming legitimately into a "chance" that has been hitherto rather withheld from them, and for which they have long and patiently waited.

My preference would be to publish first, one after the other, four of the earlier novels, not absolutely in the order of their original appearance but with no detrimental departure from it; putting *The American,* that is, first, *Roderick Hudson* second, *The Portrait of a Lady* third, and *Princess Casamassima* fourth. After this would come three or four volumes of the longer of my short stories—to be followed by *The Tragic Muse* in two volumes, a book which closes, to my mind, what I should call as regards my novels, my earlier period. I think, though as to this I am not positive, that I should then give three or four more volumes to completing the group of such minor productions; and should wind up with my five later novels, *The Awkward Age, The Wings of the Dove,*

The Ambassadors and *The Golden Bowl* in the order of their appearance. And I repeat that I am proposing nothing but my fiction.

If a *name* be wanted for the edition, for convenience and distinction, I should particularly like to call it the New York Edition if that may pass for a general title of sufficient dignity and distinctness. My feeling about the matter is that it refers the whole enterprise explicitly to my native city—to which I have had no great opportunity of rendering that sort of homage. And—last of all—I should particularly appreciate a single very good plate in each volume, only one, but of thoroughly fine quality. I seem to make out (though I have not been able yet to go into the whole of the question) that there would not be an insuperable difficulty in finding for each book, or rather for each volume, some sufficiently interesting illustrative subject.

There are two or three points more.

Messrs. Scribner's complete edition of Rudyard Kipling offers to my mind the right type of form and appearance, the right type of print and size of page, for our undertaking. I could desire nothing better than this, and should be quite content to have it taken for model. (But I think, also, by the way, that I should like a cover of another colour—to differentiate—than the Kipling.)

As for time of delivery of first copy I should find it convenient to be able to take from the present date to the 25th September to send the two first books, completely revised (with the very *close* revision and re-touching that for these cases I have spoken of) and with their respective Prefaces, of from 3000 to 5000 words. The revision, the re-manipulation, as I may call it, of *The American* and *Roderick Hudson* is demanding of me, I find, extreme (and very interesting) deliberation; which will tend, however, absolutely to improvement (and not to say, perhaps, even to making of the works in question, in their amended state, unique—and admirable, exemplary—curiosities of literature).

I should not omit, finally, to note that in the foregoing I have, inevitably left the question open of the inclusion or the non-inclusion of my longer novel *The Bostonians.* I cannot take time, have not freedom of mind to decide this minor matter just now; but I shall do so later on, and if in the affirmative a convenient place in the whole order will be found for the book.

Henry James

July 30 1905

152 · To Hendrik C. Andersen

Ms Barrett

Lamb House, Rye
May 31st 1906

Carissimo Enrico Mio.

Of course, I've had punctually all your beautiful and blessed missives, and of course I've tenderly loved you, and yearningly embraced you, and passionately thanked you for them—but equally of course I've had to wait till tonight to do these things otherwise than all silently and hinderedly and, oh, so distantly. I won't take up precious time and space in telling you why I've *waited*—for you will feel always a felicity in this, as in the sense of the beautiful consciousness of something to happen, in good and fortunate time between us; your looking for my letter on the one hand, and my having the sense of its going forth to you on the wings of my affection, and your at last taking it in and being glad of it, there by your yellow Tiber, on the other. In short here we are together again—after a meagre and dismal and frustrated fashion I admit; but more at least than when neither of us is thus, with a poor vain pen, invoking the other. Your brave and charming letter of last month gave me much greater joy than my delay can, after all, have suggested to you, and that, and the numerous little photographs of your work, and the wondrous architectures and elevations and now, within a few days, the beautiful little new note with the three kodak-views of your self, your mother and the friend, have immensely comforted and cheered me. For they tell, and you speak so handsomely yourself, of your health and energy and *might*—so that I wonder at you and am proud of you, and send up hosannas and hymns of praise to the skies. I take your word for it that when you say you are well—with your old ailments conjured away—and say it so emphatically, you really mean it, dearest boy, and are not talking in the air. So I feel that you *must* be well, for if you weren't, with your prodigious and heroic production, which implies such a possession of life and sanity (don't read that word as *vanity*), you would by this time be sleeping in the cold tomb. Your production *is* prodigious and heroic and very beautiful and interesting to me—so much so that, dearest Hendrik, I affectionately and heartily declare, even while seeing less than ever where this colossal multiplication of divinely naked and intimately associated gentlemen and ladies, flaunting their bellies and bottoms and their other private affairs, in the face of day, is going, on any *American* possibility, to land you. I won't attempt to go into this last question now—you know already how it perplexes and even not a little distresses me. So I content myself with paying my tribute to your noble imagination and your splendid sense of the body and the members, your wealth of composition, combination, creation! The small photographs, as I say, immensely interest me, just as the rate at which you go takes away my breath. I look your kodaks (as I suppose them) over again, while I write, and they make me groan, in spirit, that I'm not standing there before the whole company with you—when I think I should find, if you would let me try, so much to say about them! There would be things, as I see the different figures thus, that I should, ever so affectionately, contend with you about, but that I can't touch on now and here. (I should go down on my knees to you, for instance, to individualize and detail the *faces,* the types ever so much more—to study, ardently, the question of doing that—the whole face-question. I should cheekily warn you against a tendency to neglect *elegance*— to emphasize too much the thickness and stoutness of limb, at the risk of making certain legs, especially from the knee down, seem too short etc.—and arms also too "stocky" and stony. The faces too blank and stony—the hair, for me, always too merely *symbolic*—and not living and *felt.* These offensive things I should say to you—in such a fashion that you would but love me better and our friendship would be but the tenderer and closer. But it's wretched work trying to talk at this damnable distance and I prefer to dwell on the things of great beauty that you constantly do. Of all the small photos accompanying your letter the two I enclose again (return by way of identifying them) strike me as the finest. But your whole overflowing vision and your whole *revel* of creation are unutterable. Delightful to me the small snapshots of your so loveable looking mother, and beautiful your own charming image with the gun on your shoulder. There, dear boy, you do look straight and strong and gallant and *valid;* for which the Powers—whoever they are—be praised. But how it only the more makes it a poor thing for me that the months are added to the months and we only don't meet. I want to ask you about your possibilities for this summer—but I have a feeling that they look bad for us. Is it your expectation that your mother will pass the summer in Italy? Will Mrs. Olivia[1] come back? Is there any chance of your being able to cross the Alps?—

by which I mean, of course, to come here for a week? Tell me of these things won't you? in some brief easy way, at your earliest opportunity. We *must* meet somehow; we must talk of it and manage it. There is no place so peaceful as here—but of course unless you do for other reasons come northward I can't dream of asking you to make the big journey. Don't, however, oh don't, pass me—so near—on the wide waters. That does cast me down. But goodnight, dearest Hendrik. I draw you close and hold you long and am ever so tenderly yours

Henry James

1. Mrs. Olivia Cushing Andersen, widow of Hendrik Andersen's brother.

153 · To Joseph Conrad

Ms Berg

Lamb House, Rye
November 1st, 1906

My dear Conrad.

I have taught you that I am lumbering and long, but I haven't, I think, yet taught you that I am base, and it is not on the occasion of your beautiful sea green volume[1] of the other day that I shall consent to begin. I read you as I listen to rare music—with deepest depths of surrender, and out of those depths I emerge slowly and reluctantly again, to acknowledge that I return to life. To taste you as I do taste you is *really* thus to wander far away and to decently thank you is a postal transaction (quite another affair), for which I have to come *back,* and accept with a long sad sigh the community of our afflicted existence. My silence is thus—after your beautiful *direct* speech to me too—but that I['ve] been away *with* you, intimately and delightfully— and my only objection to writing to you in gratitude is that I'm not reading you, but quite the contrary, when I do it. But I *have* you now, and the charm of this process of appropriation has been to me, with your adorable book for its subject, of the very greatest. And I am touched in the same degree by the grace of your inscription,[2] all so beautifully said and so generously felt. *J'en suis tout confus,* my dear Conrad, and can only thank you and thank you again. But the book itself is a wonder to me really—for it's so bringing home the prodigy of

367

your past experience: bringing it home to me more personally and directly, I mean, the immense treasure and the inexhaustible adventure. No one has *known*—for intellectual use—the things you know, and you have, as the artist of the whole matter, an authority that no one has approached. I find you in it all, *writing* wonderfully, whatever you may say of your difficult medium and your *plume rebelle*. You knock about in the wide waters of expression like the raciest and boldest of privateers,—you have made the whole place your own and *vous y avez, en même temps que les droits les plus acquis et vous y avez les plus rares bonheurs*. Nothing you have done has more in it the root of the matter of *saying*. You stir me in fine to amazement and you touch me to tears, and I thank the powers who so mysteriously let you loose with such sensibilities, into such an undiscovered country—*for* sensibility. That is all for tonight. I want to see you again. Is Winchelsea a closed book? Are the Ford Madoxes still away? (What a world *they* must then have been let loose into!) I am looking for some sign of them, and with it perhaps some more contemporary news of you. I hope the smaller boy is catching up, and your wife reasserting herself, and your "conditions" favourable? Ah, one's conditions! But we must *make* them, and you have on every showing, *de quoi!* I pat you, my dear Conrad, very affectionately and complacently on the back and am yours very constantly

Henry James

P.S. *Milles amitiés* to the fireside and the crib!

1. *The Mirror of the Sea* (1906).
2. Conrad had inscribed the book in French, writing the equivalent of a letter on the endpapers. See Joseph Conrad, *Lettres Françaises*, ed. Jean-Aubry (1929), 77.

154 · To W. Morton Fullerton

Ms Texas

58 Rue de Varenne
Monday A.M. 22d [22 April 1907]

My dear Morton.

Mrs. Wharton[1] has written you twice, I believe on the subject of breakfasting here on Wednesday to meet a man who *raffoles* of your Book and longs to know you, and I add my entreaty that you will make her some sign—if you are not absent or *remarié!* Don't, I beseech you, be any of these things and do do come; for I also languish to see you even on this comparatively artificial basis. It seems settled that I stay here—but *here*—till May 10th or 12th—so that I can then make place for seeing you more and better. But cull with me, with *us,*—*for* me, for us—these passing hours.

Ever yours

H.J.

1. HJ was staying with Mrs. Wharton during his Paris visit and was apparently trying to prod Fullerton into answering his hostess's letters. For details of Fullerton's correspondence with Mrs. Wharton see *The Library Chronicle of the University of Texas,* New Series, no. 31.

155 · To W. Morton Fullerton

Ms Princeton

Lamb House, Rye

November 14*th* 1907

My dearest Morton.

I have had your letter since yesterday, and if I have waited a little since, for a free hour to articulate, its immensely interesting and touching, its really overwhelming *contenu,* has only the more deeply sunk into my spirit, so that, verily, the waves of my emotion have closed over it as those of some clear tropic sea might over some imperilled swimmer striking out for the moment below the surface. When I say "overwhelming," of all the sense of your troubled words, I only mean—very simply—that you stir my tenderness even to anguish: a fig for any tenderness (for that matter) that isn't so stirrable. Regret what you must and what you may, but for God's sake waste no further mere vain semblance of sense ever again on any compunction for the fact of your having so late, so late, after long years, brought yourself to speak to me of what there was always a muffled unenlightened ache for my affection in my not knowing—simply and vaguely and ineffectually guessing as I did at complications in your life that I was utterly powerless to get any nearer to, even though I might have done so a little helpfully.[1] I seem to feel now that if I had been nearer to you—by your admission of me (for I think *my* signs were always there) something might have been advantageously different, and I think of the whole long mistaken

369

perversity of your averted *reality* so to speak, as a miserable *personal* waste, that of something—ah, so tender!—in *me* that was only quite yearningly ready for you, and something all possible, and all deeply and admirably appealing in yourself, of which I never got the benefit. The clearing of the air lifts, it seems to me, such a load, removes such a falsity (of defeated relation) between us, that I think *that* by itself is a portent and omen of better days and of a more workable situation. The difference, I agree, is largely that of my "aching," as I say, intelligently now, where I only ached darkly and testified awkwardly before; but I can't believe I can't somehow, bit by bit, help you and ease you by dividing with you, as it were, the heavy burden of your consciousness. *Can* one man be as mortally, as tenderly attached to another as I am to you, and be at the same time a force, as it were, of some value, without its counting effectively at some right and preappointed moment for the brother over whom he yearns? I launch that question at you, and I believe in your solid basis and your final *trempe;* in other words in your assured future. I wish to God I could say on the spot *the* thing, the mere practical plain thing that would clear the air of your nightmare more than anything—that thus and so the sense you mention can be imaginably compassed. But even as to that light will break and patience find its account. Don't worry over *worrying*—nothing takes the *particular* inconvenient form we fear; it only, at the worst, takes some other—in which we don't know it and fear it for the same. The letter I return to you—exquisite and sacred—represents a value of devotion, a *dedication* to you, so absolute and precious that I should feel but one thing about it in your place (as for that matter I perceive you to feel)—that it will be more than anything else, than all together, the thing to see you through. So sit tight and sit firm and *do* nothing—save indeed look for that money; for [which] I wish to goodness I could *help* you to look, better than my present impotence permits. But even this may miraculously happen. I am losing this evening's post after all—this won't go till tomorrow A.M. But it takes you, my dearest Morton, the ever so much less wasted and wandering wealth of affection of yours, all and always,

Henry James

P.S. *Destroy* these things—when you've made them yours.

1. This and the next letter reveal that, under pressure from a blackmailer, Fullerton had finally told HJ the details of some of his sexual involvements. The blackmailer was his

former mistress, who had rifled Fullerton's desk and found correspondence relating to his bisexuality. See Edel, *The Master* (1972), and R. W. B. Lewis, *Edith Wharton* (1975).

156 · To W. Morton Fullerton

Ms Princeton

The Reform Club
November 26*th* 1907

Dearest Morton.

I returned but last night (to find your letter here) from a four days' ordeal—lugubrious and funereal—of "going to meet" an old American Friend (Lawrence Godkin) at Liverpool and seeing him through the dreary and complicated business of effecting the internment of a near relation (the mortal *dépouille* brought over)—who was a still older friend of mine—in a terribly out of the way and inaccessible part of the Midlands—a *pays perdu* of Northamptonshire twelve miles from a station—and such bleak and dreary and dreadful and death-dealing miles. But it's over—only my letters have been piling up here *en attendant*—and yours is the first, *bien entendu*, that I (oh so tenderly and responsively, my dear Morton, my hideously tormented friend) deal with. Sickened as I am by what *you* have to deal with, and with no pang of your ordeal muffled or dim or faint, to me, I yet find myself very robustly conscious of two things. (1) That you are *hypnotized* by nearness and contact and converse—hypnotized by the utterly wrong fact of being—of remaining—under the same roof with the atrocious creature into a belief in her possible *effect* on any one she may so indecently and insanely approach that has no relation to any potential reality. She can possibly appear to no one but as a mad, vindictive and obscene old woman (with whom, credibly, you may well, in Paris, have lived younger, but who is now only wreaking the fury [of] an *idée fixe* of resentment on you for not having perpetrated the marriage with her that it was—or would be—inconceivable you *should* perpetrate). She can only denounce and describe and exhibit *herself*, in the character of a dangerous blackmailer, and thereby render very dangerous and absolutely compromising *any* commerce held with her. If you were not breathing the poisoned air of her proximity and her access you would *see* this and feel it—and the whole truth and reality and proportion and measure of things. The woman can *do* nothing but get (in literal truth) "chucked out," with refusal to touch or look at her calumnious wares—her overtures to your people at home, e.g. simply burned on the spot, unlooked at, as soon as *smelt*. And so throughout, she can absolutely in the very nature of the case and on the very face of it— but inspire a *terror* not only of intercourse, credence or reciprocity— but of the act or appearance *of attention* itself—for she will reek with every sign of vindictive and demented calumny. No one will *touch*, or listen to, e.g., anything with the name of the Ranee[1] in it—it will serve only to scare them. As for R[onald] G[ower],[2] he is very ancient history and, I think, has all the appearance today of a regularized member of society, with his books and writings everywhere, his big monument (not so bad) to Shakespeare, one of the principal features of Stratford on Avon. However, I didn't mean to go into any detail—if you [have] known him you've known him (R.G.); and it is absolutely your own affair, for you to take your own robust and frank and per- fectly manly stand on. Many persons, as I say, moreover, knowing him at this end of Time (it is my impression); the point is what I especially insist on as regards your falsified perspective and nervously aggravated fancy. I have a horror-stricken apprehension of your *weakening*, mor- bidly to her: the one and only thing that could lose you. You have but one course—to say: You most demented and perverted and unfortu- nate creature, *Do* your damnedest—you *m'en donnerez des nouvelles*. If after this you make any pact or compromise with her in the interest of an insane (for it would be *that* in you), compassion, *then*, dearest Mor- ton, it would be difficult to advise or inspire you. It is detestable that you should still be under the same roof with her—but if you should remain so after she had lifted a finger to attempt to *colporter* her calum- nies—you would simply commit the folly of your life. My own belief is that if you really *break* with her—utterly and absolutely—you will find yourself *free*—and leave her merely beating the air with grotesque *gestes* and absolutely "getting" nowhere. If any echo of her deportment should come back to you send anyone to *me*—they will find *à qui par- ler*. But for God's sake after any *act* (though her dealings with you are indeed now all acts) don't again in any degree however small or indi- rect, temporize an inch further, but take your stand on your honour, your manhood, your courage, your decency, your intelligence and on the robust affection of your old, old, and faithful, faithful friend

Henry James

1. Margaret Brooke, Ranee of Sarawak. See Letter 94, note 5.
2. Lord Ronald Sutherland Gower (1845–1916), younger son of the second Duke of Sutherland, sculptor, politician, author, and art critic. He was the sculptor of the Shakespeare memorial in Stratford-on-Avon. See Letter 91.

157 · To Edith Wharton

Ms Yale

Lamb House, Rye
October 13*th* 1908

My very dear Friend!

I cabled you an hour ago my earnest hope that you *may* see your way to sailing with Walter B[erry][1] on the 20th—and if you *do* manage that this won't catch you before you start. Nevertheless I can't not write to you—however briefly (I mean on the chance of my letter being useless) after receiving your two last, of *rapprochées* dates, which have come within a very few days of each other—that of October 5th only today. I am deeply distressed at the situation you describe[2] and as to which my power to suggest or enlighten now quite miserably fails me. I move in darkness; I rack my brain; I gnash my teeth; I don't pretend to understand or to imagine. And yet incredibly to you doubt-less—I am still moved to say "Don't *conclude!*" Some light will *still* absolutely come to you—I believe—though I can't pretend to say what it conceivably may be. Anything is more credible—conceiv-able—than a mere inhuman *plan*. A great trouble, an infinite worry or a situation of the last anxiety or uncertainty are conceivable—though I don't see that such things, I admit, can explain *all*. Only sit tight yourself *and go through the movements of life*. That keeps up our connec-tion with life—I mean of the immediate and apparent life; behind which, all the while, the deeper and darker and the unapparent, in which things *really* happen to us, learns, under that hygiene, to stay in its place. Let it get out of its place and it swamps the scene; besides which its place, God knows, is enough for it! Live it all through, every inch of it—out of it something valuable will come—but live it ever so quietly; and—*je maintiens mon dire*—waitingly! I have had but that one letter, of weeks ago—and there are *kinds* of news I can't ask for. All this I say to you, though what I am really hoping is that you'll be on your voyage when this reaches the Mount. If you're not you'll be so very soon afterwards, won't you?—and you'll come down and see me here and we'll talk *à perte de vue,* and there will be something in that for both of us—especially if we are able then in a manner to "conclude."

Believe meanwhile and always in the aboundingly tender friendship—the understanding, the participation, the *princely* (though I say it who shouldn't) hospitality of spirit and soul of yours more than ever

Henry James

P.S. I can't tell you what hearty joy I take in Walter B.'s beautiful appointment. I delight—I revel—in it—and I infinitely desire to see him. I expect to be in London for a few days from Nov. 3d or 4th. If you can only be there too!

1. See Letter 150, note 6. Berry had just been named to the International Tribunals in Egypt.
2. The situation was that of her difficult marriage to Teddy Wharton and her involvement with the volatile Morton Fullerton.

158 · *To Anne Thackeray Ritchie*
Ms Harvard

Lamb House, Rye
December 3d 1908

Dearest old Friend![1]

A brave and delightful postscript to our too-brief meeting your little grey card superscribed with mystic and intricate characters! I take it as a token and symbol of your beautiful fidelity and undying grace and should like to wear it round my neck like some mystic figured amulet or consecrated charm. I make out on its kind, gentle, vivid words— and, rather than not, the fact that you were amused and beguiled (by the aid of your unquenchable fancy and humour) at Lady Pollock's afternoon sing-song. There also flushes through the crushed strawberry glow of Vanessa's beauty and credulity, and the promise of Virginia's printed wit and the felicity of Hester's return.[2] These things I note as items of your always enviable sense of the things about you—of which I wish it were often given me to partake. But the so sweet and savoury *to be,* perceptibly and spiritually, you—and when I am with you I get all the fragrance and all the distinction. Therefore I *must* be with you again soon—as soon as the dire complications of our massive maturity (that is of *mine*) show the first sign of intermitting a little. I am scribbling this in my little old celibatoirean oak-parlour before being called to dinner—and oh so wish I were going to hand you in—to cold beef and pickles! for which you will say Thank-you! Here comes the mild announcement, and I proceed to munch and mumble alone—such a contrast to that bloated last Monday. However, *you* saved that, and now there is *nobody* to save your fondly clinging old friend

Henry James

1. Anne Isabella Thackeray, Lady Ritchie, was a sister of Leslie Stephen's first wife, Harriet Marion Thackeray, who died in 1875.

2. HJ alludes here to Vanessa Bell and the future Virginia Woolf and to Mrs. Ritchie's daughter Hester. Vanessa and Virginia had spent some weeks at Rye; in a letter to Sara Norton Darwin, 11 September 1907, HJ had written: "Leslie Stephen's children three of them—the three surviving poor dear mild able gigantic Thoby, gathered in his flower—have taken two houses near me (temporarily) and as I write the handsome (and most loveable) Vanessa Clive-Bell sits on my lawn (unheeded by me) along with her little incongruous and disconcerting but apparently very devoted newly acquired sposo. And Virginia, on a near hilltop, writes reviews for the *Times*—and the gentle Adrian interminably long and dumb and "admitted to the bar," marches beside her like a giraffe beside an ostrich—save that Virginia is facially most fair. And the hungry generations tread me down!"

159 · To Max Beerbohm

Ms Harvard

Lamb House, Rye
December 19*th* 1908

My dear Max Beerbohm.[1]

I won't say in acknowledgment of your beautiful letter[2] that it's exactly the sort of letter I like best to receive, because that would sound as if I had *data* for generalizing—which I haven't; and therefore I can only go so far as to say that if it belonged to a class, or weren't a mere remarkable individual, I *should* rank it with the type supremely gratifying. On its mere lonely independent merits it appeals to me intimately and exquisitely, and I can only gather myself in and up, arching and presenting my not inconsiderable back—a back, as who should say, offered for any further stray scratching and patting of that delightful kind. I can bear wounds and fell smitings (so far as I have been ever honoured with such—and indeed life smites us on the whole enough, taking one thing with another) better than expressive gentleness of touch; so you must imagine me for a little while quite prostrate and overcome with the force of your good words. But I shall recover, when they have really sunk in—and then be not only the "better," but the more nimble and artful and alert by what they will have done for me. You had, and you obeyed, a very generous and humane inspiration; it charms me to think—or rather so authentically to know, that my (I confess) ambitious Muse does work upon you; it really helps me to believe in her the more myself—by which I am very gratefully yours

Henry James

1. Max Beerbohm (1872–1956), writer and caricaturist, who drew many affectionate cartoons of HJ.

2. "I could not resist writing to Henry James about 'The Jolly Corner' and about his writings in general, and I have had such a *very* lovely letter from him." Max Beerbohm, *Letters to Reggie Turner*, ed. Hart-Davis (1964), 178. The tale had just appeared in the December issue of *English Review*.

160 · To Bernard Shaw

Dictated Ts Harvard

Lamb House, Rye
20th January 1909

My dear Bernard Shaw.

Your delightful letter is a great event for me,[1] but I must first of all ask your indulgence for my inevitable resort, today, to this means of acknowledging it. I have been rather sharply unwell and obliged to stay my hand, for some days, from the pen. I am, thank goodness, better, but still not penworthy—and in fact feel as if I should never be so again in presence of the beautiful and hopeless example your inscribed page sets me. Still another form of your infinite variety, this exquisite application of your ink to your paper! It is indeed humiliating. But I bear up, or try to—and the more that I *can* dictate, at least when I absolutely must.

I think it is very good of you to have taken such explanatory trouble, and written me in such a copious and charming way, about the ill-starred *Saloon*. It raises so many questions, and you strike out into such illimitable ether over the so distinctly and inevitably circumscribed phenomenon itself—of the little piece as it stands—that I fear I can meet you at very few points; but I will say what I can. You strike me as carrying all your eggs, of conviction, appreciation, discussion etc., as who should say, in one basket, where you put your hand on them all with great ease and convenience; while I have mine scattered all over the place—many of them still under the hens!—and have therefore to rush about and pick one up here and another there. You take the little play "socialistically," it first strikes me, all too hard: I use that word because you do so yourself, and apparently in a sense that brings my production, such as it is, up against a lion in its path with which it had never dreamed of reckoning. Yes, there literally stands ferocious at the mouth of your beautiful cavern the very last formidable beast with any sop to whom I had prepared myself. And this though I thought I had so counted the lions and so provided the sops!

But let me, before I say more, just tell you a little how *The Saloon* comes to exist at all—since you say yourself "WHY have you done this thing?" I may not seem so to satisfy so big a Why, but it will say at least a little How (I came to do it); and that will be perhaps partly the same thing.

My simple tale is then that Forbes-Robertson and his wife a year ago approached me for the production of a little old one-act comedy written a dozen years or so previous, and that in the event was to see the light but under the more or less dissimulated form of a small published "story."[2] I took hold of this then, and it proved susceptible of being played in three acts (with the shortest intervals)—and was in fact so produced in the country, in a few places, to all appearances "successfully"; but has not otherwise yet affronted publicity. I mention it, however, for the fact, that when it was about to be put into rehearsal it seemed absolutely to require something a little better than a cheap curtain raiser to be played in front of it; with any resources for which preliminary the F.R.'s seemed, however, singularly unprovided. The matter seemed to be important, and though I was extremely pressed with other work I asked myself whether I, even I, mightn't by a lively prompt effort put together such a minor item for the bill as would serve to help people to wait for the major. But I had distractingly little time or freedom of mind, and a happy and unidiotic motive for a one-act piece isn't easy to come by (as you will know better than I) offhand.

Therefore said I to myself there might easily turn up among all the short tales I had published (the list being long) something or other naturally and obligingly convertible to my purpose. That would econ-omise immensely my small labour—and in fine I pounced on just such a treatable idea in a thing of many years before, an obscure pot-boiler, "Owen Wingrave" by name—and very much what you have seen by nature. It was treatable, I thought, and moreover I was in possession of it; also it would be very difficult and take great ingenuity and expert-ness—which gave the case a reason the more. To be brief then I with consummate art lifted the scattered and expensive Owen Wingrave into the compact and economic little Saloon—very adroitly (yes!) but, as the case had to be, breathlessly too; and all to the upshot of finding that, in the first place, my friends above-mentioned could make neither head nor tail of it; and in the second place that my three-act play, on further exploitation, was going to last too long to allow anything else of importance. So I put *The Saloon* back into a drawer; but so, likewise, I shortly afterwards fished it out again and showed it to Granville-Barker,[3] who was kind about it and apparently curious of it, and in consequence of whose attention a member of the S[tage] S[ociety] saw it. That is the only witchcraft I have used!—by which I mean that that was the head and front of my undertaking to "preach" anything to anyone—in the guise of the little Act—on any subject whatever. So much for the modest origin of the thing—which, since you have read the piece, I can't help wanting to put on record.

But, if you press me, I quite allow that this all shifts my guilt only a little further back and that your question applies just as much, in the first place, to the short story perpetrated years ago, and in the re-perpetration more recently, in another specious form and in the greater (the very great alas) "maturity of my powers." And it doesn't really matter at all, since I am ready serenely to answer you. I do such things because I happen to be a man of imagination and taste, extremely in-terested in life, and because the imagination, thus, from the moment direction and motive play upon it from all sides, absolutely enjoys and insists on and incurably leads a life of its own, for which just this vi-vacity itself is its warrant. You surely haven't done all your own so in-teresting work without learning what it is for the imagination to *play* with an idea—an idea about life—under a happy obsession, for all it is worth. Half the beautiful things that the benefactors of the human species have produced would surely be wiped out if you don't allow this adventurous and speculative imagination its rights. You simplify too much, by the same token, when you limit the field of interest to what you call the scientific—your employment of which term in such a connection even greatly, I confess, confounds and bewilders me. In the one sense in which *The Saloon could* be scientific—that is by being done with all the knowledge and intelligence relevant to its motive, I really think it quite supremely so. That is the only sense in which a work of art can be scientific—though in that sense, I admit, it may be so to the point of becoming an everlasting blessing to man. And if you waylay me here, as I infer you would be disposed to, on the ground that we "don't want works of art," ah then, my dear Bernard Shaw, I think I take such issue with you that—if we didn't both *like* to talk—there would be scarce use in our talking at all. I think, frankly, even, that we scarce want anything else at all. They are capable of saying more things to man about himself than any other "works" whatever are capable of doing—and it's only by thus saying as much to him as possible, by saying, as nearly as we can, all there is, and in as many ways and on as many sides, and with a vividness of presentation that "art," and art alone, is an adequate mistress of, that we enable him to pick and choose and compare and know, enable him to arrive at any sort of synthesis that isn't, through all its superficialities and vacancies, a base and illusive humbug. On which statement I must rest my sense that all *direct* "encouragement"—the thing you enjoin on me—encouragement of the short-cut and say "artless" order, is really more likely than not to be shallow and misleading, and to make him turn on you with a vengeance for offering him some scheme that takes account but of a tenth of his attributes. In fact I view with suspicion the "encouraging" *representational* work, altogether, and think even the question not [an] *a priori* one at all; that is save under this peril of too superficial a view of what it is we have to be encouraged or discouraged *about.* The artist helps us to know this,—if he have a due intelligence—better than anyone going, because he undertakes to represent the world to us; so that, certainly, if *a posteriori*, we can on the whole feel encouraged, so much the better for us all round. But I can imagine no scanter source of exhilaration than to find the brute undertake that presentation without the most consummate "art" he can muster!

But I am really too long-winded—especially for a man who for the last few days (though with a brightening prospect) has been breathing with difficulty. It comes from my enjoying so the chance to talk with you—so much too rare; but that I hope we may be able before too long again to renew. I am comparatively little in London, but I have my moments there. Therefore I look forward—! And I assure you I have been touched and charmed by the generous abundance of your letter. Believe me yours most truly,

Henry James

1. George Bernard Shaw (1856–1950), the Anglo-Irish dramatist, wrote to HJ on 17 January 1909 as a committee member of the Incorporated Stage Society to explain why HJ's one-act ghost play, *The Saloon*, was being rejected. Shaw argued that the young man in the play should kill the ghost of his ancestor in the haunted room, instead of being killed by it. "People don't want works of art from you," Shaw wrote, "they want help, they want above all encouragement . . ." For the further correspondence between the two see HJ, *The Complete Plays* (1949). Shaw's pocket diaries reveal that a quarter of a century before he wrote his letter to HJ, the Irish dramatist spent a night in a haunted house in behalf of the Society for Psychical Research. The diary records "Slept there. Terrific nightmare." No further details are given. See Bernard Shaw, *The Diaries*, ed. Weintraub (1986), I, 121. HJ's play, based on his earlier short story "Owen Wingrave" (1892) about a young pacifist in a military family, was produced by Gertrude Kingston in 1911.

2. HJ refers here to another play, originally called *Summersoft*, which became the three-act *The High Bid*, produced by Sir Johnston Forbes-Robertson in 1908.

3. Harley Granville-Barker (1877–1946), stage director and dramatist.

161 · To Edith Wharton

Ms Yale

Lamb House, Rye
July 26th 1909

Dearest Edith.

I could really cry with joy for it!—for what your note received this noon tells me: so affectionate an interest I take in that gentleman. How admirable a counsellor you have been, and what a *détente*, what a blest and beneficent one, poor tortured and tethered W.M.F. must feel! It makes me, I think, as happy as it does you. And I hope the consequence will be an overflow of all sorts of practical good for him— it *must* be. Of course, I shall breathe, nor write, no shadow of a word of what I have been hearing from you to him—but if he should in time—and when he *has* time (he can't have now), the pleasure I shall take in expressing my sentiments to him will be extreme.[1]

Your telegram arrived in time to keep me from writing Macmillan otherwise than in the sense it expressed; but I have now written him in *this* sense: that I am aware of matters in Morton's situation that make me think a sum of money will be highly convenient to him, I named them a little, and that if M. write to propose an advance I shall like greatly to send them, the Macmillans, a cheque for £100 that they may remit him the amount of as from themselves, I remaining, and wishing to remain, wholly unmentioned in the affairs. But send me no cheque, please, not only till I have let you know what reply I have had from Macmillan, but till Morton tells you he *has* made the request.[2]

I hope the sum he has to pay to the accursed woman isn't really a very considerable one, or on which the interest for him to pay will be anything like *as* burdensome as what he has been doing. And 53 rue de Varenne?—But you will tell me of that at your leisure. I'm delighted you're to have Miss Bahlmann[3] with you. Paul Harvey[4] comes to me here for the night and I think will be able to give me some news of Walter B[erry]. I am greatly touched by your so gentil little *envoi* of the étude of the Praslin story. I haven't immediate time to master it, but have sampled it a little, and have known it more or less before. I remember Mrs. Deluzy Field in the U.S., and her coming one day to see my mother when I was there—a very expressive and demonstrative white-puffed person, impressing *les miens* as a Frenchwoman of the most insinuating and dazzling manners. She was a méridionale Protestant (of origin), I think—and that worked badly for her relations with the Duchess etc. But how when we were *tout-jeunes* in Paris the closed and blighted and *dead* closed *hôtel* P[raslin] used to be pointed out to us as we walked in the Rue St. Honoré![5]

Ever and always yours
Henry James

1. Morton Fullerton was still threatened by the blackmail he had first mentioned to HJ in 1907 (see Letter 155).

2. Frederick Macmillan, the publisher, at the suggestion of Edith Wharton and HJ, offered a contract to Morton Fullerton for a book about Paris. HJ suggested that Fullerton receive an advance, and Mrs. Wharton said she would supply £100. Macmillan refused and paid this sum as part of the firm's contract. Fullerton never completed the book.

3. Anna Bahlmann, Mrs. Wharton's childhood governess, who served as Mrs. Wharton's secretary after 1904.

4. Paul Harvey (1862–1948), whom HJ had known as a boy in France, was now in the British Embassy in Cairo. See Letter 36, note 4.

5. Mrs. Wharton had sent HJ an account of the celebrated murder in which the Duc de Choiseul, Charles Laure Hugues Theobald Praslin (1805–1847), stabbed his Duchess, Altarice Rosalba Fanny Sebastiani, to death. Mrs. Deluzy Field was the former Henriette Deluzy-Desportes, a governess in the Duke's household, who created the friction between the ducal pair that ultimately resulted in the Duke's using three knives to dispose of the Duchess. The crime occurred in 1847, and the James family, in Paris in 1855, still heard echoes of it. The Duke committed suicide after the crime; Mlle Deluzy was arrested as an accessory but was released. She married an American, the Reverend Henry M. Field, and became renowned in New York as hostess and conversationalist. In 1875 (10 June, *Nation*) HJ noticed Mrs. Fields' posthumous *Home Sketches*. See HJ *Literary Criticism*, Library of America (1984), p. 272. Mrs. Wharton toyed with the idea of using the story in a novel; a descendant of Mlle Deluzy, Rachel Lyman Field, wrote a successful novel based on this family history, *All This and Heaven Too* (1938).

162 · To John Galsworthy

Ms Unknown

[Lamb House, August 1909]

I answer your appeal on the censor question[1] to the best of my small ability. I *do* consider that the situation made by the Englishman of letters ambitious of writing for the stage has less dignity—thanks to the Censor's arbitrary rights upon his work—than that of any other man of letters in Europe, and that this fact may well be, or rather *must* be, deterrent to men of any intellectual independence and self-respect. I think this circumstance represents accordingly an impoverishment of our theatre; that it tends to deprive it of intellectual life, of the *importance* to which a free choice of subjects and illustration directly ministers, and to confine it to the trivial and the puerile. It is difficult to express the depth of dismay and disgust with which an author of books in this country finds it impressed upon him, in passing into the province of the theatre with the view of labouring there, that he has to reckon anxiously with an obscure and irresponsible Mr. So-and-So who may by law peremptorily demand of him that he shall make his work square, at vital points, with Mr. So-and-So's personal and, intellectually and critically, speaking, wholly unauthoritative preferences prejudices and ignorances, and that the less original, the less important and the less interesting it is, and the more vulgar and superficial and futile, the more it is likely so to square. He thus encounters an arrogation of critical authority and the critical veto, with the power to enforce its decisions, that is without a parallel in any other civilised country and which has in this one the effect of relegating the theatre to the position of a mean minor art, and of condemning it to ignoble dependences, poverties and pusillanimities. We rub our eyes, we writers accustomed to freedom in all other walks, to think that this cause has still to be argued in England.

1. A Joint Select Committee of Lords and Commons held an inquiry in 1909 into the question of licensing of plays in England. From the early eighteenth century control of the stage had been exercised by the Lord Chamberlain. The committee recommended that he should continue to license plays, but that it should be optional to submit a play for license and legal to perform an unlicensed play. However, no legislative action followed the report of this committee. On 12 August 1909 John Galsworthy read, as part of the testimony given by authors and dramatists during the hearings, HJ's letter of protest. The letter is reproduced in the committee's report of 1909, published by His Majesty's Stationery Office. The Lord Chamberlain continued to be responsible for the licensing of plays until 1968.

163 · To Mrs. J. T. Fields

Ms Huntington

Lamb House, Rye
January 2nd 1910

Dear Mrs. Fields.[1]

How long I have been in answering your good note on the subject of dear Sara Jewett's letters, and how much ashamed I am! But there have been reasons, and my delay rather inevitable! I was making a long stay in London when your inquiry came, and I wanted to make *sure* before replying that my fear of having kept nothing from her hand was a justified fear: which I could do only by waiting till I could get back here—where my papers and possessions abide. So I waited, and when I came home found that I have preserved nothing—(I never had *many* letters from her at all) even as I supposed was the case. And that depressed and abashed me, in respect of writing to tell you so—and then came the pressure of rather urgent and overwhelming Christmas postal matter (a very formidable business by the good old British tradition); so that from these sad deterrents or delays my hand has been considerably stayed. Well, such now is the rather sad and sorry little case—that I find our admirable friend's occasional communications have submitted to the law that I have made tolerably absolute these last years and as I myself grow older and think more of my latter end: the law of not leaving personal and private documents at the mercy of any accidents, or even of my executors! I kept almost all letters for years—till my receptacles would no longer hold them; then I made a gigantic bonfire and have been easier in mind since—save as to a certain residuum which *had* to survive. You see that of Sara Jewett's, even beloved as one felt her, there were very few—and those ante-dating her accident and her illness; when I never expected to survive her and wish to deal with her memory. *After* those troubles I scarcely heard from her at all—or only in two or three painful and pathetic fragments, as it were, which it was pure sadness to keep. I wish I could help you more. I will with the greatest joy in any *other* way—if any memorial of her is in course of taking shape to which I might contribute a few pages. So the case has shaped itself. I wish you strength and cheer to do anything and everything to which you may put your wise and tender hand, and am, dear Mrs. Fields, your all-faithful old friend

Henry James

P.S. I would for instance with pleasure address you a letter, as Editor—a "letter" of reminiscence and appreciation and making twenty-five pages of print or so, which would serve, if you cared, as Introduction to your Volume: a thing very frank, familiar, *as* a thorough Friend, etc.; and oh so tender and so *admiring*—as I *do* admire her work!

1. Mrs. Fields (1834–1915), the former Annie Adams, was the widow of the editor and publisher J. T. Fields. Her close friend Sarah Orne Jewett had died in 1909.

164 · To Hugh Walpole

Ms Texas

Lamb House, Rye
May 13th 1910

Dearest, Dearest Hugh.[1]

I have been utterly, but necessarily, silent—so much of the time lately quite too ill to write. Deeply your note touches me, as I needn't tell you—and I would give anything to be able to have the free use of your "visible and tangible" affection—no touch of its tangibility but would be dear and helpful to me. But, alas, I am utterly unfit for visits—with the black devils of Nervousness, direst, damnedest demons, that ride me so cruelly and that I have perpetually to reckon with. I am mustering a colossal courage to try—even tomorrow—in my blest sister-in-law's company (without whom and my brother, just now in Paris, I couldn't have struggled on at all) to get away for some days by going to see a kind friend in the country—in Epping Forest.[2] I feel it a most precarious and dangerous undertaking—but my desire and need for change of air, scene and circumstance, after so fearfully overmuch of these imprisoning objects, is so fiercely intense that I am making the push—as to save my life—at any cost. It *may* help me—even much, and the doctor intensely urges it—and if I am able, afterwards (that is if the experiment isn't disastrous), I shall try to go to 105 Pall Mall for a little instead of coming abjectly back here. Then I shall be able to see you—but all this is fearfully contingent. Meanwhile the sense of your personal tenderness to me, dearest Hugh, is far from not doing much for me. I adore it.

I "read," in a manner, "Maradick"[3]—but there's too much to say about it, and even my weakness doesn't alter me from the grim and battered old *critical* critic—no *other* such creature among all the "reviewers" do I meanwhile behold. Your book has a great sense and love of life—but seems to me very nearly as irreflectively juvenile as the Trojans, and to have the prime defect of your having gone into a subject—i.e. the marital, sexual, bedroom relations of M. and his wife— the literary man and his wife—since these *are* the key to the whole situation—which have to be tackled and faced to mean anything. You don't tackle and face them—you *can't*. Also the whole thing is a monument to the abuse of voluminous dialogue, the absence of a plan of composition, alternation, distribution, structure, and other phases of presentation than the dialogue—so that *line* (the only thing *I* value in a fiction etc.) is replaced by a vast formless featherbediness—billows in which one sinks and is lost. And yet it's all so loveable— though not so *written*. It isn't written *at all*, darling Hugh—by which I mean you have—or, truly, only in a few places, as in Maradick's dive—never got expression *tight* and in close quarters (of discrimination, of specification) with its subject. It remains loose and far. And

385

you have never made out, recognized, nor stuck to, *the centre of your subject.* But can you forgive all this to your fondest old reaching-out-his-arms-to you

H.J.?

1. Walpole (1884–1941) was beginning his career as a novelist. HJ met him in 1908 and was charmed by his youth, naïveté, and literary zeal, but remained critical of his work.

2. To Hill Hall, country house of Mrs. Charles Hunter, hostess of celebrities and sister of the composer Ethel Smyth.

3. *Maradick at Forty,* just published, was Walpole's second novel, preceded the previous year by *The Trojan Horse.* Of HJ's criticisms Walpole's biographer, Sir Rupert Hart-Davis, wrote in *Hugh Walpole* (1952): "many young writers would have quailed before such devastating strictures, but for Hugh they were spurs to fresh endeavour." See also Leon Edel's essay on Walpole, dealing with the cumulative effect of such criticisms, in *Stuff of Sleep and Dreams* (1982).

165 · To Harley Granville-Barker

Ms Taylor

Lamb House, Rye, Sussex
August 1st 1910

Dear Granville Barker.

I shall be obliged indeed if you will rescue the cut copy of my ill-starred comedy[1] for me from the limbo of the vague. These cuts were the result of an heroic effort—and I am afraid I shouldn't be able to *see* them at all again. (Besides which, however, I don't really see them, in their profusion, now.) I know of no intimation on the part of Frohman that he will interest himself again in my play—he has conveyed none such to me. He paid me a modest forfeit for non-production and I have resumed my possession of it (or *shall* when I get those three lean copies). That, for me, is the sense of what has happened, and I have only now to think ruefully and gloomily, what other use I shall—or can—make of it. I wish you, for yourself, some prompter inspiration than I strike myself as likely to find. But *my* first course must be to get the cuts—by which I mean the ensanguined corpse—washed and laid out clean. I leave this place for the U.S. on the 10th.

Yours most truly
Henry James

1. Harley Granville-Barker, the playwright-director, had started preparations to produce HJ's new play, *The Outcry,* as part of a repertory season planned by the American producer Charles Frohman (1860–1915), which was also to have included plays by Shaw, Galsworthy, Masefield, Maugham, and Barker. The death of Edward VII and the period of mourning that followed proved a death-blow to Frohman's plans. Barker experienced difficulty in casting HJ's play and also demanded certain essential cuts. "He hated doing it, of course," Granville-Barker wrote to Leon Edel on 9 December 1929, "and had to be induced to part with first one bit, then after a while another." During his stay in the United States, HJ turned the recovered script into a novel with the same title, which was published in 1911.

166 · To Grace Norton

Ms Harvard

Chocorua, N.H.
August 26*th* 1910

Dearest Grace.

I am deeply touched by your tender note—and all the more that we have need of tenderness, in a special degree, here now. We arrived, William and Alice and I, in this strange sad rude spot, a week ago tonight—after a most trying journey from Quebec (though after a most beautiful, quick, in itself auspicious, voyage too), but with William critically, mortally ill and with our anxiety and tension now (he has rapidly got so much worse) a real anguish. The main mark of his state is a difficulty of breathing that it's painful and terrible to see—and he at present lies constantly, as the only thing possible, under the influence of morphia. Alice is, and has been for weeks (he had gone down and down so before we sailed), of a miraculous devotion, but we have the defense well organized, for all the remoteness and isolation that strikes me here as almost sinister; the "local" Doctor, nine miles off, being really very good and competent, and his son, an excellent young physician as well, installed in the house as valuable and efficient nurse and taker of responsibilities. The telephone and automobile make nothing *very* difficult, and last night we had up from Boston a very intelligent and I think able heart specialist, or more or less such, one Smith by name, for consultation and further light. He went back this A.M. early, but with a good effect on the situation left behind him (he holds that dear William has "a fighting chance"—though my own

387

heart sinks down and down over it); and we are further to have today a trained woman-nurse in addition to young Doctor Shedd—so that, in this better air (though the heat has been suffocating), we are probably in more favoring (and as practicable) conditions than we should find in Irving Street. Alice is terribly exhausted and spent—but the rest she will be able to take must presently increase, and Harry, who, after meeting us at Quebec, started with a friend on a much-needed holiday in the New Brunswick woods (for shooting and fishing) was wired to yesterday to come back to us at once. So I give you, dear Grace, our dismal chronicle of suspense and pain. My own fears are of the blackest, I confess to you, and at the prospect of losing my wonderful beloved brother out of the world in which, from as far back as in dimmest childhood, I have so yearningly always counted on him, I feel nothing but the abject weakness of grief and even terror. But I forgive myself "weakness"—my emergence from the long and grim ordeal of my own peculiarly dismal and trying illness isn't yet absolutely complete enough to make me wholly firm on my feet. But *my* slowly recuperative process goes on despite all checks and shocks, while dear William's, in the full climax of his intrinsic powers and intellectual ambitions, meets this tragic, cruel arrest. However, dear Grace, I won't further wail to you in my nervous soreness and sorrow—still, in spite of so much revival, more or less under the shadow as I am of the miserable, damnable year that began for me last Christmas-tide and for which I had been spoiling for two years before. I will only wait to see you—with all the tenderness of our long, long unbroken friendship and all the host of our common initiations. I have come for a long stay—though when we shall be able to plan for a resumption of life in Irving Street is of course insoluble as yet. Then, at all events, with what eagerness your threshold will be crossed by your faithfullest old

Henry James

P.S. It's to-day blessedly cooler here—and I hope you also have the reprieve!

P.S. I open my letter of three hours since to add that William passed unconsciously away an hour ago—without apparent pain or struggle. Think of us, dear Grace—think of us!

167 · To Thomas Sergeant Perry

Ms Colby

Chocorua, N.H.
September 2nd 1910

My dear old Thomas.

I sit heavily stricken and in darkness—for from far back in dimmest childhood he had been my ideal Elder Brother, and I still, through all the years, saw in him, even as a small timorous boy yet, my protector, my backer, my authority and my pride. His extinction changes the face of life for me—besides the mere missing of his inexhaustible company and personality, originality, the whole unspeakably vivid and beautiful presence of him. And his noble intellectual vitality was still but at its climax—he had two or three ardent purposes and plans. He had cast them away, however, at the end—I mean that, dreadfully suffering, he wanted only to die. Alice and I had a bitter pilgrimage with him from far off—he sank here, on his threshold, and then it went horribly fast. I cling for the present to *them*—and so try to stay here through this month. After that I shall be with them in Cambridge for several more—we shall cleave more together. I should like to come and see you for a couple of days much, but it would have to be after the 20th, or even October 1st, I think; and I fear you may not then be still in *villeggiatura*. If so I *will* come. You knew him—among those living now—from furthest back with me. Yours and Lilla's all faithfully,

Henry James

168 · To Theodora Bosanquet

Ms Harvard

105 Pall Mall, S.W.
October 27th 1911

Dear Miss Bosanquet.

Oh if you *could* only have the real right thing to miraculously propose to me, you and Miss Bradley, when I see you on Tuesday at 4.30! For you see, by this bolting—in horror and loathing (but don't *repeat* those expressions!) from Rye for the winter—my situation suddenly becomes special and difficult; and largely through this, that having got

back to work and to a very particular job, the need of expressing myself, of pushing it on, on the old Remingtonese terms, grows daily
stronger within me. But I haven't a seat and temple for the Remington
and its priestess—*can't* have here at this club, and on the other hand
can't now organize a permanent or regular and continuous footing for
the London winters, which means something unfurnished and taking
(*wasting, now*) time and thought. I want a small, very cheap and very
clean *furnished* flat or trio of rooms etc. (like those we talked of under
the King's Cross delusion—only better *and* with some, (a very few)
tables and chairs and fireplaces), that I could hire for two or three—
three or four—months to drive ahead my job in—the Remington
priestess and I converging on it and meeting there morning by morning—and it being preferably nearer to her than to me; though near
tubes and things for both of us![1] I must keep on *this* place for food and
bed etc.—I have it by the year—till I really *have* something else—by
the year—for winter purposes—to supersede it (Lamb House abides—
for long summers). Your researches can have only been for the *unfurnished*—but look, *think, invent!* Two or three decent little tabled and
chaired and lighted rooms would do. I catch a train till Monday, probably late. But on Tuesday!

Yours ever,
Henry James

1. On his return from the United States, HJ settled for the winter into his room at the
Reform Club, where however he was not permitted to have his female typist. Miss Bosan-
quet found two rooms adjoining her own residence at 10 Lawrence Street, Cheyne Walk,
Chelsea, and HJ went there daily by taxi from his club to work on his autobiography. See
Theodora Bosanquet, *Henry James at Work* (1927).

169 · To James Jackson Putnam

Ms Countway

Lamb House, Rye
January 4th 1912

My dear Putnam.

This is a *delayed* word—partly because I have been designedly and
watchfully waiting, partly by reason of the avalanche of correspondence that descended on me at the New Year, and with which I am

still a little at a disadvantage in struggling. I meant it to have reached you on New Year's day—whereas it does not start toward you even punctually then. But it takes with it, and in it, my strong sense of owing you some faithful report of myself after so long—and after your last winter's great sympathy in particular; and also my great gladness that the report can be so bright. For I want you to know that I am quite enormously better, and so far as possible how I have come to be able to say so. It's perhaps easier for me to say now, however, why it is and *wasn't* better—I mean during those weary months of last year, when I occasionally saw you.[1] The following time has thrown some light on that—a good deal in fact: I began really to be better from the day I went back to London to *stay*—though even that was only some three months ago. I had evil times, many of them, in America, after last seeing you, and the summer conditions proved formidable to me in the extreme—I had at Nahant, e.g. in July (early) to send at short notice [for] Dr. Winslow there, my almost worst distresses had so come back to me. The heat, the confinement (by reason of the same), my sense of being caught in an almost fatal *trap* (I had put off my sailing to Europe from June to early in August), all *that* had brought me once more to a bad crisis, and the whole season was really but a mitigated nightmare. Things were also very unpropitious here when I first returned—the heat and drought and other *convulsions*[2] that I found poor dear old England given over to were very disconcerting and arresting, and the weeks I began by spending in this place (for I really write this from the country) saw me but little way further. I had in fact another crisis and thereupon fled to London at once, to settle and stick fast for the winter (without waiting for a later part of it, as I had tried to resign myself to doing). The big Babylon, with its great spaces for circulation, for movement, and for variety, has proved an absolute specific—the only one that was adequate for me and worthy, so to speak, of my powers and my infirmities, on the *scale* of them and proportionate to them—the contracted circle and the scant variety and the narrow circulation had comparatively done little. I have recovered myself further in consequence, during the past twelve or fourteen weeks, than I had done in any period of six or eight months before, and am in fact now really better than I have been not only since I was taken so acutely ill, (two years ago) but than I have been for at least four years. I have liabilities to relapse a little at times, but I recognize now perfectly the conditions that produce them and know how to manage, minimise and stave them off. I have got back to work, am working well, and that is an unspeakable aid and support and blessing. Speaking in a summary manner I have a *big* enough surface to expand myself nervously upon—and if I had had a bigger one at the time you were seeing me, I probably should have got forward much more continuously. It has been a matter of the *big* rhythm and the long beat, if you know what I mean—but I wish I were sitting with you again in Marlborough Street (on this basis of improvement only though!) on one of those rather melancholy winter evenings of a year ago—and just long *enough* to appeal to your comprehension and interest a little more vividly. I have at any rate worked the troubled history pretty well out for myself—in especial since that second time of my being with Joseph Collins[3] in New York—in April—after the last time of my seeing you. I had a bad crisis again there—and beyond being very kind and interested he did nothing for me at all: so that it was *then* I began to get hold of things more intimately for myself and more or less to grasp the real clue to the labyrinth. Difficult outside conditions caused it still at times to be very bewildering, as I say, but I more persistently grasped the logic of the matter and saw that the basis of my recovery was, first, the basis of all adequately and all precautionarily *feeding* (so as to *forestall* any approach to inanition); second, the basis of feeding *at the same time* as little *fatteningly* as possible; third, the basis of as much *movement,* or circulation, and multiplication of contact, and variety of vision, as much (roughly speaking) beguilement, as possible. If I stoked without movement I got too high "blood pressure" and great increase of chronic panting and heaving. If I moved (*much*) without stoking I got collapse and *bed,* in straight resumption of the effect of the Fletcherized starvation which was the *fons et origo* of all my woes and which had so nearly done me to death. If I took too much meat (as least fat-making) I distressfully and dreadfully panted and heaved: if I took too little I sooner or later fainted by the wayside and laid me down in sick despair as to die. If, *to eat enough,* I took certain other things I felt the oppression and injury of overweight—promptly and easily produced. But the worst thing of all was: first the not finding opportunity and atmosphere for the circulation and locomotion I required; and second the superstition of *fatigue,* which was more or less forced upon me from roundabout, and was very delusive and misleading and injurious (not the fatigue, but the mistake). I was only fatigued when I moved too little—I wasn't when I did so enough or too much. "Rest" was a mockery when I could stoke enough (and stoking a mockery when I couldn't be restless enough and adequately and rightly—otherwise than by heaving—work it off). I had been resting from my starvation all the years of my starvation—it was the only thing but starve that I could do. Spending most of June and July at Nahant with my extraordinarily kind old friend G. A. James,[4] a wondrous good Samaritan to me at that unholy time, I almost went mad from the desolation (I mean the narrow confines and *yet supposed extent!*) of the deadly (yet luxurious!) scene, and the sickening torrid heat that, with other hindrances, made any choice or range of circulation impossible. However, I am boring you to death (if I am not really interesting you!) and I only risk the former effect to possibly invoke the latter. It's a flood of egotism—but what are the Patient class but egotistic, especially in proportion as it's grateful? You tided me over three or four bad places during those worst months. Now everything is changed and you will after all be certainly glad to hear it, and that I am really, for a still too obese mortal, master of the situation. I hope you yourself are in good heart and hope. I hear you were in these parts in the summer, and wish I had been here to receive you. Collins spent an evening with me in the late autumn and much admired me—as an independent work of art! Soon I am hoping for Bill and his bride. But I quickly reapply the remedy of London—of the blessed miles of pavement, lamplight, shopfront, apothecary's beautiful and blue jars and numerous friends' teacups and tales! Don't think it necessary to "answer" this the least little bit. I have written to possibly strike a light for another forlorn brother—even on your professional altar, though I shall be delighted at a word of cheer from you. Yours, my dear Putnam all faithfully,

Henry James

1. This letter reveals that HJ, in consulting the eminent psychiatrist James Jackson Putnam (1846–1918) in Boston, was exposed briefly and beneficially to early Freudian therapy. Putnam, professor of neurology at Harvard, had been in touch with Freud, Ernest Jones, and Morton Prince; and he seems to have gone into James's prolonged "Fletcherizing," which had proved in the end debilitating and demoralizing. (This was a food-chewing fad invented by Horace Fletcher, a nonmedical person, to which HJ became addicted.) James's own testimony in this letter, while focusing on externals, suggests that he was able to respond to the deeper psychological problems that undermined his well-being—the loss and mourning for his elder brother, the sense of aging, the deep loneliness he had come to experience in the isolation of Rye.

2. Coal and railway strikes and public discontent.

3. Dr. Joseph Collins, the fashionable New York pseudo-psychiatrist, who wrote a series of books, "The Doctor Looks at . . ." His comments on HJ as patient are in *The Doctor Looks at Biography* (1925). He prescribed, as HJ put it, "baths, massage and electrocutions."

4. George Abbot James (no relative) was a classmate of HJ's at Harvard in 1862. See *Notes of a Son and Brother,* chapter X.

170 · To Theodate Pope Riddle

Ms Hillstead

105, Pall Mall, S.W.
January 12*th* 1912

My dear Theodate.[1]

I return you the dreadful document,[2] pronouncing it without hesitation the most abject and impudent, the hollowest, vulgarest, and basest rubbish I could possibly conceive. Utterly empty and illiterate, without substance or sense, a mere babble of platitudinous phrases, it is beneath comment or criticism, in short beneath contempt. The *commonness* of it simply nauseates—it seems to have been given to those people to invent, richly, new kinds and degrees of commonness, to open up new oceans or vast dismal deserts of it. And that these are those for whom such lucubrations represent a series of *values,* and who spend their time and invite others to spend theirs over them, makes me wonder—well, makes me wonder at more things than I shall now undertake to tell you. I shall just simply tell you *one* of them, if you'll let me—which is the prodigy of the "effect of America" in producing a sense of proportion, a kind of perspective, a flatness of level and thinness of air, in which a person of your fine and true quality finds it natural to pass on such a tissue of trash to another. Where in such an air are criticism and comparison and education and taste and tradition, and the perception a measure and standard of—well, again of more things than I can name to you? See how you make me write—as if I were writing *at* you! But I'm not, my dear Theodate, nor expressing myself with resentment—only with a bewildered sense of strangeness through which I look at you as over the abyss of oddity of your *asking* about that thing to which I hate to accord the dignity even of sending it safely back to you! But I brush the strangeness away—as a momentary blur, and it instantly goes, and I see you again in that charming light of last summer and of all the Farmington hospitality and beauty and of the wondrous motor-days in particular, and the prodigious Hill-stead to Cambridge one most of all; and in the clearance I embrace you tenderly and respectfully, if you let me—as a sign of all the grati-tude I've cherished for you, and all my fond hope of our renewing some such occasion here—or such a pale image of them as poor old "here" may make possible. I am spending this winter practically in London, which is doing me a world of good—in a different way from the world dear Hillstead did me but still very valuably. I saw L. a little some time ago and found her as hard as all the nails of old Jewry put up to auction. She wouldn't have sent me that document, no; but she would have sent me cold poison and then charged me Ten Pounds for it. The really nice one of that family is G. who is velvet-soft and has much more talent than the poisoner, too. I make out that you are leading a life in N.Y., and I wish indeed I could sprawl on the red cretonne. Do take in Peggy and feed her from the pink and silver, and it will all be blest to you and to *her* and all delightful to her poor old uncle and your

Affectionate old friend,
Henry James

P.S. I should so like to send my very best love to the beautiful boun-tiful graceful Parents.

1. HJ met Theodate Pope Riddle during his 1905 trip to the United States and saw her again during the visit of 1910–1911. She was an architect and had built Avon Old Farms at Farmington, Connecticut, where HJ enjoyed inspecting her collection of Impressionist paintings.
2. The document was a report of a séance in which it was claimed William James had tried to communicate with his family.

171 · To Howard Sturgis

Ms Harvard

105. Pall Mall S.W.
Feb. 20th 1912

Dearest Howard.[1]

You have the art of writing letters which make those who already adore you to the verge of dementia slide over the dizzy edge and fairly sit raving their passion. One doesn't "thank" for such pages as I just receive from you—but one is prouder than ever of having always *enter-tained* a passion for the exquisite spirit capable of them. Yes, I *have* been unwell to rather a wretched degree, and have had a couple of times over to scramble down to Lamb House and put myself to bed. I came back thence last five days ago and have within the last two felt distinctly better. When I *am* at all better London is best for me—I could weep tears over the thought of starting on your premises a new infirmary ward. What an angel of bounty you are, and what handsome advantage is taken of it! I shall not add by a touch, dearest Howard, to that handsomeness—the scene at Qu'Acre strikes me as rich and rounded, to the ideal point, as it is. I have an impression that I am really now crawling out of my hole—and also one that I *needn't* so absolutely, some five weeks ago, have tumbled into it. I slipped and lost my footing, as it were, and then a series of mistakes, which I might very well have left unmade, precipitated the rest of my descent. I really don't think it need *so stupidly* occur again. But it's dire to have to recognise that one *could* still be so stupid, after all one has paid for a grain of wit. I have to buy it, you see—that article; while to you it comes nat'ral—like every other grace and generosity.

Yes, but I can't *think* of Teddy's Victim[2] when I'm myself down and *affaibli*. I need *all* my resources—physical, moral, and financial—to look the situation in the face at all, and even then I don't stare at it very hard, but give it every chance to cut me if it will. I can neither *do* anything, write to her or be written to, about it—and ask myself why therefore cultivate, in the connection, a mere platonic horror—which permits me neither to hold her hand nor to kick his tail. I have got back to work here again—at my little Chelsea *trou*—within three or four days; and that, when I can really do it, does me far more good than anything. Did any echo come to you of my having gone down to Wancote for the week end on Saturday Jan. 27th and having had to ask to be allowed to go to bed the hour after I arrived?—where I remained till the Monday A.M., when Mrs. Julian [Sturgis] very kindly sent me home (to town) in her motor-car. Your sister May was to have come—that had been the grand occasion of *my* going; but she failed at the eleventh hour and so precipitated—by the shock of not finding her—my collapse. And the cold was zeroic—as my resistance was *not!*

To my Nephew Bill and his bran-new Bride I have lent Lamb House for as long as they will stay—and their being there is a great joy and pacification to me.

Yes, I *have* heard (from Gaillard Lapsley)[3] that dear Arthur[4] is lecturing on Symonds "with the disagreeable side left out!" But it supremely characterizes Symonds that that was just the side that *he* found most supremely agreeable—and that to ignore it is therefore to offer to our yearning curiosity a Symonds exactly *uncharacterized.* However, Arthur is clearly doing him in the Key of Pink.[5] But if a course of lectures, generally, might be made of all the things, disagreeable *and* agreeable, he "leaves out," it might stretch almost to the length of his whole *oeuvre*—so far as at present perpetrated. But, dearest Howard, HERE is perpetration enough; so good-night; it's a joy to be told you're *sound.*

Ever your fond old
H.J.

1. Howard Sturgis (1854–1920), youngest son of the expatriate head of Baring Brothers, bankers, lived all his life in the family's Georgian villa, Queen's Acre (Qu'Acre), on the edge of Windsor Park. His companion was William Haynes Smith, known as "the Babe."

2. HJ is referring to the developing divorce between Edith Wharton and her husband, Edward (Teddy).

3. Gaillard T. Lapsley (1871–1949), American-born fellow of Trinity College, Cambridge, where he was a preeminent authority on medieval constitutional history. He was an intimate of the Edith Wharton circle and ultimately Edith Wharton's literary executor.

4. Arthur Christopher Benson (1862–1925), editor of Queen Victoria's letters, a master at Eton until 1905 and subsequently master of Magdalene College, Cambridge.

5. The "disagreeable side" was John Addington Symonds's homosexuality. HJ's reference to "the Key of Pink" is an ironic allusion to Symonds's book of essays, *In the Key of Blue* (1892).

172 · To Hendrik C. Andersen

Ms Barrett

[The Athenaeum]
April 14th 1912

Dearest Hendrik.

Not another day do I delay to answer (with such difficulty!) your long and interesting letter. I have waited these ten days or so just *because* of the difficulty: so little (as you may imagine or realise on thinking a little) is it a soft and simple matter to stagger out from under such an avalanche of information and announcement as you let drop on me with this terrific story of your working so in the colossal and in the void and in the air![1] Brace yourself for my telling you that (*having*, these days, scrambled a little from under the avalanche) I now, staggering to my feet again, just simply flee before the horrific mass, lest I start the remainder (what is hanging in the air) afresh to overwhelm me. I say "brace yourself," though I don't quite see why I need, having showed you in the past, so again and again, that your mania for the colossal, the swelling and the huge, the monotonously and repeatedly huge, breaks the heart of me for you, so convinced have I been all along that it means your simply burying yourself and all your products and belongings, and everything and Every One that is yours, in the most bottomless and thankless and fatal of sandbanks. There is no use or application or power of absorption or assimilation for these enormities, beloved Hendrik, anywhere on the whole surface of the practicable, or, as I should rather say, impracticable globe; and when you write to me that you are now lavishing time and money on a colossal ready-made City, I simply cover my head with my mantle and turn my face to the wall, and there, dearest Hendrik, just bitterly *weep* for you—just desperately and dismally and helplessly water that dim refuge with a salt flood. I have practically said these things to you before—though perhaps never in so dreadfully straight and sore a form as today; when this culmination of your madness, to the tune of five hundred millions of tons of weight, simply squeezes it out of me. For that, dearest boy, is the dread Delusion to warn you against—what is called in Medical Science MEGALOMANIA (look it up in the Dictionary!) in French *la folie des grandeurs*, the infatuated and disproportionate love and pursuit of, and attempt at, the Big, the Bigger, the Biggest, the Immensest Immensity, with all sense of proportion, application, relation and possibility madly *submerged*. What am I to say to you, gentle and dearest Hendrik, *but* these things, cruel as they may seem to you, when you write me (with so little *spelling* even—though that was always your wild grace!) that you are extemporizing a World-City from top to toe, and employing forty architects to see you through with it, etc.? How can I throw myself on your side to the extent of employing to back you a single letter of the Alphabet when you break to me anything so fantastic or out of relation to any reality of any kind in all the weary world??? The idea, my dear old friend, fills me with mere pitying dismay, the unutterable Waste of it all makes me retire into my room and lock the door to howl! Think of me as doing so, as howling for hours on end, and as not coming out till I hear from you that you have just gone straight out on to the Ripetta and chucked the total mass of your Paraphernalia, planned to that end, bravely over the parapet and well into the Tiber. As if, beloved boy, any use on all the mad earth can be found for a ready-made city, made-while-one-waits, as they say, and which is the more preposterous and the more delirious, the more elaborate and the more "complete" and the more magnificent you have made it. Cities are *living* organisms, that grow from within and by experience and piece by piece; they are not bought all hanging together, in *any* inspired studio anywhere whatsoever, and to attempt to plank one down on its area prepared, as even just merely projected, for use is to—well, it's to go forth into the deadly Desert and talk to the winds. Dearest Hendrik, don't ask me to *help* you so to talk—don't, don't, don't. I should be so playing to you the part of the falsest, fatallest friend. But do *this*—realise how dismally unspeakably much these cold hard, desperate words, withholding sympathy, cost your ever-affectionate, your terribly tender old friend

Henry James

1. Andersen had sent HJ his elaborate plan to create a "world city," for which he had enlisted the aid of many European notables. The plan was published in 1913 in two deluxe privately printed volumes (300 copies) titled *The World City,* designated as "a world centre of communications." It contained extensive architectural drawings of buildings and public squares, including the "Fountains of Life and of Immortality," on which Andersen had been working for some time.

173 · *To Hugh Walpole*

Ms Texas

The Reform Club
May 19th 1912

Beloved little Hugh.

Your letter greatly moves and regales me. Fully do I enter into your joy of sequestration, and your bliss of removal from this scene of heated turmoil and dusty despair, which, however, re-awaits you! Never mind; sink up to your neck into the brimming basin of nature and peace, and teach yourself—by which I mean let your grandmother teach you—

that with each revolving year you will need and make more piously these precious sacrifices to Pan and the Muses. History eternally repeats itself, and I remember well how in the old London years (of *my* old London—*this* isn't that one) I used to clutch at these chances of obscure flight and at the possession, less frustrated, of my soul, my senses and my hours. So keep it up; I miss you, little as I see you even when here (for I *feel* you more than I see you); but I surrender you at whatever cost to the beneficent powers. Therefore I rejoice in the getting on of your work—how splendidly copious your flow; and am much interested in what you tell me of your readings and your literary emotions. These latter indeed—or some of them, as you express them, I don't think I fully share. At least when you ask me if I don't feel Dostoieffsky's "mad jumble, that flings things down in a heap," nearer truth and beauty than the picking and composing that you instance in Stevenson, I reply with emphasis that I feel nothing of the sort, and that the older I grow and the more I *go* the more sacred to me do picking and composing become—though I naturally don't limit myself to Stevenson's *kind* of the same. Don't let anyone persuade you—there are plenty of ignorant and fatuous duffers to try to do it—that strenuous selection and comparison are not the very essence of art, and that Form *is* [not] substance to that degree that there is absolutely no substance without it. Form alone *takes*, and holds and preserves, substance—saves it from the welter of helpless verbiage that we swim in as in a sea of tasteless tepid pudding, and that makes one ashamed of an art capable of such degradations. Tolstoi and D. are fluid pudding, though not tasteless, because the amount of their own minds and souls in solution in the broth gives it savour and flavour, thanks to the strong, rank quality of their genius and their experience. But there are all sorts of things to be said of them, and in particular that we see how great a vice is their lack of composition, their defiance of economy and architecture, directly they are emulated and imitated; *then*, as subjects of emulation, models, they quite give themselves away. There is nothing so deplorable as a work of art with a *leak* in its interest; and there is no such leak of interest as through commonness of form. Its opposite, the *found* (because the sought-for) form is the absolute citadel and tabernacle of interest. But what a lecture I am reading you—though a very imperfect one—which you have drawn upon yourself (as moreover it was quite right you should). But no matter—I shall go for you again—as soon as I find you in a lone corner.

You ask for news of those I "see"; but remember that I see but one person to ninety-five that you do. A. Bennett I've never to this day beheld[1]—and certain *American* papers of his in *Harper,* of an inordinate platitude of journalistic cheapness, have in truth rather curtailed in me any such disposition. There he writes about what I *know,* and makes me ask myself whether his writing about what I *don't* know mayn't have, after all, that same limitation of value. Lucy Clifford gallantly flourishes—on all fine human and personal lines; Jocelyn P[ersse] continues to adorn a world that is apparently so easy for him. I lately dined and went to a play with him (*Rutherford and Co.,*[2] or whatever, very helpless, but more decent than anything else that's going); and he was, as ever, sympathy and fidelity incarnate. On the whole, however, I've had very little chance to talk of you. Little May Sinclair[3] drew me to her rather desolately vast blank Albemarle Club to tea—in a dim and dumb literary circle as of pale ink-and-water; but the high tide of blankness submerged us all. So blank may the naiads and Ladies of the ink-and-water stream become! I've called on the little Gräfin,[4] but missed her—unconsoledly—or call it inconsolably—as yet. From the great [prose] Minstrel of the Gallery (there's Form for you!) I've had a letter—but this is an instance that I must wait to impart to you at leisure: it has *such* a harmony with—everything else! Well, dearest Hugh, love me a little better (if you *can*) for this letter, for I am ever so fondly and faithfully yours

Henry James

1. Arnold Bennett (1867–1931), author of *The Old Wives' Tale* (1908) and *Clayhanger* (1910) as well as successful plays, and a prolific journalist who contributed to English and American journals articles on the arts and general comment. He was one of Pinker's clients, and HJ met him in Pinker's office in January 1913. See *The Journals of Arnold Bennett 1911–1921,* ed. Newman Flower (1932).
2. *Rutherford and Company,* a play by G. Sowerby.
3. May Sinclair (1865?–1946), a novelist.
4. Gräfin Arnim (d. 1941), the former Elizabeth Mary Beauchamp, Countess Arnim in her first marriage and later Countess Russell, whose amusing and successful novel *Elizabeth and Her German Garden* was published in 1898.

174 · *To Howard Sturgis*

Ms Harvard

Lamb House, Rye
August 9th 1912

Beloved Howard!

The Firebird[1] perches on my shoulder while I bend, all eagerly, to acknowledge your delightful letter—yet, luckily, not to the point of my having to deprive that beautiful record of a response as free as itself. She has been with me since last evening, and was to have remained till tomorrow, but within this afternoon the horoscope has not unnaturally shifted, and Frank Schuster and Claude Phillips[2] having been with us, from Folkestone, for a couple of hours, she moves off, as soon as we have had tea, to rejoin them there for the night—they have just dashed away in their own car—and I retreat upon my now forever inexpungable base, after wriggling out of every net cast to draw me into the onrush. She embarks tomorrow morning to all appearance—in order to arrive, at tea, at 5, with the Jacques Blanches[3] in Normandy—after which my comprehension sinks exhausted in her wake. She has held us, F.S., C.P. and I, spell-bound, this pair of hours, by her admirable talk. She never was more wound up and going, or more ready, it would appear, for new worlds to conquer. The only thing is that none at this rate will soon be left a lady who consumes worlds as you and I (*don't* even) consume apples, eating up one for her luncheon and one for her dinner. That is indeed, as your charmingly, your touchingly vivid letter so expresses, the terrible thing about (and *for*) a nature and a life in which a certain saving accommodation or gently economic bias seem able to play so small a part. She uses up everything and every one either by the extremity of strain or the extremity of neglect—by having too much to do with them (when not for *them* to do), or by being able to do nothing whatever, and passes on to scenes that blanch at her approach. She came over to us only the other day in order to help herself (and us!) through part of an embarrassing and unprovided summer, to put in a block of time that would bridge over her Season; but she has already left us in raggs (as they used to, and I inadvertently happen to, write it)* and tatters—we ground to powder, reduced to pulp, consumed utterly, and she with her summer practically still to somehow constitute. That is what fairly terrifies me for her future, possessed as I am, as to the art of life, with such intensely economic, saving, sparing, making-everyone-and-everything-go-as-far-as-possible instincts—doubtless in comparison a quite ignoble thrift. I feel as if I shouldn't know *where* I might be if I didn't somehow or other make every occasion serve—in *some* degree or other. Whereas our Firebird is like an extravagant dandy who sends thirty shirts to the wash where you and I (forgive, dear Howard, the collocation!) send one; or indeed even worse—since our Firebird dirties her days (pardon again the image!) at a rate that no laundry will stand; and in fact doesn't seem to believe in the washing, and still less in the ironing—though she does, rather inconsistently in the "mangling"!—of any of her material of life. Well, let us hope that the Divine Chemisier will always keep her supplied straight and to sufficiency with the intimate article in which he deals!—All thanks for your wishes and inquiries about my pectoral botherations. They will be better enough, I feel sure, when a sordid peace again reigns. All I want for that improvement is to be *let alone,* and not to feel myself far aloft in irresistible talons and under the flap of mighty wings—and about to be deposited on dizzy and alien peaks. "Take me *down*—and take me home!" you saw me having to cry that, too piteously, the other day to the inscrutable and incomparable Cook—rescuer as well as destroyer. I am really inditing these last remarks *after* our friend's departure; the after-dinner evening has now closed about me—and the sight of poor heroic Gross[4] (who had again, for the millionth time, polished off her packing and climbed to her forward perch, but with the light of near Folkestone and fresh disintegrations in her aged eye) has already become a pathetic memory. They are all—the Firebird, Frank S., Claude P., and their respective cars to cross from Folkestone together tomorrow, as I understand, Schuster and Phillips proceeding then by that means to a Strauss festival at Stuttgart. In a wonderful age—for the Firebirds, Claudes and Shoos [Schusters]—do we verily live! I have as much as I can do to live at my own very advanced one—and to that end must now get me to a belated bed; where you must take me for dreaming of you with all the devotion, dearest Howard, of your faithfullest

Henry James

*I shall recover my orthography, and other powers, only little by little.

P.S. *Please* destroy all this gross profanity!

1. Edith Wharton.

2. Claude Phillips (1846–1924) was keeper of the Wallace Collection. Frank Schuster (1840–1928) was a wealthy music lover, patron, and friend of composers and performers.

3. Jacques-Émile Blanche (1861–1942), a fashionable French painter, whose portrait of HJ is now in the National Portrait Gallery, Smithsonian Institution, Washington.

4. Mrs. Wharton's maid. Mrs. Wharton had come to Lamb House on August 8th and spent the night, proceeding on the 9th to Folkestone on her way to the Continent.

175 · To Edmund Gosse

Dictated Ts Congress

Lamb House, Rye
October 15*th* 1912

My dear Gosse.

Here I am at it again—for I can't not thank you for your two notes last night and this morning received. Your wife has all my tenderest sympathy in the matter of what the loss of her Brother cost her. Intimately will her feet have learnt to know these ways. So it goes on till we have no one left to lose—as I felt, with force, two summers ago, when I lost my two last Brothers within two months and became sole survivor of all my Father's house. I lay my hand very gently on our friend.

With your letter of last night came the Cornhill with the beautifully done little Swinburne chapter.[1] What a "grateful" subject, somehow, in every way, that gifted being—putting aside even, I mean, the value of his genius. He is grateful by one of those arbitrary values that dear G[eorge] M[eredith] for instance, doesn't positively command, in proportion to his intrinsic weight; and who can say quite why? Charming and vivid and authentic, at any rate, your picture of that occasion; to say nothing of your evocation, charged with so fine a Victorian melancholy, of Swinburne's time at Vichy with Leighton, Mrs. Sartoris and Richard Burton;[2] what a felicitous and enviable image they do make together—and what prodigious discourse must even more particularly have ensued when S. and B. sat up late together after the others! Distinct to me the memory of a Sunday afternoon at Flaubert's in the winter of '75–'76, when Maupassant, still *inédit*, but always "round," regaled me with a fantastic tale, irreproducible here, of the relations between two Englishmen, each other, and their monkey![3] A picture the details of which have faded for me, but not the lurid impression. Most deliciously Victorian that too—I bend over it all so yearningly; and to the effect of my hoping "ever so" that you are in conscious possession of material for a series of just such other chapters in illustration of S., each a separate fine flower for a vivid even if loose nosegay.

I'm much interested by your echo of Haldane's[4] remarks, or whatever, about G[eorge] M[eredith]. Only the difficulty is, of a truth, somehow, that *ces messieurs,* he and Morley and Maxse and [Leslie] Stephen,[5] and two or three others, Lady Ulrica included, really never knew much more where *they* were, on all the "aesthetic" ground, as one for convenience calls it, than the dear man himself did, or where *he* was; so that the whole history seems a record somehow (so far as "art and letters" are in question) of a certain absence of point on the part of every one concerned in it. Still, it abides with us, I think, that Meredith was an admirable spirit even if not an *entire* mind; he throws out, to my sense, splendid great moral and ethical, what he himself would call "spiritual," lights, and has again and again big strong whiffs of manly tone and clear judgment. The fantastic and the mannered in him were as nothing, I think, to the intimately sane and straight; just as the artist was nothing to the good citizen and the liberalised bourgeois. However, lead me not on! I thank you ever so kindly for the authenticity of your word about these beastly recurrences (of my disorder). I feel you floated in confidence on the deep tide of Philip [Gosse]'s experience and wisdom. Still, I *am* trying to keep mainly out of bed again (after forty-eight hours just renewedly spent in it). But on these terms you'll wish me back there—and I'm yours with no word more,

Henry James

1. Gosse's essay on Swinburne appeared in the October 1912 *Cornhill Magazine* and was reprinted in *Portraits and Sketches* (1912).

2. Frederick Lord Leighton, painter; Mrs. Adelaide Sartoris, sister of Fanny Kemble; Sir Richard Burton (1821–1890), Victorian swordsman, explorer, anthropologist.

3. Gosse replied on 16 October 1912: "The Monkey story . . . relates to a Page whom Swinburne or Powell (they are not distinguished in the story) brought to Etretat and who became jealous of a Monkey, which was also a member of the household, and how after a scene (oh! what a scene!) the Page hanged the Monkey outside the master's bedroom door, and then rushed out and drowned himself. Whereupon the master raised a marble monument not to the Page, but to the Monkey. Is this the little horror which you heard Maupas-

sant relate? Or was it the completely anodyne absurdity of Swinburne's having killed and roasted his own pet monkey as a feast for Maupassant? . . . I believe you to be the only person left who can give a first-hand report." Charteris, *Life and Letters of Sir Edmund Gosse,* 343.

4. Richard Burdon Viscount Haldane (1856–1928), lawyer, statesman, philosopher, Lord Chancellor (1912–1915).

5. John Morley, later Viscount, an author and statesman; Admiral Frederick Augustus Maxse (d. 1900), famous for his exploits in the Crimean War.

176 · To Mrs. William James

Dictated Ts Harvard

21 Carlyle Mansions, S.W.
April 1st [and 16th] 1913

Dearest Alice.

Today comes blessedly your letter of the 18th written after the receipt of my cable to you in answer to your preceding one of the 6th (after you had heard from Robert Allerton of my illness). You will have been reassured further—I mean beyond my cable—by a letter I lately despatched to Bill and Alice[1] conjointly, in which I told them of my good and continued improvement. I am going on very well, increasingly so—in spite of my having to reckon with so much chronic pectoral pain now so seated and settled, of the queer "falsely anginal" but none the less when it is bad, distressing order. It comes directly from no heart-trouble—for I haven't any—that is one element of mitigation of my consciousness of it—and it is more or less controllable by certain kinds of care: care above all as to what I eat, and above all drink (very little liquid), and care never to consent to hurry (in the *least*) or flurry or worry—care to sleep almost sitting, on a bed-rest— and care to move (walk, circulate) as much as I can while doing so very slowly and gently and *alone* (not talking at the same time). So I manage, and have got back to work, and can go about to some extent in the afternoon (to see friends) with the aid of the blest taxis of the low London tariff, the long strike in that business being over: though of course the whole thing deprives me of much sense of *margin.* I neither *ever* lunch out nor dine out—though I not infrequently dine, for change and ventilation, at the Club. *And* I shall get better, improve further still I pretty well believe—very possibly with some further control of the pectoral question: which meanwhile remains in abeyance (as regards any sharpness of it) during my hours of quietude, hours of deliberate movements only. Moreover too it is astonishing with how much pain one can with long practice learn constantly and not too defeatedly to live. Therefore, dearest Alice, don't think of this as too black a picture of my situation; it is so much brighter a one than I have thought at certain bad moments and seasons of the past that I should probably ever be able to paint. The mere power to work in such measure as I can is an infinite help to a better consciousness—and though so impaired compared to what it used to be it tends to *grow,* distinctly—which by itself proves that I have *some* firm ground under my feet. And I repeat to satiety that my conditions *here* are admirably helpful and favouring. (Now that Kidd is back from so much absence at Rye—her distracted mother having come to an end in my cottage—there is no hitch in our household order or ease, and the value of the good little apartment shines out brightly again.)

You can see, can't you? how strange and desperate it would be to "chuck" everything up, Lamb House, servants, Miss Bosanquet, *this* newly acquired and prized resource, to come over, by a formidable and expensive journey, to spend a summer in the (at best) to me torrid and (the inmost inside of 95 apart) utterly arid and vacuous Cambridge. Dearest Alice, I could come back to America (could be carried back on a stretcher) to *die*—but never, never to live. To say how the question affects me is dreadfully difficult because of its appearing so to make light of you and the children—but when I think of how little Boston and Cambridge were of old ever *my* affair, or anything but an accident, for me, of the parental life there to which I occasionally and painfully and losingly sacrificed, I have a superstitious terror of seeing them at the end of time again stretch out strange inevitable tentacles to draw me back and destroy me. And then I could never either make or afford the journey (I have no margin at all for *that* degree of effort—especially with the more and more, the eternally babyish Burgess to look after, whose powers—apart from his virtuous attachment—to take care of me is *nil,* compared with my perpetual need of taking care of *him.* He gets the wages of a good valet (here) and is incapable of any of the responsibilities.) But you will have understood too well—without my saying more—how little I can dream of any *déplacement* now—especially for the sake of a milieu in which you and Peg and Bill and

Alice and Aleck would be burdened with the charge of making up *all* my life. Not one grain of it should I be able to pick up outside of you. I haven't a single other tie in America that means ten cents to me—*really* means it. You see my capital—yielding all my income, intellectual, social, associational, on the old investment of so many years—my capital is *here,* and to let it all slide would be simply to become bankrupt. Oh if you only, on the other hand, you and Peg and Aleck, *could* walk beside my bathchair down this brave Thames-side I would get back into it again (it was some three weeks ago dismissed), and half live there for the sake of your company. I have a kind of sense that you would be able to live rather pleasantly near me here—if you could once get planted. But of course I on my side understand all your present complications.

April 16*th!* It's really too dismal, dearest Alice, that, breaking off the above at the hour I *had* to, I have been unable to go on with it for so many days. It's now more than a fortnight old still, though my check was owing to my having of a sudden, just as I rested my pen, to drop perversely into a less decent phase (than I reported to you at the moment of writing) and have had with some difficulty to wriggle up again, I am now none the less able to send you no too bad news. I have wriggled up a good deal, and still keep believing in my capacity to wriggle up in general.—Suffice it for the moment that I just couldn't, for the time, drive the pen myself—when I am "bad" I feel too demoralised, too debilitated, for this; and it doesn't at all do for me then to push against the grain. Don't feel, all the same, that if I resort this morning to the present help, it is because I am *not* feeling differently—for I really am in an easier way again (I mean of course specifically and "anginally" speaking) and the circumstances of the hour a good deal explain my proceeding thus. I had yesterday a Birthday, an extraordinary, prodigious, portentous, quite public Birthday, of all things in the world, and it has piled up acknowledgments and supposedly delightful complications and arrears at such a rate all round me, that in short, Miss Bosanquet being here, I today at least throw myself upon her aid for getting on correspondentially—instead of attending to my proper work, which has, however, kept going none so badly in spite of my last poor fortnight. I will tell you in a moment of my signal honours, but want to mention first that your good note written on receipt of *A Small Boy* has meanwhile come to me and by the perfect fulness of its appreciation gave me the greatest joy. There are several things I want to say to you about the shape and substance of the book—and I will yet; only now I want to get this off absolutely by today's American post, and tell you about the Honours, a little, before you wonder, in comparative darkness, over whatever there may have been in the American papers that you will perhaps have seen; though in two or three of the New York ones more possibly than in the Boston. I send you by this post a copy of yesterday's *Times* and one of the *Pall Mall Gazette*—the two or three passages in which, together, I suppose to have been more probably than not reproduced in N.Y. But I send you above all a copy of the really very beautiful Letter (expressed with singular grace and felicity and sobriety, I think, and from the hand of dear delightful Percy Lubbock), ushering in the quite wonderful array of signatures (as I can't but feel) of my testifying and "presenting" friends: a list of which you perhaps can't quite measure the very charming and distinguished and "brilliant" character without knowing your London better. What I wish I *could* send you is the huge harvest of exquisite, of splendid sheaves of flowers that converted a goodly table in this room, by the time yesterday was waning, into such a blooming garden of complimentary colour as I never dreamed I should, on my own modest premises, almost bewilderedly stare at, sniff at, all but quite "cry" at. I think I must and shall in fact compass sending you a photograph of the still more glittering tribute dropped upon me—a really splendid "golden bowl," of the highest interest and most perfect taste, which would, in the extremity of its elegance, be too proudly false a note amid my small belongings here if it didn't happen to fit, or to sit, rather, with perfect grace and comfort, on the middle of my chimney-piece, where the rather good glass and some other happy accidents of tone most fortunately consort with it. It is a very brave and artistic (exact) reproduction of a piece of old Charles II plate; the bowl or cup having handles and a particularly charming lid or cover, and standing on an ample round tray or salver; the whole being wrought in solid silver-gilt and covered over with quaint incised little figures of a (in the taste of the time) Chinese intention. In short it's a very beautiful and honourable thing indeed; and if the said American movement that Bill and Harry and I had a couple of weeks ago so flurriedly to inter-cable about, could but have proposed itself in, and resolved itself into, some such aspect as that of a not too expensive presentation object or "artistic memento," I could have faced *that* music with the very best grace I could muster. That is the only thing I *consented* to face here. Against the *giving to me* of the Portrait, presumably by Sargent, if I do succeed in being able to sit for it, I have absolutely and successfully protested. The possession, the attribution or ownership of it, I have insisted, shall be only their matter that of the subscribing friends (whose individual subscriptions were kept down, by the scheme, to the very lowest figure, most of them consisting but of a sovereign and a half-sovereign); my participation being that of the sitter alone, and not a bit of the acquisitor. And they must first catch their hare; the portrait must first come into being. Sargent, most beautifully, as a member of the Committee, tried to insist on doing it for nothing; but had to yield to the representation, of course, that if this were allowed the work would become practically *his* present altogether, and not that of the Friends. "Where," they naturally ask, "should *we* then come in?"—So he agreed, with the one condition, that, when I should have sat, he was to be free to tear the canvas straight up if he himself doesn't like the result. This is a part of the matter which will greatly appeal to Bill—appeal perhaps more than any other part; and at any rate, you see, I may perhaps after all never figure—! I tell you all this partly because I kind of want to have it clear that what I couldn't dream of accepting from Boston and New York was the crude raked-together *offrand* of a lump of money.[2] I have had a good letter from Bill since the hour of our cables, and his mention of two or three of the names, alone, connected with the question in Boston, have made me quite gasp with dismay. It's invidious to specify, but the idea of being beholden to the rummaged pockets of Sturgis Bigelow and of Barrett Wendell,[3] for instance, would have been simply intolerable to me. If I don't feel that way about all these good people here, I can only say that somehow I *don't*—on the basis that is, of the "piece of plate." On the other hand I should thoroughly have felt so had their approach been, like the projected one we got wind of, with the crude money-lump! *And,* moreover, I haven't, you see, anything like any such number of real personal acquaintances, of individual friendly *relations,* in N.Y. and Boston as I have roundabout me here. Counting my nearest and dearest out (that is all my nearest relatives) there are not more than half a dozen persons in either city whom I should in the least care to look at as subjects of such an appeal, or to "take" anything from. The sad part of the matter of the other day is that I fear I have incurred the grave reprobation and almost resentment of the friend[4] (on this side of the world) at whose instance you heard of the attempt's being launched. That is a sorry result—though I hasten to add a "probably" but short-lived one. What is infelicitous is that she purposely kept out of the "movement" here, in order to associate herself with the American one; but now, as it happens, the American one is, thank goodness, squashed—so, though really one of the best friends I have in the world, she fails to figure in either. However, I am drenching you with this—though I shall have probably done no more than sate your just curiosity and sympathy. I am hoping now each day for a happy echo of Otis Place[5]—and supposing it, perhaps mistakenly, a little overdue. Otis Place, at any rate, has my perpetual fond thought—and the echo will happily come! I am sending Harry a copy of the Letter too—but do send him on this as well. You see there *must* be good life in me still when I can gabble so hard. The Book[6] appears to be really most hand-somely received hereabouts. It is being treated in fact with the very highest consideration. I hope it is viewed a little in some such man-nerly light roundabout yourselves, but I really call for no "notices" whatever. I don't in the least want 'em. What I *do* want is to person-ally and firmly and intimately encircle Peg and Aleck and their Mother and squeeze them as hard together as is compatible with squeezing them so tenderly! With this *tide* of gabble you will surely feel that I shall soon be at you again. And so I shall! Yours, dearest Alice, and dearest all, ever so and ever so!

Henry James

P.S. I have just heard from Alice Edgar,[7] Wilky's Alice, that she dashes out to these parts, London and Paris, for a very few weeks only (devoted mainly to Paris) and with a couple of "lady friends" (which expression, to do her justice, she doesn't use). But she writes me very sweetly and nicely, and I shall be very glad to see her and to do for her the very limited whatever that my circumstances of every kind admit of. I really want to know her—for the poor Wilky-ghost's sake.

1. William (Billy) James, WJ's second son, and his wife, the former Alice Runnells. Robert Allerton, an art collector, was a friend of Billy's wife.

2. Edith Wharton and her circle solicited a gift of money for HJ in the United States in the hope that he would invest it in an automobile, then still a high luxury. This gift was vetoed by HJ.

3. William Sturgis Bigelow (1850–1926), a cousin of Mrs. Henry Adams, who had embraced Mahayana Buddhism, and Barrett Wendell, professor of English at Harvard, of whose writings (and apparently personality) HJ was critical.

4. Probably Mrs. Wharton.

5. Where Billy James and his bride were living.

6. *A Small Boy and Others.*

7. Alice Edgar (b. 1875), daughter of HJ's younger brother Garth Wilkinson (Wilky) James. She married David Alexander Edgar, a Canadian, in 1910.

177 · To Bruce Richmond

Ts Lubbock

21 Carlyle Mansions, Cheyne Walk, S.W.

Wednesday A.M. [4 June 1913]

My dear Bruce!

I have done it *tant bien que mal*—though feeling it thereby bleeds.[1] But it's a bloody trade. I don't quite see the lower numeral consort with the II at the head. Kindly notice.

H.J.

1. For Richmond (1871–1964), editor of the *Times Literary Supplement*, HJ had written a review of Emile Faguet's *Balzac,* and Richmond had asked him to cut it. HJ reprinted it in full in *Notes on Novelists* (1914).

178 · To Hugh Walpole

Ms Texas

Lamb House, Rye

August 21*st* 1913

Belovedest Hugh.

It's a proof of your poor old infatuated friend's general and particular difficulties that a couple of days, rather than a couple of hours, have elapsed, and that he has had to let them do so, since your dear letter came to bless him. But here he is with you now, though too late at night—he has had to sink to slumber awhile since dinner; and he hardly knows how to put it strongly enough that he rejoices even across this dire gulf of space in your company and conversation. You give him, it would seem, a jolly good account of yourself, and he fairly gloats over the picture. Beautiful must be your Cornish land and your Cornish sea, idyllic your Cornish setting, this flattering, this wonderful summer, and ours here doubtless may claim but a modest place beside it all. Yet as you have with you your Mother and Sister, which I am delighted to hear and whom I gratefully bless, so I can match them with my nephew and niece[1] (the former with me alas indeed but for these ten or twelve days), who are an extreme benediction to me. My niece, a charming and interesting young person and *most* conversable, stays, I hope, through the greater part of September, and I even curse that necessary limit—when she returns to America. Cultivate with me, darlingest Hugh, the natural affections, so far as you are lucky enough to have matter for them. I mean don't wait till you are eighty to do so—though indeed *I* haven't waited, but have made the most of them from far back. I like exceedingly to hear that your work has got so bravely on, and envy you that sovereign consciousness. When it's finished—well, when it's finished let some of those sweet young people the *bons amis* (yours) come to me for the small change of remark that I gathered from you the other day (you were adorable about it) they have more than once chinked in your ear as from my poor old pocket, and they will see, *you* will see, in what coin I shall have paid them. I too am working with a certain shrunken regularity—when not made to lapse and stumble by circumstances (damnably physical) beyond my control. These circumstances tend to come, on the whole (thanks to a great power of patience in my ancient organism), rather *more* within my management than for a good while back; but to live with a bad and chronic anginal demon preying on one's vitals takes a great deal of doing. However, I didn't mean to write you of that side of the picture (save that it's a large part of that same), and only glance that way to make sure of your tenderness even when I may seem to you backward and blank. It isn't to exploit your compassion—it's only to be able to feel that I am not without your fond understanding: so far as your blooming youth (*there's* the crack in the fiddle-case!) *can* fondly understand my so otherwise-conditioned age. However, there's always understanding enough when there's affection enough, and you touch me almost to tears when you tell me how I touched the springs of yours that last time in London. I remember immensely wanting to. I gather that that planned and promised visit of dear Jocelyn P[ersse]'s hasn't taken place for you (from your not naming it); it's a Jocelyn P. so whirlable into space at any incalculable moment that no want of correspondence between the bright sketch and the vague sequel is ever of a nature to surprise. And the bright sketches are so truly genial, and even the dim vaguenesses without the invidious sting. "We'll see him again, we'll see him again!" as the old Jacobite song says of bonny Prince Charlie. Perhaps I shall achieve seeing him here in the course of the autumn—and perhaps, oh be-loved Hugh, *you* will achieve, for my benefit, a like—or more likely—snatch of pilgrimage. My desire is to stay on here as late into the autumn as may consort with my condition—I dream of sticking on through November even if possible: Cheyne Walk and the black-barged yellow river will be the more agreeable to me when I get back to them. I make out that you will then be in London again—I mean *by* November, though such a black gulf of time intervenes; and then of course I may look to you to come down to me for a couple of days. It will be the lowest kind of "jinks"—so halting is my pace; yet we shall somehow make it serve. Don't say to me, by the way, apropos of jinks—the "high" kind that you speak of having so wallowed in previ-ous to leaving town—that I ever challenge you as to *why* you wallow, or splash or plunge, or dizzily and sublimely soar (into the jinks ele-ment), or whatever you may call it: as if I ever remarked on anything but the absolute inevitability of it for you at your age and with your natural curiosities, as it were, and passions. It's good healthy exercise, when it comes but in bouts and brief convulsions, and it's always a kind of thing that it's good, and considerably final, to *have* done. We must know, as much as possible, in our beautiful art, yours and mine, what we are talking about—and the only way to know is to have lived and loved and cursed and floundered and enjoyed and suffered. I think I don't regret a single "excess" of my responsive youth—I only regret, in my chilled age, certain occasions and possibilities I *didn't* embrace. Bad doctrine to impart to a young idiot or a duffer; but in place for a young friend (pressed to my heart), with a fund of nobler passion, the preserving, the defying, the dedicating, and which always has the last word; the young friend who can dip and shake off and go his straight way again when it's time. But we'll talk of all this—it's abominably late. Who is D. H. Lawrence,[2] who, you think, would interest me? Send him and his book along—by which I simply mean Inoculate me, at your convenience (don't address me the volume); so far as I can be inoculated. I always *try* to let anything of the kind "take." Last year, you remember, a couple of improbabilities (as to "taking") did worm a little into the fortress. (Gilbert Cannan[3] was one.) I have been reading over Tolstoi's interminable *Peace and War* and am struck with the fact that I now protest as much as I admire.[4] He doesn't *do* to read over, and that exactly is the answer to those who idiotically proclaim the impunity of such formless shape, such flopping looseness and such a denial of composition, selection and style. He has a mighty fund of life, but the *waste,* and the ugliness and vice of waste, the vice of a not finer *doing,* are sickening. For me he but makes "composition" throne, by contrast, in effulgent lustre!

Ever your fondest of the fond,
H.J.

1. HJ's niece Peggy and her youngest brother Aleck were staying at Lamb House.
2. D. H. Lawrence (1885–1930) had just published *Sons and Lovers.*
3. Gilbert Cannan (1884–1955), a novelist.
4. See Letter 173.

179 · To Fanny Prothero and Stark Young

Ms *Tintner*

Lamb House, Rye
September 14*th* 1913

This, please, for the delightful young man from Texas,[1] who shows such excellent dispositions. I only want to meet him half way, and I hope very much he won't think I don't when I tell him that the following indications as to five of my productions (splendid number—I glory in the tribute of his appetite!) are all on the basis of the Scribners' (or Macmillans') collective and revised and prefaced Edition of my things, or that if he is not minded somehow to obtain access to *that* form of them, ignoring any other, he forfeits half or much more than half, my confidence. So I thus amicably beseech him—! I suggest to him as alternatives these two slightly differing lists.

1   Roderick Hudson
2   The Portrait of a Lady
3   The Princess Casamassima
4   The Wings of a Dove
5   The Golden Bowl.

1   The American
2   The Tragic Muse
3   The Wings of a Dove
4   The Ambassadors
5   The Golden Bowl.

The second list is, as it were, the more "advanced." And when it comes to the Shorter Tales the question is more difficult (for characteristic selection) and demands separate treatment. Come to me about that, dear Young Man from Texas, later on—you shall have your little tarts when you have eaten your beef and potatoes. Meanwhile receive this from our admirable friend Mrs. Prothero.

Henry James

1. Stark Young (1881–1963), later drama critic of the *New Republic*. By the end of the letter HJ addresses Young directly.

180 · To Hugh Walpole

Ms Texas

21 Carlyle Mansions, S.W.
January 6*th* 1914

Darlingest and delightfullest old Hugh!

There you are—and what else is it I hinted at? but that Edinburgh should, in your writing to me, have moved you to expression and not simply to telling me that your disgust at it moved you to none.[1] Your letter this A.M. received is none other than a portion of the letter that I expressed my preference for over the mere statement of a no-letter—expressed it, that is, by a personal squeeze, so to speak, of such supreme tenderness of intentions that your feeling in it a "reproach" prompts me to declare myself most reproachful then when I am exactly most—well, I'll call it single heartedly affectionate. May you never suffer from harsher usage than these sentiments of mine assault you withal. I delight in your outbreak against the singular gift for irritation possessed by the race that surrounds you—you see it's a reaction—*the* reaction—of which I invited you to give me the benefit, and now that you have given me that I thank you for it ever so kindly. I could have done even with more detail—as when you say "*Such* parties!" I want so to hear exactly what parties they are. When you refer to their "immorality on stone floors," and with prayerbooks in their hands so long as the exigencies of the situation permit of the manual retention of the sacred volumes, I do so want the picture developed and the proceedings authenticated. But I feel with you about the whole impression! It *is*, no doubt, a damnably graceless people when you're up against them as in this grim time, and one is the more exasperated by them somehow from their being in general so damnably successful and well doing. Well, *I've* been among them for the last time—never, never again!

I'm awfully amused by your "amazement" at my being struck with C. Mackenzie's novel[2]—and can only say that I have been *so* struck, and seemed to know *why*, all along, this was the case. He has a large imperfection, I think, in his remarkable inability to *select*, his need to keep putting it all down and down and down, whatever it is and however it comes, his general irresponsibility as to the reasons and connections and relations—relations to the whole and to other aspects of the story—of the things he does. But he seems to me *to do the things* with extraordinary, or at least with the most unusual, reality and truth and salience, with a singular possession of the schoolboy consciousness and character, a singular saturation with the whole sense of them and power to develop them and carry them far. He has energy and sensibility and humour and imagination in all that exhibition, I think, and he has what is so rare in all the crew in general, a sense of style and a gift for it which lapses at times in his culpable *longueurs* and promiscuities, but which frequently picks itself up with really almost admirable art and instinct. Thanks to this, some of his episodes—and he has so many—are so *done*. Isn't this so—and isn't the force and the skill of him, and the evocation of the figure and scene and sound again and again of an energy truly commendable? You will tell me later on—and it will be very interesting to talk of him; for you will have lights that I don't possess to throw. And meantime I don't think "theatrical" describes him, though he's peculiarly interesting, to my sense, as coming from the third rate theatre-nest he does. However, all this will keep, and you must slate him for all he's (or isn't) worth, to me— or all you are—if you feel me too wrong. I mean to read *Carnival* if I can. I have been struck enough for that! Have patience with me, meanwhile—and believe in all my sympathy with your present ordeal. Think of me as hanging about you in it from afar—as none of your standers-off dream of the sense of and as ever, dearest boy, your all faithfullest old

H.J.

1. Walpole had just visited Edinburgh (where his father was Anglican Bishop) and had made derogatory remarks to HJ about John Gray (1866–1934), a poet and a friend of Oscar Wilde's, about whom an unconfirmed rumor existed that he was the original of Dorian Gray. Gray was an ordained priest with a diocese in Edinburgh.

2. Compton Mackenzie (1883–1972) had published his first novel, *Carnival*, in 1912 and was writing *Sinister Street*. He was the son of HJ's actor friends Edward Compton and Virginia Bateman, who had produced *The American* in 1890.

181 · *To Edith Wharton*

Ms Yale

21 Carlyle Mansions, S.W.
February 25*th* 1914

Dearest Edith,

The nearest I have come to receipt or possession of the interesting volumes you have so generously in mind is to have had *Bernstein's* assurance, when I met him here some time since, that *he* would give himself the delight of sending me the Proust production, which he learned from me that I hadn't seen.[1] I tried to dissuade him from this excess, but nothing would serve—he was too yearningly bent upon it, and we parted with his asseveration that I might absolutely count on this tribute both to poor Proust's charms and to my own. But *depuis lors*—! he has evidently been less *en train* than he was so good as to find *me*. So that I shall indeed be "very pleased" to receive the *Swann* and the *Vie et l'Amour*[2] from you at your entire convenience. It is indeed beautiful of you to think of these little deeds of kindness, little words of love (or is it the other way round?). What I want above all to thank you for, however, is your so brave backing in the matter of my disgarnished gums. That I am doing right is already unmistakeable. It won't make me "well"; nothing will do that, nor do I complain of the muffled miracle; but it will make me mind less being ill—in short it will make me better. As I say, it has already done so, even with my sacrifice for the present imperfect—for I am "keeping on" no less than eight pure pearls, in front seats, till I can deal with them in some less exposed and exposing conditions. Meanwhile tons of implanted and domesticated gold etc. (one's caps and crowns and bridges being *most* anathema to Des Vœux,[3] who regards them as so much installed metallic poison) have, with everything they fondly clung to, been, less visibly, eradicated; and it is enough, as I say, to have made a marked difference in my felt state. That is the point, for the time—and I spare you further details. I greatly rejoice to think that Percy [Lubbock] is with you. I understand but well the impulse that moved him—and it's so interesting to me that Vienna has sung its song. I like to hear of the limits of joys (the Vienna joy) that I haven't had. I shall perhaps even hear of those of the Algerian joy[4]—and then I shall *gloat!* Yet I want inconsistently to hurry up Coopersale.[5] All love of course to Percy.

Yours *de cœur*
Henry James

1. Henry Bernstein (1876–1953) was a French dramatist.
2. Mrs. Wharton promptly sent HJ the two volumes of *Du Côté de chez Swann* recently published by Marcel Proust and also *Vie et l'amour* by Abel Bonnard (1883–1968). On 2 March 1914 HJ wrote her "I shan't yet for a little fall upon Proust and Co." He added that "perusal" of current fiction had become impossible to him. These are the only references to Proust in HJ's letters. Mrs. Wharton in *A Backward Glance* (1934) writes that James "seized" on the Proust "and devoured it in a passion of curiosity and admiration." But James was having his teeth extracted at this time, and his general ill-health and the coming of the war suggest that he may not have had the opportunity to read the opening sections of what would become Proust's multivolumed novel.
3. Dr. Des Vœux was now HJ's attending physician.
4. Mrs. Wharton had announced her impending journey to North Africa.
5. Mrs. Wharton was attempting to purchase a handsome villa, Coopersale, near Mrs. Charles Hunter's Hill Hall. The negotiations in due course collapsed.

182 · To Henry Adams

Ms Mass. Historical

21 Carlyle Mansions, S.W.
March 21st 1914

My dear Henry.

I have your melancholy outpouring of the 7th,[1] and I know not how better to acknowledge it than by the full recognition of its unmitigated blackness. *Of course* we are lone survivors, of course the past that was our lives is at the bottom of an abyss—if the abyss *has* any bottom; of course too there's no use talking unless one particularly *wants* to. But the purpose, almost, of my printed divagations was to show you that one *can,* strange to say, still want to—or at least can behave as if one did. Behold me therefore so behaving—and apparently capable of continuing to do so. I still find my consciousness interesting—under *cultivation* of the interest. Cultivate it *with* me, dear Henry—that's what I hoped to make you do, to cultivate yours for all that it has in common with mine. *Why* mine yields an interest I don't know that I can tell you, but I don't challenge or quarrel with it—I encourage it with a ghastly grin. You see I still, in presence of life (or of what you deny to be such), have reactions—as many as possible—and the book I sent you is a proof of them. It's, I suppose, because I am that queer monster the artist, an obstinate finality, an inexhaustible sensibility. Hence the reactions—appearances, memories, many things go on playing upon it with consequences that I note and "enjoy" (grim word!) noting. It all takes doing—and I *do.* I believe I shall do yet again—it is still an act of life. But you perform them still yourself—and I don't know what keeps me from calling your letter a charming one! There we are, and it's a blessing that you understand—I admit indeed alone—

Your all-faithful
Henry James

1. HJ sent *Notes of a Son and Brother* to Adams, who said the book "reduced me to a pulp." Adams wrote to his friend Mrs. Cameron: "Poor Henry James thinks it all real and actually still lives in that dreary, stuffy Newport and Cambridge with papa James and Charles Eliot Norton."

183 · *To Rhoda Broughton*

Ms Chester

Lamb House, Rye
August 10th 1914

Dearest Rhoda!

It is not a figure of speech but an absolute truth that even if I had not received your very welcome and sympathetic script I should be writing to you this day. I have been on the very edge of it for the last week—so had my desire to make you a sign of remembrance and participation come to a head; and verily I must—or may—almost claim that this all but "crosses" with your own. The only blot on our unanimity is that it's such an unanimity of woe. Black and hideous to me is the tragedy that gathers, and I'm sick beyond cure to have lived on to see it. You and I, the ornaments of our generation, should have been spared this wreck of our belief that through the long years we had seen civilization grow and the worst become impossible. The tide that bore us along was then all the while moving to *this* as its grand Niagara— yet what a blessing we didn't know it. It seems to me to *undo* everything, everything that was ours, in the most horrible retroactive way— but I avert my face from the monstrous scene!—you can hate it and blush for it without my help; we can each do enough of that by ourselves. The country and the season here are of a beauty of peace, and loveliness of light, and summer grace, that make it inconceivable that just across the Channel, blue as *paint* today, the fields of France and Belgium are being, or about to be, given up to unthinkable massacre and misery. One is ashamed to admire, to enjoy, to take any of the normal pleasure, and the huge shining indifference of Nature strikes a chill to the heart and makes me wonder of what abysmal mystery, or villainy indeed, such a cruel smile is the expression. In the midst of it all at any rate we walked, this strange Sunday afternoon (9th), my niece Peggy, her youngest brother and I, about a mile out, across the blessed grass mostly, to see and have tea with a genial and garrulous old Irish friend (Lady Mathew, who has a house here for the summer), and came away an hour later bearing with us a substantial green volume, by an admirable eminent hand, which our hostess had just read with such a glow of satisfaction that she overflowed into easy lending.[1] I congratulate you on having securely put it forth before this great distraction was upon us—for I am utterly pulled up in the midst of a rival effort by finding that my job won't at all consent to be done in the face of it. The picture of little private adventures simply fades away before the great public. I take great comfort in the presence of my two young companions, and above all in having caught my nephew by the coat-tail only *just* as he was blandly starting for the continent on August 1st. Poor Margaret Payson[2] is trapped somewhere in France—she *having* then started, though not for Germany, blessedly; and we remain wholly without news of her. Peggy and Aleck have four or five near maternal relatives lost in Germany—though as Americans they may fare a little less dreadfully there than if they were English. And I have numerous friends—we all have, haven't we?—inaccessible and unimaginable there; it's becoming an anguish to think of them. Nevertheless I do believe that we shall be again gathered into a blessed little Chelsea drawing-room—it will be like the reopening of the salons, so irrepressibly, after the French revolution. So only sit tight, and invoke your heroic soul, dear Rhoda, and believe me more than ever all-faithfully yours,

Henry James

1. Rhoda Broughton's novel was *Concerning a Vow* (1914).
2. Peggy James's American friend, with whom she had shared lodgings in London.

184 · *To Edith Wharton*

Ms Yale

Lamb House, Rye
August 19*th* 1914

Dearest Edith.

Your letter of the 15th has come—and may this reach you as directly, though it probably won't. No I won't make it long—the less that the irrelevance of all remark, the utter extinction of everything, in face of these immensities, leaves me as "all silent and all damned" as you express that it leaves *you.* I find it the strangest state to have lived on and on for—and yet—with its wholesale annihilation, it *is* somehow life. Mary Cadwal[ader] is admirably here—interesting and vivid and helpful to the last degree, and Bessie Lodge and her boy had the heavenly beauty, this afternoon, to come down from town (by train *s'entend*) *rien que* for tea—she even sneakingly went first to the inn for luncheon—and was off again by 5.30, nobly kind and beautiful and good. (She sails in the *Olympic* with her aunt on Saturday.) Mary C. gives me a sense of the interest of your Paris which makes me understand how it must attach you—how it would attach me in your place. Infinitely thrilling and touching such a community with the so all-round incomparable nation. I feel on my side an immense community here, where the tension is proportionate to the degree to which we feel engaged—in other words up to the chin, up to the eyes—if necessary. Life goes on after a fashion, but I find it a nightmare from which there is no waking save by sleep. I *go* to sleep, as if I were dogtired with action—yet feel like the chilled *vieillards* in the old epics, infirm and helpless at home with the women, while the plains are ringing with battle. The season here is monotonously magnificent—and we look inconceivably off across the blue channel, the lovely rim, toward the nearness of the horrors that are in perpetration just beyond. I can't begin to think of exerting any pressure upon you in relation to coming to the "enjoyment" of your tenancy—your situation so baffles and beats me that I but stare at it with a lack of lustre! At the thought of *seeing* you, however, my eye does feel itself kindle—though I dread indeed to see you at Stocks[1] but restlessly chafe. I manage myself to try to "work"—even if I *had*, after experiment, to give up trying to make certain little *fantoches* and their private adventure *tenir debout. They* are laid by on the shelf—the private adventure so utterly blighted by the public; but I have got hold of something else, and I find the effort of concentration to some extent an antidote.[2] Apropos of which I thank you immensely for D'Annunzio's frenchified ode[3]— a wondrous and magnificent thing in its kind, even if running too much—for my "taste"—to the vituperative and the execrational. The Latin Renascence mustn't be too much for and by *that*—for which its facile resources are so great. However, the thing is splendid and makes one wonder at the strangeness of the genius of Poesy—that it should be able to pour through that particular rotten little skunk! What's magnificent to me in the French themselves at this moment is their lapse of expression. I hear from Howard [Sturgis][4]—flanked by Mrs. Maquay and more and more uplifted about William; and I've had some beautiful correspondence with White.[5] Try to want *greatly* to come to him—enough greatly to do it, and then I shall want enormously to urge you. I put here in fact a huge store of urgence—all ready for you the moment you can profitably use it. The *conditions* of coming seem now steadily to improve—though a pair of American friends of ours crossed nine days ago (or upward) via Dieppe—having come *comfortably* from Paris thither and slept there—in a very tranquil, even if elongated, manner. May this not fail of you! I am your all-faithfully tender and true old

H.J.

P.S. So many, and *such* things to Walter [Berry] and to Morton [Fullerton].

1. The country home of the Humphry Wards.
2. Probably HJ's notes for the unfinished novel *The Sense of the Past*.
3. Gabriele D'Annunzio (1863–1938), Italian poet and novelist, had been living in France since 1910, occupied with cinema and plays.
4. See Letter 171.
5. Probably Henry White at the American Embassy in London.

185 · To Edward Marsh

Ms Berg

21 Carlyle Mansions, S.W.
April 24*th* 1915

My dear dear Eddie.

This is too horrible and heart-breaking.[1] If there was a stupid and hideous disfigurement of life and outrage to beauty left for our awful conditions to perpetrate, those things have been now supremely achieved, and no other brutal blow in the private sphere can better them for making one just stare through one's tears. One had thought of one's self as advised and stiffened as to what was possible, but one sees (or at least I feel) how sneakingly one had clung to the idea of the happy, the favouring, hazard, the dream of what still might be for the days to come. But why do I speak of my pang, as if it had a right to breathe in presence of yours?—which makes me think of you with the last tenderness of understanding. I value extraordinarily having seen him here in the happiest way (in Downing Street, etc.) two or three times before he left England, and I measure by that the treasure of your own memories and the dead weight of your own loss. What a price and a refinement of beauty and poetry it gives to those splendid sonnets—which will enrich our whole collective consciousness. We must speak further and better, but meanwhile all my impulse is to tell you to en-tertain the pang and taste the bitterness for all they are "worth"—to know to the fullest extent what has happened to you and not miss one of the hard ways in which it will come home. You won't have again any relation of that beauty, won't know again that mixture of the ele-ments that made him. And he was the breathing beneficent man—and now turned to this! But there's something to keep too—his legend and his image will hold. Believe by how much I am, my dear Eddie, more than ever yours,

Henry James

1. The death of Rupert Brooke on a French hospital ship in the Aegean Sea on 23 April 1915.

186 · *To Burgess Noakes*

Dictated Ts Harvard

21, Carlyle Mansions, S.W.

June 13th 1915

My Dear Burgess.

If I haven't worried you with letters it has been because I didn't want you to have anything on your mind to answer, and because I also knew that Minnie has two or three times written to you. This, at present, isn't to press you for any sort of answer at all, but only to tell you that we hope you keep on doing well and perhaps begin to see some glimpse of your being allowed to leave for a convalescent furlough here. If that comes in sight you will of course let us know—and meantime I hope you are as happy as you can be in such rather hampered conditions. If your deafness[1] tends to diminish now that you are out of those hideous sounds we shall be very glad to hear it, and I feel convinced, at any rate, that it will gradually improve: I have seen, all winter, too many men, in hospital, slowly throw it off, even when it has been bad at first; not to have faith in your doing so. Meanwhile we go on as conveniently here as people can hope to do at this terrible time, and are thinking of getting to Rye by some sort of date in the early part of July. I have just lent the house again for a couple of weeks (from toward the end of next), to an old friend and her invalid officer son, for whom it will be a good place of convalescence; but that will probably not extend beyond a dozen days or so. Otherwise we go on, and are having a wonderful beginning of summer, with week after week of fine weather. May it do you some good even in stuffy Leicester—if it *is* stuffy, as I fear. We keep on wishing immensely that you were not so far away, and that I could get somehow to see you. If you would like to see either Minnie or me, one of us would come; though it would be probably easier for her than for me. I am not in worse health than a year ago—I am even, strange to say in decidedly better; but I have to be very careful, and anything in the nature of rushing about remains impossible to me. If you *can* manage ten words on a post card I shall, after all, be glad; and am faithfully yours,

Henry James

1. Burgess Noakes, HJ's valet, had been wounded by a shell-burst and, in addition to numerous injuries, lost his hearing. He was now in a hospital at Leicester.

187 · To Henry James III

Dictated Ts Harvard

21 Carlyle Mansions, S.W.
June 24*th* 1915

Dearest Harry.

I am writing you in this fashion even although I am writing you "intimately"; because I am not at the present moment in very good form for any free play of hand, and this machinery helps me so much when there is any question of pressure and promptitude, or above all of particular clearness. That *is* the case at present—at least I feel I ought to lose no more time.

You will wonder what these rather portentous words refer to—but don't be too much alarmed! It is only that my feeling about my situation here has under the stress of events come so much to a head that, certain particular matters further contributing, I have arranged to seek technical (legal) advice no longer hence than this afternoon as to the exact modus operandi of my becoming naturalized in this country. This state of mind probably won't at all surprise you, however; and I think I can assure you that it certainly wouldn't if you were now on the scene here with me and had the near vision of all the circumstances. My sense of how everything more and more makes for it has been gathering force ever since the war broke out, and I have thus waited nearly a whole year; but my feeling has become acute with the information that I can only go down to Lamb House now on the footing of an Alien under Police supervision—an alien friend of course, which is a very different thing from an alien enemy, but still a definite technical outsider to the whole situation here, in which my affections and my loyalty are so intensely engaged. I feel that if I take this step I shall simply rectify a position that has become inconveniently and uncomfortably false, making my civil status merely agree not only with my moral, but with my material as well, in every kind of way. Hadn't it been for the War I should certainly have gone on as I was, taking it as the simplest and easiest and even friendliest thing; but the circumstances are utterly altered now, and to feel with the country and the cause as absolutely and ardently as I feel, and not offer them my moral support with a perfect consistency (my material is too small a matter) affects me as standing off or wandering loose in a detachment of no great dignity. I have spent here all the best years of my life—they practically have *been* my life: about a twelvemonth hence I shall have been domiciled uninterruptedly in England for forty years, and there is not the least possibility, at my age, and in my state of health, of my ever returning to the U.S. or taking up any relation with it as a country. My practical relation has been to this one for ever so long, and now my "spiritual" or "sentimental" quite ideally matches it. I am telling you all this because I can't not want exceedingly to take you into my confidence about it—but again I feel pretty certain that you will understand me too well for any great number of words more to be needed. The real truth is that in a matter of this kind, under such extraordinarily special circumstances, one's own intimate feeling must speak and determine the case. Well, without haste and without rest, mine has done so, and with the prospect of what I have called the rectification, a sense of great relief, a great lapse of awkwardness, supervenes.

I think that even if by chance your so judicious mind should be disposed to suggest any reserves—I think, I say, that I should then still ask you not to launch them at me unless they should seem to you so important as to balance against my own argument and, frankly speaking, my own absolute need and passion here; which the whole experience of the past year has made quite unspeakably final. I can't imagine at all what these objections should be, however—my whole long relation to the country having been what it is. Regard my proceeding as a simple act and offering of allegiance and devotion, recognition and gratitude (for long years and innumerable relations that have meant so much to me), and it remains perfectly simple. Let me repeat that I feel sure I shouldn't in the least have come to it without this convulsion, but one is *in* the convulsion (I wouldn't be out of it either!) and one must act accordingly. I feel all the while too that the tide of American identity of consciousness with our own, about the whole matter, rises and rises, and will rise still more before it rests again—so that every day the difference of situation diminishes and the immense fund of common sentiment increases. However, I haven't really meant so much to expatiate. What I am doing this afternoon is, I think, simply to get exact information—though I am already sufficiently aware of the question to know that after my long existence here the process of naturalisation is very simple and short. I have put myself in relation with J. S. Sargent's, and the de Glehns' excellent solicitor (he is also that of several other good people I know), Nelson Ward, a most sympathetic and competent person, whom I have often met at the Sargents', (and who has about him the "picturesque" association that he is, by the left-hand, great-great-grandson, or whatever, of Horatio Nelson being the not at all remote descendant of his daughter Horatia, of whom Lady Hamilton was the mamma). He will tell me definite things today—but I probably shall not instruct him to do anything at once or till I can turn round again (though I've indeed been turning round and round all these months). I shall at any rate write you again if I *have* said to him "Go ahead." My last word about the matter, at any rate, has to be that my decision is absolutely tied up with my innermost personal feeling. I think that will only make you glad, however, and I add nothing more now but that I am your all-affectionate old Uncle

Henry James

188 · To H. H. Asquith

Ms Bodleian

21 Carlyle Mansions, S.W.

June 28th 1915

My dear Prime Minister and Illustrious Friend.

I am venturing to trouble you with the mention of a fact of my personal situation, but I shall do so as briefly and considerately as possible. I desire to offer myself for naturalization in this country, that is, to change my status from that of American citizen to that of British subject.[1] I have assiduously and happily spent here all but forty years, the best years of my life, and I find my wish to testify at this crisis to the force of my attachment and devotion to England, and to the cause for which she is fighting, finally and completely irresistible. It brooks at least no inward denial whatever. I can only testify by laying at her feet my explicit, my material and spiritual allegiance, and throwing into the scale of her fortune my all but imponderable moral weight— "a poor thing but mine own." Hence this respectful appeal. It is neces- sary (as you may know) that for the purpose I speak of four honorable householders should bear witness to their kind acquaintance with me, to my apparent respectability, and to my speaking and writing English with an approach of propriety. What I presume to ask of you is whether you will do me the honour to be the pre-eminent one of that gently guaranteeing group? Edmund Gosse has benevolently consented to join it. The matter will entail on your part, as I understand, no expen- diture of attention at all beyond your letting my solicitor wait upon you with a paper for your signature—the affair of a single moment; and the "going through" of my application will doubtless be propor- tionately expedited. You will thereby consecrate my choice and deeply touch and gratify yours all faithfully,

Henry James

1. To each of his sponsors HJ sent a memorandum, "Henry James's reasons for Natu- ralization July 1915": "Because of his having lived and worked in England for the best part of forty years, because of his attachment to the Country and his sympathy with it and its people, because of the long friendships and associations and interests he has formed there—these last including the acquisition of some property: all of which things have brought to a head his desire to throw his moral weight and personal allegiance, for what- ever they may be worth, into the scale of the contending nations' present and future fortune."

189 · To H. G. Wells

Dictated Ts Bodleian

21 Carlyle Mansions, S.W.
July 10th 1915

My dear Wells.

I am bound to tell you that I don't think your letter makes out any sort of case for the bad manners of *Boon*,[1] so far as your indulgence in them at the expense of your poor old H. J. is concerned—I say "your" simply because he has *been* yours, in the most liberal, continual, sacrificial, the most admiring and abounding critical way, ever since he began to know your writings: as to which you have had copious testimony. Your comparison of the book to a waste-basket strikes me as the reverse of felicitous, for what one throws into that receptacle is exactly what one *doesn't* commit to publicity and make the affirmation of one's estimate of one's contemporaries by. I should liken it much rather to the preservative portfolio or drawer in which what is withheld from the basket is savingly laid away. Nor do I feel it anywhere evident that my "view of life and literature," or what you impute to me as such, is carrying everything before it and becoming a public menace—so unaware do I seem, on the contrary, that my products constitute an example in any measurable degree followed or a cause in any degree successfully pleaded: I can't but think that if this were the case I should find it somewhat attested in their circulation—which, alas, I have reached a very advanced age in the entirely defeated hope of. But I *have* no view of life and literature, I maintain, other than that our form of the latter in especial is admirable exactly by its range and variety, its plasticity and liberality, its fairly living on the sincere and shifting experience of the individual practitioner. That is why I have always so admired your so free and strong application of it, the particular rich receptacle of intelligences and impressions emptied out with an energy of its own, that your genius constitutes; and *that* is in particular why, in my letter of two or three days since, I pronounced it curious and interesting that you should find the case I constitute myself only ridiculous and vacuous to the extent of your having to proclaim your sense of it. The curiosity and the interest, however, in this latter connection are of course for my mind those of the break of perception (perception of the vivacity of *my* variety) on the part of a talent so generally inquiring and apprehensive as yours. Of course for myself I live, live intensely and am fed by life, and my value, whatever it be, is in my own kind of expression of that. Therefore I am pulled up to wonder by the fact that for you my kind (my sort of sense of expression and sort of sense of life alike) doesn't exist; and that wonder is, I admit, a disconcerting comment on my idea of the various appreciability of our addiction to the novel and of all the personal and intellectual history, sympathy and curiosity, behind the given example of it. It is when that history and curiosity have been determined in the way most different from my own that I myself want to get at them—precisely *for* the extension of life, which is the novel's best gift. But that is another matter. Meanwhile I absolutely dissent from the claim that there are any differences whatever in the amenability to art of forms of literature aesthetically determined, and hold your distinction between a form that is (like) painting and a form that is (like) architecture for wholly null and void. There is no sense in which architecture is aesthetically "for use" that doesn't leave any other art whatever exactly as much so; and so far from that of literature being irrelevant to the literary report upon life, and to its being made as interesting as possible, I regard it as relevant in a degree that leaves everything else behind. It is art that *makes* life, makes interest, makes importance, for our consideration and application of these things, and I know of no substitute whatever for the force and beauty of its process. If I were Boon I should say that any pretence of such a substitute is helpless and hopeless humbug; but I wouldn't be Boon for the world, and am only yours faithfully

Henry James

1. Wells had sent HJ his newly published satirical book *Boon, The Mind of the Race,* containing a chapter titled "Of Art, of Literature, of Mr. Henry James," in which he mocked and parodied his friend. The best-known passage described a novel by HJ as being "like a church but without a congregation to distract you, with every light and line focused on the high altar. And on the altar, very reverently placed, intensely there, is a dead kitten, an egg-shell, a bit of string . . ." HJ had written a letter to Wells, 6 July 1915, saying he found it difficult to accept the idea that "a mind as brilliant as yours *can* resolve me into such an unmitigated mistake." Wells apologized and claimed he had written the book to relieve tension produced by the war. There was no further correspondence between the two novelists.

190 · *To John Singer Sargent*

Ms Unknown

21 Carlyle Mansions, S.W.

July 30*th* 1915

My dear John.

I am delighted to hear from you that you are writing and sending to Mrs. Wharton in the good sense you mention. It will give her the greatest pleasure and count enormously for her undertaking.

Yes, I daresay many Americans *will* be shocked at my "step"; so many of them appear in these days to be shocked at everything that is not a reiterated blandishment and slobberation of Germany, with re-calls of ancient "amity" and that sort of thing, by our Government. I waited long months, watch in hand, for the latter to show some sign of intermitting these amiabilities to such an enemy—the very smallest would have sufficed for me to throw myself back upon it. But it seemed never to come, and the misrepresentation of *my* attitude becoming at last to me a thing no longer to be borne, I took action myself. It would really have been *so* easy for the U.S. to have "kept" (if they had cared to!) yours all faithfully,

Henry James

191 · To Margaret Mary James

Dictated Ts Harvard

21, Carlyle Mansions, S.W.
December 1st 1915

Dearest Pegg.

I don't lose an hour, or scarcely, in thanking you more intensely than I can say for your two letters that have just come in together, one of November 15th, and the second, smaller one, of the 19th, telling me of the note to me that you have given the young doctor; whom I shall be very glad to see if he brings me news of you, and has time, and above all, takes me as I am. I am not in these days very rewarding to visitors—so little so in fact that I am obliged to manage to have al-most none at all, and haven't for a long time been able to exercise the least hospitality. The point is, however, that hearing from you does me a world of good—weeks and weeks of all this latter difficult time, ever since I have been in [Dr.] Des Vœux's hands, having somehow, and doubtless largely by my own fault, represented a sad lapse of com-munication with your Mother and Harry. I say by my own fault, be-cause I doubtless might have written more—at the same time that my poor old state has made writing very difficult, and yet has, withal filled me with a kind of morbid desire to be, consolingly, in touch with you. Some ten days ago, or perhaps it was only a week, I could stand the great void of the post no longer, and cabled suppliantly to Harry to cable me back a few words that I could kind of try to go on with. This he at once blessedly did, and more will now doubtless come, though it hasn't done so yet, save indeed to this happy extent of *your* news, which is so interesting and illuminating. I learn by it for the first time what you are doing in Cincinnati, and very remarkable and valiant does it seem—if the inspiration and the reward to sustain you through those aspects of it which must sometimes, in their multiplication of bad cases, bad specimens, hopeless subjects etc., rather minister to doubt. Likewise I groan over your doom of having been fitted out with a kind of practical equivalent to M.P.[1]—similarly depressing, I fear, even though spotted with different spots. How they do grow on you, as it were; I don't mean the spots, but the spotted and the inconvertibles themselves; with the big reservoir of them, that seems to surround you, to draw upon. I can quite imagine what you mean by the panting freshness and readiness of such an American community as that, with its desire for the public good and the energy of its contribution to the same, of which you have become so brave an agent. It's all a good bit bewildering seen from here—where, however, God knows, our own bewilderments are not wanting. I shan't attempt to speak of these now—and the sign of the wondrous in yours, as it most strikes me, is such a fact as that F. Duveneck[2] is at this time of day still being "lionised"; anything there may have been to lionise him *for* goes back into such an antediluvian past. His only good work was done in his very few first years, nearly fifty of these ago—at least the long interval since has always looked like a deadly desert. I daresay, however, in fact I must often have heard, that he has flourished at Cincinnati during a large part of that time as an excellent teacher so it's doubtless all right—and it isn't of him I dreamed of writing you.

There is no good in my trying to go on without allowing to you that I am having difficult days, and weeks, and even months,—for only on that basis can I really send you any coherent news. I am having a troubled, new heart-condition, but it is being very well taken care of by Des Vœux, and I get, and evidently shall get, a good deal of relief. One feels very abject, at our pitch of life and public pain, in the midst of the huge tremendous things that press upon us, to have disqualifying personal and physical troubles; or I should, at least, if I weren't so ancient and for a long time past so *éprouvé*. My greatest *épreuve* just now, alas, by which I mean very much for all these past months, though under great present aggravation, is the fact of my almost impossibility of sleep; which has me for the moment in its clutches. Take in consideration for this letter—written in the only way I *can* write now, or shall ever, I fear, write again—that I this A.M. left my bed at 8:30, unable to stick it out longer, after not having closed my eyes the whole blessed night, from the moment I first propped myself up there on my pillows, and that this has followed upon a series of nights different only by a little. I don't tell you this for dreariness, but more, rather, to show you how I bear it than how I don't. (Des Vœux promises me improvement as to that, but it doesn't come yet.) And the great thing I want above all to say to you is that to have heard you would like so much to come out to me moves me deeply and gratefully, and that one of these months I shall intensely and rejoicingly welcome you and clutch you and keep you. Only we must wait for that, wait for some less heavy and horrible time. The idea of your dreaming of anything of the sort in these actual conditions simply sickens and flattens me out; therefore stick to your present noble work and feel *that* your actual right mission. I shall keep afloat here successfully, I feel, with the good help I get; counting Des Vœux, that is, and also counting my admirable household, in which I venture to include Miss Bosanquet, as wonderfully helpful. I have definitely now got Burgess back—not discharged, but on indefinite and renewable leave, and with his army pay of course stopped; and I should be utterly unable to get on without him, as his service is a matter of any and every hour, and his devotion boundless and most touching.

I fear I see none of your old friends with the exception, once in a while, of Fanny P[rothero]; all social life has gone to smash; nothing exists but *the* huge enormity. George Prothero is a haggard hero of labour and courage, and she as wonderful as ever in her indefatigability. But it's all applied now to the general situation—save that she'll be intensely interested to hear about you. I rejoice unspeakably that your Mother has gone on to be with Harry, and I live in the deferred hope of a New York, in default of a Cambridge, letter from her. Let me say that what you wrote from California must really all have come—only it was difficult, all the summer long, to make the proper recognitions. Your photographs of the San Francisco house perfectly reached me, and were as interesting as possible, so that I am horrified that I didn't, and couldn't, tell you so. But this is all now—save that I am extremely glad that Aleck, bless him, wasn't able to carry out that Red Cross idea. The difficulties for Neutrals in France now are overwhelming— but the pen drops from my hand![3]

Your all-affectionate old Uncle
Henry James

1. Margaret Payson, Peggy James's friend.
2. The painter Frank Duveneck (1848–1919), some time after the death of his wife, Elizabeth Boott, in 1888, had returned to his home city and for many years had been teaching painting at the Cincinnati Academy of Arts.
3. This letter to WJ's daughter was HJ's last. He had a stroke the following morning and died three months later, on 28 February 1916.

Index